SANTA FE, TAOS & ALBUQUERQUE

ZORA O'NEILL

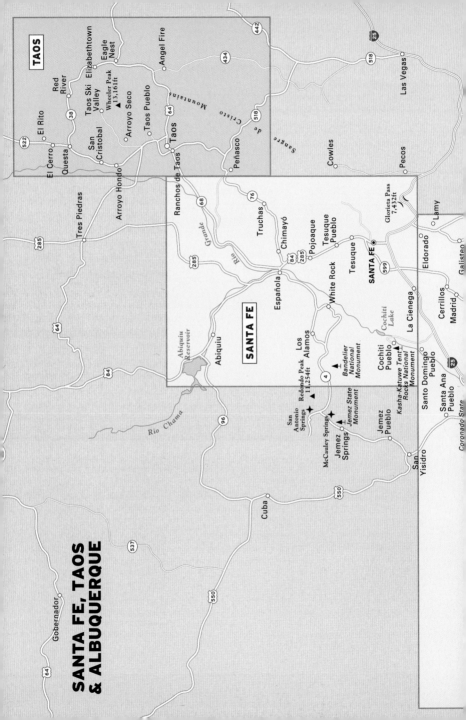

SANTA FE, TAOS & ALBUQUERQUE

TAOS

Red River
Elizabethtown
Eagle Nest
Angel Fire
El Cerro
El Rito
Questa
Taos Ski Valley
Wheeler Peak 13,161ft
Arroyo Seco
San Cristobal
Taos Pueblo
Arroyo Hondo
Taos
Ranchos de Taos
Sangre de Cristo Mountains
Peñasco
Cowles
Pecos
Las Vegas

SANTA FE

Tres Piedras
Rio Grande
Truchas
Chimayó
Pojoaque
Tesuque Pueblo
Tesuque
Española
White Rock
SANTA FE
Glorieta Pass 7,432ft
Lamy
Eldorado
Galisteo
Cerrillos
Madrid
La Cienega
Cochiti Lake
Abiquiu Reservoir
Abiquiu
Redondo Peak 11,254ft
Los Alamos
Bandelier National Monument
Kasha-Katuwe Tent Rocks National Monument
Cochiti Pueblo
Santo Domingo Pueblo
Santa Ana Pueblo
Coronado State
Rio Chama
San Antonio Springs
McCauley Springs
Jemez Springs
Jemez State Monument
Jemez Pueblo
San Ysidro
Cuba
Gobernador

ALBUQUERQUE

State Park

© AVALON TRAVEL

20 mi

20 km

Contents

Discover Santa Fe, Taos & Albuquerque

When I tell people I grew up in Albuquerque, I often get a blank stare, and sometimes a Bugs Bunny joke. "That's New Mexico, right?" some say cautiously. "I've never met anyone from there." Yes, it's *New* Mexico, it's part of the United States, and for some reason, we don't get out much.

Maybe we're lazy from a lack of oxygen – Albuquerque is 5,352 feet above sea level, but Wheeler Peak, which overshadows Taos, hits 13,161 feet. More likely, it's because New Mexico, and particularly the stretch between Albuquerque and Taos, is so astonishingly beautiful: austere mesas, red sandstone canyons, pine-studded mountain ranges. Why go anywhere else, when you can smell lilacs in spring, ozone after summer thunderstorms, spicy roasting green chile, and fragrant piñon crackling in fireplaces? Why stray, when coyotes yelp in the night, western tanagers warble in the trees, and the drums boom at pueblo ceremonies? Why move an inch, when you live under this singular sky: by day, a cloudless, turquoise dome; by night, a velvet backdrop clotted with stars.

I strayed, but I feel fortunate to have this place to return to. It may not be another country, but it is another world. Nicknamed the Land of Enchantment, New Mexico may as well be Wonderland. Sixteenth-century Spanish is spoken in tiny mountain towns north of Santa Fe, while in Albuquerque, people fight to preserve Route 66 motor courts built in the 1950s. Santa Fe is an adobe-looking utopia where the economy magically thrives on nothing but art and politics, and the hippie homesteaders of Taos aim to get off the grid – the same way the neighboring pueblo has been, for hundreds of years.

Visitors might need time to adjust – to the altitude, but maybe also to the laid-back attitude – but there's a point of entry for everyone. Outdoor adventurers can hike for an hour or a week, along mountainsides thick with yellow-leafed aspens, and skiers can plunge through armpit-deep powder at Taos Ski Valley, one of the country's most thrilling downhill runs. Culture mavens thrive in Santa Fe, with its world-class contemporary art scene and an eclectic calendar of international film and music. History buffs can climb to ancient cave dwellings, wander among crumbling Franciscan mission churches, or ogle vintage neon signs in Albuquerque.

At the end of the day, you can always pull yourself back into the present with a cold margarita and cuisine with a hot-chile kick – but that's no guarantee you'll shake off northern New Mexico's spell.

Planning Your Trip

▶ WHERE TO GO

Santa Fe

A network of little streets and thick-walled adobe homes, New Mexico's picturesque capital has a human scale and a golden glow (partly from the loads of money spent here). Museums are a major draw—for state history, folk art, and more—as are the scores of galleries lining Canyon Road. Great hiking trails are just a few minutes' drive—or head farther, to the cliff dwellings at Bandelier National Monument; to Abiquiu, where the scenery inspired painter Georgia O'Keeffe; or to Los Alamos, birthplace of the A-bomb.

Taos

A small town of 4,800 people adjacent to an ancient pueblo, Taos melds artists, trust-fund hippies, spiritual seekers, and ski bums (Taos Ski Valley is a pilgrimage site)—plus the Spanish and American Indian families who've

called the place home for centuries. There's little sightseeing; instead, its atmosphere, cultivated in mellow coffee shops and hidden hot springs, is the real attraction. Make a day drive around the Enchanted Circle, a loop of two-lane roads through high valleys where elk graze.

Albuquerque

A modern Western city, the state's biggest, Albuquerque sprawls at the base of the Sandia Mountains. It's proud of its Route 66 vintage style but it's also preserving farmland along the Rio Grande and redesigning itself as a green burg. To the west, Acoma Pueblo sits atop a monolithic mesa, while the wetlands of the Bosque del Apache National Wildlife Refuge to the south attract thousands of birds. Head north to Santa Fe through the ghost towns of the Turquoise Trail or to the red rocks of the Jemez Mountains.

ruins on the valley floor at Bandelier National Monument

▶ WHEN TO GO

With 300 days of sunshine annually, New Mexico doesn't have a bad time to visit. High season is mid-May to mid-September. Starting in July, the day's heat is squelched with a strong, brief rainstorm in the afternoon, and nights are still cool. Summer is the only time to hike at higher elevations, as many trails are still snow-covered as late as May. If you want to go rafting, plan on late May and early June, when the snowmelt makes the rivers run high and wild. Winter sees a surge of visitors heading straight to the ski trails, but the towns stay uncrowded, and traditional celebrations preceding Christmas are wonderful; many sights are closed or have limited hours, however.

The shoulder seasons have their own appeal and can be cheaper, particularly in April, when ski season has wound down, and in November, when it hasn't gotten started. But note that Taos Pueblo is closed to visitors for about 10 weeks between February and April; the precise dates change every year. Spring weather can also be extreme, varying from snowfall to ceaseless, hot winds—and lots of mud. In the fall, the crowds disperse, leaving crisp temperatures and generally clear skies through late October. In the mountains, the aspen leaves turn a brilliant yellow, accessible by the many beautiful hiking trails.

IF YOU HAVE. . .

- **THREE DAYS:** Pick one place – probably Santa Fe – and stay there.
- **FIVE DAYS:** Visit Santa Fe, with an overnight trip to Taos.
- **ONE WEEK:** Add a day trip to Abiquiu and Bandelier.
- **TWO WEEKS:** Add Albuquerque, the Jemez Mountains, and Acoma Pueblo.

the red rocks of the Jemez Mountains

If you're planning a visit between Christmas and New Year's, during Santa Fe's summer art markets, or for the October balloon fest in Albuquerque, book a hotel at least six months in advance.

hot-air balloonists readying for a dawn ascension at the Albuquerque International Balloon Fiesta

▶ BEFORE YOU GO

Getting Around

If you'll be just in Albuquerque or Santa Fe, you can get around on foot and public transport—easily in Santa Fe and with a little planning in Albuquerque. A commuter rail line links the two cities, with handy stops in each downtown area. Parking in downtown Santa Fe can be expensive and difficult, so it's best to rent a car only for day trips out of the city. Taos, however, has only minimal bus service, so a car will make things much easier.

The Climate and What to Take

The contents of your suitcase will be determined largely by the time of year, but be prepared for a wide range of temperatures—with a variety of layers—whenever you visit. Many people wrongly assume that New Mexico's desert setting means heat all day, all year round. In fact, the altitude yields both extremely hot and cold weather. Winter temperatures can dip well below freezing even in the relatively low elevations of central Albuquerque, though it sees little snow. If you think you'll attend pueblo ceremonial dances during the winter, pack mittens, long underwear, double-thick wool socks, and a hat with earflaps—there's a lot of standing around outside.

Spring is mud season—if you hike or head to rural areas during this time, save a clean pair

hiking on Sandia Peak outside of Albuquerque

of shoes for around town. Summers are hot by day (July's average temperature is 92°F), but as soon as the sun dips below the horizon, the temperature can drop 20°F or more, especially outside of city centers; always keep a sweater on hand. Brief afternoon "monsoons" in July and August sometimes warrant an umbrella or rain slicker. In the sun, you'll be more comfortable in long-sleeve, light-colored shirts and pants in silk or cotton rather than skimpy tank tops and shorts—covering up will help deflect the glare. In fact, you should guard against the sun any time of year, as the thin atmosphere at this altitude means you'll burn more quickly than you're used to. You should never be without sunglasses, heavy-duty sunscreen, and a brimmed hat.

As for style, anything goes. New Mexicans are very casual in their dress. Only if you'll be hobnobbing with Santa Fe's upper echelon need you pack something dressy—the local formalwear for men is clean jeans, shined cowboy boots, and a bolo tie. When visiting churches and pueblos, it's respectful to not show excessive skin—women should avoid obvious cleavage and supershort skirts.

winter on Sandia Peak

Explore Santa Fe, Taos & Albuquerque

▶ THE BEST OF SANTA FE, TAOS & ALBUQUERQUE

While you could conceivably explore Santa Fe, Taos, and Albuquerque for several weeks, seeking out ever more obscure hiking trails and sweeping vistas, 12 days gives just enough time to appreciate the distinct character of each community and enjoy the surrounding rural areas and bumpy back roads. This itinerary involves a lot of driving to cover all of the area's most scenic routes, but you'll still have plenty of opportunities for leisurely lunches and other out-of-car activities.

Day 1

Arrive at Albuquerque's Sunport airport; transfer directly to Santa Fe. If you want old-school style, stay at La Fonda—it's that much easier to get to bed after dinner at The Shed nearby and a margarita in the hotel lobby bar.

Day 2

Start with an early breakfast at the Plaza Café and then tour the surrounding blocks, including the Palace of the Governors, the St. Francis Cathedral, and the Loretto Chapel. Around happy hour, wander down to the Dragon Room Lounge on Old Santa Fe Trail, and then have a casual dinner at Upper Crust Pizza across the street while you watch the sun glow on San Miguel Chapel.

Day 3

Take in Santa Fe's more contemporary culture, with shopping, gallery hopping, or a visit to the Museum of International Folk Art.

End up on Canyon Road, with drinks and tapas, and maybe even dancing at El Farol.

Day 4

Drive to Bandelier National Monument to see the ancestral Puebloan ruins. Have a late lunch on "the hill" in Los Alamos or down in the valley in Española. If you're up to more driving, head for Abiquiu, where the cliffs glow red in the sunset. Return to Santa Fe to sleep.

Day 5

Drive to Taos via the high road, stopping at the pilgrimage site of Chimayó and in the villages of Truchas and Las Trampas. In Taos, head to the Stakeout Grill & Bar for an early dinner and a view of the sunset, and then settle into your hotel after a de rigueur margarita at the Adobe Bar.

LIFE IMITATES ART

Both Santa Fe and Taos have long histories of fostering creative output, much of it inspired by the surrounding landscape. Tour northern New Mexico with a creative eye, and soon you'll be recognizing locations from paintings and maybe find yourself ready to buy. . . or to dive into some work of your own.

ART IS WHERE YOU FIND IT

Taos is the best place to see where and how artists lived: **Mabel Dodge Luhan House** is now a bed-and-breakfast, but Mabel's own bed is still in place in her sunlit room with views of Taos Mountain. Elsewhere in town, the **Blumenschein Home and Museum** and **Taos Art Museum at Fechin House** both show how resident artists adapted their homes to their personal styles; the wood carving at Fechin House is especially rich.

Northwest of Santa Fe lies Abiquiu, turf that painter Georgia O'Keeffe called her own – even if she had only a small house in town and a studio at **Ghost Ranch.** But everything under the sway of flat-topped Pedernal Peak – often depicted in her work – was grist for her creativity.

But perhaps the most illuminating spot is Dorothy Brett's miniscule cabin at the **D. H. Lawrence Ranch,** barely big enough for a bed and a woodstove. Across the yard, in front of Lawrence's only slightly larger home, is the towering pine depicted in Georgia O'Keeffe's *The Lawrence Tree.* Get her perspective, and the curving lines of the painting come into focus: "There was a long weathered carpenter's bench under the tall tree in front of the little old house that Lawrence had lived in there. I often lay on that bench looking up into the tree. . . past the trunk and up into the branches. It was particularly fine at night with the stars above the tree."

ART IN ACTION

Art lovers need not spend all their time in museums (though there are some great ones) – it can be just as rewarding to visit studios, talk with artists, and see how objects are made. Time your trip around the **High Road Arts Tour,** for instance, and you'll get to see woodworkers' studios in an area that's usually quite closed and private feeling. The **New Mexico Potters Trail** is a year-round route of open studios, most between Santa Fe and Taos – participating artists do some of the finest contemporary work in the state, an excellent complement to the traditional pottery from the pueblos.

Curious about the process? Just north of Santa Fe, **Shidoni** and **Tesuque Glassworks** sit side by side – the former is a bronze foundry, with demonstrations on weekends, and the latter has an open glass-blowing studio where you'll usually see some craftspeople at work. It's remarkable to see such heavy technology creating what are often very delicate pieces. If you're truly inspired, head to **Sunrise Springs,** just south of the city, for classes in its ceramics studio.

sculpture at Tesuque Glassworks

San Francisco de Asis Church in Taos

Day 6

Start with breakfast at Gutiz or a pastry from Loka, and then stop by San Francisco de Asis Church, followed by a tour of La Hacienda de los Martinez. Stop for lunch in Arroyo Seco, at Maverick County Food Co., and then head up the mountain for a hike.

Day 7

Visit Taos Pueblo. Then check out some other indigenous architecture: Tour an Earthship on the Solar Survival Tour at Greater World Earthship Development, pausing to peer down into the Rio Grande Gorge on the way. Have dinner at Lambert's, Taos's favorite white-tablecloth spot.

Day 8

Pack a picnic lunch and take a leisurely drive around the Enchanted Circle, stopping for a hike along the back side of Wheeler Peak. Depending on your timing, you can get your green-chile fix in Questa or back in Taos at Orlando's.

Day 9

Fueled with a to-go breakfast burrito from Mante's Chow Cart, drive down to Albuquerque via the low road along the Rio Grande, then along the Turquoise Trail, stopping for lunch in Madrid and at Tinkertown Museum. Stay the night in Albuquerque, either at the Mauger Estate near downtown or in a rural-feeling Corrales B&B.

Day 10

Weather permitting, take a hot-air balloon ride first thing in the morning and then have breakfast at Sophia's Place. Or start with a hearty meal and then take a bike ride along the Paseo del Bosque. In the afternoon, visit the National Hispanic Cultural Center.

Day 11

Drive to Acoma Pueblo, west of Albuquerque. Return by afternoon and take a sunset ride up the Sandia Peak Tramway. Enjoy dinner and drinks downtown.

Day 12

Have a big breakfast at the Frontier before catching your plane out of the Albuquerque airport.

The Sandia Peak Tramway runs more than 2,000 vertical feet up from the Albuquerque foothills.

▶ WEEKEND GETAWAYS

Even if you have only a few days, getting away to northern New Mexico can be exceptionally refreshing, an easy way to disconnect from your regular routine by immersing yourself in the state's otherworldly architecture and rich history. Just an hour from the Albuquerque airport, Santa Fe lends itself perfectly to a romantic escape. Settle in at one of the many remarkable hotels, and make reservations at a couple of the city's best restaurants (those mentioned here are just a few of the possibilities). With planning, you could also spend an evening at the Santa Fe Opera in the summer. Isolated, countercultural Taos is worth the extra 90-minute drive if you're really looking to get off the map and off the grid, while Albuquerque offers a fun and funky city break, along with great outdoor activities. These itineraries are for three days, but of course a four-day weekend would be better—the extra day will be a big help as you adapt to the elevation and the slow pace.

Santa Fe

DAY 1

Fly into Albuquerque; head to Santa Fe via the scenic Turquoise Trail and check in to your hotel: The Inn of the Five Graces is an exotic, utterly luxurious hideaway, or hole up in the Hacienda wing of the Hotel Santa Fe. If it's summertime, head to Canyon Road for the gallery crawl, which gets started around 5 P.M. If it's wintertime, curl up for a bit by the fire at Staab House, at La Posada de Santa Fe, and then walk over to dinner at Café Pasqual's.

DAY 2

Pick up breakfast at the French Pastry Shop and then spend the morning sightseeing (New Mexico Museum of Art, Museum of International Folk Art) and the afternoon in a private hot tub at Ten Thousand Waves, finishing with a massage and spa treatment. Around happy hour, head to La Casa Sena—have a drink in the flower-filled patio and then move inside for a candlelit dinner. If you're up for more, head over to the bar at El Mesón for a drink.

gallery on Canyon Road

NOT JUST HOT TAMALES

Given the region's distinctive cuisine – from only-in-New-Mexico hot chile to gourmet creativity – it would be easy to plan a vacation entirely around eating.

BEST TRADITIONAL NEW MEXICAN

"Green or red?" is the official state question, referring to the dilemma diners face when they order enchiladas, huevos rancheros, or anything else that can be drowned in an earthy red chile sauce or a chunky, vegetal green one.

- **Tia Sophia's:** History was made in this greasy-spoon spot near the Santa Fe Plaza – allegedly where the breakfast burrito was invented (page 55).

- **Orlando's:** The Taos favorite is known for its green-chile sauce – deceptively smooth and velvety, considering it's often the hottest thing in town (page 123).

- **Duran Central Pharmacy:** An Albuquerque institution, this lunch counter is known for its hearty green-chile stew (page 167).

- **Perea's Tijuana Bar & Restaurant:** In Corrales, in Albuquerque's North Valley, this bar serves rich *carne adovada*, or red-chile-marinated pork, for lunch only (page 172).

- **Barelas Coffee House:** Here's another spot in Albuquerque for excellent red chile, especially when it flavors traditional stews such as posole and menudo (page 172).

BEST GREEN-CHILE CHEESEBURGERS

This greasy treat is perhaps the best use of the indigenous green chile outside of standard enchiladas and burritos. The cheese both anchors the chunks of green goodness and softens their spicy punch.

- **Bobcat Bite:** Just outside Santa Fe is this restaurant that grinds its own meat and shapes the enormous patties by hand. There are other items on the menu, but they're just window dressing (page 61).

- **The Frontier:** With the all-you-can-ladle pot of green-chile stew at the condiment counter, you can add as much heat as you want to your burger at this colossal diner in Albuquerque (page 169).

- **Owl Café:** Often cited as the best GCCB in the state, the Owl's version requires a drive way down south of Albuquerque to the village of San Antonio. Once you're there, though, you can also sample the Owl's main rival, from Manny's Buckhorn, across the street (page 178).

- **Blake's Lotaburger:** A New Mexico chain, this place is far more accessible than the Owl and (heresy) almost as delicious. No individual Blake's is reviewed in this book – just keep an eye out for the icon of the man in the red-white-and-blue top hat.

BEST LOCAL AND ORGANIC

New Mexico's extreme climate makes farming difficult – perhaps why locally grown produce is so treasured by the foodie set.

- **Treehouse Pastry Shop & Café:** Set on the grounds of a Santa Fe nursery, the Treehouse gets a lot of its ingredients from right out its back door (page 60).

- **Blue Heron:** The chef honed his skills in bountiful Portland, Oregon, but he has adapted well to his new setting outside Santa Fe (page 61).

- **Joseph's Table:** Chef Joseph Wrede pioneered local cuisine when his Taos restaurant opened in 1995. It's still one of the state's best (page 124).

- **Los Poblanos:** Guests at this historic farm inn in Los Ranchos de Albuquerque enjoy fresh eggs for breakfast, among other treats (page 165).

- **The Grove:** Using eggs and greens from the Rio Grande Valley, this Albuquerque café whips up all-day breakfasts in a chic atmosphere (page 168).

OFFBEAT NEW MEXICO

Fringy, countercultural, freakish, or just plain quirky – whatever you want to call the offbeat side of northern New Mexico, there sure is a lot of it. In places such as **Madrid**, a ghost town made good, the do-what-you-like spirit has taken over an entire community in the past few decades, inspiring art galleries and assorted odd projects such as the *Nude Geezers* fund-raising calendar – no wonder the locals call themselves "Madroids."

Farther north, outside of Taos, a similar independent ethos drives the **Greater World Earthship Community,** where all the houses function off the power grid. But what's most remarkable about these homes is their curvy design, with walls built into hills, around glass bottles, and into whimsical waves. More distinctive architecture can be seen at **Dar Al Islam,** a retreat partially built by an Egyptian master of earthen architecture – his adobe work looks both at home and exotic in the hills near Abiquiu.

Albuquerque contributes to bizarre architecture too, with the excellent "pueblo deco" of the **KiMo Theater** (go inside to see the Southwest theme taken to its logical extreme) and the more contemporary **Bart Prince House,** the work of a brilliant local architect whose home and studio resembles a spaceship.

Speaking of spaceships, you could probably

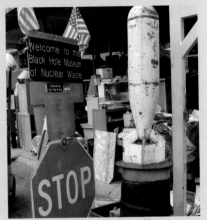
Cold War relics at The Black Hole, Los Alamos

build your own with bits collected from **The Black Hole,** a salvage yard in Los Alamos that stocks used lab equipment and office supplies, as well as a heavy dose of Cold War paranoia. You can have a similar time-warp experience in **Mary's Bar** in Cerrillos, where it seems as if the Wild West never faded, or at **Tinkertown Museum,** outside Albuquerque, a folk-art project that presents old-time whittling as a source of entertainment.

DAY 3

Take an early-morning hike on the Dale Ball Trails or, less strenuously, around the Santa Fe Canyon Preserve. Treat yourself to brunch at Harry's Roadhouse, a little south of town, for high-end diner-style goodies (and pie), and then drive back down I-25 to catch your flight out.

Taos
DAY 1

Fly into Albuquerque; head to Taos via I-25 and the low road. Pick a prime plaza-view room at La Fonda de Taos, or, more luxuriously, a suite at El Monte Sagrado. After

you check in, stroll the plaza and visit the Blumenschein Home and Museum and the galleries on Ledoux Street. Have green chile for dinner at Orlando's.

DAY 2

Visit Taos Pueblo in the morning. In the afternoon, tour the Taos Art Museum at Fechin House and the Millicent Rogers Museum. If you'd rather hike, head for the West Rim Trail along the Rio Grande Gorge—it's fairly level, so you shouldn't have too much trouble, despite the elevation. Be dazzled by dinner at Byzantium.

The Blumenschein Home and Museum in Taos shows a painter's life.

DAY 3

Get up early for a dip in Blackrock Springs. Drop by San Francisco de Asis Church later in the morning and then prep yourself for the drive back south with breakfast at El Taoseño or, more lavishly, with brunch at Joseph's Table. Head out along the high road to Santa Fe and then I-25 to the airport, which takes about four hours without much stopping; a straight shot back down the low road will shave about 40 minutes off the trip.

Albuquerque

DAY 1

Arrive at Albuquerque airport; transfer to your hotel. Try Los Poblanos Historic Inn or another rural-feeling inn in the North Valley, or The Hotel Blue downtown if you want to be in the middle of the action. Stroll around Old Town and then dine at Chef du Jour, or head up to New Mexican favorite El Patio near the university.

DAY 2

If you're feeling ambitious, get an early start to drive straight west to Acoma Pueblo, which takes about an hour and a half. On your way back to Albuquerque, stop off on the West Mesa to clamber up the dormant volcanoes and then drive around the base to see Petroglyph National Monument. Or stay in the city and spend the morning at the Indian Pueblo Cultural Center, followed by late lunch at Mary & Tito's. Spend the evening in Nob Hill or downtown.

DAY 3

Get up early again to head for Sandia Peak. Either take the tramway up from the foothills or drive around the back side of the mountain and up the winding scenic highway. Allow about three hours for the outing and then stop off at The Frontier for a late lunch before catching your flight.

Acoma Pueblo

► AMERICAN INDIAN HERITAGE

The culture that developed before the arrival of the Spanish in the 16th century is visible in both ruined and inhabited pueblos and in excellent museums that hold some of the region's finest treasures. Even if you're visiting only one city on your trip, there's a lot of Indian history to see in and around each place—but definitely try to schedule a visit around a dance ceremony, as this will give you the most memorable impression of the living culture. If you're serious about buying art and jewelry, you may want to time your visit with the Santa Fe Indian Market, which takes place every August and showcases more than 1,200 Native American artisans. Otherwise, be sure to visit the gift shops at the Institute of American Indian Arts Museum in Santa Fe or the Indian Pueblo Cultural Center in Albuquerque to get an idea of prices and quality; you can also buy directly from craftspeople at the pueblos.

Albuquerque

Use the city as a base for getting to know the culture, starting with a visit to the Indian Pueblo Cultural Center, with its excellent museum and café. All the other sights, though, are on the edge of town or well beyond. On the

REGIONAL IDENTITY

New Mexicans have particular ways of identifying themselves and the elements of the state's unique cultural mix. The people who have lived in the highlands and along the Rio Grande for millennia most commonly refer to themselves as Indians, or American Indians in formal situations; or they will call themselves by their pueblo's specific name – Jemez or Santa Clara, for instance. The term "Native American" appears occasionally, but most New Mexican Indians see it as just another inaccurate label.

Those who trace their roots to the conquistadors call themselves Spanish or Hispano. The latter is not to be confused with Hispanic, which refers to Spanish speakers regardless of background. Hispano is also distinct from Mexican and Latino.

The third category is the catch-all term Anglo, which really just means "none of the above" – whether you're white, Asian, or even African American, you could be considered Anglo, a relative latecomer to the state of New Mexico.

west mesa, Petroglyph National Monument has trails past hundreds of ancient rock carvings, while on the north edge, in Bernalillo, you can climb down into a ceremonial kiva at Coronado State Monument.

Mesa-top Acoma Pueblo is well worth the drive west of the city—along with Taos Pueblo, it's the most scenic (and oldest) in New Mexico; you can break up the trip with a stop at Laguna Pueblo to see its mission church. You can also drive south and east through the Manzano Mountains to the Salinas Pueblo Missions, ruined villages that didn't survive the Spanish conquest. North of the city, the Jemez Mountain Trail runs through Jemez Pueblo—sure, the red-

Critters adorn the rocks at Petroglyph National Monument in Albuquerque.

American Indian art – and artist – in Santa Fe

the excellent contemporary art collection at the Institute of American Indian Arts Museum, perhaps picking up some craftwork at the gift shop. Even Hotel Santa Fe, co-owned by Picurís Pueblo, showcases tribal art.

The pueblos north of the city offer more in the way of casinos than they do in traditional sightseeing, but the Poeh Museum at Pojoaque is worth a stop, and collectors will want to make the drive to San Ildefonso Pueblo for its stunning black-on-black pottery. Finally, Bandelier National Monument is a must—this lush protected canyon was once inhabited by the ancestors of today's Pueblo people, and an easy hike leads past the traces of their settlement on the valley floor; a more difficult one takes you up to their cliff-face homes.

rock scenery is beautiful, but don't miss the Indian frybread from the vendors set up in front of the Walatowa Visitors Center.

Rest up from your road trips at the beautiful Hyatt Regency Tamaya resort, owned by Santa Ana Pueblo, or Casita Chamisa in Albuquerque's North Valley, which has a small ruin on its grounds, excavated by the owner.

Santa Fe

On Museum Hill, the Wheelwright Museum of the American Indian and the Museum of Indian Arts & Culture are two fascinating exhibitions of arts and crafts. Then visit

Taos

Head straight to Taos Pueblo—one of the most beautiful spots in the state, the organic adobe structures seemingly untouched by time (only *seemingly*—in fact, they get a fresh coat of mud nearly every year). Also don't miss the excellent weaving and pottery collections at the Millicent Rogers Museum. And to put it all in context, stay the night at Little Tree B&B, all built by Taos Pueblo artisans; the owner can give you a history lesson on the area, along with a comfortable bed.

► MESAS AND MOUNTAINTOPS

Not only is New Mexico's mountain scenery stunning, but the population is sparse, so it's very easy to get out of town and enjoy the natural splendor all on your own. This route, which takes nine days, caters to hikers who want to spend as much time as possible outside of the cities. When you arrive in New Mexico and see the scenery, it's tempting to put on your boots and head straight out, but unless you're coming from a comparable

elevation, stick to clambering in foothills and scenic drives for the first couple of days. Drink plenty of liquids, and head to bed early.

If you'd prefer not to do the overnight backpacking trip suggested below, take a day hike in Bandelier National Monument instead and then stay the night in nearby Los Alamos or camp at the monument. In the morning, you can squeeze in another quick day hike at Bandelier or drive on toward Jemez and hike to San Antonio Springs. As for timing, don't try this itinerary any earlier than mid-May; even then you will still encounter snowpack at higher elevations. If you're especially interested in rafting, the early part of the summer, when the river is fullest, is the best time to do it. Visiting in the fall may be colder, but the glowing yellow aspen groves that stud the mountains are a major attraction.

Day 1

Arrive at Albuquerque's Sunport; pick up your rental car and head north to your hotel in Santa Fe. If you arrive on an early flight, take a detour to Kasha-Katuwe Tent Rocks National Monument for an easy, hour-long hike—but don't push yourself too hard.

Day 2

Rent a bike and get oriented downtown, and then head down the rail trail to Lamy or cruise around the Dale Ball Trails in the Sangre de Cristo foothills. Return to Santa Fe for a leisurely and hearty barbecue dinner at The Cowgirl.

Day 3

Take your pick of several hikes in the Santa Fe area: The Rio en Medio trail north of Tesuque is a good one, or make the trek along Raven's Ridge if you can handle the elevation. At night, relax in the hot tubs at Ten Thousand Waves, and then have a late dinner at Mu Du Noodles.

Day 4

Drive to Taos via the high road, spending the afternoon around town or on a short hike in Hondo Canyon near Taos Ski Valley (grab a burrito at Abe's Cantina y Cocina in Arroyo Seco when you head up this way). At night, meet other outdoorsy types at Eske's Brew Pub. Bunk at the casual Laughing Horse Inn.

Kasha-Katuwe Tent Rocks National Monument

Day 5

Hike or mountain bike along the South Boundary Trail, or go rafting through the white water in the Taos Box. Around sunset, head out to Blackrock Springs. Spend the night in Taos.

Day 6

Drive back south via the low road and take an afternoon hike in Valles Caldera National Preserve; stay the night in Los Alamos or at the campground at Bandelier National Monument.

Day 7

Head into Bandelier National Monument for an overnight backpacking trip to ancestral Puebloan ruins at the Shrine of the Stone Lions.

Day 8

Hike out to your car and drive south along the Jemez Mountain Trail. Stay overnight in Jemez Springs, soothing your muscles with a rest in the hot springs here.

Day 9

Return to Albuquerque via the Jemez Mountain Trail; grab a last bite of green-chile stew at The Frontier if you have time before your flight.

SANTA FE

One of Santa Fe's several nicknames is "Fanta Se," a play on the name that suggests the city's disconnection from reality. This small cluster of mud-colored buildings in the mountains of northern New Mexico does indeed seem to subsist on dreams alone, as more than 20 percent of the 67,000 people who live here are engaged in some sort of creative endeavor—a larger proportion of writers, artists, and performers than in any other city in the United States. The local Yellow Pages gives some indication of the scale: "Art galleries" take up five pages, and "Artists" have their own heading, with subheadings for painters, sculptors, and so on. In all, nearly half of the city is employed in the larger arts industry. (Cynics would lump the state legislature, which convenes in the capitol here, into this category as well.)

The city fabric itself is a byproduct of this creativity—many of the "adobe" buildings that make up the distinctive downtown area are in fact plaster and stucco, built in the early 20th century to satisfy a collective vision of what the city ought to look like to appeal to tourists. And the mix of old-guard Spanish, Pueblo Indians, groovy Anglos, and international jetsetters of all stripes has even developed a soft but noticeable accent—a vaguely Continental intonation, with a vocabulary drawn from the 1960s counterculture and alternative healing.

What keeps Santa Fe grounded, to use the local lingo, is its location, tucked in the foothills of the Sangre de Cristos. The outside is never far, even if you're just admiring the mountain view from your massage table at a Japanese-style spa or dining on succulent locally raised

COURTESY OF SANTA FE CONVENTION & VISITORS BUREAU/© JACK PARSONS

HIGHLIGHTS

◖ Palace of the Governors: The state history museum is set in Santa Fe's original government offices, a thick-walled adobe first built in the Spanish colonial era. A new wing, opening in May 2009, will hold even more fascinating exhibits (page 28).

◖ La Fonda: The Santa Fe Trail trade route ended on the doorstep of this hotel, which has witnessed the city's fluctuating fortunes – and harbored its assorted characters – for centuries (page 31).

◖ Canyon Road: This winding street of galleries is the heart of Santa Fe's art scene – and its social life – when it's packed with potential collectors and party hoppers on summer Friday nights (page 33).

◖ Museum of International Folk Art: In the main exhibition hall, all the world's crafts, from Appalachian quilts to Zulu masks, are jumbled together in an inspiring display of human creativity (page 36).

◖ Bandelier National Monument: The hidden valley of Frijoles Canyon was home to the ancestors of today's Puebloans, in an elaborate city complex and cliff-side cave apartments (page 72).

◖ Ghost Ranch: The spread where Georgia O'Keeffe kept a house occupies a patch of dramatic red-rock cliffs and wind-blown pinnacles. Hike up to Chimney Rock for the best view across Abiquiu (page 79).

◖ Chimayó: Faith is palpable in this village north of Santa Fe, where a chapel is known as "the Lourdes of America," thanks to the heal-

ing powers attributed to the holy dirt found here (page 80).

◖ Las Trampas: In this remote mountain village on the high road to Taos, the San José de Gracia Church is a pure example of colonial Spanish adobe design (page 83).

LOOK FOR ◖ TO FIND RECOMMENDED SIGHTS, ACTIVITIES, DINING, AND LODGING.

SANTA FE

0   0.5 mi
0   0.5 km

To Santa Fe Airport
AIRPORT RD

To Rancho de las Golondrinas, Sunrise Springs, and Blue Heron

HORSEMAN'S HAVEN

GENOVEVA CHAVEZ COMMUNITY CENTER

STAGE COACH MOTOR INN

MARISCOS LA PLAYA

JACKALOPE

TREEHOUSE CAFÉ

SILER RD

OSAGE AVE

W ALAMEDA ST

Santa Fe River

AGUA FRIA ST

PAOLO SOLERI OUTDOOR AMPHITHEATER

EL REY INN

RAMBLIN' CAFÉ

FELIPE'S TACOS

FILM CENTER AT CINEMACAFE

THE SCREEN

COLLEGE OF SANTA FE

LLANO ST

GIG

COUNTER CULTURE

BACA ST

DUNE ST

LENA ST

HIGH MAYHEM

MU DU NOODLES

SANTA FE INTERNATIONAL HOSTEL

SANTA FE BAKING CO

MARISCOS LA PLAYA

TINY'S

DON DIEGO AVE

DON GASPAR ST

BODY

CORDOVA RD

CERRILLOS RD

ZIA RD

SIRINGO RD

ST. MICHAEL'S DR

ST. FRANCIS DR

SAN MATEO RD

ST. VINCENT HOSPITAL

RODEO RD

PUBLIC LANDS INFORMATION CENTER

To Hwy 14 and Albuquerque

SEE "DOWNTOWN SANTA FE" MAP

ANNAPURNA

Railyard Park

PALACE AVE

PASEO DE PERALTA

HICKOX ST

To Tesuque

84 285

ALEXANDER'S INN

CANYON ROAD

CANYON RD

CAMINO DEL MONTE SOL

EL FAROL

CRISTO REY CATHOLIC CHURCH

To Santa Fe Canyon Preserve

HYDE PARK RD

GONZALES RD

475

To Ten Thousand Waves and Dale Ball Trails

ST. JOHN'S COLLEGE

MUSEUM OF INDIAN ARTS & CULTURE

MUSEUM OF INTERNATIONAL FOLK ART

MUSEUM OF SPANISH COLONIAL ART

WHEELWRIGHT MUSEUM OF THE AMERICAN INDIAN

CCA/BATAAN MEMORIAL/ CHILDREN'S MUSEUM

CAMINO LEJO

OLD SANTA FE TRAIL

OLD PECOS TRAIL

To Rancheros de Santa Fe and Galisteo

HARRY'S ROADHOUSE

BOBCAT BITE

SILVER STARLIGHT

AVALON TRAVEL

25

84 285

14

lamb at an elegant restaurant. You can be out of town at a trailhead in 10 minutes, skiing down a precipitous slope in 30, or wandering among the red cliffs you've seen in Georgia O'Keeffe's paintings of Abiquiu in 60. To the east of the city is the border of Pecos Wilderness Area, a couple of hundred thousand acres of dense forest studded with alpine summits such as Santa Fe Baldy and Truchas Peak.

Santa Fe's history, too, gives the community strong roots—established in 1609, it's the second-oldest city in the United States (St. Augustine, Florida, beats it by 44 years). The city is surrounded by American Indian pueblos that have been inhabited since well before the Spanish arrived, alongside the remnants of much older cities, such as Tyuonyi in Bandelier National Monument. As the former capital of the Spanish territory of Nuevo México, Santa Fe was the gateway to the wilder, emptier lands to the north—and it still is, with two scenic routes running north to Taos: The high road winds along mountain ridges through old Hispano villages, while the low road follows the Rio Grande through apple orchards and canyons.

If you need a break from Santa Fe and all its history, head for the town of Española, a modern and unlikely mix of lowrider-proud cruisers and convert Sikhs and a great place for New Mexican food. Or seek out isolated Los Alamos, home of the atomic bomb—the biggest reality check of all.

PLANNING YOUR TIME

If you're looking at a short trip, a three-day weekend in the city is a perfectly good getaway; add a few days more to take a hike outside of town or make the drive to Taos, Los Alamos, or Abiquiu. Mobs arrive in July and August, especially for Spanish Market and Indian Market (the latter coincides with closing night at the Santa Fe Opera), so you'll find the city a bit calmer—and the heat less overpowering—in spring and fall. Choose spring if you'll be primarily in the city—lilacs bloom in May, tumbling over adobe walls and filling the air with scent—but opt for the fall if you plan to do

a lot of hiking, because October is when the dense groves of aspen trees on the Sangre de Cristo Mountains turn bright yellow, a gorgeous sight enhanced by the crisp, spicy air at that time of year. If you do come in the summer, however, you'll find the gallery scene in full swing—plan to be in the city on a Friday night, when Canyon Road galleries have their convivial openings.

HISTORY

La Villa Real de la Santa Fé (The Royal City of the Holy Faith) was built to be the capital of Spain's northernmost territory in the New World. The Camino Real, the route that connected the outpost with Mexico, dead-ended in the newly built plaza. Barely 70 years later, the 1680 Pueblo Revolt set back the Spanish settlers' plans, but not for long: Don Diego de Vargas returned with troops in 1693, bent on reconquering the city. After a pitched battle, the Spanish moved back in (ousting the Indians from the statehouse, which they'd turned into storerooms and apartments) and established a shaky truce with the local population, after which more Spaniards began to settle in small villages north of Santa Fe.

Mexico's independence from Spain in 1821 marked a major shift in the city's fortunes, as the new government opened its northernmost territory to outside trade—something the Spanish had refused to do. Soon enough, the Santa Fe Trail, a route from Missouri to New Mexico first blazed in 1792, was booming with trade, and the city was a cosmopolitan commercial hub where Mexicans and Americans swapped goods and hard currency. But not without a little turmoil: In 1836, the Mexican government appointed Albino Pérez to the governorship—unlike previous leaders, he wasn't a native New Mexican, which angered the populace. A group of protesters fought Pérez's disorganized militia on Black Mesa (the same place a crew of Puebloan holdouts prolonged De Vargas's *reconquista* in 1694), northwest of Santa Fe. Pérez was then hunted down and killed in the Palace of the Governors. This incident helped the Americans earn an easy victory in New Mexico during the Mexican-American War, when General Stephen Kearny peaceably brought the territory under U.S. control in 1846.

But Santa Feans still had to contend with the more domineering figure of Bishop Jean Baptiste Lamy, appointed in 1850. For more than three decades, the Frenchman struggled with the local culture (both Spanish Catholic and Indian), and his attempts to "elevate" the city to European standards can be seen in the grandiose stone St. Francis Cathedral.

The Americans had a little more luck taming the frontier capital when the railroad came through, in 1880. Although it effectively killed the Santa Fe Trail (and the trade economy with it), it opened up the city to what's still its lifeblood today: tourism. As locals moved south to do business in the boomtown of New Albuquerque, where the train tracks went right by their front doors, loads of curious Easterners, who weren't deterred by the 18-mile rail spur up from Lamy, took their places. Along with them came freight cars full of odd materials, such as bricks and timber, to build new houses that were the most visible evidence that New Mexico was no longer a Spanish colony.

Some of these early visitors were artists who helped popularize Santa Fe as a retreat well before the territory was granted official statehood in 1912. In that same year, a council of city planners decided to promote Santa Fe as a tourist destination and preserve its distinctive architecture. By 1917, the Museum of Fine Arts (now the New Mexico Museum of Art) had opened, and the first Indian Market was held in 1922 in response to the trend of Anglos' collecting the local craftwork. Los Cinco Pintores—a crew of intrepid painters who built their own houses on Canyon Road—were just a handful of the artists who now called the city home.

A new element was added to Santa Fe's mix in 1943, when the building at 109 East Palace Avenue became the "front office" and only known address for Los Alamos, where the country's greatest scientists were developing the atomic bomb under a cloud of confidentiality. But the rational scientists left little mark on Santa Fe—right-brain thinking has continued to flourish, and the city is now a modern, creative version of its old self, a meeting place where international art dealers swap goods and ideas.

ORIENTATION

For all the things to see and do in Santa Fe, it's easy to forget you're in a small town. Not only are most of the major sights within walking distance from the central plaza, but visitors will have little reason to see large swaths of town. Generally, you'll find yourself within the oval formed by Paseo de Peralta, a main road that almost completely circles the central district. On its southwest side it connects with Cerrillos Road, a main avenue lined with motel courts, shopping plazas, and chain restaurants. Compared with the central historic district, it's unsightly, but there are some great local places to eat along this way, as well as the few inexpensive hotels in town.

Sights

DOWNTOWN

The city's most visited sights are within a few blocks of the central plaza.

Santa Fe Plaza

When Santa Fe was established in 1610, its layout was based on the standard Spanish laws regulating town planning in the colonies—hence the central plaza fronted by the Casas Reales (Palace of the Governors) on its north side. The plaza is still the city's social hub, and the blocks surrounding it are rich with history. In the center of the plaza is the **Soldiers' Monument,** dedicated in 1867 to those who died in "battles with…Indians in the territory of New Mexico"—the word "savage" has been neatly excised, a policy applied to historic markers throughout the state.

DOWNTOWN SANTA FE

To Santa Fe Opera, Española, and Taos

To Hwy 599

CLAFOUTIS ▼

N GUADALUPE ST

JEFFERSON

PASEO DE PERALTA

SAN FRANCISCO ST

BUMBLE BEE'S BAJA GRILL

W ALAMEDA ST

Santa Fe River

Santa Fe River State Park

AQUA SANTA ▼

W WATER ST

IRVINE ST

CLOSSON ST

DE FOURI ST

SANTUARIO DE GUADALUPE ‡

RISTRA ▼

BERT'S LA TAQUERIA ▼

THE COWGIRL

AZTEC CAFÉ ▼

EL TESORO ▼

AZTEC ST

S ST FRANCIS DR

AGUA FRIA ST

ROMERO ST

Santa Fe Southern Railway/ NM Rail Runner

NM FILM ■ MUSEUM

SNOWDEN'S ▼

MONTEZUMA AVE

WILLEE'S ▼

SFSR/NM RAIL ■ RUNNER DEPOT

GARFIELD ST

SANDOVAL ST

W MANHATTAN AVE

JUANITA ST

READ ST

W MANHATTAN AVE

VICTORIA PRICE CONTEMPORARY ART & DESIGN ■

SANTA FE ● MOTEL & INN

FARMERS MARKET ■

EL PARADERO B

BOX GALLERY ■

■ EVO GALLERY

HOTEL ● SANTA FE

▼ SAGE BAKEHOUSE

★ SITE SANTA FE

PASEO DE PERALTA

NINITA ST

Railyard Park

CERRILLOS RD

SANTA FE ● SAGE INN

CAMINO SIERRA VISTA

0   200 yds

0   200 m

© AVALON TRAVEL

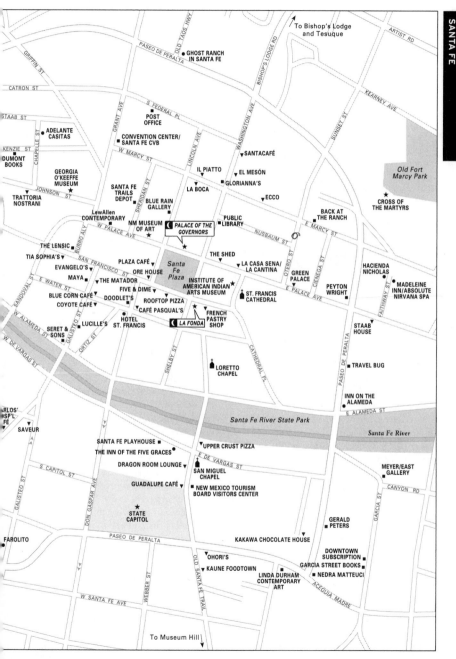

To Bishop's Lodge
and Tesuque

ARTIST RD

GRIFFIN ST
PASEO DE PERALTA

OLD TAOS HWY.

GHOST RANCH
IN SANTA FE

BISHOP'S LODGE RD
KEARNEY AVE

CATRON ST

STAAB ST
S FEDERAL PL
POST
OFFICE

WASHINGTON AVE

SUNSET ST

Old Fort
Marcy Park

CHAPELLE ST
ADELANTE
CASITAS
CONVENTION CENTER/
SANTA FE CVB
W. MARCY ST

KENZIE ST
DUMONT
BOOKS

GRANT AVE

SANTACAFÉ

GEORGIA
O'KEEFFE
MUSEUM

LINCOLN AVE

IL PIATTO
EL MESÓN

CROSS OF
THE MARTYRS

JOHNSON ST
SANTA FE
TRAILS
DEPOT
BLUE RAIN
GALLERY

SHERIDAN ST

GLORIANNA'S
LA BOCA

ECCO

TRATTORIA
NOSTRANI

LewAllen
CONTEMPORARY

BURRO ALLEY

NM MUSEUM
OF ART
W. PALACE AVE

PALACE OF THE
GOVERNORS

PUBLIC
LIBRARY

NUSBAUM ST

E. MARCY ST

BACK AT
THE RANCH

OTERO ST

THE LENSIC
TIA SOPHIA'S

SAN FRANCISCO ST

PLAZA CAFÉ
ORE HOUSE

Santa
Fe
Plaza

THE SHED
LA CASA SENA/
LA CANTINA

CIENEGA ST

HACIENDA
NICHOLAS

EVANGELO'S
MAYA
E. WATER ST
THE MATADOR
FIVE & DIME

GREEN
PALACE

PEYTON
WRIGHT

E. PALACE AVE

FAITHWAY ST

MADELEINE
INN/ABSOLUTE
NIRVANA SPA

SANDOVAL ST

BLUE CORN CAFÉ
COYOTE CAFÉ

GALISTEO ST

DOODLET'S

INSTITUTE OF
AMERICAN INDIAN
ARTS MUSEUM

ROOFTOP PIZZA
CAFÉ PASQUAL'S

ST. FRANCIS
CATHEDRAL

W. ALAMEDA ST

SERET &
SONS

LUCILLE'S

ORTIZ ST

HOTEL
ST. FRANCIS

LA FONDA

FRENCH
PASTRY
SHOP

STAAB
HOUSE

W. DE VARGAS ST

SHELBY ST

LORETTO
CHAPEL

CATHEDRAL PL

PASEO DE PERALTA

TRAVEL BUG

INN ON THE
ALAMEDA

ARLOS'
SP'L
FE
SAVEUR

E. ALAMEDA ST

Santa Fe River State Park

Santa Fe River

S CAPITOL ST

SANTA FE PLAYHOUSE
THE INN OF THE FIVE GRACES
DRAGON ROOM LOUNGE

UPPER CRUST PIZZA

E. DE VARGAS ST

SAN MIGUEL
CHAPEL

MEYER/EAST
GALLERY

CANYON RD

GALISTEO ST

DON GASPAR AVE

GUADALUPE CAFÉ

NEW MEXICO TOURISM
BOARD VISITORS CENTER

GARCIA ST

FAROLITO

STATE
CAPITOL

PASEO DE PERALTA

OLD SANTA FE TRAIL

KAKAWA CHOCOLATE HOUSE

GERALD
PETERS

DOWNTOWN
SUBSCRIPTION
GARCIA STREET BOOKS
NEDRA MATTEUCI

OHORI'S
KAUNE FOODTOWN

WEBBER ST

W. SANTA FE AVE

LINDA DURHAM
CONTEMPORARY
ART

ACEQUIA MADRE

To Museum Hill

© ZORA O'NEILL

The plaza is the city's main gathering spot.

◖ Palace of the Governors

The former seat of Santa Fe's government is now the state history museum (105 W. Palace Ave., 505/476-5100, www.palaceofthegovernors .org, 10 A.M.–5 P.M. Tues.–Sun., $8, free 5–8 P.M. Fri.). Built 1610–1612, it's one of the oldest government buildings in the United States, giving it plenty of time to change character (from Spanish colonial adobe to Greek revival wood trim in the territorial era to a brief Victorian phase and back to spiffier adobe in 1909) and accumulate stories: De Vargas fought the Indian rebels here room by room when he retook the city in 1693, ill-fated Mexican governor Albino Pérez was beheaded in his office in 1837, and Governor Lew Wallace penned *Ben Hur* here in the late 1870s.

Eighty percent of the museum's collection is in storage, so an expansion, slated to finish in May 2009, will add a little breathing room. What you can see in the meantime: trinkets and photos from the 19th century, including the oldest daguerreotype in the state—which happens to be a portrait of Padre Antonio

Martinez, a folk hero of Taos. You'll also see the beautiful 18th-century Segesser hide paintings, two wall-size panels of buffalo skin depicting, on one, a meeting between two Indian tribes, and on the other, a battle between the French and a Spanish expedition in Nebraska. These works, along with the room they're in (trimmed with 1909 murals of the Puyé cliffs) are worth the price of admission. In a couple of the restored furnished rooms, you can compare the living conditions of the Mexican leadership circa 1845 to the relative comfort the U.S. governor enjoyed in 1893.

Walking tours depart from the Lincoln Avenue side of the museum at 10:15 A.M. (Mon.–Sat. summer only, $10), covering all the plaza-area highlights in about two hours. You can also buy a **museum pass** here for $18 that grants you admission to this and four other exhibition spaces—the New Mexico Museum of Art, the Museum of Indian Arts & Culture, the Museum of International Folk Art, and the Museum of Spanish Colonial Art; the pass is good for four days. A $12 pass gets you entrance just to this place and the New Mexico Museum of Art.

St. Francis Cathedral

Santa Fe's showpiece cathedral (131 Cathedral Pl., 505/982-5619, 7 A.M.–6 P.M. daily, free), visible from the plaza at the end of East San Francisco Street, was built over about 15 years in the late 19th century. It represents a bit of a folly for Jean Baptiste Lamy, who initiated the project. The French priest had been assigned by the church to a newly created post that would formally separate New Mexico's Catholics from those in Mexico, but when he arrived in 1851 full of fire and zeal to uplift the barbarous population, he promptly alienated much of his would-be flock.

Lamy was not only shocked by the locals' ways of worship (the cult of the Virgin of Guadalupe was already well established, and the Penitente brotherhood was performing public self-flagellation), but he was also horrified by their aesthetics. How could a person possibly reach heaven while praying on a dirt floor

IT'S NOT *ALL* ADOBE

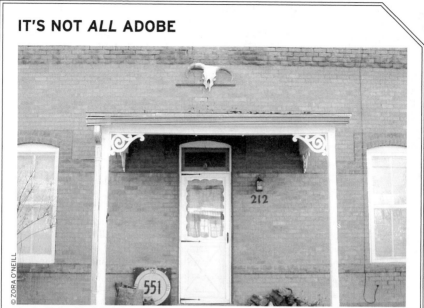

© ZORA O'NEILL

Santa Fe territorial style

Santa Fe maintains its distinctive historic core through the stringent Historic Styles Ordinance, which dictates even the shade of brown stucco finish required for buildings around the plaza. But look closely, and you'll see several different styles. **Colonial** is the term applied to adobe (or adobe-look) buildings, usually one story, with their typical rounded edges and flat roofs supported by vigas – long crossbeams made of single tree trunks. The style was developed by the Spanish colonists in the 16th, 17th, and 18th centuries, based on their previous experience with adobe architecture and forms they saw in the pueblos.

In the 19th century, when New Mexico became a territory of the United States, American influence came in the form of timber-frame houses, often two stories with balconies, and ornamented with brick cornices or coping and Greek revival details, such as carved wood fluted columns and pediments above windows. This **territorial** style, as it's called, can still be seen on the plaza at the two-story Catron Building on the northeast side, but a lot of the best examples were lost during the **pueblo revival** period in the early part of the 20th century. Architects such as John Gaw Meem and Isaac Rapp (the latter designed the Museum of Fine Arts on the northwest corner of the plaza) took their inspiration from both the Spanish colonial-era mission churches and the traditional pueblo buildings, where they saw a clean-lined minimalism that was in keeping with the developing modernist sensibilities. Because they used contemporary frame construction, pueblo revival buildings could be much bigger – Meem's additions to La Fonda make it five stories tall. The architectural trend coincided with the city's aggressive move to court tourism and the idea of developing a comprehensive "look" for the city, so many of the wood-frame territorial houses were simply covered over in a thick layer of plaster. The result is not precisely "historic," but the city planners achieved their goal: Santa Fe looks like no other city in the United States.

© ZORA O'NEILL

St. Francis Cathedral

inside a building made of mud? Lamy took one look at the tiny adobe church dedicated to St. Francis of Assisi and decided he could do better. Construction on the Romanesque revival St. Francis Cathedral began in 1869, under the direction of architects and craftsmen from Europe—they used the old church as a frame for the new stone structure and then demolished all of the adobe save for a small side chapel.

Lamy seems to have financed his very expensive project through a loan from one of the city's wealthiest men, Abraham Staab, one of Santa Fe's leading Jewish merchants. This is the alleged reason for the Hebrew inscription "Yahweh" over the cathedral's main doors and the two six-pointed stars in the place: one visible from the pulpit, another in the vestuary. Even so, Lamy ran short of cash—hence the stumpy aspect of the cathedral's corners, which should be topped with spires.

Inside is all Gothic-inspired light and space and glowing stained-glass windows, but that could never truly replace the local traditions.

The salvaged adobe chapel remains, off to the left of the altar. It is dedicated to the figure of La Conquistadora, a statue brought to Santa Fe from Mexico in 1625, carried away by the retreating Spanish during the Pueblo Revolt, proudly reinstated in 1693, and honored ever since for inspiring the Spanish to stick with their colonizing project. She glows in her purple robes, under a heavy viga ceiling—all of which probably makes Lamy shudder in his crypt in front of the main altar (he died in 1888).

Loretto Chapel

Step inside this small chapel (207 Old Santa Fe Tr., 505/982-0092, 9 A.M.–6 P.M. Mon.–Sat., 10:30 A.M.–5 P.M. Sun., $2.50), and you leave the Southwest behind. Initiated by Bishop Lamy in 1873, the building was the first Gothic structure built west of the Mississippi. Lamy was occupied with building the St. Francis Cathedral, so this was a side project, perhaps a way to keep his French architects employed. The decorative elements reflect his fondness for all things European: the stations of the cross rendered by Italian masons, the harmonium and stained-glass windows imported from France. Even the stone from which it was built was hauled at great expense from quarries up to 200 miles south.

But what really draws the eye is the marvelously simple and elegant—and allegedly miraculous—spiral staircase leading to the choir loft. Made entirely of wood, it makes two complete turns without a central support pole. It was built in 1878 by a mysterious carpenter who appeared seemingly at the spiritual behest of the resident Sisters of Loretto. These nuns—who had in 1853 trooped to New Mexico from Missouri to found a school at Lamy's request—had resorted to prayer because the funding from Lamy hadn't been quite enough. The carpenter toiled in silence for six months, the story goes, and then disappeared, without taking any payment. He was never heard from again—though some historians claim to have tracked him down to Las Cruces, where he met his end in a bar fight. The Sisters of Loretto finally went broke in 1968; the chapel was desanctified when it was sold in 1971, but it's still a popular wedding spot. The chapel closes at 5 P.M. every day in winter.

New Mexico Museum of Art

Famed as much for its building as for the art it contains, the New Mexico Museum of Art (107 W. Palace Ave., 505/476-5072, www.nmart museum.org, 10 A.M.–5 P.M. Tues.–Sun., $8, free 5–8 P.M. Fri.) is dedicated to work by state artists. Built in 1917, it is a beautiful example of pueblo revival architecture, originally designed as the New Mexico pavilion for a world expo in San Diego two years earlier. The curvaceous stucco-clad building is an amalgam of iconic pueblo mission churches: The bell towers, for instance, mimic those found at San Felipe. Inside, the collection varies from Gerald Cassidy's *Cui Bono?*, a perpetually relevant oil painting that questions the benefits of pueblo tourism (it has been on display since the museum opened in 1917), to contemporary video installations. Look out for an excellent collection of Awa Tsireh's meticulous watercolors of ceremonial dances at San Ildefonso pueblo, alongside work of other local American Indian artists.

On your way out, don't miss the adjacent St. Francis Auditorium, where three artists adorned the walls with art nouveau murals depicting the life of Santa Fe's patron saint. It's rare to see a secular style usually reserved for languorous ladies in flowing togas used to render such scenes as the apotheosis of Saint Francis and Santa Clara's renunciation, and the effect is beautiful.

Georgia O'Keeffe Museum

Opened in 1997, this museum (217 Johnson St., 505/946-1000, www.okeeffemuseum.org, 10 A.M.–5 P.M. Thurs.–Tues., open daily May–Aug., $8, free 5–8 P.M. Fri.) honors the artist whose name is inextricably bound with New Mexico. The contrary member of the New York avant-garde ("Nothing is less real than realism," she famously said) first visited the state in the 1920s and then moved to Abiquiu permanently in 1949, after the death of her lover, photographer Alfred Stieglitz.

Initially, the museum was a bit of a hollow monument, as O'Keeffe's finest works—her signature sensuous, near-abstract flower blossoms, for instance—have already been ensconced in other famous museums the world over, leaving only the rarities here (who knew she did illustrations for a Dole Fruit Co. ad campaign?) to hang alongside loosely related special exhibitions on her contemporaries, or those whose work she influenced or admired. But in mid-2005, the museum received the collection of the Georgia O'Keeffe Foundation, the trust that had been managing the artist's assets since her death in 1986. The transaction brought some exciting new treasures—although much of the space is still given over to exhibitions on her contemporaries or on those whose work she influenced or admired.

Institute of American Indian Arts Museum

Set in the city's former post office building, this museum (108 Cathedral Pl., 505/983-8900, www.iaia.edu, 10 A.M.–5 P.M. Mon.–Sat. and noon–5 P.M. Sun., $5) is the showcase for students, professors, and alumni of the prestigious IAIA. Come here if you're burned out on old pots in glass cases—instead you'll see the contemporary American Indian experience rendered in oil, charcoal, glass, bronze, and conceptual installations. The collection of works by confident colorist and the institute's most famous professor, Fritz Scholder, is particularly strong. And while the work on the walls is often very experimental, the gift shop stocks a good blend of modern and traditional styles (as well as the iconic "Frybread Power" T-shirt), and it is quite well priced.

◖ La Fonda

"The Inn at the End of the Trail," on the corner of San Francisco Street and Old Santa Fe Trail (100 E. San Francisco St., 505/982-5511, www.lafondasantafe.com), has been offering respite to travelers in some form or another since 1607. This hotel boomed in the early years of the Santa Fe Trail and the gold-digging era with a casino and saloon; it hosted the victory ball

© ZORA O'NEILL

La Fonda, the inn at the end of the Santa Fe Trail

following General Kearny's takeover of New Mexico in the Mexican-American War; and during the Civil War it housed Confederate general H. H. Sibley during his short-lived attempt to claim New Mexico for the South. Lynchings, shootings, and all the other signatures of Wild West life took place in the lobby. In the 1920s, it got a bit safer for the average tourist, as it became part of the chain of Harvey Houses along the country's railways. Since the 1960s, it has been a family-owned hotel.

The stacked pueblo revival place you see today dates from 1920, and its interior still hums with history—something about the tile floors, painted glass, and heavy furniture conveys the pleasant clamor of conversation and hotel busyness the way more modern lobbies do not. Guests still pick up their keys at an old wood reception desk, drop their letters in an Indian-drum-turned-mailbox, and chat with the concierge below the poster for Harvey's Indian Detours car-tour service. Also look around at the great art collection, including wall-size portraits of Kit Carson and Native American dancers, as well as a mural of a Santa

Fe Trail wagon train. La Plazuela restaurant, in the sunny center courtyard, is a beautiful place to rest, and the bar is timeless.

Cross of the Martyrs

This white cross at the top of a hill overlooking downtown Santa Fe is a memorial to the Spanish settlers who were killed in the Pueblo Revolt. It's actually a newer version of a first cross, raised in 1920 a little bit to the west, off Paseo de la Loma. This new cross is at the end of a zigzagging paved path uphill, each switchback marked with a plaque explaining various points in the city's history. It's not a strenuous walk, and the bird's-eye view from the hilltop is excellent. Behind the cross is **Old Fort Marcy Park,** site of the remnants of the first American fort in the Southwest, built in 1847 by General Stephen Kearny and then abandoned in 1894. The path up to the cross begins on Paseo de Peralta just east of Otero Street.

NEW MEXICO STATE CAPITOL

A round building with an entrance at each of the cardinal points, the 1966 state capitol (411

Old Santa Fe Tr., 505/986-4589, 8 A.M.–5 P.M. Mon.–Fri.) mimics the sun symbol, called a *zia*, used on the state flag. Inside it's a maze of concentric halls, many of which are lined with an excellent collection of art by the state's best-known creative types—all accessible for free. On the ground level, check out the halls on the senate side; upstairs galleries combine folk art and rugs with more contemporary work, such as Holly Hughes's giant buffalo-head sculpture. Head to the fourth-floor Governor's Gallery (505/476-2200), established in 1973, for more traditional work and a rotating series of exhibits curated by the New Mexico Museum of Art, and don't forget to look up at the stained-glass skylight over the rotunda, which has an Indian basket-weave pattern. The floor of the rotunda is a mosaic rendition of the state seal: the Mexican brown eagle, grasping a snake and shielded by the American bald eagle. When the legislature is in session—late January through February in even-numbered years, late January through March in odd—you're welcome to sit in the galleries and watch the proceedings.

C CANYON ROAD

Ground zero for Santa Fe's art market is the intersection of Paseo de Peralta and Canyon Road, the beginning of a half-mile strip of more than 80 galleries. In the summer, Canyon Road is a sea of strolling art lovers, aficionados and amateurs alike. It's especially thronged on Friday evenings, when most galleries have an open house or an exhibition opening. There's a city parking lot at the north end of the road, and public restrooms (9:30 A.M.–5:30 P.M. daily) are near the south end, in the complex at 225 Canyon Road, behind Expressions gallery.

Hard to believe, but this street wasn't always chockablock with thousand-dollar canvases. It used to be farmland (irrigated by the "Mother Ditch," Acequia Madre, which runs parallel one block to the south), and only a few decades ago, it was still unpaved, a muddy gully when it rained. In addition to the galleries, you'll also pass the mid-19th-century house **El Zaguán**, which contains the offices of the **Historic Santa Fe Foundation** (545 Canyon Rd., 505/983-2567, www.historicsantafe.org, 9 A.M.–noon and 1:30–5 P.M. Mon.–Fri., free). Named for its long internal hallway *(zaguán),* the building was the home of a local merchant, James L. Johnson, from 1854, and then occupied by several other city bigwigs after he lost his fortune in 1881. Its garden, laid out in the late 19th century, is a lovely place to rest in the summer. At 630 Canyon Road, the **Quaker meetinghouse** is the former home of Olive Rush, who painted the Santa Fe Trail mural at La Fonda and willed her house to the Quakers after her death. In the 1920s, Los Cinco Pintores, the band of young realist painters who also called themselves the "five little nuts in five mud huts," lived in houses they built around the intersection with Camino del Monte Sol. (Will Shuster is the best known of the five today, in part because he started the Zozobra tradition; Walter Mruk, Fremont Ellis, Joseph Bakos, and Willard Nash were the other four.)

Head beyond the shops and through a residential stretch to the far north end of the road to see John Gaw Meem's enormous **Cristo Rey Catholic Church** (1120 Canyon Rd.), built of 180,000 adobe bricks around a steel frame. It opened in 1940 but looks as if it could be much older; inside is a dramatic mid-18th-century baroque stone altarpiece, salvaged from La Castrense, the military chapel that used to occupy the south side of the plaza.

GUADALUPE AND THE RAILYARD DISTRICT

Guadalupe Street runs south and north from just west of the plaza; its southern stretch developed around the depot for the 18-mile rail spur up from the main line at Lamy, but today it is lined with a clutch of cafés and shops that feel quite different from the plaza, as Guadalupe is just outside of the historic center, beyond the reach of the most stringent adobe-look codes. The area around the railroad tracks, from Sanbusco Center southwest, has been recently redeveloped, with Santa Fe's newest green space, Railyard Park, inaugurated in late 2008. On the north end of the park are numerous arts spaces, the city farmers market hall, and the **Santa Fe Southern Railway** (410 S. Guadalupe St., 505/989-8600, www.sfsr .com) depot—where vintage trains depart to Lamy. This is also the spot where commuter trains from Albuquerque arrive.

Santuario de Guadalupe

Built 1776–1796, this is the oldest shrine to the Virgin of Guadalupe in the United States (100 S. Guadalupe St., 505/988-2027, 9 A.M.–4 P.M. Mon.–Sat., free). A century later, it got an odd makeover, with a New England–look wood steeple, tall neo-Gothic arched windows, even a white picket fence—but a renovation in 1975 restored a lot of its original details and shored up its three-foot-thick adobe walls. The interior is spare, just folding chairs set up on the wood floor in front of a Mexican baroque oil-on-canvas altar painting from 1783. Mass is still said regularly, and musical groups, particularly the Santa Fe Desert Chorale, take advantage of the space's excellent acoustics. A museum in the small anteroom displays relics of the old building, such as Greek-style columns carved in wood, and shows exposed pieces of the adobe walls. The chapel is closed on Saturdays during the winter.

SITE Santa Fe

In sharp contrast to the Guadalupe chapel, this boxy, modern exhibition space (1606 Paseo de Peralta, 505/989-1199, www.site santafe.org, 10 A.M.–5 P.M. Wed., Thurs., and Sat., 10 A.M.–7 P.M. Fri., noon–5 P.M. Sun., $10, free on Fri.) is dedicated to all things new in the art world. It puts on high-concept one-off shows that make use of its very flexible space. In even-numbered years, SITE hosts the Santa Fe Biennial, curated by hip critics such as Dave Hickey.

Railyard Park

A massive change for Santa Fe, Railyard Park, which extends along the tracks southwest of Paseo de Peralta, has transformed a previously barren space in the center of the city into a green haven. And not just literally green

(because that waxes and wanes according to the seasons), but also figuratively—the park has innovative water-use guidelines and functions as a sort of living museum, with heritage-breed apple trees and other local plants, as well as a restored piece of an acequia, a centuries-old irrigation ditch. A bike path runs along the acequia, which extends off the southwest end of the park.

OLD SANTA FE TRAIL

From its end at La Fonda, the historic trade route runs off to the east; just past Paseo de Peralta and the small Santa Fe River, it passes through Barrio de Analco, one of Santa Fe's oldest residential neighborhoods, established by the Tlaxcala Indians, who came from Mexico as servants of the first Spanish settlers. The road then runs past the state capitol and to a junction with Old Pecos Trail, the main route to I-25 (and historically the cattle drivers' route to Mexico).

San Miguel Chapel

This sturdy adobe building (401 Old Santa Fe Tr., 505/983-3974, 9 A.M.–5 P.M. Mon.–Sat., 10 A.M.–4 P.M. Sun., $1) is the oldest church structure in the United States, built around 1610 and then partially rebuilt a century later, after it was set aflame in the Pueblo Revolt. Its stone buttresses are the product of a desperate attempt to shore up the sagging walls in the late 19th century. The interior is snug and whitewashed, with painted buffalo hides on the walls and a splendid altar screen that was restored in 1955 after having been covered in house paint for decades. The late-18th-century work is attributed to the anonymous Laguna Santero, a Mexican artist who earned his name from the intricately carved and painted screen at the Laguna Pueblo church, near Albuquerque. The screen functions like an enormous picture frame, with both oil paintings and *bultos* (painted wood statues of saints) inserted in the openings. Below the altar, you can look down into cutouts made into the floor to see the original foundations of the building. On your way out, take a look at the old church bell, now on display in the side room. Allegedly cast in Spain in 1356, it was brought to the New World and installed at San Miguel in the early 19th century.

Bataan Memorial Military Museum and Library

The Bataan Death March, just one of World War II's many atrocities, was a particular tragedy in New Mexico, because most of the state's national guard, which was drafted as the 200th Coast Artillery, was among the more than 70,000 U.S. and Filipino soldiers subject to torture, malnourishment, random execution, malaria, "friendly fire," and three years' imprisonment. Of the 1,800 who started in the regiment, fewer than 900 came home, and a full third of those men died in the first year back. The catastrophe is recalled with newspaper clippings, maps, and testimonials at this home-grown museum (1050 Old Pecos Tr., 505/474-1670, 9 A.M.–4 P.M. Tues., Wed., and Fri., 9 A.M.–1 P.M. Sat., free), which also contains Civil War memorabilia and exhibits on Native American contributions in U.S. wars, such as the Choctaw and Navajo codetalkers. The museum opens one hour later and closes one hour earlier in winter.

Santa Fe Children's Museum

Across the parking lot from the Bataan Memorial, kids can have tons of hands-on fun at the Santa Fe Children's Museum (1050 Old Pecos Tr., 505/989-8359, 10 A.M.–5 P.M. Wed.–Sat., noon–5 P.M. Sun., $4). Fitting for New Mexico, pint-size looms give a chance for kids to learn to weave. And then there are the globally appealing bits: a giant soap-bubble pool, face painting, and fun-house mirrors.

Center for Contemporary Arts

Behind the Children's Museum, this multimedia arts space (1050 Old Pecos Tr., 505/982-1338, www.ccasantafe.org, 10 A.M.–6 P.M. Mon.–Sat., free) screens films and mounts small temporary shows of New Mexican artists.

MUSEUM HILL

The life-size bronze sculpture *Journey's End*, commemorating the Santa Fe Trail and the hardy mule teams that traversed it, marks the entrance to Camino Lejo, a strip of major exhibition spaces on Santa Fe's southeast side. With the Museum of Indian Arts & Culture just next door to the Museum of Spanish Colonial Art, it's an interesting opportunity to compare the two depictions of New Mexican culture and history. One of the city's best tourist deals, a $18 **museum pass**, good for four days, grants access to three of the institutions on the hill (the fourth is free), as well as to the Palace of the Governors and the New Mexico Museum of Art on the plaza. You can buy it at any of the five participating museums. Or buy a $12 pass to both the Museum of International Folk Art and the Museum of Indian Arts & Culture.

Museum of Spanish Colonial Art

The Museum of Spanish Colonial Art (750 Camino Lejo, 505/982-2226, www.spanish colonial.org, 10 A.M.–5 P.M. Tues.–Sun., $6) opened in 2002 with a strong collection of folk art and historical objects dating from the earliest Spanish contact. The collection had been growing since the Spanish Colonial Arts Society was established in Santa Fe in 1925, and it now has about 3,000 pieces. The one-of-a-kind treasures—such as the only signed *retablo* by the 19th-century *santero* Rafael Aragón— are shown alongside more utilitarian items from the colonial past, such as fine tortoiseshell combs, silk mantas, wool rugs, and decorative tin. New work by contemporary artisans is also on display—don't miss Luis Tapia's meta-*bulto, The Folk-Art Collectors.* The museum is also open Mondays in the summer.

Museum of Indian Arts & Culture

This excellent museum (710 Camino Lejo, 505/476-1250, www.indianartsandculture.org, 10 A.M.–5 P.M. Tues.–Sun., $8) is devoted to Native American culture from across the country, though the cornerstone is the permanent exhibit Here, Now & Always, which traces the New Mexican Indians from their ancestors on the mesas and plains up to their present-day efforts at preserving their culture—all through inventive spaces (looking into a HUD-house kitchen on the rez, or sitting at desks in a public schoolroom), sound clips, and stories. Another wing is devoted to contemporary art, while the halls of craftwork display gorgeous beaded moccasins, elaborate headdresses, and more. The gift shop is particularly extensive, stocked with beautiful jewelry and other tidbits from local artisans. The museum is also open Mondays in the summer.

C Museum of International Folk Art

This marvelous hodgepodge of a museum (708 Camino Lejo, 505/476-1200, www.international folkart.org, 10 A.M.–5 P.M. daily, $8) is one of Santa Fe's biggest treats—but the easily overwhelmed should steer clear of the main exhibition space, the collection of modernist designer Alexander Girard. About 10 percent of his collection—10,000 pieces from more than 100 countries—is on permanent display in one hall, hung on walls, set in cases, even dangling from the ceiling. Pieces are juxtaposed to show off similar themes, colors, and materials, an approach that initially seems jumbled but in fact underscores the universality of certain concepts and preoccupations around the world.

Elsewhere in the museum, a wing is dedicated to northern New Mexican Hispano crafts—a good complement to the Museum of Spanish Colonial Art—and a lab area where you can see how pieces are preserved. Temporary exhibits take up the rest of the space, usually with colorful, interactive shows on Carnival celebrations around the world, for instance. Don't skip the gift shop, which stocks some smaller versions of the items in the galleries, along with a great selection of world-music CDs. Like the MIAC, the place closes on Mondays in the low season.

Wheelwright Museum of the American Indian

Mary Cabot Wheelwright, an adventurous East Coast heiress, made her way in the early 1920s to New Mexico, where she met a Navajo medicine man named Hastiin Klah. Together they devised this museum (704 Camino Lejo, 505/982-4636, www.wheelwright.org, 10 A.M.–5 P.M. Mon.–Sat., 1–5 P.M. Sun., free), which opened in 1937 as the House of Navajo Religion. The mission has since been broadened to incorporate all Native American cultures, with exhibits of new work by individual artists rotating every few months. The building—modeled after the typical Navajo hogan, with huge viga timbers supporting the eight-sided structure—has two levels: the ground-floor exhibition space and the basement gift shop, really a re-creation of a 19th-century trading post. The shop would feel like a tourist trap if it weren't for the authentically creaky wood floors and the beautiful antique jewelry on display in the overcrowded cases.

SANTA FE METRO AREA
Rancho de las Golondrinas

The "Ranch of the Swallows" (334 Los Pinos Rd., 505/471-2261, www.golondrinas.org,

outdoor waiting area at Lamy station, a real Wild West rail stop

10 A.M.–4 P.M. Wed.–Sun. June–Sept., $5), about 15 minutes' drive southeast of Santa Fe, is a 200-acre museum in the form of a restored Spanish colonial *paraje*, a way station on the Camino Real. Museum staff members in period costumes demonstrate crafts and other aspects of early New Mexican history in the blacksmith shop, the schoolhouse, and the mills. The ranch hosts big to-dos—a sheep-shearing fair in early June and a frontier-theme horse show in August—and outside the regular season, it opens just for special theme weekends such as a Civil War reenactment in late April and an October harvest festival.

Lamy

Dedicated rail fans, and anyone wanting a break from a drive, will want to head out to this tiny settlement southeast of Santa Fe—the Amtrak train lets passengers off at a lone depot. Parked on the tracks outside, the **Lamy Station Café** (505/466-1904, 11 A.M.–3 P.M. Wed.–Fri., 8:30 A.M.–3 P.M. Sat., 9:30 A.M.–3 P.M. Sun., $8) occupies a vintage dining car, complete with a mod mauve-and-turquoise color scheme and loads of chrome; the menu is American standards, such as a delicious pulled-pork sandwich. Just across the street, the old Legal Tender Saloon is now the **Lamy Railroad & History Museum** (505/466-3519, 11 A.M.–3 P.M. Fri.–Sun. June–Aug., $2). It's worth a visit just for its glam wood interior, dating from 1881; the bar was imported from Bavaria.

Entertainment

BARS

With balmy summer evenings and a populace that always seems to knock off work a little early, Santa Fe is a great place to savor happy hour. The patio at **The Cowgirl** (319 S. Guadalupe St., 505/982-2565, 11 A.M.–2 A.M. Mon.–Fri., 11:30 A.M.–2 A.M. Sat., 8:30 A.M.–midnight Sun.) is packed 5–7 P.M. with neighbors swilling margaritas; pool tables in a side room (called the Corner Pocket) keep people around later. Sunset is also a great time to hit **The Ore House** (50 Lincoln Ave., 505/983-8687, 2:30–11 P.M. daily), on the plaza, where the upstairs balcony bar serves more than 40 kinds of margaritas (happy hour is only 4–6 P.M., though—and you have to request fresh lime juice). Over at La Fonda hotel, the outdoor **Bell Tower Bar** (100 E. San Francisco St., 505/982-5511, 4 P.M.–sunset Mon.–Thurs., 2 P.M.–sunset Fri.–Sun., Apr.–Oct.) provides a fine view from its fifth-floor patio, one of the highest spots in the center of town. In wintertime, the regulars decamp to the lobby watering hole, **La Fiesta Lounge** (11 A.M.–midnight Mon.–Sat., noon–11:30 P.M. Sun. year-round), decorated with portraits of rodeo queens; live local country acts grace the small corner stage. Another good winter haunt is the dimly lit **Dragon Room Lounge** (406 Old Santa Fe Tr., 505/983-7712, 11:30 A.M.–2 A.M.

The Cowgirl's patio is popular at happy hour and beyond.

Mon.–Sat., 5 P.M.–midnight Sun.), where guys in cowboy hats chat with mountain bikers and dressed-up cocktail drinkers, especially during happy hour. Green-chile stew and other snacks are available till 9 P.M., and there's live music Tuesday, Thursday, and Saturday.

For any time of the night, **El Farol** (808 Canyon Rd., 505/983-9912, 11:30 A.M.–3 P.M. and 5 P.M.–2 A.M. Mon.–Sat., noon–midnight Sun.) is a perennial favorite. A bar since 1835, it's the gallery owners' clubhouse after quitting time. A very respectable Spanish restaurant (lots of tasty tapas) serves until 10 P.M., and exuberant dancing occasionally breaks out on the tiny dance floor.

The vintage glam **Staab House** (330 E. Palace Ave., 505/986-0000, 11:30 A.M.–11 P.M. daily), at La Posada de Santa Fe, has history of another kind. The 1882 Victorian home of the prominent Jewish merchant Abraham Staab, it still bears mezuzahs on the doorframes, along with the original ornate woodwork and gas chandelier fixtures. The elegant setting is perfect for a postprandial cognac.

¡Chispa! at El Mesón (213 Washington St., 505/983-6756, 5 P.M.–midnight Tues.–Sat.) has live music five nights a week, with a particularly devoted crew of regulars on Tuesday, for tango night. You can order traditional tapas, or bigger dishes from El Mesón's excellent dinner menu at the bar, or just join in the dancing on the small wood floor.

Several funkier venues round out the downtown bar scene: **Evangelo's** (200 W. San Francisco St., 505/982-9014), one block off the plaza, usually has its big windows open, letting the band's blues jam or country tunes spill out into the street. When there's no band, the pool tables and a couple of hundred kinds of beer provide distraction. Hidden in plain sight just off the plaza, **The Matador** (116 W. San Francisco St., no phone) is not on the normal tourist circuit. Those who descend the stairs (actually around the corner on Galisteo Street) to the basement-level dive are a good cross-section of Santa Fe's younger artists, among other renowned drinkers. If there's not a live band, there's punk rock on the stereo

to match the concert posters on the walls. Down on Guadalupe Street, **Willee's** (401 S. Guadalupe St., 505/982-0117, 6 P.M.–2 A.M. Mon.–Sat.) is another eclectic spot, with hip-hop and Latin DJ nights early in the week and live blues bands on the weekends.

A bit cheesier but chummier is **La Cantina** (125 E. Palace Ave., 505/988-9232, www.la casasena.com, seatings at 5:30 and 8 P.M.), next to La Casa Sena, where the boa-clad waitstaff belt out show tunes while they serve you drinks and light snacks. You have to make reservations at one of the seatings. Finally, **Silver Starlight** (500 Rodeo Rd., 505/428-7777, 5–10 P.M. Tues.–Sat.), the bar at the RainbowVision gay retirement community, draws a great mix of locals and visitors, with occasional drag revues and high camp (and great cocktails) pretty much any time you go.

PERFORMING ARTS

The 2,128-seat **Santa Fe Opera** (U.S. 84/285, 800/280-4654, www.santafeopera.org) is the city's premier arts venue. The elegant open-air amphitheater seven miles north of Santa

the Lensic Performing Arts Center, Santa Fe's most diverse stage

© ZORA O'NEILL

Fe acts as summer camp for the country's best singers to perform a mix of repertory and modern works during July and August. Even if you think opera is all about tuxes, plush seats, and too-long arias, you shouldn't miss the SFO, where half the fun is arriving early to "tailgate" in the parking lot—a chummy, artsy picnic that involves gourmet goodies, lots of champagne, and time to mill around and check out other attendees' bolo ties. In addition to your picnic dinner, also pack blankets to ward off the chill after the sun sets. If you have kids to entertain, visit on a designated "youth night," a special dress rehearsal with extra info to introduce young ones to the art form.

Set in a fantastical 1931 Moorishly curlicued palace, the **Lensic Performing Arts Center** (211 W. San Francisco St., 505/988-1234, www.lensic.com) is Santa Fe's best stage after the opera house, with everyone from Ladysmith Black Mambazo to the Santa Fe Chamber Orchestra playing to the 821-seat house. The

GOOD-BYE, OLD MAN GLOOM!

Every fall, on the weekend after Labor Day, a raucous chant fills the air in Santa Fe's Fort Marcy Park: "Burn him! Burn him! Burn him!" It's not a witch hunt, but the ritual torching of Zozobra, a 50-foot-tall marionette with long, grasping arms, glowering eyes, and a growly voice. Zozobra, whose name comes from the Spanish word for gloom or anxiety, is said to represent the accumulated worries, sorrows, and chronic problems of the populace; burning him to ashes purges these troubles and allows for a fresh start.

This type of burning ritual has ancient roots, but the tradition in Santa Fe dates only from the 1920s, when artist Will Shuster (a.k.a. "Shus") and a few friends wanted to liven up the annual Fiesta de Santa Fe. Shuster, who had moved to Santa Fe in 1920 to treat the tuberculosis he'd developed in World War I, was inspired by the Mummers Parade, a fixture in his native Philadelphia. He also drew on the traditions of the Yaqui Indians in Tucson, Arizona, who perform a ritual burning of an effigy of Judas during Semana Santa, the week preceding Easter.

The first Zozobra, built in 1924, was just 18 feet high, with a disproportionately small head. By 1926, Shuster had perfected the scale and developed the spectacle. A *Santa Fe New Mexican* article from that year relates:

Zozobra...stood in ghastly silence illuminated by weird green fires. While the band played a funeral march, a group of Kiwanians in black robes and hoods stole around the figure.... [Then] red fires blazed at the foot of the figure... and leaped into a column of many colored flames. As it burned,...there was a staccato of exploding fireworks from the figure and round about, and throwing off their black robes the spectators emerged in gala costume, joining an invading army of bright-hued harlequins with torches in a dance around the fires as the band struck up "La Cucaracha."

Shus oversaw the building of Zozobra nearly every year until 1964, when he ceded responsibility to the Kiwanis Club. In the late 1930s, Errol Flynn, in town with Olivia de Havilland and Ronald Reagan to film *The Santa Fe Trail*, set Zozobra aflame. A few years later, during World War II, the puppet's face had the features of the era's baddies – and was called Hirohitlomus. In 1950, Zozobra appeared on the New Mexico state float in the Rose Bowl parade and won the national trophy.

Shus, who died in 1969, is now a local legend – he's also credited with inventing piñon-juniper incense and starting the tradition of citywide bonfires on Christmas Eve. And thanks in part to another of the artist's innovations – collecting and stuffing the figure with outdated police reports, pictures of ex-girlfriends, papers from paid-off mortgages, and other anxiety-inducing scraps of paper – the 30,000 people who gather to watch the conflagration are happy to see Zozobra go up in smoke.

two-month-long **Santa Fe Chamber Music Festival** (www.sfcmf.org) schedules events here and at the St. Francis Cathedral, with performances nearly every day in July and August. For the rest of the year, the chamber orchestra of **Santa Fe Pro Musica** performs in Loretto Chapel and other intimate venues (505/988-4640, www.santafepromusica.com). The eclectic organization also sponsors performances by the likes of Loudon Wainwright.

Also check the schedules at **Gig** (1808 2nd St., 505/690-9408, www.gigsantafe.com), where singer-songwriters and other acoustic acts take the stage, and **High Mayhem** (1703-B Lena St., 505/501-3333, www.highmayhem .org), a raw community arts space that hosts all-ages rock shows, experimental jazz, and lots more. And **Paolo Soleri Outdoor Amphitheater** (1501 Cerrillos Rd., 505/989-6318), on the grounds of the Santa Fe Indian School, is a beautiful setting for a summer concert. With some 2,500 seats, the venue attracts big touring bands and festivals.

If it's live theater you want, visit the historic **Santa Fe Playhouse** (142 E. De Vargas St., 505/988-4262, www.santafeplayhouse .org), which occupies a small adobe in Santa Fe's oldest neighborhood. It stages a selection of melodrama, folk plays, and work by Latino and gay playwrights. Sundays are "pay what you wish."

CINEMA

Santa Fe has a number of excellent film outlets in addition to the megaplexes. Closest to the center of town, the **New Mexico Film Museum** (418 Montezuma St., 505/476-5760, www.nmfilmmuseum.org) is an archive for the state on and in film, wedged into a charming vintage single-screen theater—screenings are infrequent but often intriguing. The most solid programming is at the College of Santa Fe's **The Screen** (1600 St. Michael's Dr., 505/473-6494, www.thescreen.csf.edu), where the enthusiastic curator brings in excellent first-run art films along with repertory gems. For a good social night out, though, **The Film Center at Cinemacafe** (1616 St. Michael's Dr., 505/988-

7414, www.santafefilmfestival.com) couples coffeehouse casual with obscure celluloid—it's run by the **Santa Fe Film Festival** (four days in early December), so the selection, from vintage animation to gay-theme hits, is inspired. Additionally, the **CCA Cinematheque** (1050 Old Pecos Tr., 505/982-1338, www.ccasantafe .org) has a film program with an emphasis on international titles, and a first-run multiplex was set to open in the new Railyard Park as this book was going to press.

FESTIVALS AND EVENTS

The city's biggest annual event is **Santa Fe Indian Market** (505/983-5220, www.swaia .org), when 1,200 Native American artisans present their jewelry, pottery, weaving, and other wares, varying from the most traditional forms to wildly inventive ones. Tented booths fill the plaza and surrounding streets, and the city swells with about 100,000 visitors. It's a bit of a frenzy during the selling proper, for one weekend near the end of August, but the atmosphere is festive, as the booths are augmented by free music and dance performances and the Native Roots and Rhythms festival (www.nrr festival.com) at the Paolo Soleri amphitheater.

Along similar lines is **Spanish Market** (505/982-2226, www.spanishmarket.org), the last weekend in July. Emphasis is primarily on traditional crafts, with New Mexico's most respected *santeros* and *santeras* selling their work alongside weavers, tinworkers, and furniture makers. Finally, the **International Folk Art Market** (505/476-1166, www.folkart market.org) showcases traditional crafts from all over the globe. Expect Bhutanese textiles, handcrafted French knives, and South African beadwork, all contributing to the largest international market in the United States. Unlike the other two markets, this one takes place off the plaza, on Museum Hill, so the city is a bit less disrupted.

After all the frenzy of summer tourism, locals celebrate the arrival of the calmer fall season with the **Burning of Zozobra** (www .zozobra.com), a neopagan bonfire on the Thursday after Labor Day that's as much a part

COURTESY OF SANTA FE CONVENTION & VISITORS BUREAU/© MARK KANE

During Fiesta de Santa Fe, there's dancing in the streets.

of Santa Fe's social calendar as the opera season. The ritual kicks off the weeklong **Fiesta de Santa Fe** (505/988-7575, www.santafe fiesta.org), which commemorates De Vargas's reoccupation of the city in 1693 after the Pueblo Revolt. The event, which has been celebrated in some form since 1712, is marked with a reenactment of De Vargas's *entrada* into the city and then a whole slew of balls and parades, including the Historical/Hysterical Parade and a children's pet parade—eccentric Santa Fe at its finest.

Rodeo Road on the south side of town isn't a nod to Beverly Hills—there really is an annual **Rodeo de Santa Fe** (3237 Rodeo Rd., 505/471-4300, www.rodeosantafe.com), which takes place near the end of June. Expect to see all the competitive events such as barrel racing and bull riding, as well as goofy clowns, trickropers, and a kids' "mutton-busting" show. The event opens with a big parade of everyone in his or her best cowboy regalia.

Foodies flock to the city in late September for the **Santa Fe Wine and Chile Festival** (505/438-8060, www.santafewineandchile .org), five days of tastings and special dinners at various venues around town. Those who want to just drink, not eat, can attend the **Santa Fe Wine Festival** (www.santafewinefestival.com), which takes place on the Fourth of July weekend at Rancho de las Golondrinas and showcases New Mexican wine producers.

Shopping

Even people who hold their purse strings tight may be a little undone by the treasures for sale in Santa Fe. The most expensive shops are more like free museums; the cheapest are shameless places eternally on the brink of "going out of business" and should be avoided. In general, you'll find assorted souvenirs and a few influential galleries downtown around the plaza, galleries of all stripes on and near Canyon Road, and more funky and fun modern stuff on South Guadalupe Street.

One of the most familiar sights of Santa Fe is the north side of the plaza, where Native American vendors from all over New Mexico spread out their wares under the *portal* at the **Palace of the Governors,** as they've been doing for more than 80 years. Some 1,000 vendors are licensed to sell here after going through a strict application process that evaluates their technical skills; every morning the 63 spots, each 12 bricks wide, are doled out by

lottery, so the selection can change wildly from day to day. Expect anything from silver bracelets to pottery to *heishi* (shell bead) necklaces to freshly harvested piñon nuts. It's a great opportunity to buy direct from a skilled artisan and learn about the work that went into a piece.

The popular **Santa Fe Farmers Market** (505/983-4098, www.santafefarmersmarket .com, 7 A.M.–noon Tues. and Sat. mid-Apr.–Oct., 9 A.M.–1 P.M. Sat. Nov.–mid-Apr.) is a great place to pick up fresh treats as well as souvenir chile *ristras.* It operates year-round from a market hall on the north end of the Railyard complex, off Paseo de Peralta near Guadalupe Street, opposite SITE Santa Fe.

Once a lovely bit of Saharan-bazaar-style chaos, the **flea market** in Tesuque Pueblo (505/670-2599, www.tesuquepuebloflea market.com, 8 A.M.–4 P.M. Fri.–Sun., Mar.–Oct.) has been tidied up considerably. But it mixes local artists with traders from Africa,

Santa Fe's adobe buildings are filled with enticing boutiques.

© ZORA O'NEILL

Guatemala, and elsewhere, and there are usually some good snacks (if not always amazing bargains) to be had. Take Exit 171 (Flea Market Rd.) off U.S. 84/285, just north of the Santa Fe Opera House.

GALLERIES

With every other storefront downtown occupied by a gallery, aimless wandering is a straight ticket to art burnout. Whether you're just browsing or actually looking to buy, decide first what you're most interested in—American Indian crafts, Taos Society of Artists' work, new abstract painting—and stick with that, at least to start with. Santa Fe's contemporary galleries are where the buzz is. Summer is the high season, with openings for new single-artist shows somewhere along Canyon Road every Friday evening, starting around 5 P.M. and lasting until 7 or 8 P.M. In the winter, spaces usually mount survey shows that change every couple of months. If you don't have a car or just don't feel like dealing with downtown parking, keep an eye out for the Art Van Go (505/570-0603, artvango@qwest.net), a free shuttle that runs daily, visiting many of the major galleries—there's not a set schedule, but you can call for details (participating galleries and art events can vary), or look for the van in the Kaune Foodtown parking lot (Paseo de Peralta at Old Santa Fe Trail) at 10 A.M. most days, or noon on Sunday.

Contemporary

Linda Durham Contemporary Art (1101 Paseo de Peralta, 505/466-6600, 10 A.M.–5 P.M. Tues.–Sat.) helped pull Santa Fe out of the mire of Western Americana with her first gallery in Galisteo, opened in the early 1980s. She has now moved to a prime spot just around the curve from Canyon Road and deals in big names such as Joel-Peter Witkin as well as up-and-comers—her taste runs to punchy, pop, and conceptual.

Similarly influential **LewAllen Contemporary** (129 W. Palace Ave., 505/988-8997, 9:30 A.M.–5:30 P.M. Mon.–Sat., 11 A.M.–5 P.M. Sun.) represents Judy Chicago

in Santa Fe as well as a range of other artists in every medium, though most are figurative to some degree. Around the corner, **Riva Yares** (123 Grant Ave., 505/984-0330, 10 A.M.–5 P.M. Tues.–Sat.) deals in *big*—massive canvases, bold images, and famous names such as Frank Stella, Milton Avery, and Esteban Vicente. The mission at **Charlotte Jackson Fine Art** (200 W. Marcy St., 505/989-8688, 10 A.M.–5 P.M. Tues.–Fri., 11 A.M.–4 P.M. Sat.), one block up from LewAllen, is simple: monochrome. But even within this limited mandate, the variety can be surprising and compelling.

On Canyon Road, real cutting-edge work is rare, but do check out **Nüart Gallery** (670 Canyon Rd., 505/988-3888, 10 A.M.–5 P.M. daily), which showcases lots of Latin American magical realism alongside more abstract work. A nice transition from some of the fustier Western galleries to the edgier contemporary scene, **Meyer East Gallery** (225 Canyon Rd., 505/983-1657, 9 A.M.–5 P.M. Mon.–Sat., 11 A.M.–4 P.M. Sun.), established in 1860 in New Haven, opened this branch in Santa Fe in the 1980s. Landscapes are popular here, though this can vary from hyperrealism to the spare geometry of Jesse Wood.

Conveniently close to SITE Santa Fe, **EVO Gallery** (554 S. Guadalupe St., 505/982-4610, 10 A.M.–5 P.M. Mon.–Thurs. and Sat., 10 A.M.–6 P.M. Fri.) puts a heavy emphasis on conceptual work and abstraction. Ed Ruscha, Agnes Martin, and Kara Walker are on the roster next to relative upstarts such as Ligia Bouton. While you're there, check neighboring **Box Gallery** (1611-A Paseo de Peralta, 505/989-4897, 10 A.M.–5 P.M. Tues.–Sat.)—like EVO, it occupies a big, airy warehouse space in the Railyard and focuses on contemporary artists, but with less familiar names.

Native American and Southwestern

Blue Rain Gallery (130 Lincoln Ave., Ste. D, 505/954-9902, 10 A.M.–6 P.M. Mon.–Sat.) showcases contemporary work from pueblo residents and beyond. In particular, see Tammy Garcia's modern takes on traditional Santa

Clara pottery forms—she sometimes renders bowls in blown glass or applies the geometric decoration to jewelry.

If you're a "pot head," go straight to **Andrea Fisher Fine Pottery** (100 W. San Francisco St., 505/986-1234, 10 A.M.–6 P.M. Mon.–Sat., noon–6 P.M. Sun.), where only the finest Native American plates, bowls, and figurines are on display—some are antique, such as works by San Ildefonso innovator María Martinez, and others are new and edgy in style. Pieces can run well into the thousands of dollars, but it's a treat to see these works up close and not behind glass.

Near Canyon Road, **Gerald Peters** (1011 Paseo de Peralta, 505/954-5700, 10 A.M.–5 P.M. Mon.–Sat.) has a bit of everything: 19th- and 20th-century American painters, Taos Society of Artists members, obligatory bronze sculptures of cowboys, and even a very solid stable of contemporary artists, which all tend toward the figurative. The space is so big that several shows are going on at any given time—you're sure to find a room that suits you.

Along with Gerald Peters, **Nedra Matteuci Galleries** (1075 Paseo de Peralta, 505/982-4631, 8:30 A.M.–5 P.M. Mon.–Sat.) is the other gigantic art dealer in town. The selection here runs more toward art of the American West, with Taos painters Ernest Blumenschein and Victor Higgins on the roster. Even if that's not your scene, the one-acre sculpture garden out back is a treat.

Sculpture and More
Definitely in the museum-quality category is **Peyton Wright** (237 E. Palace Ave., 505/989-9888, 10 A.M.–5:30 P.M. Mon.–Sat.), a large house where one-off shows deal in modern American masters (need a Marsden Hartley for your foyer?) as well as Old World treasures that look as if they've been culled from a czar's forgotten vault. For quite the opposite feel, lighten up at **Chuck Jones Studio Gallery** (135 W. Palace Ave., 505/983-5999), where you can see original cels and sketches from early Disney films as well as more recent animated hits such as *SpongeBob SquarePants* and *The Simpsons*.

Or you can just chill out and watch the good stuff on TV.

North of Santa Fe in the village of Tesuque, the bronze foundry **Shidoni** (Bishop's Lodge Rd., 505/988-8001, 9 A.M.–5 P.M. Mon.–Sat.) has been active since 1972. The main attraction is two large gardens full of metalwork sculpture. The gardens are open from sunrise to sunset every day, but if you want to see the foundry in action, show up at noon on a weekday or anytime between 9 A.M. and 5 P.M. on Saturday. Immediately adjacent, **Tesuque Glassworks** (Bishop's Lodge Rd., 505/988-2165, 9 A.M.–5 P.M. daily) has been operating almost as long, since 1975. It functions as a co-op, with a whole range of glass artists using the furnace and materials and displaying their work in the small gallery. To get to Tesuque, head north out of Santa Fe on Washington Avenue, which becomes Bishop's Lodge Road; Shidoni will be on the left side of the street.

CLOTHING AND JEWELRY
Get the Santa Fe look at **Maya** (108 Galisteo St., 505/989-7590, 10 A.M.–6 P.M. Mon.–Sat., 11 A.M.–6 P.M. Sun.) and **Lucille's** (223 Galisteo St., 505/983-6331, 10 A.M.–6 P.M. Mon.–Sat., 11 A.M.–4 P.M. Sun.), two stores that deal in flowing cotton skirts, bohemian tunics, and chunky jewelry. Maya also has lots of cute shoes and poppier items, while Lucille's always has good stuff on the sale rack.

On Canyon Road, artist Richard Campiglio of **Cruz Jewelry Studio** (618 Canyon Rd., 505/986-0644, 10 A.M.–5 P.M. daily) makes heavy, distinctive jewelry in silver and semiprecious stones—Goth cross pendants as well as drop earrings that look like sea urchins. The studio also has a small gallery space and a café in the back.

Back near the plaza, don't miss **Glorianna's** (55 W. Marcy St., 505/982-0353, 10 A.M.–4:30 P.M. Mon., Tues., and Thurs.–Sat.), a treasure trove of beads, packed to bursting with veritable eggs of raw turquoise, trays of glittering Czech glass, and ropes of African trade beads, as well as boxes full of smaller treasure, such as delicate iridescent seed beads and antique sequins. (It's often closed for lunch 1–2 P.M., though.) And you can pick up a pair of boots fit for the Opry at **Back at the Ranch** (209 E. Marcy St., 505/989-8110, 10 A.M.–5:30 P.M. Mon.–Sat., noon–5 P.M. Sun.), stocked floor-to-ceiling with ostrich-skin ropers and loads of belt buckles.

GIFTS AND HOME DECOR

If it's an odd knickknack, it's at **Doodlet's** (120 Don Gaspar St., 505/983-3771, 9:30 A.M.–5 P.M. Mon.–Sat.), a long-established corner shop filled to the brim with goodies: toy accordions, oven mitts emblazoned with Day of the Dead–esque Mexican skeletons, and every sort of novelty lights you can imagine. Endless browsing potential—and kids can practice the xylophone while you shop.

Traditional New Mexican folk art is the stock in trade at **Móntez** (125 E. Palace Ave., 505/982-1828, 10 A.M.–5 P.M. Mon.–Wed., 10 A.M.–6 P.M. Thurs.–Sat., 1:30–5 P.M. Sun.), where you can find not only elaborate painted-glass-and-tin saints' portraits but also inexpensive colorful votive holders. (In wintertime, the shop opens an hour later.)

The owner of **Seret & Sons** (224 Galisteo St., 505/988-9151, 9 A.M.–5:30 P.M. Mon.–Wed., 9 A.M.–7 P.M. Thurs.–Sat., 9:30 A.M.–5 P.M. Sun.) is a Santa Fe icon who's reputed to have invented Jimi Hendrix's signature global-boho look when he brought groovy fabrics back from his travels through Turkey, Afghanistan, and Iran. Today he concentrates on dealing finely woven rugs, antique doors, and life-size wooden elephants from his cavernous warehouse just south of the plaza. Each room of the warren is dedicated to a particular item—chances are you haven't seen so many rugs in one place outside of Istanbul. For funky folk art that won't break the bank, head for the equally gigantic **Jackalope** (2820 Cerrillos Rd., 505/471-8539, 9 A.M.–6 P.M. Sun.–Thurs., 9 A.M.–7 P.M. Fri. and Sat.), where seemingly acres are given over to mosaic-topped tables, wooden chickens, Mexican pottery vases, and inexpensive souvenirs. Sharing the space is a community of prairie dogs—good distraction for children while adults cruise the breakables.

For the perfect (if short-lived) Santa Fe souvenir, visit **Todos Santos** (125 E. Palace Ave., 505/982-3855, 10 A.M.–6 P.M. Mon.–Sat., 11 A.M.–4 P.M. Sun.), a chocolate shop in Sena Plaza that makes *milagros,* the traditional Mexican Catholic prayer charms shaped like body parts, here rendered in Valrhona chocolate and covered in a delicate layer of gold or silver leaf. The closet-size shop blends high and low in the world of confection: Mexican-wrestler Pez dispensers are on the shelves next to Leone pastilles imported from Italy; the glass case is stocked with decadent hand-dipped artisanal truffles, but you can also get a tin full of milk chocolate "sardines." If your preference is for nuts and chews, head to long-time candy vendor **Señor Murphy's** (100 E. San Francisco St., 505/982-0461, 10 A.M.–5:30 P.M. daily) for some "caramales" (chewy balls of caramel and piñon nuts wrapped up in little corn husks) and other New Mexico-inspired sweet treats.

COLLECTORS' BOOKS AND MAPS

Nicholas Potter, Bookseller (211 E. Palace Ave., 505/983-5434, 10 A.M.–6 P.M. Mon.–Sat., 11 A.M.–4 P.M. Sun.) is a rambling bungalow packed to the rafters with books—a few dog-eared paperbacks, but mostly rare hardbacks. It's eminently browsable, with an owner who knows his stuff. **Snowden's** (333 Montezuma St., 505/820-2665, 10 A.M.–5 P.M. Mon.–Sat.) specializes in Native American and Southwestern titles, while Western history buffs will love **Dumont Maps and Books of the West** (314 McKenzie St., 505/986-6114, 10 A.M.–5 P.M. Mon.–Sat., also noon–5 P.M. Sun. July and Aug.), where first-edition true tales of cowboy life are stacked up against New Mexico travel brochures from the 1920s. **Garcia Street Books** (376 Garcia St., 505/986-0151, 9:30 A.M.–6:30 P.M.) caters to broader interests, and many of the finds in its antiquarian editions (particularly strong on art) are just as juicy.

Sports and Recreation

It's no accident *Outside* magazine has its offices here. On weekends, Santa Feans leave the town to the tourists and scatter into the surrounding mountains on foot or bike. You'll find something to do all four seasons, though high-altitude hikes shouldn't be attempted till mid-May at least. If you're in town in the fall, don't miss the leaves turning on the aspens, usually in mid-October (for a great view, ride the lift at the ski basin if you're not up for anything more strenuous). The main access route for most activities is Highway 475—it starts out from the north side of Santa Fe as Artists Road, then the name changes to Hyde Park Road, and farther north locals call it Ski Basin Road.

The **Public Lands Information Center** (1474 Rodeo Rd., 505/438-7840, www.public lands.org, 8 A.M.–5 P.M. Mon.–Sat.) is the best starting point for any outdoor activity. It's closed on Sundays, though, and on Saturdays in the winter. If you'd like to head out with a guide and perhaps a larger group, contact **Outspire!** (505/660-0394, www.outspire.com), which organizes full- and half-day outings—hiking in summer, snowshoeing in winter. And if you need gear, look no farther than local favorite **Santa Fe Mountain Sports** (607 Cerrillos Rd., 505/988-3337, 9 A.M.–6 P.M. Mon.–Sat., 9 A.M.–5 P.M. Sun.), which stocks all the accoutrements for summer and winter activities.

SKIING AND SNOWSHOEING

Sixteen miles northeast out of town in the Santa Fe National Forest, **Ski Santa Fe** (Hwy. 475, 505/982-4429, www.skisantafe.com, $54 full-day lift ticket) is a well-used day area (no rental cabins) with 44 fairly challenging trails. A major selling point: virtually no lift lines.

The only regularly groomed trails for cross-country skiers are the **Norski Trails,** about a quarter of a mile before the Ski Santa Fe parking lot, off the west side of the road. The standard route is about 2.5 miles, winding through the trees and along a ridgeline, and you can shorten or lengthen the tour by taking

various loops and shortcuts, as long as you follow the directional arrows—important here because the network sees a lot of use. If you want to blaze your own trail, **Aspen Vista,** on Highway 475 just after mile marker 13, is a wide 10-mile-long road with a gradual climb and good views—great for either skiing or snowshoeing. It's closed to motorized vehicles, so it's relatively peaceful too.

Just seven miles out of town along the road to the ski area, **Hyde Memorial State Park** has a couple of nicely maintained **sledding** runs, as well as some shorter cross-country ski routes. **Cottam's Ski Shop** (Hwy. 475, 505/982-0495, www.cottamsskishops.com) is the biggest rental operation in the area—it's handily situated on the way up to Aspen Vista.

HIKING

Some hikes start very near the center of town, while others call for a half-hour drive at the most. The most popular are the trails in the Sangre de Cristo foothills: the Atalaya, Dale Ball, and Winsor Trails. The Dale Ball and Winsor Trails are described in detail in the *Mountain Biking* section.

Atalaya Mountain

One of the most accessible trails in the Santa Fe area (you can even take the "M" city bus to the trailhead on the campus of St. John's College) is also one of the more challenging. The hike heads up to a 9,121-foot peak, starting out as a gentle stroll along the city's edge and then becoming increasingly steep, for a round-trip of approximately seven miles.

Santa Fe Canyon Preserve

For an easy saunter close to town, head for this 190-acre patch of the foothills managed by The Nature Conservancy (505/988-3867). The area is open only to people on foot—no distracting mountain bikes, and no pets allowed either. The preserve covers the canyon formed by the now-diverted Santa Fe River, which farmers

Randall Davey Audubon Center

Birders of course will want to start a hike here, but even general visitors will also be intrigued by the house of artist Randall Davey (1800 Upper Canyon Rd., 505/983-4609, 8 A.M.–4 P.M. daily) and two very pretty trails that lead into the forest and canyons behind ($2). The beautifully painted back rooms of the house are open for a guided tour at 2 P.M. every Friday ($5), and a free guided bird walk departs from the parking lot at 8:30 A.M. every Saturday.

Aspen Vista

As you head farther up the mountain, Aspen Vista Picnic Area (13 miles up the road from town) marks the start of the most popular trail in the Sangre de Cristos. But don't be put off by the thought of crowds, as the promised views of golden aspen groves are indeed spectacular—in the densest spots, when the sun is shining through the leaves, the air itself feels yellow. Though at a high elevation, it's an easy hike, on a wide path with a very gradual slope across the 10 miles.

Raven's Ridge

This is another local favorite, though not too heavily traveled, with great views of Santa Fe Baldy (elev. 12,622 feet)—while you're busy slogging up and over several peaks yourself. The trail starts at the Winsor trailhead (no. 254) in the Santa Fe ski area parking lot, but when you reach the wilderness boundary fence, the Raven's Ridge Trail heads to the right along the outside of the fence. The trail shows up on only one local map (Drake Mountain Maps' *Map of the Mountains of Santa Fe*), but it's easy to follow once you're up there. When in doubt, just head uphill: You'll bag Deception, Lake, and Tesuque peaks in a total of seven miles and a top elevation of 12,409 feet, returning to the ski area parking lot by walking down along the Tesuque chairlift. But this final stretch isn't particularly scenic, so you may want to take in only one or two of the peaks (Lake Peak, the second you reach, is the highest), and then retrace your steps.

FALL IN NORTHERN NEW MEXICO

With all its evergreens and scrub trees, New Mexico doesn't seem a likely spot for a vivid display of fall colors. But the deciduous trees that flourish here – aspen, maple, cottonwood – are particularly vibrant and dramatic, wild pockets of color against the rocky landscape, often bright gold against red rocks.

You don't have to drive far to see the colors, which are usually at their peak in mid-October. In Albuquerque, head to the east face of the Sandia Mountains and up the road to the peak, stopping off at Cienega Picnic Area and Las Huertas Picnic Area, about midway up the mountain. Or head southeast to the Manzano Mountains. Much of this area was marred by a forest fire in 2008, but Fourth of July Canyon, where maple leaves turn shades of pink and crimson, is still a beautiful color show. The drive along the Jemez Mountain Trail, between Bernalillo and Los Alamos, is especially nice, with the cottonwoods contrasting with the red canyon walls and with plenty of other deciduous trees around Valles Caldera National Preserve (the latter is also easily reached from Santa Fe). Closer to Santa Fe, just drive up Highway 475 (the road to the ski basin), where pullouts are positioned for the best vistas of the many colorful aspen stands. Abiquiu's dramatic rock formations are also a great backdrop for cottonwoods. From Taos, the entire Enchanted Circle drive passes through various patches of color.

---

once attempted to tame by building a two-mile-long rammed-earth dam (a herd of goats did the ramming). An easy interpretive loop trail leads around the area for 1.5 miles, passing the remnants of the dam and winding through dense stands of cottonwoods and willows. The trailhead is on Cerro Gordo Road just north of its intersection with Upper Canyon Road.

Rio en Medio

You can lose the crowds just by heading a little farther from town: Rio en Medio Trail (no. 163) begins north of Tesuque and leads along a clear stream to a series of waterfalls and then up some rather strenuous switchbacks to a large meadow that's filled with wildflowers in springtime. From the trailhead to the first cascade is 1.7 miles; the meadow is at the 3.5-mile mark, and then the trail converges half a mile later with Nambe Trail (no. 160), where you'll probably want to turn around, for a hike that will take a total of four or five hours.

To reach the trailhead, drive north out of Santa Fe on Washington Avenue, which becomes Bishop's Lodge Road (Highway 590). Drive straight through the village of Tesuque and then turn right in less than a mile onto Highway 592, following signs for the village of Rio en Medio. In the village, which you reach after 6.5 miles, the road turns into County Road 78-D, a very unpromising-looking dirt track that winds through front yards for 0.8 mile before ending in a small parking area. A forest road carries on from there for a short stretch, and then the trail proper heads off to the right and down along a stream.

BIKING

Mountain bikers have fantastic outlets very close to Santa Fe, while those who prefer the open road will love the challenges in the winding highways through the mountains north of the city. **Rob & Charlie's** (1632 St. Michael's Dr., 505/471-9119, 9:30 A.M.–6 P.M. Mon.–Sat.) is a reliable shop for road bikers, and closer to the plaza, **Mellow Velo** (638 Old Santa Fe Tr., 505/995-8356, 9:30 A.M.–5 P.M. Mon.–Sat., 10 A.M.–4 P.M. Sun.) is a good friendly shop downtown that rents both mountain and road models and also runs shuttles and tours. The shop is closed Sundays in the winter and open later during the summer—it's best to call ahead.

Mountain Biking

The **Dale Ball Trails** are a 30-mile network of single-track routes used by both hikers and mountain bikers, winding through stands of piñon and juniper in the foothills. Two trailheads give access to the North, Central, and South Sections of the trail: From the northern trailhead, on Sierra del Norte (immediately off Highway 475 after mile marker 3), the North Section trails vary a bit in elevation, but the Central Section (south from the parking area) is more fun because it's a longer chunk of trails. The southern trailhead, on Cerro Gordo just north of its intersection with Canyon Road, gives access to the Central Section and a newer South Section, which is very difficult, for advanced riders only. Note that the trail that starts at the southern trailhead lot, part of the Santa Fe Canyon Preserve, is for foot traffic only—ride your bike one-tenth of a mile down Cerro Gordo to the start of the Dale Ball system.

A very popular run is **Winsor Trail** (no. 254), which provides a great range of scenery and terrain. It has become best known as an awesome downhill joyride, with a local shuttle service providing drop-offs at the top. But local riders strongly discourage this tactic—the Forest Service has considered closing the trail to bikes because of accidents and damage done by sloppy skidding. Instead, it's recommended you earn the great descent by pedaling up first—there are few deadly steep ascents, so it's tiring but not impossible, and you'll rarely have to hike-a-bike.

The main trail begins near Tesuque: Take Washington Avenue north out of the center of Santa Fe, continuing as it becomes Bishop's Lodge Road (Highway 590). After not quite four miles, turn right onto County Road 72-A, also signed as Big Tesuque Canyon. There are two small pullout areas for parallel parking, and the trail starts about one-tenth of a mile up the road from the second parking area—the first half mile is through private land. It's not cheating too badly to shorten the uphill leg by starting at Chamisa Trail, six miles up Highway 475 (Hyde Park Road), which connects with Winsor after 2.5 miles—but you'll need to arrange a pickup at the bottom.

If you just want an easy out-and-back cruise, the **Santa Fe Rail Trail** is perfect. The wide gravel path begins at Rabbit Road (take St. Francis Drive south and under I-25) and runs along the railroad tracks through town and on to Lamy, a trip of about 11 miles that's almost completely level. If you're feeling especially leisurely, you can bike down and then take a train back with the Santa Fe Southern Railway tours (see *Guadalupe and the Railyard District* in the *Sights* section).

Road Biking

Make sure you're acclimated to the altitude before you set out on any lengthy trip—the best tour, along the **high road to Taos,** will take you through some of the area's highest elevations. Find the full driving route in the *Outside Santa Fe* section in this chapter. Starting in Chimayó shaves some not-so-scenic miles off the ride and gives you a reasonable 45-mile jaunt all the way to Taos. The annual **Santa Fe Century** (www.santafecentury.com) ride takes place every May, running a 104-mile loop south down the Turquoise Trail and back north via the old farm towns in the Galisteo Basin, southeast of Santa Fe.

ROCK CLIMBING

Diablo Canyon is the closest climbing area to Santa Fe, a set of two facing cliffs with more than 70 bolted routes and a number of traditional routes, ranging in difficulty from 5.8 to 5.13, with most rated 5.10. The longest one stretches 300 feet. Sun exposure on the cliffs is such that you should be able to find a comfortable spot to climb at any time of day, from early spring through the fall. Farther back is the Grotto, a slot canyon that's shaded most of the day—great during the hottest part of the summer. Be careful, though, as the basalt is loose in spots, particularly on the south-facing cliffs—you must wear a helmet because rock fall is very common.

The canyon is due west of Santa Fe. Drive north on St. Francis Drive, then at the highway junction, double back south on Highway 599 about four miles to the exit for Camino la Tierra. Head west on Camino la Tierra 4.6 miles, where you need to bear gently right on a dirt road (the main road takes a sharp turn left). Continue 7.6 miles until you reach a parking area. Don't be tempted to drive farther than the designated parking area—flash floods from the canyon and falling rocks can do serious damage, even if your car doesn't get stuck in the sand.

If you want to polish your skills before you tackle the crags, head to **Santa Fe Climbing Center** (825 Early St., 505/986-8944), where you can play around alone on the walls ($13 for a day pass) or sign up for a guided group trip to a nearby climbing site (starting at $70 for half a day).

GOLFING

Marty Sanchez Links de Santa Fe (205 Caja del Rio Rd., 505/955-4400, www.linksdesantafe.com) is a "water-aware" course that uses indigenous grasses and other plants to minimize water use. It offers great views of the mountains as you tour the 18 holes designed by Baxter Spann; there's also "The Great 28," an additional par-3 nine-holer that's exceptionally challenging. With five sets of tees, the course is good for both beginners and experts. Greens fees are reasonable, starting at $31 for weekday play.

RAFTING

Most excursions on the Rio Grande put in or end in Pilar (see the *Low Road to Taos* section later in this chapter). **Santa Fe Rafting Co.** (888/988-4914, www.santaferafting.com) runs half-day float trips and white-water runs down the Rio Grande for $50 per person, as well as three-day trips down the relatively placid Rio Chama for $375 per person. **Kokopelli Rafting** (800/879-9035, www.santafeadventure.com) runs a day trip through the Rio Chama's White Rock Canyon on Class II and III rapids, combined with a hike through Bandelier National Monument ($119 per person). Both companies also do runs through the excellent white water of the Taos Box, with departures from Santa Fe.

FISHING

Trout teem in the Rio Chama, northwest of Santa Fe. Visit the fly shop **The Reel Life** (500 Montezuma St., 505/995-8114, 10 A.M.–6 P.M. Mon.–Sat., noon–5 P.M. Sun.), in Sanbusco Center, where you can also arrange a day trip to nearby waters ($300 for two).

SPAS

Ten Thousand Waves (3451 Hyde Park Rd., 505/992-5025, www.tenthousandwaves.com, 9:15 A.M.–10:30 P.M. Wed.–Sun., 4–10:30 P.M. Tues.) is such a Santa Fe institution that it could just as well be listed under the city's major attractions. This traditional Japanese-style bathhouse just outside of town has two big communal pools (one for women only, one co-ed) and several smaller private ones tucked among the trees so as to optimize the views of the mountains all around; many have adjoining cold plunges and saunas. Rates are reasonable ($19 for as long as you like in the communal tubs; New Mexico residents and their guests get a discount on Wednesdays), and the place also offers excellent massages, facials, and body scrubs. In the wintertime (Nov.–June), hours are shorter Monday–Wednesday.

Just out of town on the south side, **Spa Samadhi** at Sunrise Springs (242 Los Pinos Rd., 505/471-3600, www.sunrisesprings .com) goes beyond the usual beautifying treatments to healing rituals with the help of staff herbalists and the like. Combine a spa session with the weekly Japanese tea ceremony (3 P.M. and 4:30 P.M. Sat., $25) for an especially restful outing.

In town, **Nirvana Spa** (106 Faithway St., 505/983-7942, www.absolutenirvana.com, 11 A.M.–6 P.M. daily) offers Balinese treatments and massages. Afterward, you can relax in the gardens with a cup of tea and some organic sweets from the adjacent tearoom.

SPORTS FACILITIES

Genoveva Chavez Community Center (3221 Rodeo Rd., 505/955-4001, www.chavezcenter .org, 6 A.M.–10 P.M. Mon.–Thurs., 5:30 A.M.–8 P.M. Fri., 8 A.M.–8 P.M. Sat., 9 A.M.–6 P.M. Sun., $5) is the city's biggest recreational facility, with a large swimming pool with a slide and a separate lap pool (both are indoors); basketball and racquetball courts; a fully equipped gym; and a year-round ice rink. In the winter, there's also a small ice-skating pond at **Hyde Memorial State Park** (505/983-7175), seven miles northeast of town on the way to the ski area.

TOURS

Stefanie Beninato (505/988-8022, www.sw guides.com) leads **walking tours** around central Santa Fe and Canyon Road, both for general history and more specialized interests, such as the Jewish-legacy tour or the garden tours; most day trips are $22 per person. If you want to head out of town, call up **Destination 505** (505/424-9500, www.destination505.com), which can organize custom daylong or multiday trips, including studio tours and excellent archaeological outings; one of the owners is a Santa Clara Pueblo member, so she has access and perspectives that a lot of other operators don't.

The nifty **Santa Fe Southern Railway** (410 S. Guadalupe St., 505/989-8600, www.sfsr .com) runs vintage train cars from the old depot on South Guadalupe to Lamy. A day train runs year-round, and during the summer, the High-Desert Highball does a 2.5-hour trip starting at sunset, with free snacks and a cash bar. Trips start at $28 per person.

© ZORA O'NEILL

Ten Thousand Waves has both public and private soaking tubs.

Accommodations

Santa Fe offers some great places to stay—historic hotels that conjure the old trading days as well as cozy, fantastically decorated bed-and-breakfasts—but none of them are very cheap. Prices quoted here for the bigger hotels are the standard rack rates—chances are, you'll be able to find substantially lower ones just by calling or by booking online, at least at the higher-end properties. Prices spike in July and August, often up to holiday rates; if you're coming for Indian Market or Christmas, try to book at least eight months in advance.

UNDER $50

As hostels go, **Santa Fe International Hostel** (1412 Cerrillos Rd., 505/988-1153, santafe hostel@comcast.net) is not the worst, but neither is it one of the more inspiring. Occupying two meandering old motel courts, it has plenty of room, including somewhat dim dorms ($15 pp), private rooms with shared ($25 s) or private bath ($35 s), and a gigantic kitchen (stocked with pantry staples for guests' use). Note that old-school hostel policy still reigns here: Daily chores are required of guests.

If you're camping, the closest tent sites to the center are at **Hyde Memorial State Park** (Hwy. 475, 505/983-7175), about seven miles northwest of the city up the road to the ski area, with both primitive ($8) and developed sites with electricity ($14). Or head to the commercial **Rancheros de Santa Fe** (736 Old Las Vegas Hwy., 505/466-3482, www.rancheros .com, mid-Mar.–Nov.), east of town about seven miles (a 20-minute drive from the plaza) and pleasantly rural. Tent sites ($20) are private and shady and well away from the RVs, and there's a pool to swim in. Be sure to make reservations in the summertime.

$50-100

A fabulous deal for anyone willing to consider an unhosted place, **Adelante Casitas** (326 Staab St., 866/476-1091, www.casitas.net)

the Mission-style arcade at Hotel St. Francis

offers by-the-night rentals just blocks from the plaza. Every house or room is a little different, varying from cozy studios ($88) to big spreads with three bedrooms ($388) and private patios—Elvira's Casita, on Staab Street, has a particularly homey, historic feel. Considering that Santa Fe hotels can't change sheets more often than every three days because of water restrictions, you're not missing too much by going it alone at a rental property—and you gain the feeling of being a Santa Fe native, waving at passersby from your front porch and mixing up margaritas in your fully outfitted kitchen.

The bones of **(Santa Fe Sage Inn** (725 Cerrillos Rd., 866/433-0335, www.santafesage inn.com, $83 d) are a standard highway motel, but the superclean rooms, all renovated in 2006, are done in sharp, modern red and black, with Southwestern rugs hung on the walls. Little touches such as free Wi-Fi, plush beds, and an above-average breakfast (fresh bagels, fruit, yogurt, and more) make this an excellent deal—the place even has a swimming pool. It may be on Cerrillos Road, but it's still walking distance to the center, and it's right across the street from the new Railyard Park.

$100-150

Physically, **Ghost Ranch in Santa Fe** (401 Old Taos Hwy., 505/821-5145, www.ghostranch .org, $90 s, $100 d), an extension of the Abiquiu Presbyterian retreat center, has all the charm of a 1970s public elementary school, but you can't beat the location just a few blocks off the plaza. If the place isn't booked with a group, you're welcome to stay in one of the small but perfectly comfortable rooms. A full breakfast is included.

Leaving aside its location, **El Rey Inn** (1862 Cerrillos Rd., 505/982-1931, www.elreyinn santafe.com, $125 d), about two miles from the plaza, counts as one of the best lodgings in Santa Fe based on charm alone. Built in 1935, the motel has been meticulously kept up and adjusted for modern standards of comfort, with beautiful gardens, a hot tub, a big swimming pool, and a fireside open-air whirlpool

tub. The 86 rooms, spread over 4.5 acres, vary considerably in style (and in price), from the oldest section with snug adobe walls and heavy viga ceilings to airier rooms with balconies, so ask to see a few before you choose. Rooms at the back of the property are preferable because of noise from busy Cerrillos Road.

In a similar vein, **Stage Coach Motor Inn** (3360 Cerrillos Rd., 505/471-0707, $100 d) dates from the 1940s, and its 14 rooms around a gravel drive are furnished with lots of pine paneling and vintage oddities such as petrified-wood coffee tables. It's a bit cheaper and feels more intimate than El Rey.

Santa Fe Motel & Inn (510 Cerrillos Rd., 800/930-5002, www.santafemotel.com, $124 d) is a good budget bet closer to the center, with rooms done up in simple, bright decor that avoids motel sameness despite the generic motor-court layout. A few kitchenettes are available, along with some more private casitas with fireplaces. Lots of nice touches—such as bread from the Sage Bakehouse across the street along with the full breakfast—give the place a homey feel without the tight quarters of a typical bed-and-breakfast.

With 12 rooms in an old adobe, plus an adjacent Victorian with two suites, **El Paradero B&B** (220 W. Manhattan St., 505/988-1177, www.elparadero.com, $110 d) has a variety of room configurations that can suit families, solo travelers, and friends traveling together. Upstairs rooms have balconies, and a few others have fireplaces.

East of the plaza, twin bed-and-breakfasts under the same ownership offer two kinds of style: The rooms at **Hacienda Nicholas** (320 E. Marcy St., 505/986-1431, www.hacienda nicholas.com, $145 d) have a tasteful Southwest flavor, decorated with a few cowboy trappings and Gustave Baumann prints; two of the rooms have fireplaces. Across the street, **(Madeleine Inn** (106 Faithway St., 505/982-3465, www .madeleineinn.com, $150 d) is set in a towering wood Victorian, but the guest rooms aren't lacy—they're done in rich Balinese fabrics and antiques. There's also a good day spa and organic tea room on the premises. If you're planning a longer stay, or just want somewhere with a kitchen, look into **Alexander's Inn** (529 E. Palace Ave., 505/986-1431, www.alexanders-inn.com, $210 d), a bit farther east. One cottage apartment has a full kitchen and a beautiful loft sleeping area; there's another casita adjacent with the same amenities, as well as two more full apartments a few blocks away. Wherever you stay, you get plush perks such as robes and slippers; breakfast is a continental spread, but that doesn't mean you'll go away hungry—the banana bread is fantastic.

$150-250

A very nice bed-and-breakfast in this category is **El Farolito** (514 Galisteo St., 505/988-1631, www.farolito.com, $210 d), where the eight rooms have private entrances, small patios, and fireplaces. Decor varies from Southwestern to international folk art (in Casita Peralta, which has two double beds), and the breakfast is very good.

Much larger (72 rooms in several interconnected buildings), but still managing an intimate feel, the **Inn on the Alameda** (303 E. Alameda St., 505/984-2121, www.innonthealameda.com, $195 d) is a good option for people who want adobe style *and* space. The big rooms have triple-sheeted beds, wireless Internet access, and overstuffed armchairs that are only lightly dusted with Southwestern flair; most also have a patio or balcony. The difference between "traditional" and "deluxe" rooms is only that the latter have a fireplace, but the premium charged for that ($75 in high season) is a bit steep. The continental breakfast spread is very generous, and there's a wine-and-cheese hour every afternoon.

Majority-owned by Picurís Pueblo, **(Hotel Santa Fe** (1501 Paseo de Peralta, 800/825-9876, www.hotelsantafe.com, $219 d) is both a successful business experiment and a very nice hotel, with one of the few large outdoor pools in town, set against the neo-pueblo hotel walls. The standard rooms are a bit small—it's worth upgrading to the junior suite if possible. If you book online, rates for the ultraluxe Hacienda wing—where the huge rooms all

have fireplaces and butler service, and where niches in the hallways are filled with Native American treasures—are a steal compared to other high-end places in town.

The gracious **Hotel St. Francis** (210 Don Gaspar Ave., 505/983-5700, www.hotelstfrancis.com, $223 d), a California mission–style building that dates from 1923, has a pleasingly authentic historic feel. The Victoriana can be laid on a little thick, but the beds, topped with fluffy duvets, are exceedingly comfortable, and extras such as free wireless Internet and *The New York Times* delivered to your door can sweeten the deal for even the most lace allergic. The 82 rooms vary considerably, from a cozy nook good for solo travelers to bigger suites with big windows, dark-wood furniture, and quilts on the brass beds. The capacious lobby bar and front veranda are excellent places to rest after a day of sightseeing.

Another restful spot is **Houses of the Moon** (3451 Hyde Park Rd., 505/992-5025, www.tenthousandwaves.com, $249 d), the guest cottages at Ten Thousand Waves spa—some have more of a local feel, with viga ceilings and kiva fireplaces, while others are straight from Japan (both samurai era and contemporary anime). There's even a tiny Airstream trailer ($119), a riff on the Japanese "capsule" hotel, that's a great value considering access to the communal hot tubs is included in the rate. Rooms all have coffeemakers, microwaves, CD players, and private patios with hibachis.

OVER $250

From the outside, **(The Inn of the Five Graces** (150 E. De Vargas St., 505/992-0957, www.fivegraces.com, $450 per suite) looks like a typical historic Southwestern lodge, a collection of interconnected adobe casitas. But inside, there's a certain air of opium dream—the sumptuous suites are done entirely in stock from Mideast exotica purveyor Seret & Sons, from the antique Turkish kilims on the walls to the pottery that was broken to make the elaborate mosaic details around the deep tubs. The result is certainly not typical "Santa Fe style," but it perfectly captures the Santa Fe aesthetic:

decadent international bohemian. A member of the exclusive Garrett Hotel Group, Five Graces offers all the luxuries that make these properties so nice to visit: a minibar stocked with free freshly made margaritas, daily walking tours and wine (also available in the small on-site tapas restaurant), and a no-tipping policy.

While other hotels have put a hip gloss on their history, **La Fonda** (100 E. San Francisco St., 505/982-5511, www.lafondasantafe.com, $269 d), just off the plaza, remains pleasantly unchanged and still family owned, its lobby of waxed saltillo tile floors and heavy Spanish-style wood decorated as it has been for decades, its bar populated by a mix of cowboys, layabouts, and lunchtime schmoozers. Despite the high price tag, this is not really a luxury hotel—you're paying for the feel of Santa Fe before it was a trendy spa-and-shopping destination. The cozy rooms are done up with the occasional New Mexican antique, and some have their original kiva fireplaces and *latilla* ceilings; open-plan deluxe rooms are actually a bit more comfortable than the subdivided suites. If you do want some modern trappings, spring for the Terraza-level penthouse suites done in chic earth tones.

Food

Dining is one of Santa Fe's great pleasures—considering the tiny population, it's remarkable what a range of flavors and what high quality you can choose from. You can always get a cheese-smothered, crazy-hot plate of green-chile chicken enchiladas, but most restaurants skew toward a more cosmopolitan "Santa Fean" cuisine that cheerfully incorporates Asian, Southwestern, and Mediterranean flavors, with an emphasis on organic and holistic. Prices included reflect the average entrée price.

DOWNTOWN

Contradicting most rules about dining in major tourist centers, restaurants on Santa Fe Plaza and right around it can be quite good—and if the fajita cart is set up, definitely stop there for lunch. The blocks within the ring formed by Alameda Street and Paseo de Peralta contain some classic Santa Fe spots to which everyone makes a trek at some point, along with a few hidden treats.

Coffee and Tea

Although Starbucks is near the plaza, disguised by an adobe facade, you might want to get your latte at a local joint such as **Ecco** (105 E. Marcy St., 505/986-9778, 7:30 A.M.–4:30 P.M. Mon.–Sat.), which is packed with coffee junkies and Wi-Fi fanatics in the mornings; later, people come in to try the exceptional gelato, varying in flavors from familiar strawberry to adventurous black sesame ($3 and up). If you don't mind a walk, head over to **Ohori's Coffee, Tea & Chocolate** (507 Old Santa Fe Tr., 505/988-7026, 8 A.M.–6 P.M. Mon.–Fri., 9 A.M.–6 P.M. Sat., $3), Santa Fe's small-batch coffee epicures. You can drink a cup of the black-as-night brew there and buy a pound or two to take home; if you're staying on Cerrillos Road, the second location at 1098½ South St. Francis Drive might be handy.

For a mellow tea-drinkers' scene, drop in at **Green Palace** (209 E. Palace St., 505/983-2239, 11 A.M.–9 P.M. Tues.–Thurs., 11 A.M.–midnight Fri. and Sat., 11 A.M.–7 P.M. Sun., $4), which also has a menu of light meals (hummus-avocado sandwiches and other hippie delights, about $8) and stays open late for acoustic strummings and open-mic nights; tea tastings on Tuesdays from 5 to 7 P.M. help guide you through the enormous list.

Breakfast and Lunch

The **French Pastry Shop** (100 E. San Francisco St., 505/983-6697, 6:30 A.M.–5 P.M. daily, $7) delivers just that, plus sweet crepes, *croque monsieurs,* and chewy baguette sandwiches. Early mornings are the best for catching a fascinating crew of Santa Fe regulars. Another solid French option is **Clafoutis** (402

N. Guadalupe St., 505/988-1809, 7 A.M.–5 P.M. Mon.–Sat., $8), a cozy, farmhouse-feeling café where you'll be greeted with a cheery "Bonjour!" This place is great at lunch, for sandwiches, and *cagettes,* platters of charcuterie or smoked fish, along with cheese and salad— sort of the French equivalent of a bento box.

Tia Sophia's (210 W. San Francisco St., 505/983-9880, 7 A.M.–2 P.M. Mon.–Sat., $6) is one of the last greasy-spoon places in the plaza area, serving old-time New Mexican plates without a touch of fusion—so authentic, in fact, the kitchen claims to have invented the breakfast burrito.

Show up early in the morning at **❮ Plaza Café** (54 Lincoln Ave., 505/982-1664, 7 A.M.–9 P.M. daily, $8) to eavesdrop on local political gossip (the mayor's phone number is posted on the wall, along with the weather forecast), as regulars roll in to read the paper and load up on coffee and great renditions of New Mexican and American diner favorites. This is no greasy spoon, though—the "harvest oatmeal" and piñon blue-corn pancakes are a great change of pace from breakfast burritos. Lunch and dinner are equally good and fresh. If you're lucky, it'll be someone's birthday, which calls for a serenade with the Mexican tune "Las Mañanitas" (though locals fondly remember the old days, when the unofficial birthday anthem was "And Then There's Maude").

For an exceptionally casual lunch, stop in at the **Five & Dime General Store** (58 E. San Francisco St., 505/992-1800, 8 A.M.–8 P.M. Mon.–Sat., 8 A.M.–7 P.M. Sun., $4), on the south side of the plaza. Formerly a Woolworth's where, allegedly, the Frito pie was invented (Frito-Lay historians beg to differ), the knick-knack shop has maintained its lunch counter and still serves the deadly combo of corn chips, red chile, onions, and cheese, all in the Fritos bag. Eat in, or, better, lounge on the plaza grass—and don't forget the napkins.

New Mexican

The Shed (113½ E. Palace Ave., 505/982-9030, 11 A.M.–2:30 P.M. and 5:30–9 P.M. Mon.–Sat., $13) has been serving platters of enchiladas since 1953—bizarrely, with a side of garlic bread. But that's just part of the tradition at this colorful, comfortable, marginally fancy place that's as popular with tourists as it is with die-hard residents. Perfectly decent distractions such as lemon-garlic shrimp and fish tacos are on the menu, but it's the red chile you really should focus on.

Standard New Mexican dishes get the modern-diner treatment at **Blue Corn Café** (133 W. Water St., 505/984-1800, 11 A.M.–9 P.M. Sun.–Thurs., 11 A.M.–10 P.M. Fri. and Sat., $10): fresh ingredients and clean flavors, all in a family-friendly, casual, slightly chain-restaurant-like setting. The chiles rellenos benefit especially well from the modernizing, and of course the tacos and enchiladas get at least a visual boost from the blue corn tortillas. Burgers and ribs are also on the menu.

Near the capitol, **Guadalupe Café** (422 Old Santa Fe Tr., 505/982-9762, 7 A.M.–2 P.M. and 5–9:30 P.M. Tues.–Fri., 8 A.M.–2 P.M. and 5–9:30 P.M. Sat., 8 A.M.–2 P.M. Sun., $8) is a morning pit stop for politicos and other busy folks who still need a shot of chile to start their day. And no, you can't get that chile on the side— the kitchen is a bit righteous on this point.

Mexican

At **Bumble Bee's Baja Grill** (301 Jefferson St., 505/820-2862, 7:30 A.M.–9 P.M. Sun.–Thurs., 11 A.M.–10 P.M. Fri. and Sat., $5) fat bumblebee piñatas dangling from the ceiling set a cheerful tone. The specialty at this upscale taco joint is Baja shrimp tacos—but made healthy by grilling rather than frying. They're garnished with shredded cabbage and a creamy sauce, plus a spritz of lime and your choice of house-made salsas. Lamb tacos are also delicious, as are the fried-fresh tortilla chips and that Tijuana classic, Caesar salad. In the morning, fresh and tasty breakfast burritos are served, and you might catch a live jazz act on Saturday nights. The place closes an hour earlier in the winter.

Spanish

Whether you want a simple plate of succulent *jamón* and plump olives or an elaborate paella,

El Mesón (213 Washington Ave., 505/983-6756, 5–11 P.M. Tues.–Sat., $19) is the place to go. The menu hits all the Spanish classics, but nightly specials show off the chef's way with seasonal ingredients—paprika-crusted pork belly on fresh fava beans, for instance. The warm dining room is a tiny bit formal; if you want just casual tapas ($5–10) and a glass of wine, the bar, ¡Chispa!, is the place to be.

La Boca (72 W. Marcy St., 505/982-3433, 11:30 A.M.–10 P.M. Mon.–Sat.) is also nominally Spanish, but its dishes can be a bit more freewheeling. It's a great place to stop in for a late-afternoon snack of bruschetta with mushrooms and egg, though you might end up staying for a dinner of grilled salmon with parsnip-bacon hash. Ranging from $3 to $12, the little plates can add up fast, but there are a four-course tasting menu for $45 and lunchtime specials for about $10.

Santa Fe Eclectic

Open since the late 1970s, **Café Pasqual's** (121 Don Gaspar St., 505/983-9340, 7 A.M.–3 P.M. and 5:30–9:30 P.M. Mon.–Sat., 8 A.M.–2 P.M. and 5:30–9:30 P.M. Sun., $29) has defined its own culinary category, relying almost entirely on organic ingredients. Its breakfasts are legendary, but the food is delicious any time of day—just brace yourself for the inevitable line, as the brightly painted dining room seats only 50 people, and loyal fans number in the thousands. Expect nearly anything on the menu: smoked-trout hash or Yucatán-style *huevos motuleños* are what's for breakfast; at dinner, sure, the mole enchiladas are good, but don't miss the Vietnamese squid salad.

Italian

Of all of the opportunities in Santa Fe to blow your rent money on a decadent dinner, **Trattoria Nostrani** (304 Johnson St., 505/983-3800, 5:30–10 P.M. Tues.–Sat., $32) is one of the most worthy—even though it incorporates none of its Southwestern surroundings. The cuisine in this four-room house with glossy wood floors and white tablecloths is pure northern Italian, executed flawlessly: delicate

fried squash blossoms to start, perhaps, then rich ravioli filled with salt cod and potato and topped with lump crab. An ethereal *panna cotta* or biscotti served with sweet *vin santo* makes the perfect finishing touch.

Locals head to amber-lit **Il Piatto** (95 W. Marcy St., 505/984-1091, 5:30–9:30 P.M. daily, $16) for casual Italian and a neighborly welcome from the staff, who seem to be on a first-name basis with everyone in the place. Hearty pastas such as *pappardelle* with duck are served in generous portions—a half order will more than satisfy lighter eaters. This is a great place to take a breather from enchiladas and burritos without breaking the bank. It's also open 11:30 A.M.–2 P.M. for lunch on weekdays.

With the options of whole-wheat crust and green chile as a topping, the pies at **Upper Crust Pizza** (329 Old Santa Fe Tr., 505/982-0000, 11 A.M.–10 P.M. daily, $12), next to San Miguel Chapel, are actually more Santa Fean than Italian. Hot deli sandwiches and big, superfresh salads round out the menu. Delivery is free, but then you'd be missing the live music on the little front deck.

Rooftop Pizza (60 E. San Francisco St., 505/984-0008, 11 A.M.–10 P.M. Sun.–Thurs., 11 A.M.–11 P.M. Fri. and Sat., $13) is a good place to enjoy a view along with your meal. This *is* Santa Fe, so you have the option of a crust with a hint of blue-corn meal, and toppings vary from plain old onions to duck and crab, and they come in combinations such as the BLT (the lettuce is added after the pie comes out of the oven, luckily). It also has a good selection of wines by the glass.

Fine Dining

As of 2008, Santa Fe's elite had anointed **Coyote Café** (132 W. Water St., 505/983-1615, 5:30–9 P.M. Wed., Thurs. and Sun., 5:30–10 P.M. Fri. and Sat., $28) as the new hot joint, after a makeover from chef Eric DiStefano—so the restaurant that started the contemporary Southwestern trend in 1987 no longer has such an obviously local bent, but the food is solid, if not quite as adventurous as it pretends to be, and portions are massive.

A long bar along the open kitchen is fun for solo diners or couples. Open summers only, the Rooftop Cantina has a more traditional (and cheaper) Mexican menu.

At elegant **La Casa Sena** (125 E. Palace Ave., 505/988-9232, 11:30 A.M.–3 P.M. and 5:30–10 P.M. Mon.–Sat., 5:30–10 P.M. Sun., $34), the emphasis is on hearty meats: chorizo-stuffed pork tenderloin, for instance, or antelope loin. Even the fish dishes need to be attacked with gusto: The trout baked in adobe gets cracked open at the table, releasing a perfectly moist and tender fish. Sunday brunch is also served (11 A.M.–3 P.M.), with dishes such as lobster ceviche and eggs Benedict with jalapeño hollandaise. There are better-value restaurants of the same caliber in town, but the patio is a dreamy place to dine in the warm months.

Set in an 1857 adobe, **Santacafé** (231 Washington Ave., 505/984-1788, 11:30 A.M.–2 P.M. and 6–10 P.M. Mon.–Sat., 6–10 P.M. Sun., $24) is an institution—which doesn't necessarily mean the food is great. But the scene, especially when the legislature is in session, is lively, with politicos seated next to ladies serious about their lunches. Stick to standards and items with a distinct Southwestern flair—the more inventive international dishes often miss the mark—or just grab a snack at the bar, frequented by a good cross-section of the city.

Groceries

For those who are self-catering, **Kaune Foodtown** (511 Old Santa Fe Tr., 505/982-2629, 8:30 A.M.–7 P.M. Mon.–Sat.) is the closest proper grocery store to the plaza. It's small but very well stocked with gourmet treats and quality meats and produce and with some prepared takeout food. (Sound like a native: The name's pronounced CON-ee, as it has been since it opened in 1896.)

GUADALUPE AND THE RAILYARD DISTRICT

An easy walk from the plaza, these few square blocks hold some of the better, quirkier dining options in town.

Cafés

In a funky wood house off Guadalupe Street, **Aztec Café** (317 Aztec St., 505/820-0025, 7 A.M.–6 P.M. Mon.–Sat., 8 A.M.–6 P.M. Sun., $5) pours java for Santa Fe's tattooed and guitar-strumming youth. An impromptu acoustic serenade on the side porch doesn't distract from the food, which is inexpensive and veggie friendly. Even coffee addicts should consider the Mexican hot chocolate. In winter, the place closes at 7 P.M. Monday–Saturday and 6 P.M. on Sunday.

Tiny **Saveur** (204 Montezuma St., 505/989-4200, 7:45 A.M.–4:45 P.M. Mon.–Fri., $7) is a cafeteria line where you're just as likely to find duck confit with a port demiglace as a big slab of meat loaf—a good place to stock up for a picnic (though it's closed on the weekends).

Make room in your morning for an almond croissant from (**Sage Bakehouse** (535 Cerrillos Rd., 505/820-7243, 7 A.M.–5 P.M. Mon.–Fri., 7 A.M.–2 P.M. Sat., $4). Washed down with a mug of coffee, these butter-soaked pastries will have you set for hours. Before you leave, pick up some sandwiches for later—classic combos such as smoked turkey and cheddar on the bakery's excellent crust. And maybe a pecan-raisin wreath. And a cookie too.

Inside the Design Center, **Carlos' Gosp'l Café** (418 Cerrillos Rd., 505/983-1841, 11 A.M.–3 P.M. Mon.–Sat., $7) is packed at lunch, as locals make a run on the fat deli sandwiches, such as the Miles Standish (turkey with cranberry, cream cheese, and mayo), or hearty Hangover Stew, a veggie green-chile chowder.

El Tesoro (500 Montezuma Ave., 505/988-3886, 8 A.M.–6 P.M. Mon.–Sat., 11 A.M.–5 P.M. Sun., $8), in the Sanbusco Center, is run by a family from El Salvador, so go for items such as banana-leaf-wrapped tamales. It's also a great spot for breakfast, for dishes such as a heavy crock of black beans topped with an egg and (the optional New Mexican touch) green chile. There are also tasty chocolate croissants and other pastries—convenient if your group has different tastes.

American

All things Texan are the specialty at **The Cowgirl** (319 S. Guadalupe St., 505/982-2565,

11 A.M.–midnight Mon.–Fri., 11:30 A.M.–midnight Sat., 8 A.M.–11 P.M. Sun., $13), a kitsch-filled spot that's as friendly to kids as it is to margarita-guzzling, rib-gnawing adults. Mesquite-smoked brisket is popular, as is the chicken-fried steak. Non-meat-eaters won't feel left out: An ooey-gooey butternut squash casserole comes with a salad on the side. Both carnivores and veggies should save room for pineapple upside-down cake and the ice-cream "baked potato."

Mexican

Festively painted in orange and yellow, **Bert's La Taqueria** (416 Agua Fria St., 505/474-0791, 11:30 A.M.–2 P.M., 5–10 P.M. Mon.–Sat., $13) is not, however, your standard Mexican party place. The tacos ($4) are modeled after what you'd get in Mexico City and come with fillings that go well beyond the usual beef to *huitla-coche* (corn truffle) and even Oaxacan-style fried grasshoppers. There's also a selection of heartier dishes, such as slow-cooked lamb. Top it all off with diverse fresh salsas and a great selection of sipping tequilas.

Fine Dining

Where Santa Fe foodies eat on a casual night, **Aqua Santa** (451 W. Alameda St., 505/982-6297, noon–2 P.M. and 5:30–9 P.M. Wed.–Fri., 5:30–9 P.M. Tues. and Sat., $18) feels like dining at a friend's house—the open kitchen occupies more than a third of the small building, leaving space for just a handful of tables in the whitewashed room with a fireplace. Dinner, served on old-fashioned flower-print plates, capitalizes on punchy combinations, such as hot baby artichokes with cool, creamy burratta cheese, and entrées are limited to five or so very strong choices—quail stuffed with chorizo, for instance. There's a solid wine list as well.

Elegant but not flashy, regulars' favorite **Ristra** (548 Agua Fria St., 505/982-8608, 5:30–9:30 P.M. daily, $27) applies a French treatment to Southwestern cuisine: Squash blossoms are fried up like ethereal beignets, while duck is spiced with a hint of pasilla chile. It's in a white-walled bungalow with tables in the front yard in warm weather; the pretty bar area is a good place to sample a special selection of appetizers, many with a Spanish influence.

CANYON ROAD

Gallery hopping can make you hungry—but there are only a handful of places to eat on Canyon Road, and not many of them are all that satisfying. For a caffeine hit, stop in the café at **Cruz Studio Jewelry** (618 Canyon Rd., 505/986-0644, 10 A.M.–5 P.M. daily), or jog off the strip to **Downtown Subscription** (376 Garcia St., 505/983-3085, 7 A.M.–6 P.M. daily), an airy coffee shop that stocks perhaps a million magazines and attracts potential readers for even the most obscure titles. Wednesday nights occasionally see poetry readings after normal hours.

You can also reenergize with a mug of "elixir"—historically accurate hot chocolate, based on ancient and medieval recipes—at the geekily obsessive (and delicious) **Kakawa Chocolate House** (1050 E. Paseo de Peralta, 505/982-0388, 10 A.M.–6 P.M. Mon.–Thurs., 10 A.M.– 8P.M. Fri. and Sat., noon–6 P.M. Sun.). It's just off Canyon Road, opposite the Gerald Peters gallery.

At the north end of Canyon Road, stalwart **El Farol** (808 Canyon Rd., 505/983-9912, 11:30 A.M.–3 P.M. and 5 P.M.–2 A.M. Mon.–Sat., noon–midnight Sun., $8) is a popular bar, but its selection of Spanish tapas is also worth noting—grilled octopus with olive pesto, for instance. You can also take in a bigger meal in a small side room that's quieter than the main bar; the *zarzuela* (fish soup) is recommended.

Santa Fe's two splurgiest restaurants are also on Canyon Road: **The Compound** (653 Canyon Rd., 505/982-4353, noon–2 P.M. Mon.–Sat. and 6–9 P.M. daily, $29) and **Geronimo** (724 Canyon Rd., 505/982-1500, 5:45–9 P.M. daily, $38). Honestly, there's far better dining value elsewhere in town, but Geronimo puts on a good show, with succulent elk tenderloin and a glitzy clientele; the place also serves lunch in the summer, and the snug bar with a fireplace is a good place to rest your feet after a Canyon Road cruise.

El Farol's front deck provides a prime view down Canyon Road.

At the very end of the galleries, **The Teahouse** (821 Canyon Rd., 505/992-0972, 8:30 A.M.–7 P.M. daily, $8) has an only-in-Santa-Fe feel, from its old-adobe setting and its specialized menu (some 13 pages devoted to teas, plus more for organic vittles) to its regular clientele of artists and even the occasional celebrity (Valerie Plame-Wilson, say). Even the service could be euphemistically described as "original Santa Fe" (i.e., "spacey"), but the food is good, and it's a great place to put your feet up after a long Canyon Road stroll. It's also open till 10 P.M. on Fridays to serve dessert during and after the gallery openings.

CERRILLOS ROAD

This commercial strip isn't Santa Fe's most scenic zone, but you'll find some great culinary gems out this way.

Cafés

Ramblin' Café (1420 2nd St., 505/989-1272, 7 A.M.–4 P.M. Mon.–Fri., 7 A.M.–2 P.M. Sat., $6) is very light on charm—it's in a near-abandoned strip mall—but its food more than makes up for it. Try the spinach-and-green-chile quesadilla or a big BLT, also laced with green chile; in the morning, a smothered breakfast burrito gets you moving.

The decor—all light pine, metal, and chalkboard menus—at **Counter Culture** (930 Baca St., 505/995-1105, 8 A.M.–3 P.M. Mon., 8 A.M.–3 P.M. and 5–9 P.M. Tues.–Sat., 8 A.M.–2 P.M. Sun.) is spartan, but the colorful crowd of, well, countercultural types fills the void. At lunch the eclectic menu runs from fat burgers to cold sesame noodles, with prices around $7; in general, Asian flavors are good, as are the soups. Dinner is a bit more formal, and a bargain, as prices max out at $15. Breakfast, served till 11 A.M., is great—then you can indulge in the gigantic muffins and coffee cakes as a main meal rather than as dessert; on Sunday, breakfast is served all day. Cash only.

Community activists need caffeine too—and they head to the **Santa Fe Baking Co.** (504 W. Cordova Rd., 505/988-4292, 6 A.M.–8 P.M. Mon.–Sat., 6 A.M.–6 P.M. Sun., $8) to get it. The scene is talkative (local radio station KSFR broadcasts a live show from here weekday mornings), and vegetarians will find a lot to eat—but so will fans of gut-busters such as chile dogs; breakfast is served all day.

Set in the Plants of the Southwest nursery, **Treehouse Pastry Shop & Café** (3095 Agua Fria St., 505/474-5543, 8 A.M.–3 P.M. Mon.–Sat., 10 A.M.–3 P.M. Sun., $9) has impeccable ecological credentials, using all local, organic ingredients, composting its waste, and even paying its workers a living wage. Fortunately, the all-veggie food, from quinoa salad to cherry pie, is delicious too. Settle in for a wait, though—as one regular says, "It's like they're just having a nice day cooking, and they only occasionally realize the customers exist."

New Mexican

The white-stucco dining room is too bright, and the beer-sign-filled lounge is too dim, but that's part of the charm at **Tiny's** (1015 Pen Rd., 505/983-1100, 11:30 A.M.–2 P.M. and 6–10 P.M. Mon.–Sat., $8), a haven of undiluted New Mexico style, right down to its name. All the old favorites are on the menu—the only concession to "modern" trends is that you might get butter with your sopaipillas. Dinner starts and ends an hour earlier in the winter.

Chile still not hot enough for you? Head to **(Horseman's Haven** (4354 Cerrillos Rd., 8 A.M.–8 P.M. Mon.–Sat., 8:30 A.M.–2 P.M. Sun., 505/471-5420, $6), which claims to serve the hottest green chile in Santa Fe. Locals grumbled when the place moved out of its gas-station-café digs into a shinier new building next door, but the chile seems to have kept its savour.

Mexican

You can tell **Mariscos La Playa** (537 Cordova Rd., 505/982-2790, 11 A.M.–9 P.M. daily, $10) is authentic Mexican because it serves ceviche and shrimp *cocktel* the standard beachfront way, with little packets of saltine crackers. If you can't decide what sort of seafood you'd like, opt for the "come back to life" soup (*caldo vuelve a la vida*), studded with shrimp, fish, calamari, clams, and more. Go at off-peak

times, or be prepared for waiting with the adoring crowds.

Asian

A little oasis of Asian-inflected organic food in a chain-restaurant part of town, **(Mu Du Noodles** (1494 Cerrillos Rd., 505/983-1411, 5:30–9:30 P.M. Tues.–Sat., $18) cuts the strip-mall glare with warm-hued walls and bamboo screens. The menu ranges from Central Asia to Japan, offering lamb pot stickers, coconutty and spicy Malaysian *laksa,* and Indian yellow curry along the way. Reviving citrus-ade with ginger is delicious hot or cold, or you can order beer or wine.

Vegetarian

At **Body** (333 W. Cordova Rd., 505/986-0362, 7 A.M.–9 P.M. daily, $9), you don't have to do yoga to enjoy a hearty meal of, say, a collard-green burrito, but once you're done with your veggie extravaganza, you just might want to—handily, there's a studio on the premises. The café caters to raw foodies (though there are hot dishes too), and it's also a bit of a social scene for Santa Fe's healthiest.

SANTA FE METRO AREA

Head farther afield for hefty burgers or enlightened spa food in a lush setting.

Mexican

In a strip mall off St. Michael's Drive, **Felipe's Tacos** (1711-A Llano St., 505/473-9397, 9 A.M.–4:30 P.M. Mon.–Fri., 9 A.M.–3:30 P.M. Sat., $5) makes soft tacos just like you get south of the border: steaming corn tortillas wrapped around grilled chicken or steak, or the chile-soaked pork *al pastor,* and then topped with radish slices, salsa, and lime. Bigger appetites will want a hefty burrito—The Original is your choice of meat, plus cheese, beans, and generous lashings of avocado. Wash it down with the fresh limeade. Breakfast burritos (9–11 A.M. only) are great, too.

Burgers and More

Perhaps the world's only burger joint owned

by a vegetarian, **Bobcat Bite** (420 Old Las Vegas Hwy., 505/983-5319, 11 A.M.–7:50 P.M. Wed.–Sat., $7) doesn't seem to suffer from the proprietor's preferences. Burgers, from freshly ground sirloin, are plenty thick, piled high with chopped green chile and oozy cheese. Berkshire pork chops and rib-eye steaks are on the menu too for heartier eaters. It's well worth the drive out this way (Old Las Vegas Highway is the frontage road on the north side of I-25) and the wait in line—try to go near the end of typical lunch hours to avoid the crowds.

For dessert, you'll want to head back toward town and ◖ **Harry's Roadhouse** (96-B Old Las Vegas Hwy., 505/989-4629, 7 A.M.–10 P.M. daily, $7), where chocolate mousse, lemon meringue, and coconut cream pies could be crowding the pastry case at any given time. And if you're looking for a reason to spend even more time on the shady front patio with a great view across the valley, the rest of the menu is solid, too: cold meat-loaf sandwiches, catfish po'boys, lamb stew, and shrimp satay, not to mention tasty margaritas and an awe-inspiring breakfast burrito.

Indian

Santa Fe vegetarians adore Albuquerque transplant **Annapurna** (905 W. Alameda St., 505/988-9688, 10 A.M.–9 P.M. Mon.–Sat., $5) for its Ayurvedic menu and mellow feel (never mind the strip-mall setting). But even folks without particular dietary needs won't say no when a giant *masala dosa,* bursting with perfectly spiced veggies, gets plopped down on the table. Wash it down with some richly spiced *chai.*

Fine Dining

Blue Heron (242 Los Pinos Rd., 505/471-6500, 7:30–10 A.M. Mon. and Tues., 7:30 A.M.–2 P.M. and 5:30–9 P.M. Wed.–Sun., $23), at the Sunrise Springs resort southwest of the city, makes an excellent romantic retreat, especially in the summer, when you can sit on the terrace overlooking shimmering ponds. The Portland, Oregon–trained chef works with local organic produce and meats and throws in Cuban and Asian flavors, and the result—in dishes such as wild mushrooms in a rich broth, topped with the lightest touch of ancho cream—is light and spa-friendly without being insubstantial.

Another beautiful dining destination is **La Mancha** (9 La Vega Rd., Galisteo, 505/466-8200, 6–9 P.M. Wed.–Sat., $24), at the old adobe Galisteo Inn, a half-hour drive southeast of Santa Fe. The small dining room, with only eight tables, is warmed by a fireplace in winter and opens onto a cottonwood-shaded courtyard in summer. The menu adds Spanish accents—mushrooms sautéed in sherry, Cabrales blue cheese—to straightforward grilled meats such as locally raised lamb chops. There's a more casual cantina menu (burgers are $9) if you don't want a megameal, and a lavish brunch is served on Sundays, but you must make reservations.

Outside Santa Fe

Less than an hour's drive from Santa Fe lie all manner of fascinating destinations, whether you're interested in the 600-year-old ruins of ancestral Puebloan culture at Bandelier or the 20th-century atomic developments in Los Alamos, home of the Manhattan Project. Abiquiu, best known as Georgia O'Keeffe country, is a landscape of rich red rocks along the tree-lined Rio Chama, while Pecos Wilderness Area, east of the city, is a great spot to hike to alpine meadows. The most popular day or overnight outing from Santa Fe is to Taos, but even that presents two possibilities: the low road along the Rio Grande or the high road that passes through tiny Hispano mountain villages.

PECOS AND VILLANUEVA

Santa Fe backs up against the vast Pecos Wilderness Area, the second-largest nature reserve

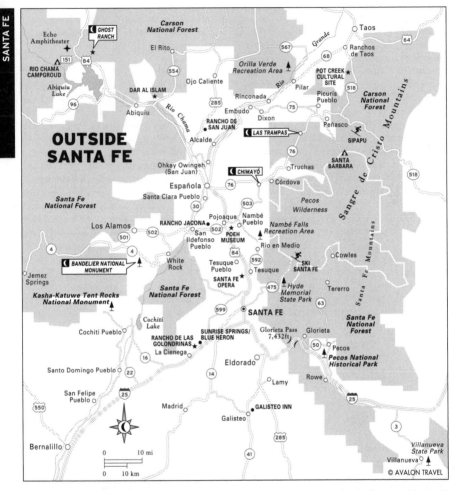

OUTSIDE SANTA FE

in the state (after the Gila, in the southwest of the state), 223,000 acres of high country where the mountain streams seethe with trout and elk ramble through emerald-green meadows. The former logging town of Pecos, where mountain men now rub shoulders with alternative healers and monks, is the jumping-off point for any trip into the woods. (While you're there, check out **San Antonio de Padua Church,** another Gothic-style project by Bishop Lamy.) To reach the village, head east along I-25 to Glorieta (Exit 299) and Highway 50; or there's an alternate route via Highway 63 (Exit 307), which passes the ruins of Pecos Pueblo, the regional power before the Spanish arrived. Villanueva, a small village near a gem of a state park, is 14 miles farther on I-25, then 10 miles south.

On the drive out, near Exit 295, you pass the site of the westernmost Civil War battle in the United States. The Battle of Glorieta Pass raged March 26–28, 1862, part of a Confederate plan to invade the West with a force of Texans—a plan that was foiled in this decisive rout. Look for annual reenactments of the fight.

OUT-OF-TOWN ESCAPES

Not that central Santa Fe is urban mayhem, but if you're visiting New Mexico for the peace and quiet, you may prefer to lodge somewhere outside of the city. These more rural escapes are especially desirable if you're visiting during a major event such as Indian Market – you can immerse yourself in the activity by day and then enjoy the silence under the stars by night. In addition to the suggestions here, see also Casa Escondida in Chimayó (page 82) and the Relais & Chateaux-operated Rancho de San Juan north of Española (page 76).

RANCHO JACONA

Only 20 minutes northwest of Santa Fe, en route to Los Alamos, this working farm (277 County Rd. 84, 505/455-7948, www.rancho jacona.com, $150 d) is dotted with 10 separate casitas, each with a kitchen, laundry, fireplace, and private patio. With trundle beds, sleeper sofas, and the like, each place sleeps at least three people, and some sleep up to eight. You'll likely get some fresh chicken eggs for breakfast, and kids can frolic in the pool. There's a three-day minimum, but chances are you'll want to stay longer.

SUNRISE SPRINGS

This resort (242 Los Pinos Rd., La Cienega, 505/471-6500, www.sunrisesprings.com, $200 d) emphasizes alternative healing and spiritual wellness, with herbal spa treatments, yoga mats in every room, even classes in pottery and Chinese calligraphy. The guest quarters are spare and soothing. Pond-view rooms

($125), each with one double bed, are perfect for people seeking a solo retreat, while the private casitas are a relative bargain compared with similar space in Santa Fe proper. It's about 20 minutes southwest of Santa Fe.

BISHOP'S LODGE

Set on the former country estate of Bishop Lamy, this country-style retreat (1297 Bishop's Lodge Rd., 505/983-6377, www.bishopslodge. com, $399 d) is the closest to Santa Fe – just 10 minutes' drive north of the plaza. More than 400 acres have room for hiking and horseback riding, plus 15 separate lodges with a variety of styles. South Lodge rooms are the oldest, with creaky porches and thick adobe walls, while Chamisa Lodge is all new, with huge bathrooms and gas fireplaces.

THE GALISTEO INN

Well worth the half-hour drive from Santa Fe, this stylish hideaway (9 La Vega Rd., Galisteo, 866/404-8200, www.galisteoinn.com, $185 d) is in the quiet village of Galisteo, where the stars crowd the sky and the crickets buzz at night. The hip guest rooms are done in vibrant turquoise and orange with a few well-chosen paintings and Western-theme antiques – style that would cost you double anywhere inside Santa Fe city limits. Three small rooms are available for solo travelers for $135 or less. Admittedly, there's not much to do in Galisteo after you've had your continental breakfast. But if you're looking for a few days of beautiful solitude, this is the place to enjoy them.

Pecos National Historical Park

The largest pueblo when the Spanish made first contact in 1540, Pecos was home to about 2,000 people, who lived among four- and five-story complexes built of stone sealed with mud. The ruins of this grand community (Hwy. 63, 505/757-6032, www.nps.gov/peco, $3) are accessible to visitors via Highway 63 and then a 1.5-mile paved interpretive trail that winds through the remnants of the Pecos Pueblo walls, a couple of restored kivas, and, most

striking, the remainder of a Franciscan mission. Free guided tours around various parts of the site run at 2 P.M. daily during the summer.

On a ridge facing out to the plains to the northeast and to the mountains behind, the park provides a beautiful view today; around 1100, when the area was being settled with the first villages, it also provided a livelihood. The ridge was part of a natural trade path between the Rio Grande farmers and the buffalo hunters of the Great Plains—both groups

TRIBAL ECONOMIES IN THE GAMING AGE

North of Santa Fe on U.S. 84/285, Cities of Gold Casino looms beside the road, a sight that would've dazzled any conquistador in search of El Dorado. This, it seems, is the true fabled jackpot of the New World.

Pojoaque opened Cities of Gold in the 1990s after much deliberation in the small pueblo. The main argument for getting into the gaming business – effectively permitted by the federal Indian Gaming Regulatory Act in 1988 and then legalized in New Mexico in 1994 – was simply a need for cash and jobs in communities that had virtually no industry. At the time, up to 72 percent of pueblo residents were jobless, and the average income in many communities was less than $10,000 per year – almost inconceivably below national standards.

Pojoaque now boasts zero unemployment as well as attractive new apartment housing and a beautifully appointed museum funded by casino profits. And it has invested in developing the even more massive (but gambling-free) Buffalo Thunder Resort. But not all pueblos have followed that community's lead down the gaming path. For instance, Picurís's social conservatism as well as more practical concerns, such as its remote location, deterred the pueblo from opening its own gambling palace; the elders did eventually agree to co-owning the Hotel Santa Fe, a venture initiated by a few Anglo entrepreneurs who saw an opportunity to capitalize on a unique relationship with a pueblo. Jemez Pueblo remains staunchly reliant on its own agriculture and crafts and does not even take advantage of its status to sell tax-free cigarettes. The divisions between gaming and nongaming pueblos are not dramatic, but they are visible – especially as they're enhanced by a difference in economic status.

Pueblloans and Anglos alike complain about the aesthetics of the gaudy, brightly lit casinos springing up on previously empty land, and others worry about the apparent loss of tradition that goes along with courting lowest-common-denominator tourism. But for many people who had previously been not much more than a scenic backdrop in New Mexico – a mute patch of "local color" – there's no incongruity at all. As George Rivera, the governor of Pojoaque, has put it, "You don't have to be poor to have your culture."

met in Pecos, itself an agricultural community, to barter. What began as a series of small villages consolidated in the 14th century into a city, with a layout so orderly it appears to have been centrally planned, and by 1450, the fortress of Pecos was the major economic power in the area.

Perhaps it was the city's trading culture and relative worldliness that made the Pecos Indians welcome Francisco Vásquez de Coronado and his men in 1540 with music and dancing rather than bows and arrows. Nearly 60 years later, Don Juan de Oñate visited the area and ordered that a mission church be built—an imposing structure with six bell towers and buttresses 22 feet thick in some spots. The building was destroyed during the Pueblo Revolt, however, and the Pecos people dug a kiva smack in the middle of the ruined convent area—symbolic architecture, to say the least. But soon enough, the Spanish were back, and they were even welcomed and aided at Pecos. When they built a new church in the early 1700s, it was noticeably smaller, maybe as a form of compromise. But even as a hybrid Pueblo-Spanish culture was developing, the Indian population was gradually falling victim to disease and drought. When the Santa Fe Trail opened in 1821, Pecos was all but empty, and in 1838, the last city dwellers marched to live with fellow Towa speakers at Jemez Pueblo, 80 miles west; their descendants live there today.

Pecos Wilderness Area

Stop in at the **ranger station** (Hwy. 63, 505/757-6121, 8 a.m.–4:30 p.m. Mon.–Fri.) on the north end of Pecos town to buy topographical maps and inquire about hiking conditions

The ruins of a Franciscan mission loom amid fallen pueblo walls at Pecos National Historical Park.

at Pecos Wilderness Area, as well as the state of various campsites—eight developed areas are usually open, though some are still recovering from bark-beetle invasions and forest fires. At this high elevation, summer temperatures are rarely above 75°F and can dip below freezing at night, so plan accordingly when you pack, especially for multiday trips.

Highway 63 runs north out of town, following the Pecos River past the tiny settlement of Tererro and several fishing access points. At the general store in Tererro, you can inquire about **horseback-riding** trips (Hwy. 63, 505/757-6193). The road then narrows and rises to reach what used to be the mining camp of Cowles—now just a wide spot in the road. Immediately north, Forest Road 223 leads 4.5 miles to Iron Gate Campground and **Mora Flats Trail,** a fairly level 3.8-mile hike to a wide-open meadow—look out for wild strawberries among the myriad wildflowers.

At the end of Highway 63 (bear right where the dirt road forks), **Cave Creek Trail,** which runs out of Panchuela Campground, is an easy

3.6-mile out-and-back that follows a small waterway up to some caves that have been carved out of the white limestone by the stream's flow. You can make this hike more ambitious by pressing on past the caves, up a steep hillside, and on to Horsethief Meadow; this adds an extra three (very strenuous) miles, and you could make this into an overnight trip, as the meadow is a beautiful place to camp. More ambitious still is the 7.5-mile trek to **Pecos Baldy Lake,** which goes out of Jacks Creek Campground and should be done as an overnight hike. All trails in this area require a $2 trailhead parking fee; additional fees apply for camping or picnicking, depending on the spot.

Food and Accommodations

At the main crossroads in Pecos, where Highway 50 meets Highway 63, **Frankie's Casanova** (Hwy. 63, 505/757-3322, 7:30 A.M.–2:30 P.M. and 5:30–9:30 P.M. Tues.–Fri., 8 A.M.–2 P.M. and 5:30–9:30 P.M. Sat. and Sun., $9) is the best all-around restaurant in town, serving massive breakfasts (pork chops!), giant lunches (burgers stuffed with green chile and cheese!), and also rather large dinners, which vary from plain old enchiladas to pasta Alfredo with shrimp. During the winter, the place is open only for breakfast and lunch.

If you want to get an early start hiking, consider staying the night in Pecos. The **Benedictine Monastery** (Hwy. 63, 505/757-6415, www.pecos monastery.org, $75 s) maintains four austere hermitages with beautiful views; the rate is a suggested donation. **Pecos Paradise Inn** (14 Hwy. 63, 505/757-3669, www.pecosparadise inn.com, $125 d) offers a few more worldly comforts: fluffy beds, a pleasant porch to lounge on, and a big fireplace in the living room. (Note that breakfast is not included.) Several mountain lodges offer multiday packages with all meals and a variety of outdoor activities; **Los Pinos Ranch** (505/757-6213, www.lospinosranch.com, $125 pp) is one of the more flexible, with a minimum stay of only two nights.

Villanueva

From Exit 323 off I-25, Highway 3 is a beautiful drive south. The two-lane road runs through a narrow valley that's a beautiful change of scenery from the mountains, with rich red earth cut into small farm plots. Villages such as Ribera and El Pueblo were founded in the late 18th century, after the establishment of the San Miguel del Vado land grant in this valley. Named for a ford *(vado)* on the Pecos River, this area later became the official customs point for caravans entering Mexican territory via the Santa Fe Trail.

You'll also pass **La Risa Café** (Hwy. 3, 575/421-3883, 8 A.M.–8 P.M. Tues.–Sat., 8 A.M.–2 P.M. Sun.), where the sunny patio is a popular stop for locals and day trippers to enjoy spicy New Mexican food, and the tiny, family-run **Madison Winery** (Hwy. 3, 575/421-8028, noon–6 P.M. Mon.–Fri., 10 A.M.–5 P.M. Sat., noon–5 P.M. Sun. in summer), between El Pueblo and Sena.

Villanueva, centered on its own historic church, is the largest settlement along the road; it has a small general store that stocks supplies for people using the nearby campground.

The small but beautiful **Villanueva State Park** (575/421-2957, $5/car) occupies a bend in the Pecos River against 400-foot-tall sandstone cliffs. Because the parkland is small, it doesn't draw big crowds—even in the summer, it's busy only on the weekends. During the week, you'll probably have the 2.5-mile Canyon Trail to yourself, and the choice of camping ($8) either on the cottonwood-shaded river bottom or up on the canyon rim amid juniper and piñon; the riverside sites are near flush toilets and a shower. The river is stocked with trout and can be deep enough for canoeing. Spring comes early in the river valley, making for flower-filled paths by late April; fall is a burst of red scrub oak and yellow cottonwood leaves, in sharp contrast to the evergreens.

THE PUEBLOS

Between Santa Fe and Taos lie a number of pueblos, each set on a separate patch of reservation land. Unlike scenic Taos Pueblo, which opens its centuries-old buildings to visitors, most of these are not worth visiting for their ancient architecture—they're typically a mix of old and new, and some are closed to outsiders all or part of the year. Do visit on feast days or for other ceremonial dances if you can, though—to confirm schedules and for other general information, contact the individual pueblos, or the **Eight Northern Indian Pueblos Council** (505/747-1593, www.eight-northern.org).

Directly north of Santa Fe, U.S. 84/285 runs right through the closest pueblos—the overpass bridges are decorated with the original Tewa names. **Tesuque** (Te Tesugeh Owingeh, "village of the cottonwood trees") is marked by **Camel Rock,** a piece of sandstone on the west side of the highway that has eroded to resemble a creature that looks right at home in this rocky desert. Though this stretch of casinos and tax-free cigarette shops isn't particularly scenic, don't be tempted to race through it—the area is a major speed trap. The old village, established in 1200, is closed to the public some days; call ahead (505/983-2667) if you're planning to visit, though the only real sight is the

Camel Rock is a landmark in Tesuque Pueblo.

new-old church, which was reconstructed after it was destroyed by arson. The new construction uses an interesting new eco-friendly building material called Rastra—a lightweight mix of concrete mixed with recycled styrofoam that takes particularly well to an adobe finish.

Pojoaque manages the **Poeh Museum** (U.S. 84/285, 505/455-5041, www.poehcenter.com, 8 A.M.–5 P.M. Mon.–Fri., 9–4 P.M. Sat., free), a striking old-style adobe building that functions as a community arts gallery, with rotating exhibits and some of the finest work for sale, as well as a permanent installation relating the Pojoaque people's path *(poeh)* through history. On summer Saturdays, dancers perform in the plaza at 11 A.M. and 1 P.M. The adjacent restaurant, **Ó Eating House** (505/455-5065, 11:30 A.M.–2 P.M. and 5:30–9 P.M. Mon.–Fri., 11:30 A.M.–2 P.M. and 5:30–10 P.M. Sat., $6), serves well-priced and tasty items such as tortilla soup and fried chicken.

San Ildefonso, best known for the black-on-black pottery of María Martinez and her husband, Julian, is off Highway 502, on the way to Los Alamos. A small **visitors center**

and museum (Hwy. 502, 505/455-3549, 8 A.M.–4 P.M. Mon.–Fri., $5/car) shows the pottery-making process, and there are several crafts shops (the latter are usually open on weekends). **Santa Clara** (Kha P'o), on Highway 30 south of Española, contains the beautiful Puyé Cliff Dwellings, but they have been closed since the Cerro Grande fire of 2000, with no stated plans to reopen; the pueblo, too, is generally closed to visitors. If you do hear that Puyé has reopened, go—the place is worth seeing. Immediately north of Española, at the junction of the Rio Chama and the Rio Grande, is **Ohkay Owingeh** (Strong Village, formerly San Juan), the birthplace of Popé, who led the Pueblo Revolt.

LOS ALAMOS

Unlike so many other sights in New Mexico, which are cloaked in centuries of history, Los Alamos is an emblem of the modern age. During World War II, what had been only an elite, rugged boys' school was requisitioned by the army to become the top-secret base for development of the nuclear bomb, home for a time

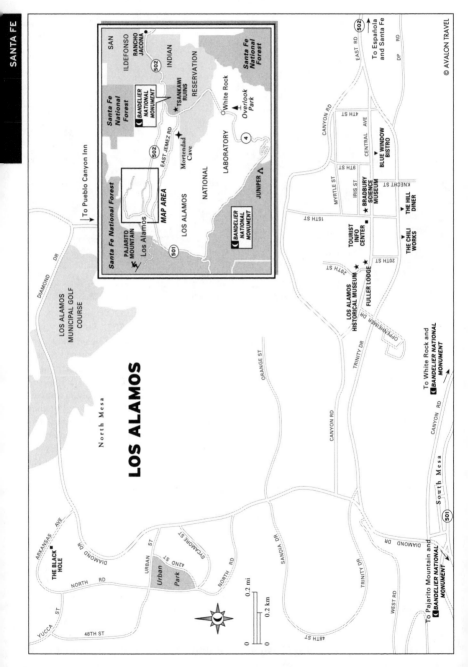

LOS ALAMOS

© AVALON TRAVEL

CEREMONIAL DANCES

This is only an approximate schedule for ceremonial dances at pueblos in the Santa Fe area – dates can vary from year to year, as can the particular dances. Annual feast days typically involve carnivals and markets in addition to dances. Confirm details and start times – usually afternoon, but sometimes after an evening or midnight Mass – with the pueblo itself or the Indian Pueblo Cultural Center (505/843-7270, www.indianpueblo. org) before setting out.

JANUARY 1
- Ohkay Owingeh (San Juan): cloud or basket dance

JANUARY 6
- Picurís: various dances

- Nambé: buffalo, deer, and antelope dances

JANUARY 22-23
- San Ildefonso: Feast of San Ildefonso, with vespers and firelight procession at 6 P.M. on the 22nd and buffalo, Comanche, and deer dances on the 23rd

JANUARY 25
- Ohkay Owingeh (San Juan), Picurís: Feast of San Pablo

FEBRUARY 2
- Picurís: various dances for Candlemas (Día de la Candelaria)

EASTER (MARCH/APRIL)
- Nambé: bow dance

- San Ildefonso: various dances

MAY
- Tesuque: corn dances for blessing of the fields

JUNE 8
- Santa Clara: buffalo dance

JUNE 13
- Ohkay Owingeh (San Juan), San Ildefonso, Santa Clara, and Picurís: Feast of San Antonio

JUNE 24
- Ohkay Owingeh (San Juan): Feast of San Juan Bautista

JULY 4
- Nambé: celebration at the waterfall

JULY 25-26
- San Ildefonso: Feast of Santiago and Santa Ana

AUGUST 9-10
- Picurís: Feast of San Lorenzo

AUGUST 12
- Santa Clara: Feast of Santa Clara

SEPTEMBER 8
- San Ildefonso: corn dance

OCTOBER 4
- Nambé: Feast of San Francisco de Asís

NOVEMBER 12
- Tesuque: Feast of San Diego

DECEMBER 12
- Pojoaque: Feast of Nuestra Señora de Guadalupe

DECEMBER 24
- Picurís and Ohkay Owingeh (San Juan): torchlight procession at sundown, followed by Los Matachines dances

- San Felipe, Tesuque, and Nambé: various dances, beginning after midnight Mass

DECEMBER 25
- San Ildefonso, Ohkay Owingeh (San Juan), Picurís, and Tesuque: various dances

DECEMBER 26
- Ohkay Owingeh (San Juan): turtle dance

DECEMBER 28
- Picurís and Santa Clara: children's dances to celebrate Holy Innocents Day

to J. Robert Oppenheimer, Richard Feynman, Neils Bohr, and other science luminaries. The Manhattan Project and its aftermath, the Cold War arms race, led to the establishment of Los Alamos National Labs (LANL). The makeshift military base soon grew into "The Nuke City," a town of nearly 20,000 people (if you count the "suburb" of White Rock, just down the hill on Highway 4).

The highway up the mountainside is wider than it used to be, but the winding ascent to "Lost Almost"—as the first scientists dubbed their officially nonexistent camp—still carries an air of the clandestine. The town itself has a jarring newness about it, only emphasized by the dramatic, timeless landscape spreading out in all directions from the mesa edge on which it's perched. The vertical mountainside that forms the backdrop for the town is still recovering from the Cerro Grande forest fire that tore through in 2000, when the entire population had to be evacuated, but it's still a beautiful starting point for hikes—after you've gone to the museums and cruised Bikini Atoll Road, Trinity Boulevard, and Oppenheimer Drive.

Orientation and Information

Los Alamos is spread out over three long mesas that jut like fingers from Pajarito Mountain. Highway 502 arrives in the middle mesa, depositing you on Central Avenue and the main downtown area; the north mesa is mostly residential, while the south mesa is occupied by the labs and two routes running back down the mountain and connecting with Highway 4. If you want to head out of town on Highway 501 (West Jemez Road), or anywhere on the south mesa, you'll get funneled through a security checkpoint—don't be alarmed, as everyone gets waved through. Stop at the **tourist information center** (109 Central Park Square, 505/662-8105, http://visit.losalamos .com, 9 A.M.–5 P.M. Mon.–Fri., 9 A.M.–4 P.M. Sat.) for maps and the handy *50 Hikes in the Los Alamos Area* booklet; in summer, it's also open 9 A.M.–3 P.M. Sunday. There's another helpful office in **White Rock** (505/672-3183, 9 A.M.–4 P.M. daily) on Highway 4.

Los Alamos Historical Museum

Even a manufactured town such as Los Alamos has a history. See what the area was like pre–Manhattan Project at this fascinating museum (1921 Juniper St., 505/662-4493, 9:30 A.M.–4:30 P.M. Mon.–Sat. and 11 A.M.–5 P.M. Sun., free), set in an old building of the Los Alamos Ranch School, the boys' camp that got the boot when the army moved in. The exhibits cover everything from relics of the early Tewa-speaking people up to juicy details on the social intrigue during the development of "the gadget," as the A-bomb was known. Afterward, pick up a flyer for a self-guided **walking tour** around the old school grounds and the lab site to see how barebones dorms meant for toughening up teens in the winter got turned into barely more luxurious apartments for the country's top physicists.

In front of the museum is historic **Fuller Lodge,** originally the Ranch School's dining room and kitchen. It was built by John Gaw Meem, who handpicked the vertical logs that form the walls and designed the cowboy-silhouette light fixtures. It houses the **Los Alamos Art Center** (10 A.M.–4 P.M. Mon.–Sat.).

The museum is just west of the main street, Central Avenue—you'll see Fuller Lodge on Central, with the museum set back behind it. During the winter, it opens half an hour later and closes half an hour earlier Tuesday through Saturday; it's open from 1 till 4 P.M. on Sundays.

Bradbury Science Museum

This LANL-sponsored exhibit (Central Ave. at 15th St., 505/667-4444, 10 A.M.–5 P.M. Tues.–Sat., 1–5 P.M. Sun. and Mon., free) on the miracles of atomic energy has the feel of a very-high-grade science fair, with plenty of buttons to push and gadgets to play with. There's also an air of a convention sales booth—the museum's mission is definitely to sell the public on LANL's work and nuclear technology in general, though a public forum corner gives space to opposing views. More interesting are the relics of the early nuclear age: the Fat Man and Little Boy shell casings, gadgetry from the Nevada Test Site, and the like.

Learn all about the A-bomb at the Bradbury Science Museum.

The Black Hole

An enormous shop dealing in engineering equipment—and everything else—tossed from LANL, The Black Hole (4015 Arkansas Ave., 505/662-5053, 10 A.M.–5 P.M. Mon.–Sat.) is more like a 17,000-square-foot museum of obsoleteness: Geiger counters, stacks of IBM punch cards, vacuum tubes, and –ometers of all kinds, not to mention every iteration of three-hole punch and desk stapler ever made. Wandering the cluttered aisles is like tumbling right into a very round-the-bend brain—a feeling enhanced by the staff's litany of conspiracy theories and the erratic click of a Geiger counter. It is true, however, that FBI agents raided the place in 2004, taking too literally a gag planted in the front display window, a computer hard drive marked "secret." Owner Ed Grothus also maintains the Omega Peace Institute next door, an antinuclear shrine. To get there, head toward the north mesa on Diamond Drive and then turn left on Arkansas Avenue.

Recreation

The mountains and canyons around Los Alamos are filled with some excellent hiking trails, in addition to those at Bandelier National Monument, farther west. One short route is **Mortendad Cave Trail,** an out-and-back (1.6 miles round-trip) that takes you to an ancestral Puebloan site consisting of an old kiva set among a cluster of cave dwellings; the ceiling of the kiva cave is carved with very well-preserved petroglyphs. You can do the route year-round, and it's easy enough for children. To reach the trailhead, turn from Highway 4 onto East Jemez Road (also known as the truck route, up the back of the hill to the labs), and then park on the right (north) after 0.7 mile. The trail begins at a gap in the fence on the opposite side of the road.

In White Rock, the **White Rock Rim Trail** runs three miles along the cliff edge—you'll have suburban tract homes to your back and a dizzying canyon out in front of you. The walk starts at Overlook Park; follow signs from Highway 4 at the first stoplight in town. You can also take a strenuous hike into the gorge along the **Red Dot Trail,** which passes a few petroglyphs on its way down to the Rio

Grande; ask at the White Rock visitors center for directions to the trailhead, which is at the back end of a subdivision.

Thanks to the canyon walls, White Rock is also popular with **rock climbers,** who most frequently head to **The Overlook,** a 65-foot basalt wall below Overlook Park. The Los Alamos Mountaineers (www.losalamos.org/climb) organization maintains a very good website with detailed route guides and information on smaller area walls; the group also helps organize the annual Meltdown climbing competition in September.

A bit of a locals' secret, **Pajarito Mountain** (505/662-5725, www.skipajarito.com, 9 A.M.–4 P.M. Fri.–Sun. and holidays) offers good skiing and snowboarding cheap ($43 for a full day), with five lifts giving access to bunny slopes as well as double-black-diamond trails. The area is just a few miles northeast of Los Alamos, off Highway 501, and luckily escaped all damage from the Cerro Grande fire.

Accommodations

The few hotels in Los Alamos cater primarily to visiting engineers, which is a shame considering the city's proximity to Valles Caldera National Preserve—it's a handy place to bunk if you want to get an early start on a hike. One very pleasant place, **Pueblo Canyon Inn** (199 San Ildefonso Rd., 505/662-9200, www.liferesources.com, $85 d), does give you ample opportunity to enjoy the town's beautiful setting, as it sits on a big lot of tall junipers and cedars on the north mesa. It's a very spacious, comfortably furnished house, with great views from the back hot tub and upstairs rooms. Otherwise, the chain hotels are all decent, but you should make reservations in case there's a conference going on.

Food

Perhaps the best-loved restaurant on the hill is **Blue Window Bistro** (813 Central Ave., 505/662-6305, 11 A.M.–2:30 P.M. and 5–9 P.M. Mon.–Fri., 5–9 P.M. Sat., $15), a cheerful place done up in bright colors. The menu is a mix of hearty burgers and healthier items, such as

veggie chili, and the ingredients are all very fresh. It's great for lunch, too; enormous sandwiches are about $8.

For breakfast or lunch, the rudimentary shack that is **The Chili Works** (1743 Trinity Dr., 505/662-7591, 8 A.M.–1 P.M. Tues.–Sat., $5) doles out breakfast burritos to junkie-like regulars. An outdoor deck is open in the summer, but most of the year, this is to-go food, heavy on hash browns and chunks of green chile.

The Los Alamos old guard favors **The Hill Diner** (1315 Trinity Dr., 505/662-9745, 11 A.M.–8 P.M. daily, $8), where the vibe is Early Cold War: wood paneling, checked tablecloths, massive slices of coconut cream pie, and hot dinners such as chicken-fried steak served with your choice of two sides (but there's a token sandwich with sprouts, dubbed the "Chia Pet"). It's open an hour later in the summer.

◖ BANDELIER NATIONAL MONUMENT

One of New Mexico's most beautiful ancient sites, Bandelier (505/672-3861, www.nps.gov/band, $12/car, plus $5 pp) comprises 23,000 acres of wilderness, including the remarkable Frijoles Canyon, which is lined on either side with cave "apartments," while the remnants of a massive settlement from the 16th century occupy the valley floor. The Edenic canyon and the fun of clambering up ladders and around caves make for a grand day out—but everyone else thinks so too, and the place is packed from late April through the end of the summer. Come early on a weekday, if at all possible, or plan an overnight hike in the backcountry to avoid the crowds. Better still, join a torch-lit, silent **night walk** into Frijoles Canyon, a trip that sparks the imagination. They typically fall on Thursday nights; check online (www.nps.gov/band) for the schedule.

Start at the **visitors center** (8 A.M.–6 P.M. daily June–Aug., 9 A.M.–5:30 P.M. Apr., Sept., and Oct., 9 A.M.–4:30 P.M. daily Nov.–Mar.), built by the Civilian Conservation Corps in the late 1930s, almost 50 years after self-taught anthropologist Adolph Bandelier first set foot

© ZORA O'NEILL

cave dwellings at Bandelier National Monument

of condo-style buildings tucked into the rock wall. Paintings and carvings decorate the cliff face above. If you're here near sunset, keep an eye on the **bat cave** near the end of the strip, home to about 10,000 of the animals.

After Long House, the trail continues another half mile to the **Ceremonial Cave,** where you can climb to a restored kiva high in the cliffs—well worth the extra mileage, unless you have trouble with heights (140 feet of ladders are involved). Rangers run free guided walks around the main loop a few times a day, or you can pick up the trail guide for a small fee in the visitors center.

Other Trails

Falls Trail, which leads southeast from the visitors center, is a showcase for the area's geology, rather than archaeology—the 2.5-mile route leads down through a canyon to two separate waterfalls. Allow about two hours for the full trip, as the going can be steep and very hot in the summer.

Well before you reach the main entrance to Bandelier, you pass **Tsankawi** on the east side of Highway 4. Unique pottery excavated in this separate section, disconnected from the main park, suggests that it was inhabited by a different people from those who settled in Frijoles Canyon, and some sort of natural border seems to have formed here, despite a shared cliff-dwelling culture: Today the pueblos immediately north of the Bandelier area speak Tewa, while those to the south speak Keresan. A 1.5-mile loop, with ladders to climb along the way, leads past unexcavated ruins, cave houses, and even a few petroglyphs.

Two popular overnight hikes are to the **Shrine of the Stone Lions,** two weathered sandstone carvings of mountain lions on a mesa top about 10 miles from the visitors center, and **Painted Cave,** which requires a 12-mile hike to see a 50-foot swath of rock covered in layers of ancient artwork.

Camping

Juniper Campground ($12), just inside the park's northern border, is usually open year-round, with 94 sites. There are no hookups or

in Frijoles Canyon, brought there by Cochiti guides. The information center has a small museum and the usual array of maps and guides; pick up a Falls Trail guide even if you're not hiking that way, as it has good illustrations of the various plants and wildflowers that grow in the area. You can also get a free backcountry permit and thorough topo maps here.

Main Loop Trail and Ceremonial Cave Trail

A paved walkway leads out the back of the visitors center into Frijoles Canyon, passing the ruins of the major settlements—or at least the ones that have been thoroughly excavated. You first reach **Tyuonyi** (chew-ON-yee), a circle of buildings that was settled for about 200 years beginning in the 1300s. Built of bricks cut from tuff (the volcanic rock that makes up most of the area) and adobe plaster, some of the 250 rooms at one time stood several stories tall.

The trail then goes up next to the cliffs, dotted with small caves dug out of the soft stone, and to **Long House,** the remnants of a strip showers—you're directed to the Los Alamos YMCA up the hill instead. No reservations are taken, but it's usually not full. The scenery up on the plateau isn't as striking as down in the canyon, but you will get an early start on the day if you stay overnight here.

ESPAÑOLA

Although it's just a few miles from San Gabriel, the first town established by Don Juan de Oñate in 1598, Española itself is a relatively modern city of about 10,000 people, founded in the 1880s as a stop on the Chili Line, the railway between Denver and Santa Fe. It's still a crossroads: Take Highway 68 (called Riverside Drive in town) north from here to Taos, or continue on U.S. 84 to Abiquiu or U.S. 285 to Ojo Caliente. Highway 76 leads east to Chimayó and then to Truchas and the other high-road towns on the way to Taos. Highway 30 is the back road to Los Alamos.

Superficially, the place is not enticing—fast-food joints line the main highway, and Wal-Mart seems to be the biggest social scene in town. One token museum, **Bond House** (706 Bond St., 505/747-8535, noon–5 P.M. daily, free), tries to scrape up some historic pride, but

really, Española is all about the food: Come here for authentic northern New Mexican cuisine, never watered down for interlopers' tastes. Española is also the state's unofficial lowrider capital—keep your eyes out for cruisers in, say, the Wal-Mart parking lot, or at the Saints and Sinners package liquor store (its neon sign should also get landmark status) on U.S. 84/285 at the south end of town.

Chimayó Trading Post

No, you haven't made a wrong turn—you're still in Española. This adobe trading post (110 Sandia Dr., 505/753-9414, 9 A.M.–4 P.M. Mon.–Sat.) on the west side of the main highway relocated here in the 1930s after several decades at its original location in Chimayó. Now it's a listed landmark, as one of the last remaining trading posts from the frontier days, and it has everything you'd expect: creaky wood floors, dim lighting, and a jumbled stock of treasures that includes not only Chimayó rugs but also ones from Iran; Nepalese silver jewelry; cut-tin candleholders, made locally; long skeins of handmade wool yarn; Edith Piaf 45s; postcards; and even free coffee. The inventory is so diverse because the elderly owner who has tended it for the past few decades with his partner was one of the original generation of jetsetters. The two worked for PanAm and Air France and picked up goodies on all their travels. You could easily spend hours in here.

Santa Cruz de la Cañada Church

Take a right turn midway through town at Highway 76 to reach the village of Santa Cruz, established in 1695. The sizable church (varied hours, free) that's here now (turn left at the traffic light after one mile) dates from 1733, and its altar screen is another colorful work attributed to the Laguna Santero, who also painted the *reredos* at San Miguel Mission in Santa Fe and the church at Laguna Pueblo. It is dated 1795 but was completely painted over—with the same images—in the mid-19th century, presenting a particular challenge to the preservationists who cleaned and restored the piece in 1995. Each panel presents a different

SANTA FE

YOGIS IN ESPAÑOLA

At first glance, Española's street culture is all lowriders, baggy pants, and blaring hip-hop. But look closer, and you'll notice a high proportion of Anglos clad in white kurtas and tightly wrapped turbans – these are members of the Sikh Dharma community in Sombrillo, just east of Española. The group is an unlikely product of the commune era, one of the oldest and largest ashrams established by Sikh Dharma's leader, Harbhajan Singh Khalsa Yogiji.

The India-born yogi first came to New Mexico in 1969 to teach yoga to the assembled hippie masses. Twinkly-eyed, white-bearded Yogi Bhajan, as he became known, had a knack for inspiring his followers not only to make their bodies strong ("healthy, happy, holy" are the tenets of his teaching, a New Age-inflected version of orthodox Sikhism), but to build up their bank accounts as well. In particular, he focused on "turning chicks into eagles" – his term for teaching women to empower themselves financially – and he encouraged all of his students to start businesses. The first Sikh Dharma-owned enterprise was Yogi Tea, followed by Golden Temple Foods, and then – in radical departures from the stereotype of Sikh

culture – Sun and Son Computers and Akal Security. The security firm was founded in Española in 1980 by a would-be police officer, turned down for jobs because of his beard and turban. "Start a company, and the police will work for you," Bhajan counseled his student. Akal has grown to become the fourth-largest security provider in the United States, with nearly every federal courthouse protected by its guards.

Based on these contributions to the state economy, as well as directly to the Democratic and Republican parties, Yogi Bhajan became very influential in New Mexico politics – his birthday party was attended every year by prominent lawmakers and former governors – and at his funeral in 2004, just after his 75th birthday, Governor Bill Richardson paid his respects in the keynote speech.

Although they might look out of place to visitors, the Sikhs are an accepted part of Española and don't merit a second glance from locals. The best evidence of their integration? The all-veggie "Khalsa Special" burrito at El Parasol takeout stand – a savvy business move that Yogi Bhajan himself surely admired.

---

combination of the original artist's work and the "fresh coat" applied half a century later.

The Wildlife Center

On the south edge of Española, this animal-rescue operation (Wheat St., 505/753-9505, www.thewildlifecenter.org, 10 A.M.–3 P.M. Wed.–Sat., $4) gives visitors the chance to see some of New Mexico's rarer mammals, such as bobcats, and birds up close and learn a bit about ecosystems in the state. Look for signs to the right just after the stoplight for La Puebla Road.

Food

Española is the place to go for hearty, inexpensive New Mexican. If you're just driving through on your way north, stop off for a quick bite at **C El Parasol** (602 Santa Cruz Rd.,

505/753-8852, 7:30 A.M.–8 P.M. daily, $3), a takeout stand with picnic tables under cottonwood trees and a Spanglish menu ("pollo with guacamole taco"). If you've got more time, head indoors to neighbor **El Paragua** (505/753-3211, 11 A.M.–9 P.M. Mon.–Thurs., 11 A.M.–9:30 P.M. Fri. and Sat., 11 A.M.–8 P.M. Sun., $15) in a big two-story hacienda filled with wagon wheels, wrought-iron bric-a-brac, and vintage newspaper clippings. The place is constantly packed with locals stuffing themselves with big plates of carnitas, chiles rellenos, and the most delectable, perfectly fried sopaipillas in the region—which doesn't mean you shouldn't also get some flan or *capirotada* (bread pudding) for dessert. Turn for both of these places at the sign for Highway 76, which is called Santa Cruz Road in town—the restaurants are immediately on the left.

For a quieter dining experience, look for **Matilda's** (424 Corlett Rd., 505/753-3200, 10:30 A.M.–8 P.M. Tues.–Thurs., 10:30 A.M.–9 P.M. Fri., 9 A.M.–9 P.M. Sat. and Sun., $7) to the southeast off the main road (if you're coming from the south, turn right at Johnny's auto parts store; if you pass the Chimayó Trading Post, you've gone too far). The place strikes a homey tone from its front steps, filled with pots of geraniums; Matilda herself, who has owned the place since the 1950s, still presides over the tables. Her family cooks up the very traditional (read: heavy on the chile, light on the cheese) northern New Mexican goods, often using ingredients they've grown themselves.

On the main drag (Highway 68/Riverside Drive), diner-style **JoAnn's Ranch O Casado** (938 N. Riverside Dr., 505/753-1334, 7 A.M.–8 P.M. Sun.–Thurs., 7 A.M.–9 P.M. Fri. and Sat., $7) serves breakfast all day, along with very good and inexpensive enchiladas, fajitas, and more. The kitsch factor is high—check out the mini-waterfall.

OJO CALIENTE

Twenty-six miles north of Española on U.S. 285, Ojo Caliente (Hot Spring) is, like Jemez Springs to the south, an old resort village based around natural mineral water, now sporting a funky, post-hippie ambience. Set among red cliffs, the pools are attractive and worth a stop if you're driving through, but they're not necessarily deserving of a day trip from Santa Fe, unless you've already been to Ten Thousand Waves there, and want more spa action. The main pools are managed by **Ojo Caliente Mineral Springs** (800/222-9162, www.ojocalientespa.com, 8 A.M.–10 P.M. daily) and built around a 1916 hotel building and several paved pools—one big public one (Mon.–Thurs. $16, Fri.–Sun. $22) and several private options ($40 for two for two hours). You can also stay the night here, in basic cottages ($199 d), in the historic hotel building ($119 d), or in the campground ($12). There's also a nice bed-and-breakfast in town, **The Inn at Ojo** (Hwy. 285, 505/583-9131, www.ojocaliente.com, $115 d).

Rancho de San Juan

En route to Ojo Caliente on U.S. 285 about 10 miles out of Española, you pass the Relais & Chateaux–managed Rancho de San Juan resort. On the grounds is **Windows in the Earth,** a warren of vaulted-ceiling caves carved into the sandstone cliffs by artist Ra Paulette; visitors may hike to the amazing structure after registering at reception (closed after noon on Sunday and all day Monday).

Gourmet diners might want to coordinate a hike with dinner at the resort's excellent **restaurant** (open to nonguests with reservations, Tues.–Sat., $35), which devises a new menu every week, with choices such as organic New Mexico lamb shank and pistachio-crusted quail. The resort itself (505/753-6818, www.ranchodesanjuan.com, $285 d), scattered over 225 acres, is quite lovely; it's 38 miles from Santa Fe but worth the drive if you're looking for luxury and solitude. Even the standard rooms have private patios and fireplaces.

ABIQUIU

Northwest of Española, along U.S. 84, the valley formed by the muddy Rio Chama is one of the most striking landscapes in northern New Mexico. Lush greenery on the river bottom clashes with bright-red mud; roaming sheep and cattle graze by the roadside. The striated hills represent dramatic geological shifts, from 200-million-year-old purple stone from the dinosaur era to red clay formed by forests, then gypsum from sand dunes, and then a layer of lava from only eight million years back. More recently, Abiquiu has become inextricably linked with the artist Georgia O'Keeffe, who made the valley her home for more than 40 years, entranced all the while by the glowing light and the dramatic skyline. It's also the birthplace of Padre Antonio Martinez, the controversial Taos priest who clashed with Bishop Lamy in the mid-1880s. Years before that, in the mid-1700s, the locals had a reputation for harboring witches, an idea that still hasn't quite worn off—the vast Ghost Ranch is better known as *el rancho de los brujos,* or "witch ranch."

SANTA FE

© ZORA O'NEILL

a Penitente *morada* (meeting house) in Abiquiu

Although Abiquiu often refers to the whole river valley, the unofficial town center is **Bode's** (505/685-4422, 6:30 A.M.–7 P.M. Mon.–Fri., 7 A.M.–7 P.M. Sat., 7 A.M.–6 P.M. Sun.), an old-fashioned general store (the name's pronounced BO-deez) where you can get gas, sandwiches, and fishing licenses and tackle. The actual village of Abiquiu, established in 1754 by *genízaros* (Hispanicized Indians) through a land grant from the Spanish Crown, is up the hill on the opposite side of the road. O'Keeffe's house forms one side of the old plaza; on the other is the Santo Tomas de Abiquiu Church, built in the 1930s after the community opted for the legal status of village rather than pueblo. Continue uphill past O'Keeffe's house to see the village *morada,* dramatically set on a hilltop. You're not really encouraged to poke around, however—the village maintains a privacy policy similar to that of the pueblos.

Poshuinge Ruin Trail

About two miles south of Abiquiu proper, on the west side of the road, this half-mile trek leads to an ancestral Tewa site, literally the "village above the muddy river," inhabited only between 1420 and 1500—why it was abandoned is unclear. The village contained about 137 rooms, as well as surrounding field grids, though there's not much to see today (thorough excavations took place in 1919, and it has been left to melt away since then). Nonetheless, it's a good place to get out and stretch your legs and take in the view from the hilltop.

Georgia O'Keeffe House

The artist's main residence, where she lived 1949–1984, fronts the small plaza in the village center of Abiquiu. The house is open to guided tours mid-March–November (505/685-4539, five times daily Tues., Thurs., and Fri., $30). The rambling adobe, parts of which were built in the 18th century, is interesting, but in many ways the surrounding landscape reflects O'Keeffe's work more than her home does. Tours depart from the Abiquiu Inn on U.S. 84; you must make reservations at least a month in advance.

Dar al Islam

In another chapter of New Mexico's long

ANCIENT EGYPT IN NORTHERN NEW MEXICO

Adobe, the word for the sun-dried mud bricks the Spanish used to build their houses for the first few centuries they lived in New Mexico, is derived from Arabic (al-tub) and Coptic, which probably has its roots in the language of the ancient Egyptians. But this shared heritage didn't help Egyptian architect Hassan Fathy communicate when he arrived in Abiquiu to build the mosque and the madrassa that would be the cornerstone of Dar al Islam, a newly established community of American-born Muslims.

Fathy had earned a reputation as a champion of vernacular architecture in the 1940s, when he built the village of New Gourna near Luxor in Egypt. His use of adobe made modernist architects scoff, but it provided cheap, efficient, and even elegant housing for people who could be easily trained to help construct the home and make their own repairs.

By the time the Dar al Islam community hired him in 1980, Fathy was in his 80s, but he nonetheless came to New Mexico to personally help build the mosque. It was his first and only commission in North America, and he was excited to work so near the pueblos, where, he noted, the proportions of the mud bricks were nearly the same as those that make up the Temple of Hatshepsut. He brought with him two Nubian assistants and hired a team of locals to help with the actual construction.

But what could've been a bonding experience over the global utility of mud-brick architecture – the very tenet Fathy had built his career on – became an awkward culture clash. Fathy was built up as an expert to local adoberos, who resented the deference, especially when he proved to be wrong. In particular, they were critical that his construction was not adapted to the cold climate, and he used techniques that could not be applied after he left. The minaret proved too expensive, and an additional plan to build individual homes in Dar al Islam had to be scrapped because of building codes that no longer permitted the use of adobe bricks without additional framing.

The innovations he did bring are lovely, though: arched doorways and roofs, and – best of all – the unsupported adobe domes and barrel vaults that were Fathy's signature, derived from ancient Nubian temples. The gentle curves of the complex's roofline and its rounded, whitewashed interior spaces echo the nearby Plaza Blanca hills, so the building seems beautifully integrated into its surroundings – so long as you don't compare it to its Spanish-style adobe neighbors.

utopian history, a few American converts to Islam established Dar al Islam (505/685-4515, www.daralislam.org), an intentional religious community, in 1979. A village for about 150 families on 8,300 acres just south of Abiquiu proper, it was meant to be a place in which Muslims could practice their religion in every aspect of life, from education to food (cattle for halal slaughter were to be raised). With funding from the Saudi royal family, the group hired renowned Egyptian architect Hassan Fathy to build the mosque and madrassa (school) that formed the core of the site. The group also established local businesses, such as the Abiquiu Inn.

The village concept never quite took off, though, and Dar al Islam has been reinvented as a retreat center that's open to visitors—but call first. Fathy's adobe mosque, all organic sinuous lines, is beautiful and harmonizes flawlessly with the land surrounding it. The most direct route to the community is via Highway 554, which runs east from U.S. 84 south of Abiquiu (follow signs for El Rito); immediately after crossing the river, turn left on County Road 155, which leads to the main entrance.

If you leave the mosque by the far side, continuing on County Road 155 on its loop back to meet U.S. 84, you pass the towering gypsum formations of **Plaza Blanca** (White Place), an oft-photographed patch of land that looks like a pile of bleached bones. You can park your car anywhere and wander among the pinnacles.

Abiquiu Lake

An Army Corps of Engineers dam project created this 4,000-acre lake with fingers running into the canyons all around. The view coming in is marred by the power station, but past that the water glimmers at the base of the flat-topped flint mountain Pedernal Peak, the distinctive silhouette that found its way into so many of O'Keeffe's paintings. ("It's my private mountain," she often said. "God told me if I painted it often enough, I could have it.") The overly paved campsites ($5) at the lake are open year-round, but water ($10) and electric hook-ups ($14) are available only in the summer.

◖ Ghost Ranch

Ghost Ranch (U.S. 84, 505/685-4333, www .ghostranch.org), a 21,000-acre retreat now owned by the Presbyterian Church, is famous for several things: First, Georgia O'Keeffe owned a small parcel of the land and maintained a studio here (a drawing she did of a cow skull is now the ranch's logo). Then, in 1947, paleontologists combing the red hills discovered about a thousand skeletons of the dinosaur *Coelophysis* ("hollow form," for its hollow, birdlike bones), the largest group discovered in the world. More recently, the dramatic red cliffs have formed the backdrop of such essential westerns as *City Slickers* and *Silverado.*

The grounds are open by day to visitors to see the **Florence Hawley Ellis Museum of Anthropology** and the **Ruth Hall Museum of Paleontology** (9 A.M.–5 P.M. Tues.–Sat., $2), which have small but interesting collections displaying the local finds, including remnants of the prehistoric Gallina culture that lived on the ridge above the valley, santos carved by sixth-generation New Mexican Max Roybal, and an eight-ton chunk of *Coelophysis*-filled siltstone in the process of being excavated. Both museums are also open 1–5 P.M. on Sundays and Mondays in the summer. Guided tours of the ranch grounds, with an emphasis on O'Keeffe's legacy, run mid-March–November (Tues., Fri., and Sat., $25).

You can also hike on your own after registering at the reception desk. The best trek, which takes about 1.5 hours round-trip, is to **Chimney Rock,** a towering landmark with panoramic views of the entire area. Don't be daunted—the steepest part of the trail is at the start—but do slather on the sunscreen, as there's no shade on this route. **Box Canyon** is an easier, shadier, all-level walk that's about four miles round-trip. **Kitchen Mesa Trail,** which starts at the same point, is much more difficult, requiring some climbing to get up the cliffs at the end (though you could hike the easy first two-thirds and then turn around).

Echo Amphitheater

This band shell–shape rock formation, a natural wonder of acoustics, is a great place to let kids run around and yell to their hearts' content. It's four miles north of Ghost Ranch; there are pleasant picnic areas tucked among the brush and a couple of campsites ($2 day-use fee).

Accommodations and Food

The **Abiquiu Inn** (888/735-2902, www.abiquiu inn.com) functions as the area's visitors center. Lodging ($140 d) consists of some pretty casitas at the back of the property, with great views of the river, and a cluster of motel rooms closer to the front (opt for rooms 2–6, which face away from the road); there are also a couple of small, twin-bed rooms for solo travelers ($80). Its restaurant (8 A.M.–8 P.M. daily, $7) serves *barbacoa* wraps and other modern Mexican dishes, as well as bigger entrées such as grilled trout. Midway between Española and Abiquiu, **Casa del Rio B&B** (505/753-2035, www.bed-and-breakfast-new-mexico.com, $119 d) is an earthy ranch house smack up against a towering red cliff. Escape out here for dense stars at night and a meditation room during the day.

You can also stay at **Ghost Ranch** (U.S. 84, 800/821-5145, www.ghostranch.org) when it's not full for retreats—cabins start at $45, or you can camp for $16. Thirteen miles down a rocky dirt track, **Christ in the Desert Monastery** (Forest Rd. 151, www.christdesert .org, $50 s) delivers on solitude; day visitors are welcome, or you can stay overnight (two-night minimum) for a suggested donation. Out the same road (at the 11.5-mile mark), **Rio Chama Campground** is remote but beautiful—preferable to Abiquiu Lake if you really want to get away from it all.

THE HIGH ROAD TO TAOS

Córdova, Truchas, Las Trampas, Peñasco—these are the tiny villages strung, like beads on a necklace, along the winding highway north through the mountains. This is probably the area of New Mexico where Spanish heritage has been least diluted—or at least relatively untouched by Anglo influence, for there has been a long history of exchange between the Spanish towns and the adjacent pueblos. The local dialect is distinctive, and residents can claim ancestors who settled the towns in the 18th century. The first families learned to survive in the harsh climate with a 90-day growing season, and much of the technology that worked then continues to work now; electricity was still scarce even in the 1970s, and adobe construction is common. These communities, closed off by geography, can seem a little insular to visitors, but pop in at the galleries that have sprung up in a couple of the towns, and you'll get a warm welcome. And during the **High Road Arts Tour** (www.highroadnewmexico.com), over two weekends in September, craftspeople famed particularly for their woodcarving skills open their home studios.

The drive straight through takes only about an hour and a half, but leave time to dawdle at churches and galleries, take a hike, or have lunch along the way. Start the driving route by leaving Santa Fe via North St. Francis Road and then continuing on U.S. 84/285 to the junction with Highway 503; turn right, following signs for Nambé Pueblo.

Nambé Pueblo

To the right off Highway 503 just a few miles is **Nambé Falls Recreation Area** (505/455-2304, $5 day-use fee), open to the public for swimming and fishing; it also has beautiful camping spots. The highlight is the falls themselves, a double cascade through a narrow

WALK ON, SANTO NIÑO

According to Spanish Catholic legend, when the Christians were battling the Moors in the medieval period, around 1300, the Muslims imprisoned a number of people after a particularly brutal battle in Atocha, near Madrid, and would not allow the captives' families to visit them. After many desperate prayers on the part of Atocha's Christian women, a mysterious child appeared, carrying food and water, to care for the prisoners, and the populace guessed that it must be the child Jesus. Thus Santo Niño de Atocha became the patron saint of prisoners, and he is still depicted carrying a pail for bread and a gourd for water and wearing a large hat emblazoned with a scallop shell, the symbol of pilgrims.

In northern New Mexico, the figure is a popular one – in Chimayó alone, Santo Niño de Atocha is installed in the main church and in a separate 1857 chapel just a block away. He is seen now as a broader intercessor, an object of prayer not just for those imprisoned but also for the chronically ill. New Mexicans have developed a unique folk practice, placing (too-small) baby shoes at the Santo Niño's feet, on the assumption that his own have worn out while he was walking in the night.

crevice, marking the break between the Sangre de Cristo Mountains and the Española Basin.

Incidentally, the Nambé line of high-end housewares has nothing to do with this pueblo of 1,700 people—weaving and micaceous pottery are some of the traditional crafts here. The biggest annual event is Fourth of July, celebrated with dances and a crafts market.

Chimayó

Continue on Highway 503 to a T junction, where you make a hard left to follow the main road and begin the descent into the valley of Chimayó, site of the largest mass pilgrimage in the United States. During

Santuario de Chimayó

Holy Week, about 50,000 people come into town on foot, starting days in advance to arrive on Good Friday and often bearing large crosses (or at least police-issued glow sticks while they're walking the highways at night). Smaller crowds participate in pilgrimages on Mother's Day and in early June.

The inspiration for the group treks, a tradition begun in 1945 as a commemoration of the Bataan Death March, is the **Santuario de Chimayó** (www.holychimayo.us, 9 A.M.–4 P.M. daily Oct.–Apr., 9 A.M.–6 P.M. daily May–Sept.), a small chapel that has gained a reputation as a healing spot, as it was built in 1814 at the place where a local farmer, Bernardo Abeyta, is said to have dug up a miraculously glowing crucifix.

Unlike many of the older churches in this area, which are now open very seldom, Chimayó is an active place of prayer, always busy with tourists as well as visitors seeking solace. (Mass is said at 11 A.M. weekdays and at noon on Sunday year-round.) As you approach from the parking area, you will see that previous visitors have woven twigs into

the chain-link fencing to form crosses, each set of sticks representing a prayer. Outdoor pews made of split tree trunks accommodate overflow crowds, and a wheelchair ramp gives easy access to the church.

But the little adobe chapel seems untouched by modernity. The front wall of the dim main chapel is filled with an elaborately painted altar screen from the first half of the 19th century, the work of Molleno (nicknamed "the Chile Painter" because forms, especially robes, in his paintings often resemble red and green chiles). The vibrant colors seem to shimmer in the gloom, forming a sort of stage set for Abeyta's crucifix, Nuestro Señor de las Esquípulas, as the centerpiece. Painted on the screen above the crucifix is the symbol of the Franciscans: a cross over which the arms of Christ and Saint Francis meet.

But most visitors make their way directly to the small, low-ceiling antechamber to the left of the altar. It holds *el posito,* the little hole where the cross was allegedly first dug up. From this pit they scoop up a small portion of the exposed red earth, to later apply to withered limbs and arthritic joints or to eat in hopes of curing internal ailments. (The parish refreshes the well each year with new dirt, after it has been blessed by the priests.) The adjacent sacristy, filled with handwritten testimonials, paintings, and abandoned crutches, is devoted to a shrine for Santo Niño de Atocha, a figurine that is also said to have been dug out of the holy ground here. At the time of research in 2008, a new museum was set to open next to the *santuario*—expect to see plenty of documentation of local miracles.

Chimayó has also been a weaving center for centuries, commercially known since 1900, when Hispano weavers started selling locally crafted "Indian" blankets to tourists. **Ortega's** (County Rd. 98, 505/351-2288, 9 A.M.–5 P.M. Mon.–Sat., 10 A.M.–4 P.M. Sun.) is one of the longest-established shops, at the intersection with Highway 76. Behind Ortega's is the tiny **Chimayó Museum** (505/351-0945, www.chimayomuseum.org, 11 A.M.–3 P.M. Tues.–Sat. Apr.–Sept., free), set on the old fortified plaza and housing a neat collection of vintage photographs.

If you want to spend the night in the area, **Casa Escondida** (Hwy. 76, 505/351-4805, www.casaescondida.com, $109 s) is a lovely place, with a big backyard, a hot tub, and a sunny garden.

For lunch head right across the parking lot from the Santuario de Chimayó to **Leona's** (505/351-4569, 11 A.M.–5 P.M. Thurs.–Mon., $2), where you can pick up bulk chile and pistachios as well as delicious tamales and crumbly *bizcochitos*. For a more leisurely sit-down lunch, 【 **Rancho de Chimayó** (County Rd. 98, 505/351-4444, www.ranchodechimayo.com, 11:30 A.M.–9 P.M. Tues.–Sun. Nov.–Apr., 11:30 A.M.–9 P.M. daily May–Oct., $11) offers great red chile on a beautiful terrace—or inside the old adobe home by the fireplace in wintertime. The place is also open for breakfast 8:30–10 A.M. on weekends, and it's a popular special-occasion spot for Santa Feans.

Córdova

Turning east (right) on Highway 76 (west takes you directly to Española), you begin the climb back up the Sangre de Cristo Mountains. Near the crest of the hill, about three miles up, a small sign points right and down into Quemado Valley to Córdova, a village best known for its unpainted, austere santos and *bultos* done by masters such as George López and José Dolores López. Another family member, **Sabinita López Ortiz** (9 County Rd. 1317, 505/351-4572, variable hours), sells her work and that of five other generations of wood-carvers. **Castillo Gallery** (County Rd. 1317, 505/351-4067, variable hours) mixes traditional styles with more contemporary work.

Truchas

Highway 76 continues to wind along the peaks, eventually reaching the little village of Truchas (Trout), founded in 1754 and still not much more than a long row of buildings set into the ridgeline and facing the expansive valley below. On the corner where the highway makes a hard left to Taos is the village *morada,* the meeting place of the local Penitente brotherhood; head straight down the smaller road to reach the old **Nuestra Señora del Rosario de Truchas Church,** tucked into a small plaza off to the right of the main street. It's open to visitors June–August only—if you do have a chance to look inside the dim, thick-walled mission, you'll see precious examples of local wood carving. Though many of the more delicate ones have been moved to the Taylor Museum in Colorado Springs, those remaining display an essential New Mexican style—the sort of "primitive" thing that Bishop Lamy hated; they're preserved today only because Truchas residents hid them in their houses during the late 19th century. Santa Lucia, with her eyeballs in her hand, graces the altar, and a finely wrought crucifix hangs to the right, clad in a skirt because the legs have broken off.

In this part of town, you'll also find the most established gallery, **Hand Artes** (505/689-2443, variable hours)—Jack Silverman's silk-screen prints of American Indian textile patterns are particularly fine. If you keep going down the road out of town, you'll eventually

Nuestra Señora del Rosario de Truchas Church

reach the beautifully isolated **Rancho Arriba Bed & Breakfast** (Hwy. 76, 505/689-2374, www.ranchoarriba.com, $70 d), a farmhouse built by hand by its owner. Guests no longer have to use an outhouse, but breakfasts are still cooked on a woodstove.

🔇 Las Trampas

Back on Highway 76, heading toward Taos, you'll reach the village of Las Trampas, which was settled in 1751, and its showpiece, **San José de Gracia Church** (10 A.M.–4 P.M. Sat. and Sun. June–Aug.), which was built nine years later. It remains one of the finest examples of New Mexican village church architecture. Its thick adobe walls, which are covered with a fresh coat of mud every year or two, are balanced by vertical bell towers; inside, the clerestory at the front of the church—a very typical design—lets light in to shine down on the altar, which was carved and painted in the late 1700s. Other paradigmatic elements: the *atrio,* or small plaza between the low adobe boundary wall and the church itself, used as a cemetery; and the dark narthex,

where you enter, confined by the choir loft above, but serving only to emphasize the sense of light and space created in the rest of the church by the clerestory and the small windows near the viga ceiling. Unfortunately, chances are slim that you'll be in town when the church is open—but it's worth trying the door anyhow.

As you leave the town heading north, look to the right—you'll see a centuries-old acequia that has been channeled through a log flume to cross a small arroyo. Less than a mile north of the village, you pass the turn for El Valle and Forest Road 207, which leads to the **Trampas Lakes** trailhead. This 6.1-mile hike goes through gorgeous alpine scenery—steep rock walls jutting from dense forest, myriad wildflowers, and the two lakes themselves, which are clear and frigid. A spur trail at the last junction leads to Hidden Lake (two miles round-trip). This route makes a very pleasant overnight trek, giving you time to fish and relax at the end, but with an early start, you could also do the trail as an intense all-day outing.

© ZORA O'NEILL

weather-beaten adobe at San José de Gracia Church in Las Trampas

Peñasco

The next community along the road is Peñasco, best known to tourists as the home of the delicious (**Sugar Nymphs Bistro** (15046 Hwy. 76, 575/587-0311, 11 A.M.–2:30 P.M. and 5:30–7:30 P.M. Wed.–Sat., 11 A.M.–2 P.M. Sun., $10), where you can get all kinds of treats such as grilled lamb, fresh-pressed cider, piñon couscous, and pizzas. Hours can be more limited in the winter, so it's best to call ahead. This is also the northern gateway to the **Pecos Wilderness Area**—turn on Forest Road 116 to reach Santa Barbara Campground and the Santa Barbara Trail to Truchas Peak, a 23-mile round-trip that requires a good amount of planning.

Picurís Pueblo

For all the signs that point to Picurís, from every possible surrounding highway, you would imagine it's a glittery tourist extravaganza. In fact, as one of the few Rio Grande pueblos that has not built a casino, Picurís Pueblo instead capitalizes on its beautiful natural setting, a lush valley where bison roam and aspen leaves

rustle. You can picnic here or fish in small but well-stocked Tu-Tah Lake. After the **San Lorenzo de Picurís Church** collapsed because of water damage in 1989, pueblo members rebuilt it by hand, following exactly the form of the original 1776 design—a process that took eight years. A museum tells the history of the pueblo, the smallest in New Mexico, with only a few hundred members, and along with Taos Pueblo, the only Tiwa-speakers. As at Nambé, local traditions have melded with those of the surrounding villages; the Hispano-Indian Matachines dances are well attended on Christmas Eve. Start at the **visitors center** (575/587-1099 or 575/587-1071, 9 A.M.–5 P.M. Mon.–Sat.) to pick up maps and perhaps hire a tour guide. The pueblo is a short detour from the high road proper: Just past Peñasco, turn left (west) from Highway 76 onto a well-marked access road, which leads to the pueblo in a few miles.

Sipapu

Detouring right (east) along Highway 518, you reach Sipapu (Hwy. 518, 800/587-2240, www.sipapunm.com), an unassuming, inexpensive **ski resort**—really, just a handful of cabins at the base of a 9,255-foot mountain. Cheap lift tickets ($39 full day), cabins from $39 per night, and utter quiet make this a bargain getaway.

You can also take a nice afternoon hike along **Cañon Tio Maes,** a two-mile trail up to a meadow filled with flowers and aspen trees—plan about 2.5 hours for a leisurely round-trip. A longer hike—more like six miles and four hours round-trip—goes to Gallegos Peak (10,258 feet), where you can look over to the snow-capped Truchas Peaks, another 2,800 feet up. The Cañon Tio Maes trailhead (no. 5) is 3.2 miles east on Highway 518 before you reach Sipapu; it's unmarked coming from this direction—look for a paved road on the left side that doubles back along the highway for a short stretch. For Gallegos Peak, drive to the Flechado Canyon Campground, 5.4 miles east of the junction, immediately past Sipapu; the trailhead is across the road.

Returning to the junction, continue to Taos via Highway 518, which soon descends into a valley and passes **Pot Creek Cultural Site** (505/587-2255, 9 A.M.–4 P.M. Wed.–Sun. July–Aug.), a mildly interesting diversion for its one-mile loop trail through ancestral Puebloan ruins from around 1100. You arrive in Taos at its very southern end—really, in Ranchos de Taos, just north of the San Francisco de Asis Church on Highway 68. Turn left to see the church, or turn right to head up to the town plaza and to Taos Pueblo.

THE LOW ROAD TO TAOS

The lush farmland around the Rio Grande is the highlight of this drive north—this valley filled with apple orchards is as green as New Mexico gets. The road is at first a bit unpromising, as it passes through the modern town of Española, but it soon winds into an ever-narrower canyon and finally emerges at the dramatic point where the high plains meet the mountains. This route is more direct than the high road and has fewer scenic stopping points, so if you're pressed for time, this is the way to go.

Alcalde

At the time of research, there was not much to see in this riverside farm town—but do look out for the historic Los Luceros ranch. In early 2008, the state had bought this beautiful territorial-style compound and the surrounding riverfront acreage, once owned by arts patroness Mary Cabot Wheelwright, and was planning to open the place as a museum and filmmaking center. Regardless, you can enjoy a lavish afternoon tea at **Ice's Tea Room** (County Rd. 1097, 505/852-2589, www.icestearoom.com, noon–5 P.M. Tues., Wed., and Thurs. Mar.–Oct., $23), made from all organic ingredients from the farm the place is set on; call ahead, though—it's by reservation only.

Embudo and Dixon

The village of Embudo is really just a bend in the river, but it offers a couple of good eating options. First up is beautiful **Embudo Station**

roadside attractions in Embudo

(Hwy. 68, 505/852-4707, 11:30 A.M.–9 P.M. Tues.–Sun. Apr.–Nov., $14), a little lodge right on the water where you can have a lunch of smoked trout under the shade of a big cottonwood; wash it down with a house-brewed beer. Friday–Sunday, **Sugar's** (Hwy. 68, 505/852-0604, 11 A.M.–7 P.M. Wed.–Mon., $5), just up the road on the right, does a big barbecue dinner with ribs, brisket, sausage, and two sides; the rest of the week you can get a simple pulled-pork sandwich or chicken-fried steak. It's takeout only, but there are a few plastic picnic tables where you can sit down. (The property was for sale in 2008—and had been for a while—so there's a chance it will shut; call ahead, or have a backup plan.)

If you're into wine, keep an eye out for the various wineries just north of here: **Vivác** is on the main highway (2075 Hwy. 68, 505/579-4441, 10 A.M.–6 P.M. Mon.–Sat., noon–6 P.M. Sun.), and **La Chiripada** (505/579-4437, 10 A.M.–5 P.M. Mon.–Sat., noon–5 P.M. Sun.) is down Highway 75 a few miles in the pleasant little town of Dixon, known for its dense concentration of artists, organic farmers, and vintners—a worthwhile detour in itself, especially in early November for the long-running **Dixon Studio Tour** (www.dixonarts.org), or on summer and fall Wednesdays (4:30–7 P.M.) for the village farmers market.

Pilar

Beginning just south of the village of Pilar and stretching several miles north, **Orilla Verde Recreation Area** ($3/car) is public land along either side of the Rio Grande, used primarily as a put-in or haul-out for **rafting,** but you can **camp** on the riverbanks as well—Petaca and Taos Junction have the best sites ($7 per night). The **Vista Verde Trail** runs about 1.2 miles one-way along the west rim, an easy walk with great views and a few petroglyphs to spot in a small arroyo about a third of the way out; the trailhead is half a mile up the hill from the Taos Junction Bridge, on Highway 567 (turn left off the highway in Pilar and then follow signs into Orilla Verde). Stop first on the main highway at the **Rio Grande Gorge Visitors Center** for maps and other information (Hwy. 68, 575/751-4899, 7:45 A.M.–4:30 P.M. daily June–Aug., 10 A.M.–3 P.M. Fri.–Sun. Sept.–May). Across the road, **Pilar Yacht Club** (Hwy. 68, 575/758-9072, 8 A.M.–6 P.M. daily Apr.–Nov., 9 A.M.–2 P.M. Thurs.–Sun. Dec.–Mar.) is the center of the action, serving food to hungry river rats and functioning as an office for a couple of outfitters; TNM&O buses running between Taos and Santa Fe can also stop here if you ask. You can also go horseback riding nearby with **Cieneguilla Stables** (505/751-2815, melcieneguillastables@hotmail.com), starting at about $40 per hour.

Information and Services

TOURIST INFORMATION

The Santa Fe Convention and Visitors Bureau (800/777-2489, www.santafe.org, 8 A.M.–5 P.M. Mon.–Fri.) hands out its visitors guide and other brochures from its offices in the Santa Fe Convention Center, at the corner of West Marcy and Grant Streets. This office is smaller but better situated than the state-run visitors center near San Miguel Chapel (491 Old Santa Fe Tr., 505/827-7336, 8 A.M.–5 P.M. Mon.–Fri.).

For info on the outdoors, head out to the comprehensive Public Lands Information Center (1474 Rodeo Rd., 505/438-7840, www.publiclands.org, 9 A.M.–4:30 P.M. Mon.–Fri.) on the far south side of town—you can pick up heaps of free flyers, including detailed route descriptions for the most popular area day hikes, as well as buy guidebooks, detailed topo maps for all the wilderness areas, and hunting and fishing licenses.

Books and Maps

Santa Fe has two particularly good bookshops right in the center of town. **Travel Bug** (839

Paseo de Peralta, 505/992-0418, 7:30 A.M.–
5:30 P.M. Mon.–Sat., 10 A.M.–3 P.M. Sun.)
specializes in maps, travel guides, gear such as
luggage and GPS gadgets, and even occasional
free advice. For more general stock, **Collected
Works** (208-B W. San Francisco St., 505/988-
4226, 9 A.M.–8 P.M. Mon.–Sat., 10 A.M.–6 P.M.
Sun.), directly across from The Lensic, is the
place to go—excellent staff recommendations,
and a trove of local-interest titles.

Local Media

The *Santa Fe New Mexican* is Santa Fe's daily
paper, which publishes events listings and gallery news in its *Pasatiempo* insert on Fridays.
For left-of-center news and commentary, the
Santa Fe Reporter is the free weekly rag, available in most coffee shops and cafés.

Radio

Santa Fe supports a number of niche radio stations: KLBU (102.9 FM) brings Ibiza-style
chill-out electronica to the mountains, while
KBAC (98.1 FM), a.k.a. Radio Free Santa Fe,
is the major community station. Tune in Friday
afternoons for news on the gallery scene.

SERVICES
Banks

First National Bank of Santa Fe (62 Lincoln
Ave., 505/992-2000, 9 A.M.–5 P.M. Mon.–
Fri.) is on the west side of the plaza. **First
Community Bank** (100 N. Guadalupe St.,
505/946-4100, 9 A.M.–5 P.M. Mon.–Thurs.,

9 A.M.–6 P.M. Sat.) is walking distance from
the plaza but also easily accessible by car.

Post Office

Santa Fe's **main post office** (120 S. Federal Pl.,
505/988-2239, 8 A.M.–5:30 P.M. Mon.–Fri.,
9 A.M.–4 P.M. Sat.) is conveniently just north
of the plaza, near the district courthouse.

Internet

Travel Bug (839 Paseo de Peralta, 505/992-
0418, 7:30 A.M.–5:30 P.M. Mon.–Sat.,
10 A.M.–3 P.M. Sun.) bookstore offers free
Internet access and also serves coffee. **Santa Fe
Public Library** (145 Washington St., 505/955-
6780, www.santafelibrary.org, 10 A.M.–9 P.M.
Mon.–Thurs., 10 A.M.–6 P.M. Fri. and Sat.,
1–5 P.M. Sun.) has several public Internet ter-
minals with free access; call ahead to reserve a
time slot if you can.

Laundry

Most self-service laundries are on or near
Cerrillos Road. One of the largest and nicest
is **St. Michael's Laundry** (1605 St. Michael's
Dr., 505/989-9375, 6 A.M.–11 P.M. daily),
across from the College of Santa Fe, a couple
of blocks east of Cerrillos Road. For drop-off
service that's a bit cheaper than what most hotels offer, try **La Unica Quality Cleaners** (647
Cerrillos Rd., 505/983-1182, 7:30 A.M.–6 P.M.
Mon.–Fri., 9 A.M.–3 P.M. Sat.) or **New Method
Cleaners** (1911 St. Michael's Dr., 505/982-0271,
7 A.M.–6 P.M. Mon.–Fri., 9 A.M.–1 P.M. Sat.).

Getting There and Around

BY AIRPLANE

Santa Fe Airport (SAF; 505/955-2900) wasn't really an option at press time, but Delta Airlines and American Eagle were considering direct flights from Los Angeles, Salt Lake City, and Dallas—the service may have started by the time you're reading this.

BY CAR

Hertz, Budget, Avis, and **Thrifty** all have branches on Cerrillos Road; only **Enterprise** (100 Sandoval St., 505/989-8859, 8 A.M.–6 P.M. Mon.–Fri., 9 A.M.–noon Sat.) has an office close to the plaza.

BY BUS AND SHUTTLE

Sandia Shuttle Express (888/775-5696, www.sandiashuttle.com) does hourly pickups from the airport 8:45 A.M.–10:45 P.M. and will deliver to any hotel ($25 one-way).

TNM&O/Greyhound (800/231-2222, www .tnmo.com) typically runs from Albuquerque's main bus station three times daily to Santa Fe, arriving in Santa Fe a little more than an hour later. Coming from Taos, TNM&O's service leaves once a day, in the early evening; the trip takes about 1.5 hours. Santa Fe's **main bus station** is at 858 St. Michael's Drive (505/471-0008, 11 A.M.–3 P.M. and 6:30–10 P.M. daily).

Within town, the reasonably useful city bus system, **Santa Fe Trails** (505/955-2001, www.santafenm.gov), can take you to all of the major sights from the handy central depot on Sheridan Street just north of the plaza. The "M" route goes to Museum Hill; Route 2 runs along Cerrillos Road; and Route 6 goes down to Rodeo Road, past the Public Lands Office and the community center. Buses on all routes don't run very frequently—generally, every 30 to 60 minutes—so check out the schedule first. The Museum Hill and Cerrillos Road buses run on Sundays. Fare is $1, or you can buy a day pass for $2.

BY TRAIN

The **Rail Runner** (866/795-RAIL, www.nm railrunner.com) connects downtown Albuquerque to central Santa Fe. Schedules for the new commuter service were being finalized at press time. The fare is $6 one way and $8 return.

Amtrak (800/872-7245, www.amtrak.com) runs the Southwest Chief through Lamy, 18 miles south of Santa Fe and a dramatic place to step off the train—you'll feel very Wild West, as there's no visible civilization for miles around. Trains arrive once daily from Chicago and Los Angeles. Amtrak provides a shuttle van for passengers coming and going to Santa Fe.

TAOS

Though adobe houses cluster around a plaza, and art galleries, organic bakeries, and yoga studios proliferate, the town of Taos is much more than a miniature Santa Fe. It's more isolated, reached by curving two-lane roads along either the winding mountain-ridge route or the fertile Rio Grande river valley, and it has a rougher, muddier feel. The glory of the landscape, from looming Taos Mountain to the staggered blue mesas dissolving into the flat western horizon, can be truly breathtaking. Add to that the intense mysticism surrounding Taos Pueblo and the often wild creativity of the artists who have lived here, and the lure is irresistible. People flock here on pilgrimages—to the ranch where D. H. Lawrence lived, to the hip-deep powder on the slopes at Taos Ski Valley, to the San Francisco de Asis Church that Georgia O'Keeffe painted—then simply wind up staying. The waitress pouring your coffee probably has a variation on this same story.

Celebrity residents such as Julia Roberts and Donald Rumsfeld have lent the place a certain reputation of wealth and exclusivity, but this is hardly the case. Farmers in Valle Valdez scrape by on their acequia-fed farm plots just as they have for centuries; the same goes for residents of old Taos Pueblo, the living World Heritage Site that still uses no electricity or running water. Add to that a strong subculture of ski bums, artists, off-the-grid eco-homesteaders, and spiritual seekers, and you have a community that, while not typically prosperous, is more loyal and dedicated to preserving its unique way of life than perhaps any other small town in the western United States.

COURTESY OF EASY TRAVELER

HIGHLIGHTS

◖ **Taos Art Museum at Fechin House:**
In the early 1930s, Russian artist Nicolai Fechin designed his home in a fantastical fusion of Tartar, Spanish, and American Indian styles. Today, his paintings hang next to the wood lintels and furniture he carved (page 97).

◖ **La Hacienda de los Martinez:** Get a taste of life in early 19th-century Taos at this restored adobe family compound, home to historic community leaders. Don't miss the fascinating display on the Penitente brotherhood (page 100).

◖ **San Francisco de Asis Church:** With its massive adobe buttresses and rich earthy glow, this 350-year-old Franciscan mission is one of the most recognizable in the world, thanks to its frequent depiction in paintings and photographs (page 102).

◖ **Taos Pueblo:** The stepped adobe buildings at New Mexico's most remarkable pueblo seem to rise organically from the earth. Don't miss the ceremonial dances here, held about eight times a year (page 103).

◖ **Rio Grande Gorge:** Think how dismayed the first homesteaders must have been when they reached "New Mexico's Grand Canyon," an 800-foot-deep channel cut through the rock to the west of Taos. Think how overjoyed today's white-water rafters are in the spring, when mountain runoff surges through the rift (page 104).

◖ **Taos Ski Valley:** This is the purist's mountain: deep powder, no pretension. Don't ski? Drive up here just to crane your neck up at the top, and consider taking lessons (page 108).

◖ **Vietnam Veterans Memorial State Park:** Set on a low ridge overlooking the bowl of a high valley, this elegant white chapel, dedicated in 1971, was built to honor one man's fallen son. Since then, it's grown to become a national monument (page 128).

LOOK FOR ◖ TO FIND RECOMMENDED SIGHTS, ACTIVITIES, DINING, AND LODGING.

North and east from Taos, the grandly named Enchanted Circle scenic byway loops around Wheeler Peak, the highest mountain in New Mexico at 13,161 feet. The area was settled primarily by miners and ranchers in the late 19th century, so it has a different atmosphere from Spanish-and-Indian Taos. Along the way, you can stop at a mining ghost town, a moving Vietnam veterans' memorial, or a

rowdy Old West–style steakhouse. Likewise, the ski resorts of Angel Fire and Red River offer a somewhat less extreme, but no less fun, alternative to Taos Ski Valley.

PLANNING YOUR TIME

Taos's busiest tourist season is the arid summer, when a day's entertainment can consist simply of gallery hopping before settling in

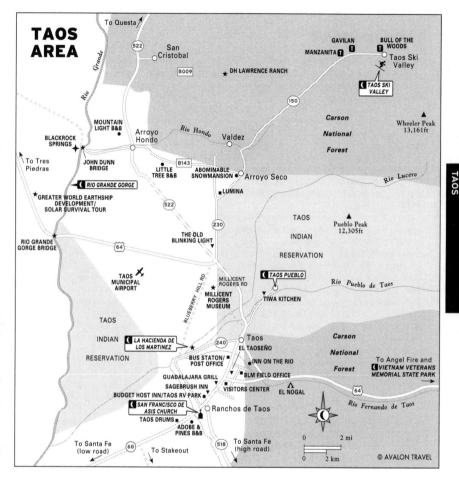

to watch the afternoon thunderheads gather and churn, and then the sun set under lurid red streaks across the broad western mesas. Wintertime is of course busy with skiers between November and April, but as they're all up on the mountain during the day, museums scale back their hours, and residents reclaim the town center, curling up with books at one of the many coffee shops. The Taos Pueblo also closes to visitors for up to 10 weeks in February and March. By May, the peaks are relatively clear of snow, and you can hike to high meadows filled with wildflowers; fall is

dominated by the smell of wood smoke and the beat of drums as the pueblo and the rest of the town turn out for the Feast of San Geronimo at the end of September.

If you're coming straight from Albuquerque, the trip takes about 2.5 hours along the slightly more direct "low road" through the river valley, or three hours along the high road; you'll want to stay over at least a couple of nights to make the drive worthwhile. From Santa Fe, it's possible to visit Taos as a day trip—as plenty of people do in the summertime—but you'll of course get a better sense of the place if you stay

TAOS

TAOS IN PRINT

Just as San Francisco de Asis Church has inspired countless painters and photographers, the people of Taos have found their way into novels and short stories.

First brush up on the basics with Bill Hemp's *Taos Landmarks & Legends* (Boulder: University Press of Colorado, 2002), which dedicates chapters to historical figures such as Kit Carson as well as more recent Taos happenings, such as the dynamics behind the New Buffalo commune. It's all served up with a generous sprinkling of anecdotes, hearsay, and even recipes.

One of Taos's more revered figures is Padre Antonio Martinez, a popular priest and leader in the mid-1800s. So some Taos residents aren't fond of Willa Cather's *Death Comes for the Archbishop* (New York: Vintage, 1990), even if it is a highly lauded literary classic. The 1927 novel is based on the mission of Jean Baptiste Lamy, who became archbishop of Santa Fe, with sympathy for his efforts to straighten out "rogue" Mexican priests such as Martinez. The *padre* gets more balanced coverage in *Lamy of Santa Fe* (Middletown, CT: Wesleyan University Press, 2003), a biography by Paul Horgan that won a Pulitzer Prize after it was published in 1975.

Frank Waters, famous Western novelist and a Taos resident for almost 50 years, fictionalized the story of Edith Warner, a woman who ran a small café frequented by the Los Alamos scientists while they were developing the nuclear bomb. *The Woman at Otowi Crossing* (Athens, OH: Swallow Press, 1987) is his portrait of a woman who seeks isolation in the New Mexico wilderness but is nonetheless drawn back into the world through the largest event of her time. The novel is true to Warner's life, but it's rounded out by a biography, *The House at Otowi Bridge: The Story of Edith Warner & Los Alamos* (Albuquerque: University of New Mexico Press, 1979), written by Peggy Pond Church, who herself lived at Los Alamos for 20 years, in the years before the area was taken over by the military.

Another Taos writer, John Nichols, earned acclaim for his comic novel *The Milagro Beanfield War* (New York: Owl Books, 2000), which was later made into a film by Robert Redford. The war of the title is an escalating squabble in a tiny village over the acequia, the traditional irrigation ditch that's still used in Valle Valdez and other agricultural communities in the area. But if you think it takes comic melodrama and a star such as Redford to make irrigation interesting, look into the beautiful and fascinating *Mayordomo: Chronicle of an Acequia in Northern New Mexico* (Albuquerque: University of New Mexico Press, 1993), Stanley Crawford's memoir about his term as "ditch boss" in the valley where he runs his garlic farm.

And if that's all too highbrow, you can find pure pulp in Ruth Laughlin's *The Wind Leaves No Shadow* (Caldwell, ID: Caxton, 1978), a bodice ripper based on the steamy life of Doña Barcelo Tules, who was born a pauper but grew up to be a powerful madam and gambling queen in 1830s Taos and then decamped to Santa Fe to run a high-end card house. She was the lover of Manuel Armijo, the last Mexican governor of New Mexico, and then attended the U.S. Victory Ball in 1846 on the arm of American general Stephen Kearny. Allegedly.

overnight. A three- or four-night visit will give you a chance to explore at a leisurely pace, with an afternoon at Taos Pueblo, a couple of mornings at galleries and museums, time for hiking or skiing, and a day tour of the Enchanted Circle. But you can also get a nice taste of Taos over a weekend, and a number of distinctive bed-and-breakfasts make it a perfect place for a short romantic getaway.

As for the Enchanted Circle, the 84-mile loop is typically done as a day trip, but you may want to stay overnight in Eagle Nest or in Red River (a.k.a. "Little Texas"), the better to take in the skiing, hiking, and rock climbing in the area. By no means attempt to visit Taos and do the Enchanted Circle loop in a single day—you'd be terribly rushed, and this is hardly the spirit of Taos.

HISTORY

The first full-time inhabitants of the area at the base of Taos Mountain were Tiwa-speaking descendants of the ancestral Puebloans (also called Anasazi) who migrated from the Four Corners area around A.D. 1000. Taos, from Tiwa for "place of the red willows," was a thriving village when Francisco de Coronado's exploratory crew arrived in 1540. By 1615, settlers had arrived and established their own small community.

The Spanish initially had difficulty getting a toehold, however. The Pueblo Revolt of 1680, led by Popé in Taos, succeeded in driving settlers out of New Mexico for 12 years. Under the heavy hand of Governor Diego de Vargas, most of the area was reclaimed in 1692, but the Taos Pueblo Indians held out for four more violent years before they formally surrendered. The only thing that held the truce was that the Pueblo people and the Spanish both had to defend themselves against Comanche and Jicarilla Apache raiders.

By the middle of the 18th century, Taos had become moderately more secure and was an integral part of a brisk trade network, thanks in part to French fur trappers who had discovered wealth in beaver pelts from the lakes in the surrounding mountains. The little village became a place to gather and swap goods brought from Mexico and in from the surrounding wilderness. At the trade fairs, rugged mountain men met and mingled with wealthy Spanish merchants, mule-train runners up from Mexico, and local Indians selling their wares.

Early in Taos's history, the population was so sparse and life so hard that it took only one energetic person to have a significant impact. Padre Antonio José Martínez, son of an established trader, was one of the area's most dynamic leaders in the first half of the 19th century. In 1835, he acquired the first printing press in the American West and began producing books and a periodical, *El Crepúsculo de la Libertad* (The Dawn of Freedom), which was published off and on well into the 20th century, eventually becoming the *Taos News*. He also established a co-ed school, a seminary, and a law school. Jean Baptiste Lamy, the Frenchman

appointed bishop of Santa Fe in 1853, earned the enmity of Taoseños by curtailing the popular Padre Martínez's work, even filing an order to excommunicate him. Although the papers don't appear to have been processed, Martínez claimed to have been cast out of the church, and he set up a private chapel at his house, from which he ministered until he died in 1867.

When Mexico declared its independence from Spain in 1821, little changed for Taos, but the transition to U.S. rule in 1846, after the Mexican-American War, caused much upheaval. Wealthy Spanish landowners and Catholic priests (including Padre Martínez) both foresaw their loss of influence under the Americans and plotted a rebellion. On January 19, 1847, the leaders incited a mob, many of them Indian, to kill New Mexico's first American governor, the veteran merchant Charles Bent; elsewhere in town and the larger region, scores of other Anglo landowners were massacred before U.S. cavalry came from Santa Fe to squelch the uprising.

The last half of the 1800s saw the establishment of a mining industry in Twining (now Taos Ski Valley) and a gold rush in nearby Elizabethtown, but the 1879 arrival of the railroad in Raton to the north bumped Taos from its role as trading hub, and the town slipped into backwater status. Nonetheless, the era brought colorful characters to Taos, some of whom would soon work their way into local legends. The six-foot-tall outlaw "Long" John Dunn, for instance, made a business in toll bridges across the Rio Grande (only one of the three survived the ravages of floodwaters), monopolizing road travel to the west; he also set up a gamblers' hotel and was the first car owner in Taos. He finally died in 1955.

Equally legendary: Bert Geer Phillips and Ernest Blumenschein, two painters on a jaunt from Denver in the summer of 1898 who "discovered" Taos when their wagon wheel snapped near town. After being happily waylaid in this inspirational place, Phillips stayed, marrying the town doctor's sister, Rose Martin. Blumenschein eventually returned with others, such as Oscar E. Berninghaus, Eadgar Irving Couse, Joseph

Sharp, and W. Herbert "Buck" Dunton. Together, the six established the Taos Society of Artists (TSA) in 1915. In the 12 years of the TSA's existence, not only did these and other artists make names for themselves as painters of the American West, but they also put Taos on the map. A deal with the Santa Fe Railway even promoted travel in exotic New Mexico with works by TSA painters in its brochures and posters. In another forward-thinking move, in 1923, Bert Phillips and Victor Higgins encouraged a wealthy local widow to donate some of her property for a permanent home for the TSA's legacy from the previous eight years; the Harwood Museum is still open on Ledoux Street. The TSA name also helped creative locals survive in the lean years. During the Depression, the Works Progress Administration funded several projects in the area, including the work of master wood-carver Patrocinio Barela, whose santos were later exhibited at the Museum of Modern Art in New York City.

More important, the TSA piqued the curiosity of influential East Coasters. One was Mabel Dodge Luhan, a well-off, freethinking woman who had fostered art salons in New York City and Florence. She then decamped to Taos in 1916, much to the fascination of cultural critics of the day. Her name is now inextricably linked with Taos's 20th-century history because she had an eye for budding artists and writers and encouraged them to come live with and meet one another at her several homes around town. By the 1920s, D. H. Lawrence, who spent some time in Taos at her behest, had taken to calling the place "Mabeltown," and figures as grand and varied as Greta Garbo, Willa Cather, Ansel Adams, Georgia O'Keeffe, Robinson Jeffers, and Carl Jung were making the long trek to this dusty mountain town. Mabel's steamy memoirs, published in the 1930s after Lawrence's death, reveal the feuds and affairs that fueled the massive creative output of this period.

The next generation, in the 1960s, was even more dedicated to living together and sharing ideas: This was when dedicated hippies, attracted by New Mexico's isolation, established several communes in the area. One, the New Buffalo commune in Arroyo Hondo, inspired Dennis Hopper when he filmed *Easy Rider*, which in turn led to another wave of countercultural immigrants. Locals, living by very traditional mores, were horrified at the naked, hallucinogen-ingesting, free-loving, long-haired aliens who had appeared in their midst; more than a decade of antagonism followed. Eventually, however, the most extreme communes disbanded and everyone mellowed a bit with age; even members of old Spanish families now talk about maximizing the solar gain of their adobe houses.

ORIENTATION

The area usually referred to as Taos encompasses not only the historic old town, which fans out from a main plaza, but a number of smaller surrounding communities. If you come via the low road, on Highway 68, you pass first through Ranchos de Taos. Once a distinct village, it's now connected to Taos proper by the least scenic part of town, a stretch of chain stores and cheap motels. Paseo del Pueblo Sur, as Highway 68 is called from Ranchos on, continues north to the central crossroads, the intersection with Kit Carson Road (U.S. 64). The main plaza lies west of this intersection; there's a pay parking lot on the east side, or a free lot a few blocks farther east on Kit Carson.

After the light, the street name changes to Paseo del Pueblo Norte; where it curves west, at the northern end of the central business district, a smaller road continues north about two miles to Taos Pueblo. Paseo del Pueblo Norte carries on through the village of El Prado (now also overtaken by greater Taos) to a four-way intersection that will forever be called "the old blinking light," even though the flashing yellow signal was replaced with a newfangled three-color job in the 1990s. Here U.S. 64 regains its name, shooting west to the Rio Grande, and Highway 522 leads northwest to the outlying village of Arroyo Hondo, then to Questa and the Enchanted Circle. Highway 150, commonly called Taos Ski Valley Road, goes north to Arroyo Seco, another peripheral town that's part of the greater Taos "metro area," and eventually to the base of the ski area.

TAOS

© AVALON TRAVEL

Sights

GUADALUPE PLAZA

Even more confusing than the patchwork of interlinked towns and highways is the fact that you can drive straight through Taos and completely miss its historic center if you're not careful. Guadalupe Plaza, enclosed by adobe buildings with deep shading *portales,* is just west of the main intersection of Kit Carson Road and Paseo del Pueblo Sur. Once an informal area at the center of a cluster of settlers' homes, the plaza was established around 1615 but then destroyed in the Pueblo Revolt of 1680. New homes were built starting in 1710, but fires repeatedly gutted the block-style homes, so the buildings that now edge the plaza all date from around 1930.

In the center is a monument to New Mexicans killed in the Bataan Death March of World War II; the U.S. flag flies day and night, a tradition carried on after an incident during the Civil War when Kit Carson and a crew of his men hoisted the flag and guarded it to keep Confederate sympathizers from taking it down. In front of the historic La Fonda hotel, a large bronze statue of local hero Padre Martinez gestures like a visionary—his enormous hands suggest his vast talent and influence. On the plaza's north side, the **old Taos County courthouse** contains a series of WPA-sponsored murals painted in 1934 and 1935 by Emil Bisttram and a team of other Taos artists. The door isn't always unlocked, but definitely try to get in: Enter on the ground floor through the North Plaza Art Center and go upstairs, toward the back of the building.

If you're curious what Guadalupe Plaza looked like before the souvenir-shop economy, stroll down Lower Ranchitos Road and turn on Valdez Road to reach **La Loma Plaza.** The center of a smaller farm settlement in the 1780s, the ring of adobe homes around a central open space is dusty and little changed

© ZORA O'NEILL

shops on Taos's Guadalupe Plaza

through the centuries. Exit the plaza by continuing uphill and bearing right—this takes you past La Loma's tiny old chapel and onto the paved San Antonio Street, which leads downhill and back to Lower Ranchitos.

MUSEUMS

The Museum Association of Taos (www .taosmuseums.org) manages five museums in town (all of those listed below except for the Governor Bent House and the Kit Carson Home and Museum). At any of the museums, you can buy a $25 pass, valid for a year, that grants you a single admission to all five. With individual admissions costing $8 or more, it can be worth it if you visit three places.

◀ Taos Art Museum at Fechin House

This sunny space (227 Paseo del Pueblo Norte, 575/758-2690, 10 A.M.–5 P.M. Tues.–Sun. May–Oct., 10 A.M.–4 P.M. Tues.–Sun. Nov.–Apr., $8), former home of artist and woodcarver Nicolai Fechin, is a showcase not only for a great collection of paintings, but also for

Fechin's lovely woodwork. When the Russia native moved to Taos in 1927, hoping to cure his tuberculosis, he bought seven acres of land, including the small two-story house, and, with the tools that are hidden in a small cabinet in the dining room, proceeded to hand carve the lintels, staircases, bedsteads, and more, in a combination of Russian Tartar and local styles. He also designed all of the metal trim and the fireplaces. His blending of traditions is flawless and natural—a small altar, also in the dining room, is set with Orthodox icons but could just as easily hold local santos. Although Fechin was devoted to traditional styles, he had no qualms about adapting the house to modern life. The stove in the kitchen is electric, installed in 1928 when power first arrived in town, and he engineered a central heating system.

The collection of paintings shown here is eclectic: Victor Higgins's 1936 *Indian Nude* recalls Gauguin, while Dorothy Brett's *Rainbow and Indians* from 1942 is more enamored of the powerful landscape. One room is dedicated to Fechin's own portrait work, characterized by broad, dynamic brushstrokes and a

TAOS

The hand-built Fechin House is as beautiful as the art collection it contains.

canny eye for distinctive facial features. One work is an etching of the same set of haggard, mustachioed twins rendered in oil by Ernest Hennings on a canvas hanging at the Harwood Museum. After all the work he did on the house, Fechin stayed in Taos only six years, leaving when his wife divorced him. He moved on to Los Angeles with his daughter, Eya (her sunny study, on the ground floor, contains the child-scale furniture that her father made for her). After her father died in 1955, Eya, by then practicing psychodrama and dance therapy, returned to live in the studio (the back building that also houses the gift shop) and helped establish the main house as a museum. While you're on the grounds, head farther back from the road to see the lobby of the Worldmark, built as a hotel in 1996—the astonishing woodwork that fills the space, all of it following Fechin's designs and planned under Eya's guidance, took 52 artisans working three years to finish.

Millicent Rogers Museum

While today's style makers jet to Dakar and Bhutan for inspiration, Millicent Rogers, a dashing, thrice-married New York City socialite and designer, moved to Taos in 1947 on a tip from a friend, Hollywood actress Janet Gaynor. Rogers brought her eye for style with her, adopting Navajo-style velvet broomstick skirts and *concho* belts and donning pounds of turquoise-and-silver jewelry for photo spreads in *Vogue* and *Harper's Bazaar*. Though she died just six years after she moved, in 1953 at the age of 51, she managed to accumulate a fantastic amount of stuff. Her namesake museum (1504 Millicent Rogers Rd., 575/758-2462, 10 A.M.–5 P.M. daily Apr.–Oct., 10 A.M.–5 P.M. Tues.–Sun. Nov.–Mar., $10) was established by her son, Paul Peralta-Ramos, and is set in the warren of adobe rooms that make up her former home. It reflects her discerning taste, with flawless pieces of pottery, rugs, and jewelry— both local works and her own designs. Peralta-Ramos contributes his own growing collection including beautiful pieces of Hispano devotional art. Aside from the individual beauty of the works, they also make up an excellent broad introduction to the artisanal work of th area, from ancient times to modern. Look for the beautiful black-on-black pottery of María Martinez, santos by Patrocinio Barela, and fine examples of the distinctive *colcha* embroidered rug style. But it's not all rooted in local culture: Rogers's goofy illustrations of a fairy tale for her children fill the last room. The gift shop here is particularly thorough and includes beautiful (though pricey) vintage jewelry and very old rugs.

Harwood Museum of Art

This museum (238 Ledoux St., 575/758-9826, www.harwoodmuseum.org 10 A.M.–5 P.M. Tues.–Sat., noon–5 P.M. Sun., $8) set in the sprawling pueblo revival–style home of the Harwood patrons, tells the story of Taos's rise as an art colony, beginning with Ernest Blumenschein's fateful wagon accident, which left him and his colleague, Bert Phillips, stranded in the tiny town in 1898. Modern Taos painters are also represented in the temporary exhibit spaces upstairs, and it's interesting to see the same material—the mountain, the pueblo, the river, local residents—depicted in different styles through the decades, from the Taos Society of Artists' early realist works with a certain genre bent to later cubist and abstract efforts. Also upstairs: a small but very good assortment of Hispano crafts, including a couple of santos by Patrocinio Barela, the Taos wood-carver who modernized the art in the 1930s, and some beautiful 19th-century tin-work. A separate back wing is dedicated to the ethereal abstractions of painter Agnes Martin, who live in Taos for 50 years before she died in 2004.

Ernest L. Blumenschein Home and Museum

Ernest Blumenschein, one of the founding fathers of the Taos Society of Artists, moved into this house (222 Ledoux St., 575/758-0505, 9 A.M.–5 P.M. daily May–Oct., 10 A.M.–4 P.M. daily Nov.–Apr., $8) in 1919 with his wife, Mary Shepard Greene Blumenschein, who was herself an accomplished artist, having earned medals at the Paris Salon for her painting.

Get a glimpse of colonial life at La Hacienda de los Martinez.

The house's decoration largely reflects her taste, from the sturdy wood furnishings in the dining room to the light-filled studio and the cozy wood-paneled library. Throughout, the walls are hung with sketches and paintings by their contemporaries; some of the finest are in the back "Green Room," including a beautiful monotype of Taos Mountain by Oscar E. Berninghaus. The main bedroom, entered through a steep arch, is decorated with Mary's lush illustrations for *The Arabian Nights*. Throughout, you can admire the variety of ceiling styles, from rough-hewn split cedar *(rajas)* to tidy golden aspen boughs *(latillas)*.

◖ La Hacienda de los Martinez

The word "hacienda" conjures a sprawling complex and rich surrounding lands, but the reality in 19th-century Taos was quite different, as this carefully restored adobe home (708 Hacienda Rd., off Ranchitos Rd., 575/758-1000, 9 A.M.–5 P.M. daily May–Oct., 10 A.M.–4 P.M. daily Nov.–Apr., $6) from 1804 shows. Its builder and owner, Severino Martinez, was a prominent merchant who hosted the Taos trade fairs at the hacienda and eventually became the mayor of Taos in the 1820s. His oldest son was Padre Antonio Martinez, the valley leader who clashed with the French bishop Jean Baptiste Lamy. Despite the family's high social standing, life was fairly rugged, cramped, and cold: 21 simple rooms arranged around two courtyards allowed room for sleeping, cooking, and, in the single room with a wood floor, dancing. Some of the spaces have been furnished to reflect their original use; others are dedicated to exhibits, such as a very interesting display on slavery in the area, and an especially creepy wood carving of Doña Sebastiana, Lady Death, with her glittering mica eyes, in the collection of Penitente paraphernalia. During the summer, local craftspeople are on hand to demonstrate weaving, blacksmithing, and the like in the house's workshops; in the fall, the trade fair is reenacted.

Kit Carson Home and Museum

Old photographs, memorabilia, and assorted trinkets from the frontier era conjure the life of the legendary scout at the Kit Carson Home and Museum (113 Kit Carson Rd., 575/758-4945, 9 A.M.–6 P.M. daily May–Oct., 9 A.M.–5 P.M. Nov.–Apr., $5, $12 family ticket). The definitive mountain man, Carson was just one of many solitary scouts, trackers, and trappers who explored the American West on foot and horseback. He was an intrepid adventurer who, after a childhood on the barely settled edge of Missouri, as a teenager joined a wagon train headed down the Santa Fe Trail; he arrived in Taos in 1826. His talent for tracking, hunting, and translating from Spanish and various Indian languages soon put him in high demand. But whether he was scouting for explorer John C. Frémont as Frémont mapped the trails west to Los Angeles or serving as an officer in the Civil War or, less heroically, forcing the Navajos on the Long Walk to Fort Sumner, he used Taos as his base camp and called the place home. He bought this house in 1843 with his third wife, Josefa Jaramillo; he and Josefa died there in 1868.

Governor Bent House and Museum

Although it's not a member of the Museum Association of Taos, this dusty little backroom exhibit space (117 Bent St., 575/758-2376, 10 A.M.–5 P.M. daily Sept.–May, $3) is definitely worth a visit. It's the former residence of Charles Bent, who was appointed the first governor of the territory of New Mexico in 1846 after the Mexican-American War. He had extensive experience as a western trader (he and his brother had built Bent's Fort, an important trading center in Colorado), but he lasted only a year in his new job, as he died at the hands of an angry mob dissatisfied with the new American government. Amid the slightly creepy clutter (a malevolent-looking ceremonial buffalo head, Inuit knives, photos of Penitente rituals from an old *Harper's* magazine, and more) is the very hole in the very wall that Bent's family quickly dug to escape while Bent tried to reason with the murderous crowd. The back room only gets stranger, with surreal taxidermy, sinister early-20th-century doctor's instruments, and lots of old guns. The whole place may feel like an antiques store where nothing's for sale, but it still gives a surprisingly good overview of the period.

OTHER ATTRACTIONS
Mabel Dodge Luhan House

Now used as a conference center and B&B, arts patroness Mabel Dodge Luhan's home (240 Morada La., 575/751-9686, 9 A.M.–7 P.M. daily, free) is open to curious visitors as well as overnight guests. Knock at the main building first; the caretaker will give you information for a self-guided tour. Bordering the Taos Reservation, the house was built to her specifications starting in 1918, a year after she had moved to New Mexico to be with her third husband (she was Mabel Dodge Sterne at that point) and then divorced him. This intrepid woman, who shaped Taos's arts culture for decades to come, also exercised a firm hand when designing her own place. Alongside a small original structure—a low row of adobe rooms that were already a century old at that point—she added a three-story main building, topped with a huge sunroom open on three sides. This, and the similarly glass-enclosed bathroom on the second floor, seemed a bit scandalous to her neighbors, the pueblo residents. One of them, however, didn't seem to mind—Tony Luhan, the foreman of the construction project, became her next husband. But Mabel's custom love nest brought out some latent prurience even in D. H. Lawrence, who objected to the curtainless bathroom windows. To soothe his sensibilities, if not Mabel's, he painted colorful swirls directly on the glass; you can still see them today.

Other parts of the house did not fare so well. After Mabel's death in 1962, subsequent residents did some serious damage. Dennis Hopper, for instance, reputedly was in the habit of riding his motorcycle across the roof of the string of guest rooms. Fittingly, the only remaining original furniture, in the second-floor bedroom, is Mabel's sturdy pine bed—perhaps simply because its Taos-style spiral posts made it too big and heavy to move.

© ZORA O'NEILL

the front gate at Mabel Dodge Luhan House

TAOS

Downstairs is a cozy reading wing as well as a vast dining room, over which portraits of Mabel and Tony preside.

Kit Carson Cemetery

After seeing where Mabel Dodge Luhan lived, you can also visit her grave, in Taos's oldest cemetery. A sprawl of headstones in a shady corner of Kit Carson Park, on Paseo del Pueblo Norte north of the Taos Inn, it was established in 1847 to bury the dead from the Taos Rebellion (the melée in which Governor Charles Bent was murdered). First known simply as El Cementerio Militar, it earned its current name when the bodies of Mr. Carson and his wife were moved here in 1869 according to his will. Many of Taos's oldest families, particularly the merchants of the late 1800s, are buried here. Mabel had been a very close friend of the trader Ralph Meyers, and they often joked about being buried together. When Mabel died in 1962, a few years after Ralph, writer Frank Waters (who had based a character in *The Man Who Killed the Deer* on Meyers) recalled their wishes and suggested that Meyers's grave be scooted over to make room for Mabel; she was the last person to be buried in the cemetery, in 1962, and her grave is squeezed into the far southwest corner. Other local luminaries at rest here include Padre Antonio Martinez, who stood up to Catholic bishop Lamy, and Englishman Arthur Manby, whose grave actually stands outside of the cemetery proper because of his lifetime of shady business deals, land grabs, and outright swindles perpetrated in town. Manby was found beheaded in his mansion in 1929, and the unsympathetic populace was happy to call it a natural causes. (Another Waters book, *To Possess the Land,* tells Manby's story.)

◖ San Francisco de Asis Church

Just as photographs of the Great Pyramid of Cheops seldom show the sprawl of modern Cairo crowding up to its base, San Francisco de Asis Church (east side of U.S. 68, Ranchos de Taos, 575/758-2754, 9 A.M.–4 P.M. daily, Mass 7 A.M., 9:30 A.M., and 11:30 A.M. Sun., donation) as depicted in, say, Emil Bisttram's or

the hulking buttresses of San Francisco de Asis Church

Georgia O'Keeffe's paintings or Ansel Adams's photographs, is always a shadow-draped fortress isolated on a hilltop. So it's often a surprise to visitors to see the cluster of buildings that ring the small plaza in front of the church, which was built in the first half of the 18th century as a Franciscan mission for the farming community of Ranchos de Taos.

Today the adobe houses around the church hold more T-shirt shops than homes, but you can nonetheless see what has fascinated so many artists. The clean lines, the shadows created by the hulking buttresses, the rich glow of the adobe in the sun—these are all appealing aesthetic details, but at bottom, the church is a sort of living architecture, as much a part of the earth as something raised above it. As with every traditional adobe structure, it must be refinished every year with a mix of clay, sand, and straw; it is then coated with a fine layer of water and sand and buffed with sheepskin.

The Shadow of the Cross

Inside, the whitewashed walls are covered with

santos and *retablos;* in an adjoining room is another, more modern attraction, an 1896 painting by a French Canadian artist named Henri Ault ($3 donation). The eight-foot-high canvas depicts Jesus in front of the Sea of Galilee; when the lights in the small room are extinguished, it begins to luminesce, and the life-size figure of Christ soon appears ready to step off the rocks and into the room. Some people also see the shape of a cross over Christ's shoulder, or a glowing halo. This "miracle" painting caused quite a sensation when Ault first made it—he claimed to be baffled by the odd phenomenon—and it was even shown at the World's Fair in St. Louis in 1904. After it spent years of exhibition in Europe, a wealthy Texan woman bought the painting, known as *The Shadow of the Cross,* and donated it to the church.

◖ TAOS PUEBLO

Even if you've been in New Mexico awhile and think you're inured to adobe, Taos Pueblo (575/758-1028, www.taospueblo.com, 8 A.M.–4:30 P.M. daily, closed for 10 weeks around Feb.–Mar., $10) is an amazing sight. Two clusters of multistory mud-brick buildings make up the core of this village, which claims, along with Acoma Pueblo, to be the oldest continually inhabited community in the United States. The current buildings, though annually repaired and recoated with mud, essentially date from the 1200s and house about 150 people year-round (the total population of the Taos reservation is about 2,000). The dedication of pueblo residents along with the town's designation as a UNESCO World Heritage Site have kept the place remarkably as it was in the pre-Columbian era, save for the use of adobe bricks as the main structural material, which was introduced by the Spanish. The apartment-like homes, stacked up in stages and connected by wood ladders, have no electricity or running water (though some use propane gas for heat and light).

As you explore, be careful not to intrude on spaces that are not clearly marked as shops, and

PUEBLO DANCES: WHAT TO EXPECT

Visiting a pueblo for a ceremonial dance or feast-day celebration is one of the most memorable parts of a visit to northern New Mexico. The animal dances are particularly transporting – dressed in pelts and mimicking the movements of a deer, for instance, the dancers transform the plaza into a forest glade. While the state's American Indian culture can occasionally seem exploited for its tourism value, a pueblo dance is not at all for the benefit of tourists. It is a ceremony and a religious ritual, not a performance – you are a guest, not an audience.

Keep this in mind as a guide to your own behavior. Applause is not appropriate, nor is conversation during the dance. Queries about the meaning of the dances are generally not appreciated. Never walk in the dance area, and try not to block the view of pueblo residents. The kivas, as holy spaces, are always off-limits to outsiders. During feast days, though, some pueblo residents may open their doors to visitors, perhaps for a snack or drink – but be considerate of others who may also want to visit, and don't stay too long. Photography is strictly forbidden at dances, sometimes with the exception of Los Matachines, which is not a religious ritual. Don't even think about trying to sneak a shot with your camera phone, as tribal police will be more than happy to confiscate it.

On a practical level, be prepared for a lot of waiting around. Start times are always approximate, and everything depends on when the dancers are done with their kiva rituals. There will usually be a main, seasonal dance – such as the corn dance – followed by several others. If you go in the winter, dress very warmly, but in layers – a Christmas Eve Mass may start inside the close-packed, overheated church and then dances may continue outside in the near-freezing cold.

stay clear of the ceremonial kiva areas on the east side of each complex. These kivas form the ritual heart of the pueblo, a private space within a private culture.

San Geronimo Church

The path past the admission gate leads directly to the central plaza, a broad expanse between Red Willow Creek (source of the community's drinking water, flowing from sacred Blue Lake higher in the mountains) and San Geronimo Church. The latter, built in 1850, is perhaps the newest structure in the village, a replacement for the first mission church the Spanish built in the 17th century. Visitors are allowed inside as long as they are respectful and quiet. The Virgin Mary presides over the room roofed with heavy wood vigas; her clothes change with every season, a nod to her dual role as the Earth Mother. Directly in front of the churchyard is where ceremonial dances take place periodically. (Taking photos is strictly forbidden inside the church at all times and, as at all pueblos, at dances as well.)

The first Spanish church, to the north behind the main house, is now a cemetery—fitting, given the tragic form of its destruction. Built in 1619 using forced Indian labor, it was first torn down during the 1680 Pueblo Revolt; the Spanish rebuilt it about 20 years later. In 1847 it was again attacked, this time by American troops sent in to quell the rebellion against the new government. As retaliation for the murder of Governor Charles Bent, the counterattack brutally outweighed what had sparked it. More than 100 pueblo residents, including women and children, had taken refuge inside the church when the Americans bombarded and set fire to it, killing everyone inside and gutting the building. Since then, the bell tower has been restored, but the graves have simply intermingled with the ruined walls and piles of dissolved adobe mud. All of the crosses—old carved wood to new finished stone—face sacred Taos Mountain.

Pueblo Crafts

You are welcome to wander around and enter any of the handful of craft shops and galleries that are open—a good opportunity to see inside the mud structures and to buy some of the distinctive Taos pottery, which is only very lightly decorated but glimmers with mica from the clay particular to this area; these pots are also renowned for cooking especially tender beans. On your way out of the pueblo, you may want to stop in at the **Oo-oonah Arts Center** (575/770-2110, 10 A.M.–4 P.M. daily Apr.–Oct.), where the gallery displays the work of pueblo children and adults enrolled in its craftwork classes—you can often find very skilled work here that's quite well priced. Twenty-five percent of the sales benefit the work of the nonprofit center, and the remainder goes to the artists. Another attraction on the road out: **Tiwa Kitchen** (575/751-1020, 11 A.M.–6 P.M. Wed.–Mon., $8), which serves simple traditional food, such as grilled buffalo and heirloom green chile.

◖ RIO GRANDE GORGE

Heading west on U.S. 64 from the "old blinking light," you pass the Taos airstrip on the left, and then, after a few more miles, the ground simply drops away. This is the Rio Grande Gorge, plunging 800 feet deep in malevolent-looking black basalt at its most alarming point. The river winds below, but it's not just millions of years of rushing water that have carved out the canyon—seismic activity has also caused a rift in the earth's surface. The crack extends north to just beyond the Colorado state line and south almost to Española. The elegant, unnervingly delicate-looking bridge that spans it was built in 1965 to supplement entrepreneur John Dunn's rickety old toll crossing eight miles north. Critics mocked it as "the bridge to nowhere" because the highway on the western bank had yet to be built, but the American Institute of Steel Construction granted it the Most Beautiful Span award in 1966. At 650 feet above the river, it was, and still is, the second-highest bridge in the United States (after the Royal Gorge Bridge in Cañon City, Colorado, and the New River Gorge Bridge in West Virginia). On either side of the bridge is the stretch of canyon called the Taos Box,

NEW MEXICO'S COMMUNES

Something about New Mexico's vast empty spaces inspires utopian thinking, as if the landscape were a blank slate, a way to start over from scratch and do things right. Spanish settlers felt it in the 16th century. Would-be gold miners banked on it in the 1800s. And in the 1960s, hippies, freethinkers, free-lovers, and back-to-the-landers fled crowded cities and boring suburbs to start life fresh in communities such as the Hog Farm and the New Buffalo Commune, both near Taos. For a while, New Mexico was the place to be: Dennis Hopper immortalized New Buffalo in his film *Easy Rider,* Janis Joplin chilled out in Truchas, and Ken Kesey drove his bus, *Further,* through the state.

Today these experimental communities and their ideals seem to have been just a brief moment of zaniness – their only legacy appears to be Hog Farm leader Wavy Gravy's consecration on a Ben & Jerry's label. But some of the ideals set down by naked organic gardeners and tripping visionaries have taken root and sprouted in unexpected ways. For instance, Yogi Bhajan, an Indian Sikh who taught mass kundalini yoga sessions in New Mexico in 1969, eventually became a major contributor to the state economy through all the businesses he established. Buddhist stupas dot the Rio Grande Valley, the product of Anglo spiritual seekers working with Tibetan refugees brought to New Mexico by Project Tibet, a non-profit organization cofounded by John Allen, who also ran the commune Synergia Ranch.

Synergia, which still exists as a retreat center, just off Highway 14 on the plateau south of Santa Fe, began as an avant-garde theater group but evolved into a hard-working cult with properties around the globe, its members dedicated to, among other things, building sustainable mini-ecosystems, or biospheres. One of the ranch's more devoted adherents was Edward Bass, renegade son of a Texas oil family. He invested some $100 million in Biosphere 2, a glass dome in the Arizona desert filled with 3,800 living species; in 1991, it was sealed up with eight people inside to test its environmental sustainability as a possible model for a Mars colony. After two two-year runs, Bio2 wasn't as inspirational as Allen and Bass had hoped, but it hasn't been a complete failure. With Bass's prodding (and funding), the place has been used as a research facility by Columbia University and now by the University of Arizona. Even as it's used as a lab to study climate change, it remains a relic of perhaps the most utopian vision yet to have sprouted in New Mexico.

two words that will inspire wild tales in any seasoned river runner. The Class III and IV rapids, which start around John Dunn Bridge to the north, are held to be the best place for white-water rafting in New Mexico.

Arroyo Hondo and Blackrock Springs

A less adrenaline-fueled way to enjoy the water here is at one of several hot springs that seep up next to the river, by-products of the seismic upsets. The easiest ones to find are those at the old John Dunn Bridge. To reach them, backtrack to the old blinking light and then head north on Highway 522. After about six miles, the road dips to the Rio Hondo; immediately after the bridge, turn left on County Road B-005, which runs along the north side of the arroyo. Drive slowly through this village, as the dirt roads are bumpy and there are often children playing. It's hard to imagine now, but this is where the New Buffalo commune was in the late 1960s—all traces of hippie influence seem to have evaporated. The road crosses the small Hondo River, then climbs a hill and descends again, winding toward the Rio Grande, where you cross John Dunn Bridge to reach the west side; turn left and then park at the first switchback. From there, it's a quarter-mile hike down the rocks and downstream to the springs. Don't crowd in if several people are already in the spring, and never leave trash behind.

TAOS

Greater World Earthship Development

If you brave the slender suspension bridge and continue on the west side of the gorge on U.S. 64, you soon see some odd apparitions along the right side of the road. These whimsically curved and creatively finished houses are Earthships: modular, low-priced homes that function entirely separately from the public utility grid by using collected rainwater and wind and solar power. Architect Michael Reynolds has been honing his Earthship design for more than three decades here in New Mexico. Whether it's due to the latent hippie culture or the awe-inspiring landscape, they have proved very popular, and you'll see them dotted around the area, as well as clustered together here at Greater World, the largest of three all-Earthship subdivisions in the area.

Although they look like fanciful Hobbit homes or Mars colony pods on the outside, Earthships are made of rather common stuff. The walls, usually built into hillsides, are stacks

View the inner workings of an eco-friendly home on the Solar Survival Tour.

of used tires packed solid with rammed earth, while bottles stacked with cement and crushed aluminum cans form front walls and colorful peepholes. Windows along the front wall are angled to maximize heat from the sun during the winter, while planters filter gray water and black water, creating a humid greenhouse atmosphere inside that's very welcome in arid New Mexico.

The Greater World subdivision maintains a visitors center, 1.8 miles past the bridge, that's the most unconventional model home and sales office you'll ever visit. You can take the self-guided **Solar Survival Tour** (575/751-0462, www.earthship.com, 10 A.M.–4 P.M. daily, $5) of a basic Earthship and watch a video about the building process and the thinking behind the design. If you're hooked, you can of course get details on buying a lot in the development or buying the plans to build your own place. Or try before you buy: Three Earthships here are for rent nightly or weekly, starting at $135.

Tres Piedras

Usually only rock climbers go the additional 26 miles to Tres Piedras, a handful of houses scattered around the intersection of U.S. 64 and U.S. 285. Its name (Three Stones) comes from the rock formations that spike up from the utterly flat plain, looking as though they should be in Australia or Greece. Otherwise, you can stop to browse at **The Old Pink Schoolhouse Gallery** (U.S. 64 at U.S. 285, 575/758-7826, erratic hours, so call ahead), an absorbing accretion of Mexican and New Mexican artwork and trinkets, all crammed in the village's former school-turned-mill.

ARROYO SECO

Bemoaning the gallerification of downtown Taos? The sheer touristy mayhem? From the old blinking light, head north on Highway 150 to the village of Arroyo Seco, a cluster of buildings at a bend in the road to the ski area, and you'll slip back a couple of decades. Sure, there's some art up here too, but this smaller community, though only a half-hour drive from the plaza, maintains an even more laid-

© ZORA O'NEILL

GREENBACKS MEET GREEN LIVING

While devoted ecoarchitect Michael Reynolds builds Earthships in isolation on Taos's western frontier, catering to a particular sort of low-budget back-to-the-lander, Tom Worrell, a media magnate turned environmental evangelist, went about the same task in the opposite way. Worrell, who hails from North Carolina but who became enamored of Taos on skiing visits, built a $20 million luxury resort. His reasoning: The term "sustainability" has a whiff of deprivation about it, which people, especially rich and influential people, want no part of.

To counter this negative association, he created El Monte Sagrado (The Sacred Mountain) as a showcase for inventions produced by his engineering company, Dharma Living Systems: Curoxin, a nontoxic alternative to chlorine, solar-panel "trees," and a seven-phase wastewater-processing system. But there's no hint you're in an "ecoresort" – no gratuitous hemp products here, just a lavish spa, a vast wine cellar, and of course, very, very high-threadcount sheets. Unless you're told, you'd never guess that the lily-covered fish ponds and babbling brooks running through the central courtyard are what Worrell calls Living Machines: a chemical-free means of treating sewage waste to produce water that is then used for the lush gardens and greenhouse plants. Worrell was ahead of the green-building trend when the resort opened in 2003 – now, ironically, guests actually expect visible signs of ecofriendliness.

Perhaps this is a sign of Worrell's success with the upper echelons, but he failed to woo the people of Taos. He antagonized some longtime locals, who saw him as swooping in and throwing around a shocking amount of cash in this not-so-well-off town. An attempt to install a Curoxin system in the town public pool failed, and in 2006, Worrell handed El Monte Sagrado's management over to a hotel group (which has chosen not to emphasize the green elements of the resort) and moved many of his operations elsewhere.

Meanwhile, Reynolds's more modest Earthships have continued to earn praise. The two men are not so different in certain elements of their visions, however. Despite the lone survivalist mentality that "off the grid" implies, both Reynolds and Worrell advocate the use of their technologies in areas with denser populations. Reynolds envisions an Earthship city of pyramid-shaped stacks of the modules, with shared cisterns and water processing. In the same vein, Worrell intentionally chose the site of El Monte Sagrado in town, half a mile from the plaza, rather than outside of Taos, to show that sustainable architecture isn't something that's "out there," in the wilderness, but something we can live with every day.

---

back and funky attitude than Taos does—if such a thing is possible. It has been a retreat for decades: Frank Waters, celebrated author of *The Man Who Killed the Deer* and *The Woman at Otowi Crossing,* lived here off and on from 1947 until his death in 1995.

"Downtown" Arroyo Seco has grown up around **La Santísima Trinidad Church,** set back from Highway 150 on the left. Built in 1834, its adobe walls are alarmingly eroded in patches, but it sports a cheery red metal roof; the spare traditional interior is decorated with santos and *retablos,* but the doors are often locked.

Better to pop in at one of the secular gathering places on the road. **Arroyo Seco Mercantile** (Hwy. 150, 575/776-8806) is the town's former general store, now a highly evolved junk shop that has maintained the beautiful old wood-and-glass display cases. Its stock varies from the practical (books on passive-solar engineering and raising llamas) to the frivolous and the beautiful, such as antique wool blankets. Across the street, **Abe's Cantina y Cocina** is a very old-style bar propped up by locals for countless decades; visit the adjacent lunch counter and peek in the side if you don't fancy making a dramatic front-door entrance to a crowd of taciturn Spanish-speaking men in cowboy hats. **Taos Cow,** the coffee shop next

TAOS

© ZORA O'NEILL

"Downtown" Arroyo Seco

door, known as "The Cow," is the hangout for everyone who doesn't fit in at Abe's—many of them guests at The Abominable Snowmansion hostel down the block.

The Rim Road and Valle Valdez

As it continues, the main road toward the ski area eventually makes a hard right, and the so-called "rim road" heads to the left. It runs the length of a canyon edge, overlooking Valle Valdez below, where tidy farm plots are set along Rio Hondo and the traditional acequia irrigation model that has been used here for more than four centuries. In typical modern real-estate distribution, the not-so-well-off native Taoseños value their fertile soil, while wealthy arrivistes (Julia Roberts, most famously) have claimed the swoon-inducing views on the rim road, which was developed only in the later part of the 20th century. On the north side of the valley, the ritzy Turley Mill development is built on the site of a still that produced the powerful bootleg hooch known as "Taos lightning" from the 1700s to 1847. It's now home

to Donald Rumsfeld and other occupants of million-dollar casitas.

TAOS SKI VALLEY

Highway 150 winds relentlessly up through Hondo Canyon, the steep mountain slopes crowded with tall, dense pines. In the wintertime, the mountaintops are often obscured by a wreath of clouds. The road dead-ends at Taos Ski Valley, a resort area that is technically an incorporated village, but only the mountain, along with the snow on top of it, matters to most people. When you finally get out of the car at the base of the ski runs and take in the vertiginous view toward Kachina Peak (elevation 12,481 feet and often white-capped even in July), you'll see why it inspires legions of reverential skiers every winter, when an average of 305 inches of snow falls on the mountain—almost 10 times the amount they get down in town. And in fact, until very recently, Taos Ski Valley permitted *only* skiers on its slopes. Snowboarders were banned, allegedly because of the seriously precipitous slopes here—more than half the trails are rated expert level, and many of them are left ungroomed. But the slopes were finally opened to all in 2008, in the last days of the ski season. It's a sea change for TSV's seriously loyal customers, and it leaves just three resorts in the country that don't allow snowboarding (Utah's Deer Valley and Alta and Mad River Glen in Vermont).

In the summertime, Hondo Canyon's many trails make for very good hiking or picnicking. The road is dotted on either side with picnic areas and campgrounds—Cuchilla del Medio is a particularly nice area for a picnic. **Rio Grande Stables** (575/776-5913, www .lajitasstables.com) does **horseback-riding trips** in the mountains around the ski valley, starting at $50 for one hour.

Entertainment

Taos is a small town—that means no glitzy dance clubs, no bars where you're expected to dress up. Nighttime fun is concentrated in a handful of places where, if you visit frequently enough, you'll get to know the regulars quickly. The various townwide celebrations—including music and dancing on the plaza on summer Thursdays—draw a full cross-section of the population.

BARS
Taos Pub Crawl

Starting around 5 P.M., the **Adobe Bar** (125 Paseo del Pueblo Norte, 575/758-2233, www .adobebar.com), in the lobby of the Taos Inn (look for the glowing thunderbird sign, the oldest neon in town), is where you'll run into everyone you've seen through the course of the day, all sipping a Cowboy Buddha ($9.50) or some other specialty margarita—the best in town. Mellow jazz or acoustic guitar sets the mood every night starting around 7 P.M. To give the poor hotel residents a break, the bar closes at 10 P.M., which forces all the regulars to move on down the road to the next phase of the evening: the dance floor at the **Sagebrush Inn** (1508 Paseo del Pueblo Sur, 575/758-2254). It gets packed with cowboy-booted couples stepping lively to decent country cover bands whose members always seem to resemble Kenny Rogers. The scene encompasses all of Taos, from artists to pueblo residents to mountain men with grizzled beards. Booze is a bargain, and the fireplace is big. After the band wraps up around midnight, the most dedicated move on to **The Alley Cantina** (121 Teresina La., 575/758-2121) for another hour or so. This warren of interconnected rooms (one of which claims to be the oldest in Taos…but don't they all say that?) can be potentially baffling after a few drinks. There are shuffleboard and a pool table for entertainment if you're not into the ensemble onstage—its name usually ends in "Blues Band"; a $3 or $4 cover applies on weekends. The kitchen is open until 11 P.M., and it's not a bad place for a burger ($6.50) at lunch either.

Other Bars

In addition to the Big Three, a few other watering holes draw a crowd, usually for live music of some kind. Wood-paneled **Eske's Brew Pub** (106 Des Georges La., 575/758-1517, 11:30 A.M.–10 P.M. daily) is across from the plaza, tucked back from the southeast corner of the intersection of Paseo del Pueblo Sur and Kit Carson Road. With live music on Fridays and Saturdays, it serves its house-made beer to a chummy après-ski crowd. You're in New Mexico—you should at least *try* the greenchile ale.

Named for its location one mile from the landmark traffic signal, **The Old Blinking Light** (1 Hwy. 150, 575/776-8787, 5–10 P.M. daily) is a casual, sprawling restaurant and bar where locals head for live bands. The food is only so-so (except for the deadly Mud Pie), but the atmosphere is very mellow and friendly, especially Monday nights for live music and on weekend afternoons, when people bring their kids to run around the back garden. If you're on the lookout for Julia Roberts (probably sans twins), this is a good bet; so far, Donald Rumsfeld hasn't been spotted.

Taos's swankiest boîte—really, the only place in town that could be called a boîte—is the moodily lit **Anaconda Bar** in El Monte Sagrado resort (317 Kit Carson Rd., 575/758-3502, from 11 A.M. daily), where deep leather booths curve around tables built of African drums. Skilled bartenders whip up pomegranate margaritas, and the list of wines by the glass is varied. Starting around 9:30 P.M. most nights, there's a not-too-intrusive live band; closing hours depend on the crowd. Another plus: the reasonably priced, wide-ranging bar menu.

Taos Mountain Casino (575/737-0777, 8 A.M.–1 A.M. Mon. and Tues., 8 A.M.–2 A.M. Wed.–Sun.) claims to be the "coziest" in New Mexico, and it certainly is an intimate gambling spot, just inside the pueblo entrance. All the basic slots plus blackjack and craps, but perhaps the biggest perk is that it's smoke free.

CINEMA AND THEATER

The Storyteller (110 Old Talpa Canyon Rd., 575/758-9715, www.transluxmovies.com) shows first-run films with an occasional arty option. Given the high concentration of artists of all stripes, it's no surprise that Taos's theater scene is very rich for such a small town. Check at the **Taos Center for the Arts** (133 Paseo del Pueblo Norte, 575/758-2052, www.taoscenterforthearts.org) to find out what shows may be on.

FESTIVALS AND EVENTS

Taos's biggest annual festivity, for which many local businesses close, is the **Feast of San Geronimo,** the patron saint thoughtfully assigned to Taos Pueblo by the Spanish when they built their first mission there in 1619. The holiday starts the evening of September 29 with vespers in the pueblo church and continues the next day with foot races and a pole-climbing contest. La Hacienda de los Martinez usually reenacts a 19th-century

Taos says "no" to generic multiplex cinemas.

Taos trade fair, with mountain men, music, and artisans' demonstrations.

The town also turns out for the **Fiestas de Taos** (www.fiestasdetaos.com), a mid-July celebration of Santiago de Compostela and Santa Ana that lasts three days, with a parade, food and crafts booths on the plaza, and the crowning of the Fiestas Queen. Also in July is the **Taos Pueblo Powwow** (www.taospueblo.com), a major get-together of Pueblo Indians and tribal members from around the country. Try to be there for the Grand Entry, the massive opening procession. The event takes place not at the pueblo but at powwow grounds off U.S. 64.

Since 1977, grape fanatics have been living it up at the 10-day **Taos Winter Wine Festival** (www.skitaos.org) at the end of January; seminars and special dinners are held at the ski valley resort center and many restaurants around town. Taos galleries put out their finest at the **Taos Arts Festival** (www.taosfallarts.com), two-week-long exhibitions in spring (Apr.–May) and fall (Sept.–Oct.), of the works

© ZORA O'NEILL

CEREMONIAL DANCES AT TAOS PUEBLO

In addition to the Feast of San Geronimo, visitors are welcome to attend ceremonial dances. This is only an approximate schedule – dates can vary from year to year, as can the particular dances. Contact the pueblo (505/758-1028, www.taospueblo.com) for times, or check the listings in the *Tempo* section of the paper for that week.

JANUARY 1
- Turtle dance

JANUARY 6
- Deer or buffalo dance

MAY 3
- Feast of Santa Cruz: corn dance

JUNE 13
- Feast of San Antonio: corn dance

JUNE 24
- Feast of San Juan: corn dance

JULY 25 AND 26
- Feast of Santiago and Santa Ana: corn dances and foot races

SEPTEMBER 29-30
- Feast of San Geronimo

DECEMBER 24
- Sundown procession and children's dance

DECEMBER 25
- Various dances

TAOS

of more than 150 Taos County artists. Since 1983, the October **Taos Wool Festival** (www.taoswoolfestival.org) has drawn textile artists as well as breeders—admire the traditional Churro sheep or an Angora goat and then pick up a scarf made from its wool. And if it's counterculture you're after, the **Taos Solar Music Festival** (www.solarmusicfest.com) takes place at the end of June at an off-the-grid stage near the Earthship development west of the Rio Grande Gorge. The event draws a wild mix of dedicated campers and sun worshippers, as well as diverse performers that have included Steve Earle, Harry Belafonte, and Los Lobos.

The glow of luminarias and torchlight on snow produces a magical effect—perhaps that's why Taos has so many winter events. On the first weekend in December, the **tree-lighting ceremony** on the plaza draws the whole town, and the rest of the season sees numerous celebrations, such as the reenactments of the Virgin's search for shelter, called Las Posadas, which take place at Our Lady of Guadalupe Church west of the plaza on the third weekend in December. At the pueblo, vespers is said at San Geronimo church on Christmas Eve, typically followed by a children's dance. On Christmas Day, the pueblo hosts either a deer dance or the Spanish Los Matachines dance.

Shopping

The main plaza is ringed with less-than-inspiring T-shirt shops and souvenir stores. Two further clusters of boutiques and art dealers lie just north of the plaza—very pleasant places to browse, though you won't find many bargains. From mid-May through October, there's a **farmers market** (8 A.M.–1 P.M. Sat.) in the town hall parking lot, next to the library just north of the plaza on Camino de la Placita.

GALLERIES

If you're in the market for something precious, pick up a copy of the *Collector's Guide,* a booklet listing the most discerning galleries, many of which are open only by appointment. If, on the other hand, you're hoping to discover Taos's next big art star, poke around smaller operations on back streets and in Arroyo Seco, or just keep your eyes out when you get your morning coffee—nearly every business doubles as a gallery in this town.

Otherwise, visiting some of the town institutions can round out your experience at the museums. **Spirit Runner** (303 Paseo del Pueblo Norte, 575/758-1132, 10 A.M.–5 P.M. Tues.–Sun.), for instance, is operated by Ouray Meyers, son of Ralph Meyers, the first Anglo man to deal in Indian art in his trading post. His gallery is as much a social hub as an art dealership, and he has some tales to tell. Summertime usually sees an all-nude show, complete with paper covering the windows and plenty of wine.

R. C. Gorman's Navajo Gallery (210 Ledoux St., 575/758-3250, 11 A.M.–5 P.M. daily) represents the best-known American Indian artist, who died in late 2005. Gorman sold art in Taos—and all over the world— since 1968, when he moved here from Chinle, Arizona. Even if you don't recognize his name, you will likely recognize his work: His fluid representations of American Indian women have achieved near-iconic status.

The town's best gallery for contemporary art is **Parks Gallery** (127-A Bent St., 575/751-0343, 10 A.M.–5 P.M. Mon.–Sat.), where the selection of styles and media is extremely varied, from Melissa Zink's bronze work to Arthur Lopez's quirky modern *bultos.*

Halfway to Arroyo Seco, turn off Highway 150 to reach **Lumina** gallery and sculpture gardens (11 Hwy. 230, 575/758-7282, 10:30 A.M.–5 P.M. Thurs.–Mon.), which has a very broad stable of artists, from a local from Santa Clara Pueblo who inlays pottery bowls with turquoise and shells to very contemporary photomontage artists. The elegant Japanese gardens are studded with monumental sculptures.

GIFTS, CLOTHING, AND JEWELRY

Gussy yourself up in Western trappings from **Horse Feathers** (109-B Kit Carson Rd., 575/758-7457, 10:30 A.M.–5:30 P.M. daily), where you can pick up a full cowpoke getup, from ten-gallon hat to jingling spurs. The big money is in the room full of vintage cowboy boots, but you can find less expensive, eclectic gift items, such as giant belt buckles or campfire cookbooks from 1900. **El Rincón Trading Post** (114 Kit Carson Rd., 575/758-9188, 9:30 A.M.–5:30 P.M. Tues.–Sun.) is crammed with stuff, some of it perhaps dating to 1909, when Ralph Meyers established his Mission Shop trading post. Today the trove is managed by his daughter, who has put aside many of the best pieces in an informal "museum," but there are still plenty of one-of-a-kind *concho* belts and other jewelry, as well as beads and baubles from elsewhere in the world. And if you want more of this odd browsing, make sure you get out to **Arroyo Seco Mercantile,** described in more detail in the *Arroyo Seco* section in *Sights.*

FX/18 (103-C Bent St., 575/758-8590, 10 A.M.–5 P.M. Thurs.–Tues., noon–5 P.M. Wed.) has a small but excellent selection of stuff you didn't know you needed, from groovy

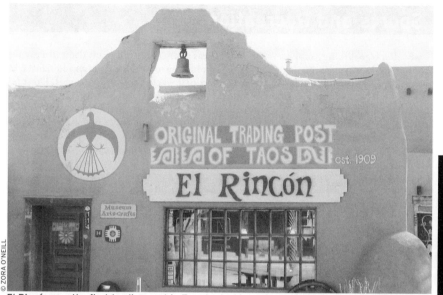

© ZORA O'NEILL

El Rincón was the first trading post in Taos to deal in crafts and jewelry from Taos Pueblo.

housewares to nifty stationery. But it doesn't forget it's in Taos—the selection of contemporary Southwest-style jewelry is some of the coolest you'll see anywhere.

Outside Taos are a number of sheep ranches, and **La Lana Wools** (136-C Paseo del Pueblo Norte, 575/758-9631, 10 A.M.–5:30 P.M. daily) shows off many of their products, from skeins of richly colored yarn (knitters will swoon) through to handwoven cloaks.

If you're not lucky enough to be staying in a hotel that uses **Desert Blends** (130 Bent St., 575/737-0770, 10 A.M.–5 P.M. Mon.–Fri., 10 A.M.–6 P.M. Sat. and Sun.) products as amenities, stop in here to stock up on locally crafted sage shampoo and red-clay face mask, for instance.

If you're overloaded on New Mexican knick-knacks, head to **Wabi-Sabi** (216-A Paseo del Pueblo Norte, 575/758-7801, 10 A.M.–6 P.M. Mon.–Sat., 11 A.M.–5 P.M. Sun.), which transcends the roadrunner paperweight with simple and beautiful Japanese (or Japanese-inspired) items for around the home. From gleaming shell knives to rough stoneware, it's all functional yet beautiful, and the store as a whole is a wonderful place to relax.

Less soothing, but a whole lot of fun, **Taos Drums** (3956 Hwy. 68, 575/758-9844, 8 A.M.–5 P.M. Mon.–Fri.) is a giant shop and factory dedicated to making Taos Pueblo–style percussion instruments, from thin hand drums to great booming ones made of hollow logs. Trying out the wares is encouraged—it's a good place to bring the kids. The shop is on the west side of the highway five miles south of the plaza (two miles south of the traffic light in Ranchos de Taos).

TOYS

Taos is also home to an exceptionally magical toy store, **Twirl** (225 Camino de la Placita, 575/751-1402, www.twirlhouse .com, 10 A.M.–6 P.M. daily). Tucked in a series of low-ceiling adobe rooms, it's crammed with everything from science experiments to wooden trains to fairy costumes. Even the kiva fireplace gets a fantastical 1,001 Nights treatment, and there's a big roster of activities on weekends.

Sports and Recreation

If you don't go hiking, mountain biking, or skiing in Taos, you're missing a lot of the town's appeal—the wild setting presses in all around, and Taos Mountain looms behind every town view. Downhill skiing is the main draw in the winter, just a 45-minute drive from central Taos, but you can also try more solitary snowshoeing and Nordic skiing. In summer, peak baggers will want to strike out for Wheeler Peak, the state's highest, while rafters, rock climbers, and mountain bikers can head the other direction to the dramatic basalt cliffs of the Rio Grande Gorge, where river runners defy death in the churning rapids of the legendary Taos Box (late May and early June is the best season for this).

Stop in at the **Carson National Forest Supervisor's Office** (208 Cruz Alta Rd., 575/758-6200, www.fs.fed.us/r3/carson, 8:30 A.M.–4:30 P.M. Mon.–Fri.) for advice, booklets on recommended trails, and maps. Just down the street, the **Bureau of Land Management Taos Field Office** (226 Cruz Alta Rd., 575/758-8851, www.nm.blm.gov, 7:45 A.M.–4:30 P.M. Mon.–Fri.) can help you prepare for a rafting or longer camping trip, with plenty of maps and brochures. A complete list of tour operators can be found online at Taos Outdoor Recreation (www.taosoutdoorrecreation.com).

Sudden thunderstorms are common in the summer, as are flash floods and even freak blizzards. Well into May, snow can blanket some of the higher passes, so wherever you go, always carry more warm clothing than you think you'll need, and don't skimp on the sunscreen, even when it's below freezing.

SKIING AND SNOWSHOEING
Taos Ski Valley (866/968-7386, www.skitaos.org, $63 full-day lift ticket) is the premier spot for Alpine skiing. The resort is open from late November through the first weekend in April, with 110 trails served by 12 lifts and snowmaking capacity on all beginner and intermediate areas in dry spells. The truly dedicated can do the hike up to Kachina Peak, an additional 632 feet past where the lift service ends. Don't be too intimidated by the trails: The highly regarded Ernie Blake Ski School is one of the best places to learn the basics or polish your skills. Novice "yellowbirds" can take one ($85) or two ($130) days of intensive instruction specially geared to new skiers. For those with some experience, a six-day improvement program costs $225, plus lift tickets. Snowboarding lessons start at $49 per day, depending on experience level. Lift tickets are half price in the two weeks after Thanksgiving.

For cross-country skiing and snowshoeing, **Enchanted Forest** near Red River offers miles of groomed trails, and there are also easy access points in the Carson National Forest—at Capulin Campground on U.S. 64, for instance, five miles east of Taos; along **Manzanita Trail** in the Hondo Canyon on the road to the ski valley; and, especially good for snowshoeing, the **Bull of the Woods Trail,** which starts off Twining Road, at the far end of the ski area parking lot, and leads in about 2.5 miles to a high pasture and then another 5.5 miles up to Wheeler Peak, if you're feeling extremely energetic.

Don't have your own gear? **Cottam's Ski & Outdoor** (207-A Paseo del Pueblo Sur, 575/758-2822, 7 A.M.–7 P.M. Mon.–Fri., 7 A.M.–8 P.M. Sat. and Sun.) has the biggest stock of rental skis, snowboards, and snowshoes. The shop also sells everything else you'll need to get out and enjoy the snow; there's another shop at the ski valley (575/776-8719) and one at Angel Fire (575/776-8256).

HIKING AND BACKPACKING
With Taos Mountain in the backyard, hiking around here varies from rambles along winding rivers to intensive hauls that gain 2,000 feet in less than four miles. Be prepared for a cold snap or storm at any time, and don't plan on doing much before May—it takes that long for the snow to thaw, though you might still

hit some of the white stuff in the highest alpine meadows even in high summer. The most accessible and varied trails are along the road to Taos Ski Valley. Off Twining Road, in the base of the ski valley, the grueling trail to **Wheeler Peak** begins, a 16-mile round-trip that only the very fit should attempt in one day. The shorter **Gavilan Trail** is plenty steep as well but leads to a high mountain meadow. The route is five miles round-trip, or you can connect with other trails once you're up on the rim. If this sounds too strenuous, you can always take the chairlift to the top of the mountain (Thurs.– Mon. late June–Sept., $7) and then wander down any of several wide, well-marked trails, all with stunning views. A variety of trails course through **Taos Canyon** east of town, with numerous campgrounds and trailheads off U.S. 64, including the **South Boundary Trail,** 22 miles up and over the pass, with views onto Moreno Valley.

If you'd like to do a backpacking trip over several days, the options are almost endless, although one popular route is to Wheeler Peak up the back of the mountain, beginning near Red River and taking two or three days to do a 19-mile loop. Consult with the BLM and the Carson National Forest offices to make sure you've got the maps you need, as well as details on campsites and water sources. If you don't want to haul all the gear yourself, you can go trekking with **Wild Earth Llama Adventures** (800/758-5262, www.llama adventures.com), which can arrange multi-day expeditions March–November with expert naturalist guides. Or you can just "take a llama to lunch" on a day hike ($89) into the surrounding mountains or down in the Rio Grande Gorge.

BIKING

A popular trail ride close to town is along the west rim of the Rio Grande Gorge, either from the suspension bridge up to John Dunn Bridge, about 15 miles round-trip, or from the suspension bridge south to the Taos Junction bridge near Pilar, about 18 miles out and back. Either way, you'll have great views and fairly level but rugged terrain. A more aggressive ride is the 22-mile South Boundary Trail (see *Angel Fire* in *The Enchanted Circle* section). **Native Sons Adventures** (1033-A Paseo del Pueblo Sur, 575/758-9342, www.nativesonsadventures .com) can provide maps and shuttle service to and from trailheads. It also runs half- and full-day tours to these and several other trails, as well as hiker-biker combo trips. Angel Fire and Red River both open their slopes to mountain bikers in the summer, with access to the peaks on the chairlift.

If you prefer road touring, you can make a pleasant loop from Taos through Arroyo Hondo and Arroyo Seco. The 25-mile route has no steep grades and is a good way to get adjusted to the altitude. Head north up Paseo del Pueblo Norte, straight through the intersection with Highway 150 and then turn right in Arroyo Hondo onto County Road B-143; this road winds up into Arroyo Seco, eventually dead-ending on Highway 230. Turn right, and you'll merge with Highway 150 in a couple of miles. The standard challenge is the 84-mile Enchanted Circle loop; every September sees the Enchanted Circle Century Bike Tour, sponsored by the Red River chamber of commerce (800/348-6444 for information). A mountain-biking race takes place the day after.

Gearing Up (129 Paseo del Pueblo Sur, 575/751-0365, 9:30 A.M.–6 P.M. daily) rents mountain and hybrid bicycles (complete with helmet, backpack, lock, and even a water bottle) for $35 per day, with discounts for longer terms. The bike-fanatic couple who own the shop are very knowledgeable and can point you to less-traveled roads and trails. If you're bringing your bicycle with you, consider having it shipped here, and they'll reassemble it and have it waiting when you arrive.

ROCK CLIMBING

From popular sport-climbing spots such as the basalt Dead Cholla Wall in the Rio Grande Gorge to the more traditional routes at Tres Piedras, Taos is a climber's dream. One of the most impressive pitches is at Questa Dome, north of Taos on Highway 378, where the

TAOS

flawless granite on the Questa Direct route is graded 5.10 and 5.11. And you're not limited to the summer, as winter sees some terrific ice climbs at higher elevations. **Taos Mountain Outfitters** (111 S. Plaza, 575/758-9292, 10 A.M.–6 P.M. Mon.–Sat., 11 A.M.–5 P.M. Sun.) can provide maps, ropes, and more details. For climbing lessons or guided tours, contact **Mountain Skills** (575/776-2222, www .climbingschoolusa.com) in Arroyo Seco.

RAFTING AND TUBING
The **Taos Box,** the 16-mile stretch of the Rio Grande south of John Dunn Bridge down to near Pilar, provides perhaps the best rafting in New Mexico, with Class III rapids ominously named Boat Reamer, Screaming Left-Hand Turn, and the like. The river mellows out a bit south of the Taos Box and then leads into a shorter Class III section called the Racecourse—the most popular run, usually done as a half-day trip. Beyond this, in the Orilla Verde Recreation Area around Pilar, the water is wide and flat, a place for a relaxing

float with kids or other water newbies; you can flop in an inner tube if you really want to chill out. **Los Rios River Runners** (575/776-8854, www.losriosriverrunners.com) leads trips to all these spots, but also see the *Rafting* section of the *Santa Fe* chapter for companies based there; Kokopelli, in particular, runs a daylong float trip in a lesser-traveled section of the river north of the Taos Box. The best season is late May and early June, when the water is high from mountain runoff.

HUNTING AND FISHING
Taos's mountain streams and lakes teem with fish; the feisty cutthroat trout is indigenous to Valle Vidal, north of Questa, or you can hook plenty of browns in the wild waters of the Rio Grande. Eagle Nest Lake and Cabresto Lake (northeast of Questa) are both stocked every year. If you'd like a guide to show you around, **Van Beacham's Solitary Anglers** (204-B Paseo del Pueblo Norte, 866/502-1700, www .thesolitaryangler.com) can't be beat; clients can have exclusive access to a few private river

The whitewater surges on the Rio Grande from Taos to Pilar.

leases, including on the Cimarron River immediately south of the Eagle Nest dam. Stop into the shop for tackle and info on flows and other conditions.

Elk are the primary target in hunters' rifle scopes, but you can also bag mule deer, bear, and antelope; **High Mountain Outfitters** (575/751-7000, www.huntingnm.com) is one of the most experienced expedition leaders, and it has access to private land for hunting exotics. Visit the website of the New Mexico Game & Fish Department (www.wildlife.state.nm.us) for details on seasons, permits, and licenses.

SPAS AND SPORTS FACILITIES

Taos Spa & Tennis Club (111 Doña Ana Dr., 575/758-1980, www.taosspa.com) is an affordable place to work out muscles made sore from skiing or biking. The $65 for a one-hour massage entitles you to free use of the hot tubs, steam room, and swimming pool for the rest of the day, or you can buy a day pass to the fitness center for $12. Facials, body scrubs, and other spa treatments are also available.

The **Taos Youth and Family Center** (407 Paseo del Cañon, 575/758-4160, 9 A.M.–9 P.M. Mon.–Sat., 10 A.M.–7 P.M. Sun.) has a big indoor pool, as well as an ice-skating rink (Nov.–Mar.).

TOURS

Roberta Meyers, who hosts a weekly storytelling hour at the Fechin Inn, also leads very dramatic walking tours around town, describing the juiciest historical moments as she goes (575/776-2562). **Rob Hawley,** co-owner of the Taos Herb Co. (710 Paseo del Pueblo Sur, 575/758-1991, www.taosherb.com) since 1979, leads daylong walks in the mountains, pointing out local wild treatments and discussing how to prepare them.

Accommodations

Because Taos is awash in centuries-old houses with impressive cultural and historic pedigrees, bed-and-breakfasts have thrived, even to the exclusion of proper chain hotels, which are typically of the generic chain variety. For those skeptical of B&Bs, don't despair: The majority of them have private bathrooms, separate entrances, and not too much country-cute decor. Certainly, just as in Santa Fe, the Southwest decor can be applied with a heavy hand, but wood-burning fireplaces, well-stocked libraries, hot tubs, and big gardens can make up for that. Also consider staying outside of Taos proper. Arroyo Seco and Arroyo Hondo are about a half-hour drive from the plaza, and some inns in these two communities, as well as in Ranchos de Taos to the south, offer excellent value. In the summer, the condos near the ski valley cut their prices by almost half—a great deal if you want to spend some time hiking in the canyon and don't mind driving into town for food and entertainment. If you're arriving in town without a car, a few good budget choices are served by Taos's Chile Line bus, which caters to skiers in the winter, from down on the southern end of town all the way up to the ski valley.

UNDER $50

The best lodging bargain in the Taos area is **The Abominable Snowmansion** (Hwy. 150 in Arroyo Seco, 575/776-8298, www.abominable snowmansion.com, $22 pp). Conveniently set midway to the Taos Ski Valley, in bustling "downtown" Arroyo Seco, this is a cheerful HI hostel offering bunks in dorm rooms or, in the summertime, tepees. As the name suggests, winter sports fanatics are the main clientele; if you don't want to be woken at the break of dawn by skiers racing for the Chile Line bus outside, opt for an individual cabin with shared bath, or a private room with en suite bathroom (the latter runs $54 in high ski season). There's also room to camp in the summer, and breakfast is included in the price.

$50-100

❮ Laughing Horse Inn (729 Paseo del Pueblo Norte, 800/776-0161, www.laughinghorseinn.com, $70 d), one of Taos's most popular budget B&Bs, cultivates an eccentric reputation, with a guest list of starving artists and Europeans on vision quests. Ten rooms in the main adobe house give new meaning to the word "snug" and share three bathrooms, while the penthouse A-frame room, which conjures some of the bygone hippie charm, has a big deck and room for six to sleep ($150 for two). An honor-system kitchen, a clothing-optional hot tub, and continental breakfasts of organic, locally farmed foodstuffs add to the throwback feel.

Budget Host Inn (1798 Paseo del Pueblo Sur, 800/323-6009, www.taosbudgethost.com, $74 s, $79 d) is the best of the string of cheapies along the highway at the southern end of Taos. The rooms in the cheerily painted two-story motel building are a little worn but kept very clean, and you get cable TV and wireless access. Try to get a room in the back for reduced traffic noise, and if you want a nonsmoking room, make sure it's between other nonsmoking rooms, as the walls are thin enough that the smell can seep through. The same owners manage the **Taos RV Park** next door, which maintains the same tidy standards. If you're on a strict budget, book well ahead here or at the Snowmansion, because many other hotels in this category can be quite grim indeed.

A good alternative to the Budget Host, the 117-room **Paragon Inn** (615 Paseo del Pueblo Sur, 575/737-0447, www.paragoninntaos.com, $80 d) was remodeled in 2007, so while its motel-style rooms aren't full of flair, they are at least clean and comfortable. The deluxe rooms do have gas fireplaces—a rare touch in this price category. There are also a small pool and whirlpool tub, and continental breakfast is included. Prices can fluctuate according to season and availability.

El Pueblo Lodge (412 Paseo del Pueblo Norte, 575/758-8700, www.elpueblolodge.com, $74 s, $89 d) is a budget operation with slightly spacey management but nice perks such as free laundry. Rooms vary wildly, from a tiny,

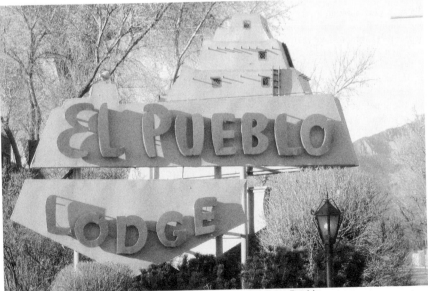

El Pueblo Lodge is conveniently located near the road to Taos Pueblo.

© ZORA O'NEILL

very atmospheric nook in the oldest adobe section to new, slick motel rooms complete with gas fireplaces; those in the 1960s motel strip are a good combo of atmosphere and tidiness. The grounds are quite pleasant, with a heated pool, a hot tub, and hammocks slung between the big cottonwoods in the summertime.

Casa Benavides (137 Kit Carson Rd., 575/758-1772, www.taos-casabenavides.com, $89 d) calls itself a bed-and-breakfast, but now it feels a bit more like a small hotel, as it sprawls down Kit Carson Road in a series of interconnected buildings, one of which is a wood Victorian built around 1900. The owners, a local family, have put a lot of care into the decoration of the 38 rooms with Taos-style furniture and Western artifacts. Each one is different, which makes the choices a little overwhelming—the artist's studios are nicely secluded, and the two small (and cheap) upstairs rooms in the Benavides family home have balconies with mountain views. Otherwise, pick the price you're comfortable with (they range up to $300), and go from there.

In addition to being a tourist attraction, the ⚫ **Mabel Dodge Luhan House** (240 Morada La., 575/751-9686, www.mabeldodgeluhan.com, $95 d) also functions as a homey bed-and-breakfast. Choose one of the snug little rooms in the oldest adobe section, all furnished with rickety antiques, floors worn down from years of treading, and tiny fireplaces; or one of the rooms in the main house: Mabel's original bedroom ($190) is the grandest (you can even sleep in her bed), but for those who don't mind waking at the crack of dawn, the upstairs solarium is gloriously sunny with gorgeous views of the mountain. Either way, you'll feel a little like you're bunking in a historical museum.

Tucked away in Arroyo Hondo, **Mountain Light B&B** (off Hwy. 522, 575/776-8474, www.mtnlight.com, $55 s, $85 d) is not only a great bargain, but it's also a wonderful place to feel like a real resident of the area. The owner, a photographer, is particularly encouraging to fellow artists (who can rent an Airstream trailer for longer retreats). Her beautiful tower-shaped house has two guest rooms, which share a bath;

they're cozy and simple, decorated with quilts and tucked in the natural curves of the house. You can eat breakfast out on the deck, with a stupendous view over Valle Valdez—one that hasn't changed much in decades.

Not a hotel at all, but simply a clutch of well-maintained one- and two-bedroom private casitas, **Taos Lodging** (109 Brooks St., 575/751-1771, www.taoslodging.com, $90 studio) is in a quiet, convenient block about 10 minutes' walk north from the plaza. The eight cottages, arranged around a central courtyard, have assorted floor plans, but all have porches, full kitchens, and living rooms, as well as access to a shared outdoor hot tub. The smallest, a 350-square-foot studio, sleeps two comfortably; the largest, at 800 square feet, sleeps up to six.

$100-150

Adobe & Pines B&B, tucked just off the road into Ranchos de Taos (4107 Hwy. 68, 575/751-0947, www.adobepines.com, $115 d), is a little out of the way, but it's especially pretty in the summer, when the large central garden is in bloom. The colors throughout are vibrant and strong, with each of the seven rooms painted a different hue. All but the tiniest (snug Puerta Azul, in the old main house, $98) have staggeringly grand bathrooms.

A relatively generic chain hotel, **Best Western Kachina Lodge** (413 Paseo del Pueblo Norte, 575/758-2275, www.kachinalodge.com, $119 d) is notable simply because it can be a great deal when booked online. Rooms are large and well kept, a full breakfast is included in the rate, and there's a big pool. It also hosts Taos dance performances every night May through October—sure, a little touristy, but nice if your trip doesn't coincide with a ceremonial dance at the pueblo itself.

Inn on the Rio (910 E. Kit Carson Rd., 575/758-7199, www.innontherio.com, $119 d) might be more accurately called Motel on the Creek. But what a motel: Each of the 12 thick-walled rooms is meticulously decorated with an artistic eye. Rich colors liven up the walls, and vintage Southwestern tchotchkes add flair without being overwhelming. The vintage wall heaters, still cranking from the old motor-court days, keep the rooms as toasty as a fireplace would. A hot tub between the two wings, plus luxe sheets and locally made bath gels, add unexpected luxury. Pair this with longtime resident owners and a great morning meal, and you have all the benefits of a bed-and-breakfast without the feeling that you have to tiptoe in late at night.

◖ **La Posada de Taos** (309 Juanita La., 575/758-8164, www.laposadadetaos.com, $144 d) hits the sweet spot between luxury comforts and casual charm—all the amenities are here, such as wood fireplaces (in five of the six rooms) and whirlpool tubs (in three), but the overall atmosphere is very homey and informal, and the decor is distinctly Taos without being heavy-handed, with sparing country touches. The price is right too, coming in on the lower end compared to other places with the same perks. El Solecito, in the older adobe section with its own back terrace, is recommended.

Of the two landmark hotels in town, **La Fonda de Taos** (108 S. Plaza, 800/833-2211, www.lafondataos.com, $134 s, $149 d) has a few more modern perks; with gas fireplaces rather than wood, the rooms don't ooze atmosphere, but the beds are very nice, there's DSL, and you can feel quite grand opening your balcony doors over the plaza (request no. 301 or 302). Don't miss the small collection of D. H. Lawrence's erotic paintings ($3 admission); they're tucked in a small room behind the front desk.

Starting in the 1890s, the **Historic Taos Inn** (125 Paseo del Pueblo Norte, 575/758-2233, www.taosinn.com, $105 s, $195 d) was the home of beloved county doctor T. P. Martin, who had a good reputation for accepting chickens or venison from his poorer patients in lieu of cash—what used to be a small plaza is now the lobby and the Adobe Bar. Many of the hotel rooms were overhauled in 2006, making it a more appealing place to stay than in years past; rooms in the main building are old-school tiny and subject to noise from the bar,

so you're better off in the courtyard section or other outbuildings, where you may also get a kiva fireplace.

$150-250

Everything at **Hacienda del Sol** (109 Mabel Dodge La., 575/758-0287, www.taoshacienda delsol.com, $155 d) is built in relation to Taos Mountain, which looms in the backyard with no other buildings cluttering the view. Even the smallest rooms feel expansive in the summer, as doors open onto a vast courtyard and, of course, the view (which you can also enjoy from the hot tub). The 11 rooms, spread over several adobe outbuildings, are cozy without being too oppressively Southwestern in their design, and perks such as robes, bathtubs, and minifridges approximate hotel service, while a collection of Taos-related books waits by the bedside.

Out near Arroyo Hondo, the house-proud owner of ◖ **Little Tree B&B** (226 Hondo–Seco Rd., 575/776-8467, www.littletreebandb .com, $155 d) is a history buff—his expertise is a perk that comes with a stay at this snug inn with four rooms. The house and its small outbuilding are rare examples of old-school adobe (no stucco finish) *without* the stamp of history; a Taos Pueblo expert built them in 1990 using a range of mud finishes and decorative techniques. The feeling is rustic, authentic, but also very comfortable. One room has a private hot tub, and three have wood-burning fireplaces or stoves; the one room without is priced at $125.

Although the location of **Casa de las Chimeneas** (405 Cordoba Rd., 575/758-4777, www.visittaos.com, $185 d) a few blocks south of the plaza is very convenient for sightseeing, the place is also a skier's delight, with snow reports via email in the winter, plus a hot tub and wet and dry saunas to soothe aching muscles. Though it calls itself a bed-and-breakfast, the layout and the generously appointed rooms feel more like a small luxury lodge than someone's adapted home. The largest suite has its own private steam sauna as well as a whirlpool tub, and skylights, fireplaces, reading nooks, and gigantic tubs are some of the perks in the other rooms, furnished in tasteful if slightly bland style.

For a larger group or a family, an excellent option in this price range is **Inger Jirby's Casitas** (207 Ledoux St., 575/758-7333, www.jirby.com, $195 suite). The two full guesthouses, side by side on historic Ledoux Street just off the plaza, are furnished very tastefully by the Swedish artist owner with colorful Indian rugs. Four people can sleep comfortably in the multilevel apartments that let in lots of light through clerestory windows. Both have a full kitchen, gas fireplace, stereo system, cable TV, wireless Internet, and even Wii.

OVER $250

A successful experiment in sustainable development is also Taos's most luxurious lodging: **El Monte Sagrado** (317 Kit Carson Rd., 575/758-3502, www.elmontesagrado.com), a soothing retreat that's still walking distance from the plaza. If they weren't pointed out to you, you'd probably never even notice the solar panels, ingenious water-reuse system, and a nonchlorinated pool. Instead, eclectic style draws the eye, whether you're in a standard casita ($279) decorated with hand-painted trout or in an ultradeluxe global suite ($659) filled with Chinese antiques. The spa offers pampering galore—it's open to nonguests as well.

Food

For a town of its size, Taos has a surprisingly broad selection of restaurants, including several splurge-worthy options; few vacationers will have the budget to sample all of them, but it's a treat to have a choice. If you're in town during a holiday or peak ski season, you might want to make reservations, but otherwise they're not necessary, and the whole Taos dining scene is exceptionally casual, with waiters often inquiring about your day skiing along with your preference for red or white wine. For less spendy meals, as with hotels, you'll find many options along Paseo del Pueblo Sur, but you won't be priced out of the center of town either. At one of the New Mexican places, be sure to try some posole—it's more common here than in Albuquerque or Santa Fe, often substituted for rice as a side dish alongside pinto beans. Also, the breakfast burrito—a combo of scrambled eggs, green chile, hash browns, and bacon or sausage wrapped in a flour tortilla—is commonly wrapped up in foil and served to go, perfect if you want an early start hiking or skiing. Note that more so than in Santa Fe, this is a cash economy—many smaller places don't take plastic.

COFFEE AND DESSERT

The location of **World Cup** on the corner of the plaza (102-A Paseo del Pueblo Norte, 575/737-5299, 7 A.M.–6:30 P.M. daily, $3) makes it a popular pit stop for both tourists and locals—the latter typically of the drumming, dreadlocked variety, lounging on the stoop. If you want a bit more room to maneuver, head to **The Bean** (1033 Paseo del Pueblo Sur, 575/758-5123, 6:30 A.M.–3:30 P.M. Mon.–Fri., 7 A.M.–3:30 P.M. Sat. and Sun., $6.50), which serves a full breakfast menu till 2 P.M., along with pastries and incredibly strong, organic coffee. This is an all-day hangout for some regulars, who start with a crossword puzzle and move on to grander projects, all while most of the rest of town files in and out.

In Arroyo Seco, most people start the day at **Taos Cow** (485 Hwy. 150, 575/776-5640, 7 A.M.–7 P.M. daily), a chilled-out coffee bar par excellence, with writers scribbling in one corner and flute players jamming in another. But it's really the ice cream that has made the Taos Cow name (you'll see it distributed all around town, and in occasional spots elsewhere in New Mexico and Colorado). The most popular flavors are tailored to local tastes: Café Olé contains cinnamon and Mexican chocolate chunks, while Cherry Ristra is vanilla with piñon nuts, dark chocolate, and cherries.

Handy for people staying on the south side

TAOS

or in Ranchos, **Mondo Kultur** (622 Paseo del Pueblo Sur, 575/751-7712, 7 A.M.–10 P.M. daily) is a major social hub, slinging fair-trade coffee, full breakfasts, rental DVDs, newspapers, and concert tickets. Free Wi-Fi and an active bulletin board provide yet another reason to hang out. A second branch north of town (36 Hwy. 522, 575/751-1994, 7 A.M.–8 P.M. daily), past the "old blinking light," serves the north side and Arroyo Hondo.

At the top of Ledoux Street, **Loka** (112-E Camino de la Placita, 575/758-4204, 8 A.M.–5 P.M. Mon.–Sat., 9 A.M.–4 P.M. Sun.) is a spacious gallery/coffee bar, a wonderfully sunny place where the baked goods are as gorgeous as the contemporary art on the walls. The food is on the pricier side ($3.50 for pastries, $8 sandwiches), but it's undeniably delicious. As a historical side note, it occupies the former offices of *El Crepúsculo de la Libertad,* the paper started by Padre Antonio Martinez.

BREAKFAST AND LUNCH

Michael's Kitchen (304-C Paseo del Pueblo Norte, 575/758-4178, 7 A.M.–2:30 P.M. daily, $7) is famous for New Mexican breakfast items such as huevos rancheros and blue-corn pancakes with pine nuts, served all day, but everyone will find something they like on the extensive menu at this down-home wood-paneled family restaurant filled with chatter and the clatter of dishes. "Health Food," for instance, is a double order of chile cheese fries. The front room is devoted to gooey doughnuts, cinnamon rolls, and pie.

At the homey **Dragonfly Café** (402 Paseo del Pueblo Norte, 575/737-5859, 11 A.M.–8 P.M. Wed.–Sat., 9 A.M.–3 P.M. Sun., $7), you can choose your table according to which novelty set of salt-and-pepper shakers you prefer. The menu is eclectic and hearty (a tender lamb kebab, for instance, or a veggie-filled bowl of Korean *bibimbop*); the brunch features delicious baked goods and fennel pancakes with orange syrup.

In the Taos Inn, elegant **Doc Martin's** (125 Paseo del Pueblo Norte, 575/758-1977, 7:30 A.M.–2:30 P.M. and 5:30–9 P.M. daily, $7)

serves all three meals, but breakfast is when the kitchen really shines—especially on dishes such as the Kit Carson (poached eggs on yam biscuits topped with red chile) or blue-corn pancakes with blueberries. The lunch menu is also tasty and doesn't reach the stratospheric prices of dinner. Despite the trendy flavor combos on the menu, the chile and beans are made by a Taos local, as they have been for decades.

Inside the Sustaining Cultures metaphysical bookstore, **Guadalupe Café** (114 Doña Luz St., 575/751-0959, 9 A.M.–5:30 P.M. Mon.–Sat., $8) is everything you'd expect in terms of earth-friendly credentials—fair trade, organic, and so on—but also especially delicious. The quiche (yes, bacon is an option) is fluffy and set in buttery crust, and it comes with superfresh salad with tamari dressing. There are also hearty soups, smoothies, and vegan baked goods.

Up in Arroyo Seco, (**Abe's Cantina y Cocina** (489 Hwy. 150, 575/776-8516, 7 A.M.–5:30 P.M. daily, $3.50), a creaky old all-purpose general store/diner/saloon, has earned fans from all over for its satisfying and cheap breakfast burritos—and don't miss the sweet, flaky empanadas (delicately spiced prune, apple, and pumpkin are the usual choices) next to the register. (For coffee, though, you'll want to go next door to Taos Cow.)

Just down the street, **Maverick County Food Co.** (480 Hwy. 150, 575/776-0900, 8:30 A.M.–4 P.M. Tues.–Sun., $10) serves eclectic sandwiches, plus bigger plates such as lamb meatballs with lentils. When the weather's nice, you can enjoy it all on a small, sunny deck, or inside the cozy sunporch. It serves espresso, gelato, and great pastries, too, if your spirits are flagging on the drive up the valley. Outside the summer season, the place is closed on Sunday.

For nourishment in Taos Ski Valley, fortify yourself with a green-chile cheeseburger at **Tim's Stray Dog Cantina** (Taos Ski Valley, 575/776-2894, 8 A.M.–9 P.M. daily, $12), which gets busy after 3 P.M., when tired skiers come down from a day on the slopes. It's a good place to start in the morning too, with breakfast burritos and chile-smothered huevos rancheros.

NEW MEXICAN

A small, brightly painted place on the north side of town, the family-run **Orlando's** (1114 Don Juan Valdez La., 575/751-1450, 10:30 A.M.–3 P.M. and 5–9 P.M. daily, $10) is invariably the first restaurant named by anyone, local or visitor, when the question of best chile comes up. That said, there have been occasional whisperings about inconsistency (the sort of talk that borders on heresy!), but Orlando's still generally serves very satisfying, freshly made New Mexican standards, such as green-chile chicken enchiladas. The posole is quite good too—perfectly firm, earthy, and flecked with oregano. It's always busy, but a fire pit outdoors makes the wait more pleasant. Cash only.

If Orlando's strikes you as a bit too fancy, **El Taoseño** (819 Paseo del Pueblo Sur, 575/758-4142, 6 A.M.–9 P.M. Mon.–Thurs., 6:30 A.M.–10 P.M. Fri. and Sat., 6:30 A.M.–2 P.M. Sun., $6.50) is a simple diner with everything from chiles rellenos to steak and eggs, all distinctly ungussied up; fittingly, it's a favorite with Taos's old, old guard (the neighboring wood-floor lounge hosts a "senior dance" on Sunday afternoons).

A drive-through never offered something so good: **Mante's Chow Cart** (402 Paseo del Pueblo Sur, 575/758-3632, 7 A.M.–9 P.M. Mon.–Thurs. and Sat., 7 A.M.–10 P.M. Fri., $4) specializes in breakfast burritos and genius inventions such as the Susie: a whole chile relleno wrapped in a flour tortilla with salsa and guacamole. Perfect road food.

It looks temporary, but the truck that houses **Mary Jane's** (616 Paseo del Pueblo Sur, 575/770-1171, $5) has been sitting in the parking lot for years. One of the off-menu specialties is *chicharrones* (fried pork skins) with "everything" (guacamole, salsa, etc.)—imagine a superdeadly version of nachos.

MEXICAN

New Mexican items may be front and center on the menu at **☐ Rellenos Café** (135 Paseo del Pueblo Sur, 575/758-7001, 10 A.M.–3 P.M. Mon.–Sat., $6–10), but the real good stuff here is from south of the border: rich *chiles en nogada* (stuffed poblano peppers in walnut sauce) and spicy, tangy tortilla soup.

Or stop in at **Guadalajara Grill** (1384 Paseo del Pueblo Sur, 575/751-0063, 10:30 A.M.–8:30 P.M. Sun.–Thurs., 10:30 A.M.–9 P.M. Fri. and Sat., $10). It may be in a strip mall, but the food transports you straight to western Mexico, with enormous portions of gooey *queso fundido* (fonduelike cheese) and shrimp sautéed in garlic. There's a branch on the north side (822 Paseo del Pueblo Norte, 575/737-0816).

ITALIAN

Hands down, **Taos Pizza Out Back** (712 Paseo del Pueblo Norte, 575/758-3112, 11 A.M.–9 P.M. Sun.–Thurs., 11 A.M.–10 P.M. Fri. and Sat., $12) serves the best pie in town, using mostly local and organic ingredients. A glance at the menu—with items such as Thai chicken, green chile and beans, and the popular portobello-camembert combo—often makes first-timers blanch, but after a bite or two they're converts, like everyone else in town. Soups and salads are also available if you want to round out your meal.

Longtime local favorite **Apple Tree** (123 Bent St., 575/758-1900, 11:30 A.M.–3 P.M. Mon. and Tues., 11:30–3 P.M. and 5–9 P.M. Wed.–Sun.) has perfectly decent Italian-ish food—but it also has one of the nicest patios in town, centrally located for a handy shopping break. Lunch here, in the dappled shade with flowers all around, is particularly lovely, and most dishes are $10 or less; most dinner entrées are under $20.

TAOS ECLECTIC

Euro-Latino might be the best catch-all term for the menu at **☐ Gutiz** (812-B Paseo del Pueblo Norte, 7 A.M.–9 P.M. Wed.–Sun., 7 A.M.–3 P.M. Tues., $8), but of course you'll find green chile in some dishes—and then there's the unclassifiable French toast, which involves raspberry cream and peanut butter (honest, it's good!). Other inventive breakfast dishes include poached eggs and salsa on subtly spiced Spanish rice. Or you can opt for a more

TAOS

traditional *croque monsieur* for lunch. Dinner service (starting at 5 P.M.) was just about to begin at the time of research, with dishes such as paella going for about $15. If the restaurant's legions of fans support the evening service, it will doubtless be a success.

Locals like **Graham's Grille** (106 Paseo del Pueblo Norte, 575/751-1350, 11 A.M.–2:30 P.M. and 5–9 P.M. Mon.–Sat.) because its menu satisfies simple cravings—for a creamy chicken salad on a buttery brioche roll, or mac-and-cheese with green chile—and some you didn't even know you had, such as one for fresh nacho chips drizzled with chocolate, a genius salty-sweet fusion. Creatively, falafel is the vegetarian option in dishes such as burritos. Spacious and airy, with lots of blond wood, the space is restful, and so are the prices—nothing's over $20. There are two entrances and two separate dining rooms—the smaller seating area at the back entrance (in the alley off the plaza) looks onto an open kitchen.

FINE DINING

Chef Joseph Wrede, of **(Joseph's Table** (108-A S. Plaza, 575/751-4512, 11:30 A.M.–2:30 P.M. and 5:30–10 P.M. daily, $32) in the La Fonda hotel on the plaza, runs the most lauded—and probably the most beautiful—restaurant in Taos. The moodily lit room glitters with gilt butterflies and pussy-willow chandeliers, the better to appreciate decadent treats such as trout with trout roe, pork liver from local pigs, and duck breast with French lentils. If you're feeling romantic, reserve one of the curtain-enclosed booths. You can also enjoy a smaller menu of more casual items (such as duck-fat french fries) at the bar, or the diverse Sunday brunch. Wrede relies on the freshest ingredients from local farms, and he does a solid vegetarian special every night.

Open since 1988, **Lambert's** (309 Paseo del Pueblo Sur, 575/758-1009, 5:30–9 P.M. Mon.–Sat., $27) is a Taos favorite, where everyone goes for prom, anniversaries, and other landmark events. Its New American menu is a bit staid, but everything is executed perfectly—trend-following foodies can't quibble

that the chile-dusted rock shrimp with house-made cocktail sauce doesn't taste good. Get the caribou if you can; otherwise, the signature pepper-crusted lamb is fantastic. A full liquor license means good classic cocktails, which you can also enjoy in the snug, clubby couch-filled lounge.

Byzantium (La Placita and Ledoux St., 575/751-0805, 5–10 P.M. Thurs.–Mon., $30) is set in a groovy room with only a few tables and a mix of Taos fixtures and ultracool modern touches—mirror tiles trim a traditional spiral pine pillar, for instance. The menu puts inventive twists on familiar dishes: Standards such as Caesar salad are presented with flair, duck gets a dressy Asian plum sauce, and Toblerone inspires an amazing dessert. Great service directly from the owner and an interesting wine list round out this offbeat dining experience. It's pricey, but portions are more than generous.

A worthwhile drive is to the **Stakeout Grill**

The long drive to the Stakeout Grill & Bar pays off with beautiful sunset views of the mountains.

& Bar (nine miles south of Taos on Hwy. 68, 575/758-2042, 5–9:30 P.M. daily, $29) for the view across the valley at sunset—the restaurant is halfway up the mountainside south of town. Unlike at many restaurants where the view is paramount, the food holds its own. Hearty steaks and rich seafood such as oysters Rockefeller are augmented with a few token vegetarian options such as ravioli with porcini mushrooms (Chef Mauro hails from Italy); there's homemade gelato for dessert, and a tasty bourbon pecan pie. A roaring fireplace adds to the ambience in the winter. Coming from town, turn left at the sign just over four miles south of the last stoplight in Ranchos de Taos.

GROCERIES AND LIQUOR

Planning a picnic? Stop at **Bravo!** (1353-A Paseo del Pueblo Sur, 575/758-8100, 11 A.M.–9 P.M. Mon.–Sat.) for Taos's best selection of wines, as well as gourmet takeout—plenty of cold salads and the like to choose from. **Cid's** grocery (623 Paseo del Pueblo Norte, 575/758-1148, 7:30 A.M.–7 P.M. Mon.–Sat.) also has great takeout food, and freshly baked bread and a whole range of organic and local goodies, from New Mexican wines to fresh elk steaks.

The Enchanted Circle

The loop formed by U.S. 64, Highway 38, and Highway 522, going past the ski resorts of Angel Fire and Red River as well as a handful of smaller towns, is perhaps too generously named, but the views of the Sangre de Cristo Mountains, including Wheeler Peak, the tallest in the state, are breathtaking. The area is also a cultural change of pace from Taos. Many of the towns along the north and east sides of the loop were settled by Anglo ranchers and prospectors in the late 1800s, and the "Wild West" atmosphere persisted well into the 20th

© ZORA O'NEILL

Some parts of the Enchanted Circle are closer to Texas than others.

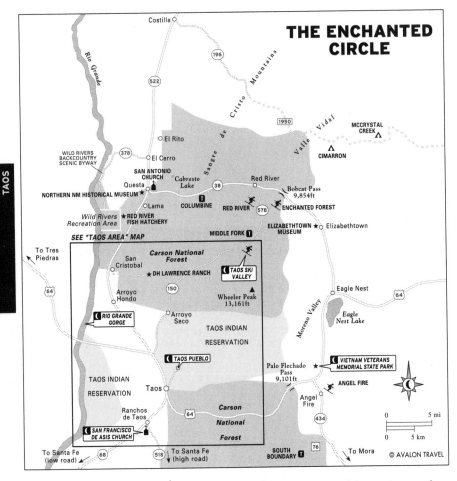

THE ENCHANTED CIRCLE

century, today reinforced by the large population of transplanted flatlander Texans enamored of the massive peaks. You can drive the 84-mile route in a very leisurely day, with time out for a short hike around Red River or a detour along the Wild Rivers scenic byway.

Most guides and maps run the route clockwise, heading north out of Taos to Questa, but if you're doing the outing as a day trip, it makes more sense to head counterclockwise, going through Angel Fire and arriving in Red River or Questa, where there's better food, around lunchtime (or you could pack a picnic

lunch to enjoy at any of the picnic areas along the small river west of Red River). You'll also enjoy fantastic views at the end of the drive, descending into the Taos Valley from Questa. If you're staying overnight, either direction will work, with the most lodging available in Red River. Because the ski areas value their customers, the roads are generally cleared quickly in the winter; the only patch that may be icy is Palo Flechado Pass west of Angel Fire.

To start, head east on Kit Carson Road, which eventually turns into U.S. 64, winding through the Taos River Valley and past numerous campgrounds and hiking trails, as well as the Institute for Buddhist Studies. At the pass, the road descends into the high Moreno Valley, a gorgeous expanse of green in the spring and a vast tundra in the winter.

ANGEL FIRE

A right turn up Highway 434 leads to this tiny ski village. The mountain here looks like a molehill in comparison with Taos Ski Valley; **Angel Fire Resort** (800/633-7463, www.angel fireresort.com, $52 full-day lift ticket) has a summit elevation of 10,677 and a vertical drop of 2,077 feet, but a large share of the runs are devoted to snowboarding, including four terrain parks and a half-pipe designed by Chris Gunnarson. For those with no snow skills at all, the three-lane, 1,000-foot-long tubing hill provides an easy adrenaline rush. Otherwise, there are few independent attractions in the cluster of timber condos at the base of the mountain. If you're around in the winter, book a sleigh ride with **Roadrunner Tours** (Hwy. 434 in town, 575/377-6416, www.rtours.com,

$25 for 35 minutes); the experienced equestrian team can also arrange trail rides into the high mountains—a great summer trip.

In the summer, in addition to the small, trout-stocked Monte Verde Lake, managed by the ski resort, the main diversion here is mountain biking. On the mountain itself, the resort maintains about 30 miles of trails. But the real challenge is the storied **South Boundary Trail,** which runs from a trailhead off Forest Road 76 south of Angel Fire. The route to Taos is about five vertical-seeming miles up and over the pass, then another 22 or so back to El Nogal trailhead on U.S. 64, a couple of miles east of Taos. (Only the truly masochistic would go the other direction—which doesn't mean it's not done.) Maps are a must; contact **Native Sons Adventures** in Taos (1033-A Paseo del Pueblo Sur, 575/758-9342, www.nativesons adventures.com).

For a lunch of burgers or brisket, stop off at **Zebadiah's** (Hwy. 434, 575/377-6358, 11 A.M.–9 P.M. daily, $8), a big wood-paneled room that caters to hungry snowboarders in

Vietnam Veterans Memorial State Park overlooks Moreno Valley.

the winter and folks fishing at Eagle Nest in the summer. The bar, which is open till about 2 A.M., is the main hangout in the area.

The Angel Fire Chamber of Commerce maintains a **visitors center** (Centro Plaza, Hwy. 434, 575/377-6661, www.angelfirechamber .org, 9 A.M.–5 P.M. Mon.–Fri.); the lobby is open 24 hours, so you can load up on glossy brochures even when the office is closed.

◖ Vietnam Veterans Memorial State Park

Back on U.S. 64, a few miles past the turn for Angel Fire, a swooping white structure rises on the hill to your left. This is the Vietnam Veterans Memorial State Park (575/377-6900, www.angelfirememorial.com, 9 A.M.–5 P.M. daily), built by Victor Westphall as a remembrance for his son David, who died in the war. When Westphall commissioned Santa Fe architect Ted Luna to design the graceful white chapel in 1968, it was the first such memorial for the casualties of Vietnam. An adjacent visitors center was built later and has expanded

through the years. The complex is a site of pilgrimage for many, and the front grounds and bulletin boards testify to veterans' and families' devotion, as they are covered with additional informal monuments and messages.

EAGLE NEST

Heading north on U.S. 64 from the Vietnam memorial, you soon see Eagle Nest Lake on the left. The lake was created in 1918 with the construction of a dam on the Cimarron River; funded by ranchers and built using Taos Pueblo labor, the 400-foot-wide structure is the largest one in the United States built with private money. In addition to agricultural and mining uses, the lake also supplied an ice-block industry in the winter. Today it's a state park, stocked with trout, and a popular summertime recreation spot (the huge Fourth of July fireworks display is legendary). Vacation homes are clustered down by the water, but the town itself is farther north, at the junction with Highway 38. A small strip of wooden buildings along Therma Drive (U.S. 64) are all that's left of a

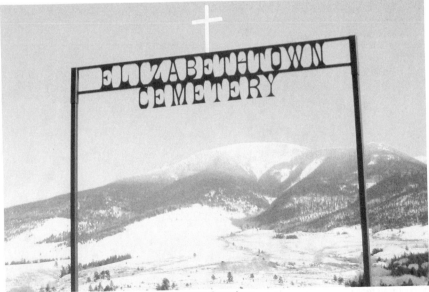

view of Mount Baldy from the Elizabethtown Cemetery

jumping (illegal) gambling town in the 1920s and 1930s, when enterprising businessmen would roll slot machines out on the boardwalks to entice travelers on their way to Raton and the train, and bars such as the Laguna Vista Saloon hosted roulette and blackjack. The Laguna Vista even claims to host its own phantom, the so-called "Ghost of Guney," a woman whose husband disappeared during their honeymoon stay at the lodge and who was forced into work as a saloon girl. The restaurant at the Guney is **Texas Reds** (575/377-2755, 5–9:30 P.M. daily, $12), a branch of the beloved restaurant in Red River; it's recommended for giant steaks or tasty burgers, but it is open for dinner only. Unfortunately, the adjoining **Laguna Vista Lodge** (575/377-6522, www.lagunavistalodge.com) doesn't rent rooms in the historic old building; instead, there are standard motel rooms connected by a screened porch ($85 d), as well as cabins and apartments with a view of the lake.

For lunch, your options include the **Kaw-Lija's Diner** (Therma Dr., 575/377-3424, 7 A.M.–8 P.M. daily May–Sept., $7), which serves chicken-fried steak in an old-fashioned ice-cream-parlor setting, and **Lucky Shoe Bar & Grille** (350 Therma Dr., 575/377-7264, 11 A.M.–late daily, $6).

The **Eagle Nest Chamber of Commerce** (54 Therma Dr., 575/377-2420, www.eaglenestchamber.org, 10 A.M.–2 P.M. Mon.–Fri.) has limited hours but an enthusiastic staff.

ELIZABETHTOWN

Blink and you'll miss it: 4.8 miles past Eagle Nest, a small sign on the right side of the road points to the left-hand (west) turn for the former gold-rush site of Elizabethtown, the first incorporated village in New Mexico. Once home to more than 7,000 people, it's now a ghost town overshadowed by the stone ruins of the Mutz Hotel, the former center of social activity. The only signs of life are, ironically, in the **cemetery**, which is still used by residents of Colfax County and contains graves dating as far back as 1880. The **Elizabethtown Museum** (575/377-3420, 9 A.M.–5 P.M. daily June–Aug., $2 donation)

TAOS

© ZORA O'NEILL

Olde Western style in Red River

details Elizabethtown's brief but lively history, from the discovery of gold in 1866 through assorted gunfights to the town's slow fade after a dredge-mining project failed in 1903.

RED RIVER

As you descend into the valley, a somewhat bizarre apparition awaits: tidy rows of wooden buildings, all done up in Old West–look facades, complete with boardwalks and swinging saloon doors. No, it's not Elizabethtown of yore; it's the ski village of Red River (the giveaway: the Alpine touches, such as Der Markt grocery store). Although Taos loyalists dismiss the **Red River Ski & Snowboard Area** (575/754-2223, www.redriverskiarea.com, $55 full-day lift ticket) as an amateur's playground, it's nothing if not convenient: The trails run right into town, so the chairlift is walking distance from anywhere. The mountain is fairly evenly divided among beginning, intermediate, and advanced trails.

Like Elizabethtown, Red River was once a community of wild prospectors, carving copper, silver, and gold out of the hillsides. When that industry eventually went bust, the town salvaged itself by renting out abandoned houses to vacationers in search of a respite from the summer heat at lower elevations (the average summer temperature is just 75°F, dipping to 38°F at night). Luckily, just when air-conditioning started to become widespread, the ski area opened in 1959, saving the town from a major slump. Red River has a year-round population of only about 450—though it can feel like a ghost town in spring and fall, when everyone's taking a collective break from the high winter and summer seasons. For an overview of the community's history, visit the 1914 **Little Red Schoolhouse Museum** (702 E. Main St., 575/754-6564, 10 A.M.–12:30 P.M. Mon., Tues., Fri., and Sat., 6–9 P.M. Thurs., donation), behind the library at the Y junction on the east side. The town hosts a rowdy Memorial Day motorcycle rally as well as a surprisingly large Fourth of July parade and a Mardi Gras street party; contact the **Red River Chamber of Commerce** for

more details (100 E. Main St., 575/754-2366, www.redrivernewmex.com).

Hiking

This is the back side of Wheeler Peak, so the ascents are much more gradual while still yielding dramatic views. Stop in at the **visitors center** (101 W. River Dr., 877/754-1708, www.redriver.org, 8 A.M.–5 P.M. daily), in the conference center next to Brandenburg Park, for area maps and trail guides. The least strenuous hiking option is Red River's chair lift, which runs in the summer, weekends only in May and early June and then daily from mid-June through September ($8, plus $15 for a day bicycle pass). It deposits you at the start of numerous hiking and mountain-biking trails back down the slope. If you prefer to stick to the lowlands, the **Red River Nature Trail** starts in town behind the conference center and runs two miles one-way, with signs identifying plants and geological formations.

West of town, the road leads past a number of trailheads that make for a good amble. **Columbine Trail,** on the left (south) 5.5 miles from the town limits, starts out easy, crossing Deer Creek, but soon moves to a series of long switchbacks that lead through a large aspen grove and then above the tree line to the ridge, a total of about five miles. If you need an incentive, wild berry bushes flourish alongside the trail in the late summer. The right side of the road, however, is a little less scenic because a molybdenum mine has stripped a good chunk of the mountain. "Molycorp: minerals for tomorrow's technology today" boasts the company, though the future looks awfully bleak right here.

Food

Business turnover can be high in Red River, and it's hard to recommend reliable options. Your choices, for the most part, are burgers and barbecue. If you're hungrier for spicy New Mexican, hold out till Questa. The town's most legendary eatery is **Texas Reds** (111 E. Main St., 575/754-2964, 5–9 P.M. daily, $18), though it's open only for dinner. If **The Hole**

TAOS

Thing (601 W. Main St., 575/754-2342, 6:30–11 A.M. daily, $1) is still open (it was changing hands in 2008), stop in for an apple fritter or a cinnamon roll, so delicious that a bear once broke in and ate a whole tray. Otherwise, **Old Tymer's Café** (210 E. Main St., 575/754-2951, 9 A.M.–9 P.M. daily, $7) is reliable, if not ground-breaking.

QUESTA

Arriving in Questa, at the junction of Highway 38 and Highway 522, you're back in Spanish New Mexico. The town, which now has a population of about 1,700, was established in 1842 and is still primarily a Hispano farming village, though a few Anglo newcomers have set up art galleries here. The heart of town is the 1841 **San Antonio Church,** a handsome white stucco structure with a red metal roof and distinctively New Mexican spiral pine columns on either side of the front door. Just south of the junction, look for signs to the **Northern New Mexico Historical Society & Museum** (noon–5 P.M. Thurs.–Sun., summer only, free), started by a Questa native who's enthusiastic about showing visitors through the restored adobe house that holds beautiful quilts and other local relics, WPA-era photos of the town, and a room dedicated to the history of the Molycorp mine.

Food

Turning south on Highway 522, you're on the final leg of the Enchanted Circle loop; the **Questa Café** (575/586-9631, 6 A.M.–10 P.M. Mon.–Sat., 6 A.M.–3 P.M. Sun., $6), about half a mile south of the junction, is the best place in town for hearty New Mexican home cooking. Or **Paloma Blanca** (575/586-2261, 7 A.M.–6 P.M. Mon.–Sat., $3), Questa's only coffeehouse, offers a pick-me-up for the end of the drive. It's about a mile farther south from Questa Café.

WILD RIVERS RECREATION AREA

Visitors usually breeze straight through Questa on their way to the Wild Rivers Recreation Area, a section of Carson National Forest that encompasses the confluence of the Rio Grande and Red River and the dramatic canyons forged by the two flows. Steep hiking trails lead down into the gorge and along the river, so you can make a full loop, and white-water rafting is very popular here in the Class III rapids of the Red River Confluence run. Five developed campgrounds (but no RV hookups) on the rim can be reached by car, or you can hike in to campsites by the river. The area feels very remote, especially once you get down one of the trails. You will probably see red-tailed hawks circling over the gnarled, centuries-old piñon and juniper trees that line the rim of the gorge. To reach the access road, head three miles north on Highway 522 from the main Questa intersection and then west on Highway 378, which leads through the town of El Cerro and to the area's **visitors center** (575/770-1600, 9 A.M.–6 P.M. daily June–Aug., $3 day-use fee, $7 camping).

VALLE VIDAL

Northeast of Questa lies Valle Vidal, a 102,000-acre section of the Carson National Forest that straddles some of the highest peaks in the Sangre de Cristo range. The access road, Highway 196, is out of the way north of Questa off Highway 522, but for those seeking pristine wilderness, Valle Vidal is perhaps the last, best place to get a sense of what New Mexico was like before mining and ranching took off in the 19th century. The place is home to the state's largest elk herd, and its watershed is essential for the rare Rio Grande cutthroat trout.

Though little visited, it is probably one of the best-known public lands in New Mexico, as it has been the topic of strenuous debate since 1982, when Pennzoil traded the land to the National Forest Service in exchange for tax breaks. Valle Vidal's status was always a bit vague, with no clear management plan for the natural-gas deposits beneath it. A strong grassroots campaign finally led to a law, passed in 2006, that prohibits mining and drilling.

There are no services in the wilderness, very few trails, and only two formal camping areas

TAOS

with no services but toilets. Coming from Highway 522, you first reach the 35 sites at **Cimarron Campground** ($10), tucked amid trees with many trout-fishing creeks nearby. Eight miles farther is **McCrystal Creek Campground** ($8), set on a flat plain, with a few ponderosas providing shade. For current conditions and advisories (parts of the valley are closed seasonally to protect the elk), contact the **Questa Ranger District office** (575/586-0520), which manages the whole area.

RED RIVER FISH HATCHERY

Back on Highway 522 heading south from Questa, after 3.5 miles you pass the turn for the Red River Fish Hatchery, an operation that produces almost 400,000 trout every year to stock lakes all over northern New Mexico. Dedicated anglers, or just people whose kids are getting antsy in the back seat, can stop into the visitors center (9 A.M.–5 P.M. daily). There's a free self-guided tour, and you can feed "trout chow" to the growing guppies.

THE D. H. LAWRENCE RANCH

After Questa, the view opens up as you descend into the valley, with mesas stretching far to the west. Just south of San Cristobal, a turn to the left (County Road B-009) leads five miles on a rutted road to the ranch where English writer and provocateur D. H. Lawrence lived in 1924 and 1925 with his wife, Frieda, and the painter Dorothy Brett. Though there's not very much to see here, it is as good a reason as any to drive up a back road and into the fragrant pine forests (though not too early in the spring—the dirt road near the end is rutted and shady, leaving it iced over often through March). The 160-acre spread, originally called the Kiowa Ranch, was a gift to Lawrence and his wife from Mabel Dodge Luhan—generous indeed, but a rough life nonetheless, as you can see from the barest-bones cabins the artists occupied: Brett's is barely big enough for her small bed and a woodstove.

Lawrence soon returned to Europe, but Frieda stayed on. After the writer died of tuberculosis in France in 1930, she eventually decided to

© ZORA O'NEILL

Pay your respects to D. H. Lawrence at his mountaintop shrine.

exhume his body and have the ashes returned to New Mexico. This plan sparked anger among Lawrence's other friends, including Mabel Dodge, who characterized Frieda's planned site for the ashes as "that outhouse of a shrine." Tales abound about how Lawrence's ashes never quite made the trip, whether by accident or sabotage, but visitors to the ranch remain undeterred. Some of the earliest to pay their respects to the place include Tennessee Williams and Georgia O'Keeffe, whose dramatic painting *The Lawrence Tree* depicts the view from the base of a gnarled pine in front of the Lawrences' cabin, farther down the hill. The aforementioned shrine is indeed small; aside from what may or may not be Lawrence's ashes mixed into a concrete slab, the modest building contains a guest book with wishes left by previous literary pilgrims, plus an official-looking certificate declaring the ashes to be genuinely Lawrence's.

To reach the ranch coming from the north, turn left at the second sign for County Road B-009 (the first is in the town of San Cristobal); coming up from Taos, look for the historic marker on the right side of the road, immediately before the turn.

Information and Services

TOURIST INFORMATION

The city-run Taos Visitors Center (1139 Paseo del Pueblo Sur, 575/758-3873, www.taosvacation guide.com, 9 A.M.–7 P.M. daily June–Aug., 9 A.M.–5 P.M. daily Sept.–May) is a helpful place on Paseo del Pueblo Sur (Highway 68) a few miles south of the plaza. Stop here for flyers and maps galore, free coffee, and a copy of the very thorough weekly news and events bulletin (also posted online), which includes gallery listings, music, and more. The staff can also advise on the Enchanted Circle. Take a peek at the side room maintained by Taos Pueblo, which displays pieces by local artisans; it's all paid for with casino money and is very tastefully done. Closer to the plaza, you can also stop in to the Taos Chamber of Commerce (108-F Kit Carson Rd., 575/751-8800, www .taoschamber.com, 9 A.M.–5 P.M. Mon.–Sat.).

Books and Maps

Moby Dickens (124-A Bent St., No. 6 Dunn House, 575/758-3050, 10 A.M.–6 P.M. Sun.–Thurs., 10 A.M.–7:30 Fri. and Sat.) is Taos's best bookstore, well informed on local history and culture and stocking plenty of maps, as well as rare books, a good CD collection, and a solid children's section. The cozy **Brodsky Bookshop** (226-A Paseo del Pueblo Norte, 575/758-9468, 10 A.M.–6 P.M. Mon.–Sat., 11 A.M.–5 P.M. Sun.) stocks both new and secondhand books; it's closed Mondays in winter.

Local Media

The *Taos News* comes out every Thursday, and it contains the *Tempo* entertainment section, with music, theater, and film listings. Many hotels offer free copies of *Tempo* to their guests. The *Albuquerque Journal* publishes a special northern edition daily, focused on local issues, but if you really want to dip in the muck of local politics, pick up a free copy of the *Horse Fly,* published monthly as the voice of cantankerous Taos.

On the northeast corner of the plaza, **Fernandez de Taos** (109 N. Plaza, 575/758-

4391, 8:30 A.M.–5 P.M. Mon.–Sat., 9 A.M.–5 P.M. Sun.) has the town's best newsstand.

Radio

While you're in town, don't miss tuning in to KTAO (101.9 FM), a local radio station that's all solar powered. The musical programming is broad, and you're sure to learn an interesting tidbit about the community in the process. KRZA (88.7 FM) is the local NPR affiliate.

SERVICES
Banks

First Community Bank (120 W. Plaza, 575/758-6652, 9 A.M.–5 P.M. Mon.–Fri.), just off the southwest corner of the plaza, is the most convenient bank and ATM while on foot. The drive-through service at **Centinel Bank of Taos** (512 Paseo del Pueblo Sur, 575/758-6700, 9 A.M.–5 P.M. Mon.–Fri.) is easily accessible from the main drag.

Post Offices

The **Taos post office** (710 Paseo del Pueblo Sur, 575/751-1801, 9:30 A.M.–5:30 P.M. Mon.–Sat.) is on the south side; there's another on the **north side** (318 Paseo del Pueblo Norte, 8:30 A.M.–5 P.M. Mon.–Fri.), next to the Dragonfly Café.

Internet

The bookstore **Sustaining Cultures** (114 Doña Luz St., 575/751-0959, 10 A.M.–5 P.M. Mon.–Sat.) has two computers for public use, plus a free wireless network. Farther afield, **Wired?** (705 Felicidad St., 575/751-9473, 7 A.M.–7 P.M. Mon.–Fri., 8 A.M.–7 P.M. Sat and Sun.), behind Raley's off La Posta Road, is a laid-back Internet café with a big garden, light snacks, and computers for $7 per hour. **Taos Public Library** (402 Camino de la Placita, 575/758-3063, noon–6 P.M. Mon., 10 A.M.–6 P.M. Tues.–Fri., 10 A.M.–5 P.M. Sat.) has less atmosphere, but it's also cheaper, at $2 per hour for users without a library card.

TAOS

Laundry

Taos has two laundries: the **Spin & Sparkle** (106 Siler Rd., 575/758-5150, 7 A.M.–7:15 P.M. daily), a few blocks south of the plaza where you can also drop off your laundry, and the **Pinch Penny Wash-O-Mat** (823 Paseo del Pueblo Norte, 575/758-1265, 6:30 A.M.–8 P.M. Mon.–Sat., 7 A.M.–5 P.M. Sun.) on the north side.

Classes

Donner Ranch offers **Fechin Art Workshops** (575/776-2622, www.fechin.com), five-day live-in retreats at a ranch just north of Taos in the mountains above the village of San Cristobal. Seminars have 14–20 students, guaranteeing personal critiques from the various instructors, most of whom specialize in oil painting, especially landscapes.

Getting There and Around

BY CAR

Enterprise has an office at 1350 Paseo del Pueblo Sur (575/758-3333, 8 A.M.–6 P.M. Mon.–Fri.).

BY BUS AND SHUTTLE

TNM&O/Greyhound (800/231-2222, www.tnmo.com) operates bus service from Albuquerque to Taos via Santa Fe. The bus station in Taos is at 710 Paseo del Pueblo Sur (575/758-1144, 9 A.M.–6 P.M. Mon.–Sat.).

Faust's Transportation (575/758-3410) runs a shuttle between Albuquerque Sunport and Taos ($45 one-way), Taos Ski Valley ($50), Angel Fire ($55), and Red River ($60); it runs only once a day Monday to Saturday, leaving the airport at 1:30 P.M. It stops in Santa Fe, so you can also use it to travel to Taos from the capital ($35). The company also provides taxi service in town.

Within Taos, the **Chile Line bus** (575/751-4459) runs north–south from the Ranchos de Taos post office to the Taos Pueblo; December–April, the route extends all the way up to Taos Ski Valley, running three times daily at 8 A.M., 11 A.M., and 3:35 P.M. seven days a week from the south end of town. Regular buses run approximately every 30 minutes 7 A.M.–9 P.M. The fare is $0.50, or $1 for an all-day pass.

ALBUQUERQUE

As a tourist destination, Albuquerque may labor in the shadow of the jet-set arts colonies to the north, but as a city, it's a thriving haven for those who pride themselves on being down-to-earth and sensible. If Santa Fe is the "City Different" (a moniker any Burqueño will razz for its pretentiozusness), then New Mexico's largest city, with more than 800,000 people in the metro area, is proudly the "City Indifferent"—unconcerned with fads, cultivated quirkiness, and flawless facades.

Which is not to say the city doesn't have its pockets of historic charm, well away from the traffic-clogged arteries of I-40 and I-25, which intersect here in a graceful tangle of looping, turquoise-trimmed bridges. The Duke City was founded three centuries ago, its cumbersome name that of a Spanish nobleman, but its character is the product of later eras: the post-1880 downtown district; the University of New Mexico campus, built in the early 20th century by John Gaw Meem, the architect who defined pueblo revival style; and Route 66, the highway that linked Albuquerque with Chicago and Los Angeles beginning in 1926.

Spread out on either side of the Rio Grande, from volcanic mesas on the west to the foothills of the Sandia Mountains along the east, Albuquerque enjoys a striking natural setting. Accessible hiking and biking trails run through diverse environments: In the morning, you can stroll under centuries-old cottonwood trees along the wide, muddy river through the center of the city; in the afternoon, you can hike along the edge of a windswept mountain range with views across the

ALBUQUERQUE

HIGHLIGHTS

◖ Rio Grande Nature Center State Park: Savor a bit of country in the city in this bird-filled sanctuary along the river. Hiking and biking trails head north and south along the cottonwood-shaded irrigation channels (page 144).

◖ KiMo Theater: A fantasia of South-western decorative styles, this former cinema is one of the few examples of pueblo deco style. Now restored and run with city money, it's the showpiece of downtown (page 145).

◖ Nob Hill: Hobnob and boutique hop in Albuquerque's quirkiest shopping district, developed in sleek modern style in the 1940s. Sidewalk cafés and bars provide a place to rest up afterward (page 148).

◖ Sandia Peak Tramway: Zip up the world's longest single-cable tram to the crest of the mountain that looms over Albuquerque. At the top, you'll get a vertigo-inducing view across the whole metro area and out to the west (page 150).

◖ Anderson-Abruzzo Albuquerque International Balloon Museum: If you're not in town for the Balloon Fiesta, come here to get some perspective on this elegant sport, with displays on history and science (page 152).

◖ Acoma Pueblo: This windswept village on a mesa west of Albuquerque is one of the oldest communities in the United States. Visit for the views as well as for the delicate black-on-white pottery made only here (page 174).

◖ Tinkertown Museum: An enthralling collection of one man's lifetime of whittling

projects, this folk-art exhibit is inspiring for adults and a delight for kids (page 180).

◖ Valles Caldera National Preserve: In the crater formed by a collapsed volcano, 89,000 acres of grassy valleys are set aside for very controlled public access. You must make reservations to hike here, but it's worth planning for (page 186).

LOOK FOR ◖ TO FIND RECOMMENDED SIGHTS, ACTIVITIES, DINING, AND LODGING.

ALBUQUERQUE

vast empty land beyond the city grid. And at the end of the day, you'll see Albuquerque's most remarkable feature, the dramatic light show as the setting sun reflects bright pink off the Sandia (Watermelon) Mountains.

The city is also an excellent (and reasonably priced) base for exploring many pueblos and natural attractions nearby, and it's just an hour's drive to Santa Fe, allowing for easy day trips or long scenic drives through the mountains in between. The main outing is the 65 miles west to Acoma Pueblo, a thousand-year-old settlement atop a natural fortress of stone. In the Manzano Mountains southeast of town lie a series of ruined pueblos, last inhabited during the early years of conquest; the road that links them also winds past a canyon known for its fall colors and a historic hotel in a distinctly New Mexican style. Naturalists will want to head south to the Bosque del Apache, one of the United States' largest bird sanctuaries, which attracts 15,000 sandhill cranes in November; drive down before dawn to see the birds at their most active and then wind your way back north via the Quebradas Backcountry Scenic Byway, a dirt route through rainbow-striped hills.

Whether you're en route to Santa Fe or just making a day loop, you have several ways to head north. The most direct is I-25, which cuts through dramatic rolling hills; take a short detour to Kasha-Katuwe Tent Rocks National Monument, where pointed white rocks tower above a narrow canyon. Beginning east of Albuquerque, the historic Turquoise Trail winds along the back side of the Sandias and then through the former mining town of Madrid, resettled as an arts colony, with galleries occupying the cabins built against the black, coal-rich hills.

The longest route north is along the Jemez Mountain Trail, a scenic byway that runs through the brick-red rocks surrounding Jemez Pueblo and then past a number of natural hot springs. The road runs along the border of Valles Caldera National Preserve, a vast, pristine valley where the daily number of visitors is controlled, so you can enjoy the vistas in solitude.

PLANNING YOUR TIME

Because Albuquerque's major historic attractions are few, the city really fares best as the primary focus of a trip, when you have time to enjoy the natural setting and the people. Ideally, you would spend a leisurely week here soaking up a little Route 66 neon, enjoying the downtown entertainment, hiking in the Sandias, taking scenic drives, and bicycling along the Rio Grande.

But given the rich history and scenic splendor farther north, it is difficult to recommend spending more than a couple of days in Albuquerque if you're also planning to visit Santa Fe and Taos in a limited time. In this case, you'll probably want to allocate only a couple of days, ideally on your way out, as Albuquerque's modern, get-real attitude is best appreciated after you've been in the adobe dreamland of Santa Fe for a bit. Spend a day driving west to Acoma Pueblo, then the next relaxing and knocking around Old Town and the shops in Nob Hill. Or if you prefer a last dose of open sky, take the tramway up to Sandia Peak and hike along the crest trail—at the end of your trip, you'll be able to handle the elevation with no problem.

Any time of year is enjoyable in the city proper—even the winters are quite mild in the basin around the river, though the Sandias start getting snow in December. As elsewhere, summer heat is usually broken by heavy afternoon rainstorms. And because Albuquerque is *not* top on tourists' lists, there's rarely a time when major attractions are unpleasantly mobbed. Hotel prices are highest in summer but not a dramatic hike from low-season rates.

HISTORY

Even before the steady traffic of tourists heading to points north, Albuquerque was a way station. It was established in 1706 as a small farming outpost on the banks of the Rio Grande, where Pueblo Indians had already been cultivating crops since 1100, and named after a Spanish duke, then a viceroy in Mexico. When the Camino Real, the main trade route north from Mexico, developed decades later, the Villa de San Felipe de Alburquerque (the first "r" was lost through the years) was ideally situated, and the town soon prospered and outgrew its original adobe fortress, the central plaza ringed with one-story haciendas and a church.

Life continued relatively quietly through the transition to U.S. rule in 1848, but then, in 1880, the railroad came through town—or near enough. The depot was about two miles from the original plaza, but investors were quick to construct "New Town," which became the downtown business district. Railroad Avenue—later named Central—connected the two communities, though increasingly "Old Town" fell by the wayside, its adobe buildings occupied primarily by the Mexican and Spanish population maintaining their rural lifestyle, while Anglos dominated commerce and the construction of the new city. Developers rapidly built up the land around the train station, with hotels, banks, shops, and more, while other visionaries looked to "the heights"—the sand hills east of the tracks—as the site for a new university. In the early 20th century, Albuquerque's crisp air became known for its beneficial effect on tuberculosis patients, and a number of sanatoriums flourished. Then Route 66 was laid down Central Avenue in the 1930s; by the next decade car traffic and business were booming, and by the 1950s, the characteristic neon signage on the numerous motor-court hotels and diners was in place.

Albuquerque's character again changed drastically after World War II, when recruits trained at Kirtland Air Force Base returned to live; at the same time, the escalating Cold War fueled Sandia National Labs, established in 1949, and engineers relocated to work on defense technology (thanks to the labs, Albuquerque still has more PhDs per capita than any other major city in the United States). Streets were carved into the northeast desert in anticipation of the tract houses these new workers would inhabit, and during the course of the 1940s, the population exploded from 35,000 to 100,000; by 1959, 207,000 people lived in Albuquerque.

Growth has been steady ever since, and in the 1990s, the city experienced another development boom, helped along by the construction of one of Intel's largest American manufacturing plants. Subdivisions have spread across the West Mesa, and small outlying communities such as Bernalillo and Placitas have been consumed by expanding sprawl. But areas in the "valley" along the river, such as Corrales and Los Ranchos de Albuquerque, retain a village feel that's not too far from the city's roots as a farming community three centuries back.

ORIENTATION

Albuquerque's greater metro area covers more than 100 square miles, but visitors will likely see only a handful of neighborhoods, all linked by Central Avenue (historic Route 66), the main east–west thoroughfare across town. Visitors typically start in Old Town: The city's best museums are clustered here, a few blocks from the Rio Grande, which runs north–south through the city. East from Old Town lies downtown, where most of the city's bars and clubs are situated, along with the bus and train depots. Central Avenue then continues under I-25 and past the University of New Mexico campus. Just east of the school, the Nob Hill shopping district occupies about 10 blocks of Central. After this, the rest of Albuquerque blurs into the broad area known as the Northeast Heights, where there are only a few attractions of note—visitors will want to come up this way, to the farthest edge of the heights, to hike in the foothills and ride the Sandia Peak Tramway to the top of the mountain. The other notable parts of town—technically, separate villages—are Los Ranchos de Albuquerque and Corrales. These are two districts in the North Valley—the stretch of the river north of Central—that contain a few of the city's better lodging options; from Old Town, head north on Rio Grande Boulevard to reach Los Ranchos and then jog west over the river and north again to Corrales.

When you're trying to get your bearings, do as the locals do and keep your eyes on the mountains, which run along the east side of the city. Additionally, street addresses are followed by the city quadrant (NE, NW, SE, SW); Central Avenue forms the dividing line between north and south, while the east–west border is roughly along 1st Street and the train tracks, with numbers increasing as they go away from the dividing lines. The two intersecting highways, I-40 (east–west) and I-25 (north–south), also divide the city into regions, though you won't need to use the freeways for much until you head east to the foothills or west to Petroglyh National Monument.

Sights

OLD TOWN AND RIO GRANDE

Until the railroad arrived in 1880, Old Town wasn't old—it was the *only* town, a cluster of one-story haciendas on the riverbank with the formal title of La Villa de San Felipe de Alburquerque. Today this area is primarily a tourist destination, the labyrinthine old adobes repurposed as souvenir emporiums and galleries. Despite all the chile-pepper magnets and cheap cowboy hats, though, the residential areas surrounding the shady plaza retain a strong Hispano flavor, and the historic Old Town buildings have a certain endearing scruffiness—they're lived in, not polished to museum-quality shine. Because there are few formal sights but plenty of lore in the neighborhood, a free walking tour with the Albuquerque Museum of Art and History is recommended if you have time. A few blocks west of Old Town runs the Rio Grande, which creates a ribbon of green space through the city and a quiet reminder of the city's agricultural history.

Albuquerque Biological Park

This-kid friendly park (505/768-2000, www.cabq.gov/biopark, 9 A.M.–5 P.M. Mon.–Fri., 9 A.M.–6 P.M. Sat. and Sun. June–Aug., 9 A.M.–5 P.M. daily Sept.–May, $7) along the riverbank just west of Old Town has several components. North of Central (2601 Central Ave. NW, to be exact) is the **Albuquerque Aquarium,** with a giant shark tank, a creepy tunnel full of eels, and displays on underwater life from the Gulf of Mexico and up the Rio Grande, and the **Rio Grande Botanic Gardens,** including a desert hothouse, a Japanese garden, and a butterfly habitat. The most New Mexico–specific installation in the gardens, and the most interesting, is the 10-acre Rio Grande Heritage Farm, a re-creation of a 1930s operation with heirloom apple orchards and rare types of livestock, such as Percheron horses and Churro sheep. Combined admission to these two areas is $7.

Across Central Avenue (but linked by a path along the river), **Tingley Aquatic Park,** known by locals as "Tingley Beach," is 18 acres of paths and ponds, including a fishing lake and a model boating lake, dug along the eastern riverbank all the way south to Iron Avenue.

one of the many courtyards in Old Town

© ZORA O'NEILL

OLD TOWN ALBUQUERQUE

To Best Western Rio Grande

BELLAMAH AVE

HOTEL ALBUQUERQUE AT OLD TOWN/Q BAR

SEASONS

NATIONAL ATOMIC MUSEUM

MOUNTAIN RD

DORA AVE

EDNA AVE

HOLLYWOOD AVE

SOTO AVE

LA CRÊPE MICHEL

ALBUQUERQUE MUSEUM OF ART AND HISTORY

CAPILLA DE NUESTRA SEÑORA DE GUADALUPE

HISPANIAE

SAINTS & MARTYRS

SAN FELIPE DE NERI CHURCH

POST OFFICE

PLAZA ST

TURQUOISE MUSEUM

MUSEUM OF NATURAL HISTORY AND SCIENCE

¡EXPLORA!

Tiguex Park

OLD TOWN RD

To Sunshine Café and Downtown

GRANITE AVE

CENTRAL AVE (ROUTE 66)

MONTEREY NON-SMOKERS MOTEL

NEW YORK AVE

ALBUQUERQUE AQUARIUM/RIO GRANDE BOTANIC GARDENS

ALHAMBRA AVE

RATTLESNAKE MUSEUM

MARBLE AVE

BÖTTGER MANSION

CHEF DU JOUR

LOMAS BLVD

GERTRUDE ZACHARY

DURAN CENTRAL PHARMACY

ALBUQUERQUE LITTLE THEATER

ROUTE 66 MALT SHOP

To Downtown

FRUIT AVE

To Tingley Aquatic Park, Rio Grande Zoo, and Sandia Peak Inn

© AVALON TRAVEL

0   200 yds
0   200 m

ALBUQUERQUE

There's no admission fee, though anyone 12 and older needs a fishing license, available at the outfitter shop on the premises.

South of Tingley Beach, **Rio Grande Zoo** (903 10th St. SW) is not particularly groundbreaking, but kids can run around among trumpeting elephants and screeching peacocks. The window into the gorilla nursery is probably the most fascinating exhibit. Admission here is $7, but $12 gets you admission to the aquarium and gardens too, plus a ride on the **Rio Line,** the miniature train that connects all sections of the Biopark. It runs every day but Monday, and tickets alone cost $2.

Albuquerque Museum of Art and History

The museum (2000 Mountain Rd. NW, 505/243-7255, www.cabq.gov/museum, 9 A.M.–5 P.M. Tues.–Sun., $4) has a permanent collection varying from a few choice Taos

Society of Artists members (compare Ernest L. Blumenschein's *Star Road and White Sun* with *Acoma Legend,* a painting by his wife, Mary Greene Blumenschein, which use similar colors and allegorical techniques but very different styles) to contemporary work by the likes of Nick Abdalla, whose sensual imagery makes Georgia O'Keeffe's flower paintings look positively literal. The history wing covers four centuries, with emphasis on Spanish military trappings, Mexican cowboys, and Albuquerque's early railroad years. Free guided tours run daily around the sculpture garden, or you can join the informative Old Town walking tour (11 A.M. Tues.–Sun. Mar.–Dec.).

American International Rattlesnake Museum

You'd never guess this small storefront just off the plaza (202 San Felipe St. NW, 505/242-6569, www.rattlesnakes.com, 10 A.M.–6 P.M.

UP, UP, AND AWAY: ALBUQUERQUE'S HOT-AIR BALLOON HISTORY

How did it come to be that one of the most iconic sights in Albuquerque is a 127-foot-tall Mr. Peanut figure floating in front of the Sandias? The city's air currents were discovered to be friendly to balloons for the first time in 1882. That was when an adventurous bartender piloted a hydrogen-filled craft into the sky as part of the New Town's Fourth of July celebrations, much to the delight of the assembled crowd, which had waited almost two days for *The City of Albuquerque*, as the balloon was dubbed, to fill. "Professor" Park Tassell, the showman pilot, went aloft alone and landed successfully; the only mishap was that a ballast sandbag was emptied on a spectator's head.

But then it took another 90 years before Albuquerque again drew attention as a place to pursue this gentle sport – in 1972, the first balloon fiesta was held, with 13 aircraft participating. The gathering, centered around a single race, was organized by a local balloon club largely as a publicity stunt for a local radio station's 50th-anniversary celebrations. The spectacle drew 20,000 spectators, most of whom had never even seen a hot-air balloon before – but within a few short years, the event was an annual spectacle of international renown.

Albuquerque, it turns out, enjoys the world's most perfect weather for navigating hot-air balloons. A phenomenon called the "Albuquerque Box," created by the steep mountains adjacent to the low river bottom, enables pilots to move at different speeds at different altitudes, and even to backtrack if necessary. Combine that with more than 300 days of sunshine per year, and it's no wonder that now more than 700 balloons – including "special shapes" such as Mr. Peanut – convene annually to show off their colors and compete in precision flying contests.

Mon.–Sat., 1–5 P.M. Sun. June–Aug., $3.50) houses the largest collection of live snakes in the world, as you have to wade through an enormous gift shop full of plush snakes, wood snakes, little magnet snakes, and snakes on T-shirts to see the real critters. You'll also see some fuzzy tarantulas and big desert lizards, and the reptile-mad staff are usually showing off some animals outside to help educate the phobic. In the off-season, September–May, the museum is open 11:30 A.M.–5:30 P.M. on weekdays.

Capilla de Nuestra Señora de Guadalupe

Tucked away in a side alley off the main street, this tiny adobe chapel (404 San Felipe Rd. NW) is dedicated to the first saint of Mexico; her image dominates the wall facing the entrance. The dimly lit room, furnished only with heavy carved seats against the walls, is still in regular use, and the air is sweet with the smell of votive candles and *milagros* placed at Mary's feet and on the modest altar, along with prayers and testimonies. Despite the building's small scale, it follows the scheme of many traditional New Mexican churches, with a clerestory that allows sunlight to shine down on the altar.

¡Explora!

This 50,000-square-foot complex adjacent to the natural history museum (1701 Mountain Rd. NW, 505/224-8300, www.explora.us, 10 A.M.–6 P.M. Mon.–Sat., noon–6 P.M. Sun., adults $7, children $3) is dedicated to thrilling—and educating—children; adults may learn something too. Its colorful geodesic-dome top sets a circuslike tone, and inside, more than 250 interactive exhibits demonstrate the scientific principles behind everything from high-wire balancing to optical illusions. Kids can even build robots using Lego systems, and, since this is the desert, a whole section is dedicated to water.

Indian Pueblo Cultural Center

Just north of I-40 from Old Town, the Indian

Pueblo Cultural Center (2401 12th St. NW, 505/843-7270, www.indianpueblo.org, 9 A.M.–4:30 P.M. daily, $6) is a must-visit before heading to any of the nearby Indian communities. The horseshoe-shaped building (modeled after the Pueblo Bonito ruins in Chaco Canyon in northwestern New Mexico) houses a large museum that traces the history of the first settlers along the Rio Grande, illustrated with some beautiful artifacts. The central plaza hosts dance performances (11 A.M. and 2 P.M. Apr.–Oct., noon Nov.–Mar.). The extensively stocked gift shop is a very good place to buy pottery and jewelry, as well as Native American music on CD. You can also have a lunch of posole and frybread at the Pueblo Harvest Café. Don't miss the south wing, which contains a gallery for contemporary art. At the information desk, check on ceremony schedules and get directions to the various pueblos.

Museum of Natural History and Science

This large exhibit space (1801 Mountain Rd. NW, 505/841-2800, www.nmnaturalhistory .org, 9 A.M.–5 P.M. daily) contains three major attractions: a planetarium and observatory; a wide-format theater screening the latest vertigo-inducing nature documentaries; and a presentation of Earth's geological history. The geology section is structured as a walk-through timeline, beginning with the Big Bang (rendered with black lights and thunderclaps) and meandering through the prehistoric era and age of volcanic activity. Some of the attractions, such the hokey "evolator" time machine, don't live up to the hype, but there's plenty of space given to the real crowd pleasers: dinosaurs. New Mexico has been particularly rich soil for paleontologists, and several of the most interesting finds are on display, such as *Coelophysis* and *Pentaceratops*. In addition, the Startup exhibit details the early history of the personal computer, in Albuquerque and elsewhere. The show was funded by former Duke City resident Paul Allen, who founded Microsoft here with Bill Gates and *then* moved to Seattle. Admission is $7 to the main exhibit

space, and $7 for the theater or the planetarium, though discounts apply if you buy tickets to more than one.

National Atomic Museum

Some Albuquerqueans have bemoaned the 69-foot-tall Redstone missile in front of this museum (1905 Mountain Rd. NW, 505/245-2137, www.atomicmuseum.com, 9 A.M.–5 P.M. daily, $5) as an eyesore, but it's a handy landmark for out of towners. And it will likely be gone by the time you read this, as the museum was slated to move to a new building in spring 2009 (and get a new name, the National Museum of Nuclear Science & History). In either location, you'll find everything you wanted to know about atomic energy, and probably a lot more, split between nuclear physics' use in daily life and a thorough recounting of the development and use of the atomic bomb, from the first tests at the Trinity Site to its use in Japan to later incidents such as the loss of several warheads over Palomares, Spain, in

entrance to Rio Grande Nature Center State Park

© ZORA O'NEILL

ALBUQUERQUE

1966. The amount of information can feel a bit crushing, but the displays are interspersed with Cold War–era comic books and other cultural artifacts—just enough colorful detail to entertain the nonscience oriented while others bone up on nuclear history. The new location is on Eubank Boulevard, at Southern Boulevard—due east of the airport, and one block south of Central.

◖ Rio Grande Nature Center State Park

Familiarize yourself with river ecology at this green haven in the center of town (2901 Candelaria Rd. NW, 505/344-7240, www.rgnc.org, 8 A.M.–5 P.M. daily, $3/car). The visitors center (10 A.M.–5 P.M. daily) is a sleek, angular concrete design by local architect Antoine Predock that's surprisingly harmonious with the surrounding greenery; you enter through a drainage culvert to an exhibit on water conservation and river ecology. Beyond, a comfortable glassed-in "living room" lets you watch birds on the pond outside from the comfort of a lounge chair and with the outdoor sounds piped in through speakers. Outside, you can walk several paved trails across the old irrigation channels and along the river, all shaded by towering cottonwood trees. In the spring and fall, the area draws all manner of migrating birdlife; borrow binoculars from the staff if you want to scout on your own, or join one of the frequent nature walks (including full-moon tours) that take place year-round.

San Felipe de Neri Church

Established in 1706 along with the city itself, San Felipe de Neri Church (2005 N. Plaza St. NW) was originally built on what would become the west side of the plaza—but it dissolved in a puddle of mud after a strong rainy season in 1792. The replacement structure, on the north side of the plaza, has fared much better, perhaps because its walls, made of adobelike *terrones* (sun-dried bricks cut out of sod) are more than five feet thick. As they have for two centuries, local parishioners attend Mass here, conducted three times a day, once in Spanish.

© ZORA O'NEILL

San Felipe de Neri Church

Like many religious structures in the area, San Felipe de Neri received a makeover from Eurocentric Bishop Jean Baptiste Lamy of Santa Fe in the second half of the 19th century. Under his direction, the place got its wooden folk Gothic spires, as well as new Jesuit priests from Naples, who later added such non-Spanish details as the gabled entrance and the widow's walk. The small yet grand interior has brick floors, a baroque gilt altar, and an elaborate pressed-tin ceiling with Moorish geometric patterns. A tiny museum (9 A.M.–4 P.M. Mon.–Sat., free) on the west side contains some historical church furnishings.

Turquoise Museum

This place (2107 Central Ave. NW, 505/247-8650, 9:30 A.M.–4 P.M. Mon.–Fri., 9:30 A.M.–3 P.M. Sat., $4) is more of a consumer's resource than a museum per se. Sure, the less imaginative may see only exhibits on the geology and history of turquoise, along with specimens from all over the world, but most folks can't help but think of all the jewelry they plan to buy. So come here to learn the distinction between "natural" and "real" turquoise and otherwise arm yourself for the shopping ahead.

DOWNTOWN

Once known as bustling New Town, the downtown area of Albuquerque, stretching along Central Avenue between the train tracks and Marquette Avenue, was the city's commercial center. Central was crowded with mule-drawn streetcars, bargain hunters, and wheeler-dealers from the East Coast. Then, in the 1950s and 1960s, shopping plazas in Nob Hill and the Northeast Heights began drawing business away; by the 1970s, downtown was a wasteland of government office buildings that was utterly desolate after 5 P.M. But thanks to an aggressive urban-renewal scheme initiated in 2000, the neighborhood has regained some of its old vigor, and Central is now a thoroughfare best known for its hip bars and lounges.

By day, you won't see too many specific attractions, but a stroll around reveals an interesting hodgepodge of architectural styles from Albuquerque's most optimistic era. At Central Avenue and 4th Street, two versions of Route 66 intersect. When the original highway was commissioned in 1926, the road from Chicago to the West Coast ran along 4th Street; after 1937, the route was smoothed so that it ran east–west along Central.

C KiMo Theater

Albuquerque's most distinctive building is the KiMo Theater (423 Central Ave. NW, 505/768-3522 or 505/768-3544 event info, www.cabq.gov/kimo). In 1927, local businessman and Italian immigrant Oreste Bachechi hired Carl Boller, an architect specializing in movie palaces, to design this marvelously ornate building. Boller was inspired by the local adobe and native culture to create a unique style dubbed "pueblo deco"—a flamboyant treatment of Southwestern motifs, in the same vein as Moorish- and Chinese-look cinemas of the same era. The tripartite stucco facade is encrusted with ceramic tiles and Native American iconography (including a traditional Navajo

© ZORA O'NEILL

The splendid KiMo Theater is preserved and managed by the city.

symbol that had not yet been completely appropriated by the Nazi party when the KiMo was built). To get the full effect, you must tour the interior to see the cow-skull sconces and murals of pueblo life; enter through the business office just west of the ticket booth, between 8:30 A.M. and 4:30 P.M. on weekdays, or 11 A.M. and 5 P.M. Saturdays.

Occidental Life Building

On Gold Avenue at 3rd Street, this one-story office building is another of Albuquerque's gems. With its curlicued facade of white ceramic tile, the ornate 1917 construction looks like the Doge's Palace in Venice rendered in marshmallow fluff. After a 1933 fire, the reconstructing architects added even more frills, such as the crenellations along the top. The entire building is surfaced in white terra-cotta; the tiles were made in a factory in Denver, which sprayed the ceramic glaze onto concrete blocks, each individually molded and numbered; the blocks were then assembled in Albuquerque according to an overall plan.

ALBUQUERQUE

DOWNTOWN ALBUQUERQUE

To University of New Mexico and NOB HILL

LOCUST ST

25

ELM ST

HIGH ST

WALTER ST

CENTRAL AVE (ROUTE 66)

ARTICHOKE CAFÉ

THE GROVE

AVE

COPPER AVE

STANDARD DINER

GOLD AVE

EDITH BLVD

IRON AVE

SILVER AVE

ARNO ST

BROADWAY BLVD

0.25 mi

0.25 km

HIGH ST

FRUIT ST

ROMA AVE

ARNO ST

MARTIN LUTHER KING JR AVE

JOHN ST

COMMERCIAL ST

CONVENTION CENTER

CAKE FETISH

ANDALUZ

JC'S

SUNSHINE THEATER

ALVARADO TRANSPORTATION CENTER

GREYHOUND/ AMTRAK

Civic Plaza

KIMO THEATER

RELISH

BURT'S TIKI LOUNGE/ATOMIC CANTINA

OCCIDENTAL LIFE BLDG

GOLD STREET CAFFE

1ST ST

2ND ST

3RD ST

STOVER AVE

BLVD

4TH ST

ROMA AVE

MARQUETTE AVE

LOMAS BLVD

PUBLIC LIBRARY

THE MAN'S HAT SHOP

SKIP MAISEL

POST OFFICE

CECILIA'S CAFÉ

COPPER AVE

7TH ST

8TH ST

KELEHER

MAUGER ESTATE

Robinson Park

THE HOTEL BLUE

LAUNCHPAD/ EL REY THEATER

GOLD AVE

FLYING STAR

SILVER AVE

LEAD AVE

COAL AVE

IRON AVE

4TH ST

5TH ST

6TH ST

7TH ST

To National Hispanic Cultural Center

9TH ST

10TH ST

11TH ST

12TH ST

KENT AVE

TIJERAS AVE

DOG HOUSE

CENTRAL AVE (ROUTE 66)

ROUTE 66 HOSTEL

To Old Town

FRUIT ST

13TH ST

14TH ST

PARK AVE

STOVER AVE

Tingley Park

Rio Grande Zoo

To Rio Grande Pool

© AVALON TRAVEL

NEW LIFE FOR "NEW TOWN"?

Long a district of desolate concrete plazas, and boarded-up shops on windblown streets, Albuquerque's downtown has taken on a new look in the last decade. The city has invested more than $350 million in a grand scheme to restore the area to its early-20th-century role as New Town, the hub of Albuquerque's commercial life.

Using the principles of New Urbanism, downtown is being promoted as a mixed-use neighborhood where residents can live, work, and play without relying on cars – ideally, everything residents need, from bars to grocery stores, should be within a 10-minute walk. For Albuquerque, a typical American city where growth has always been out rather than up and people are used to spending hours in their cars every day, the plan is revolutionary. The city built a new public transport hub – including a commuter-rail line – while developers have converted office buildings into residential lofts. The old Albuquerque High School building just east of the railroad tracks on Central Avenue (the microneighborhood dubbed EDo,

short for "east downtown") had the chalk dust blown out of its lofty halls and now provides chic living space.

But for all the energy and activity, as of 2008, downtown is still not quite there. The holdup? Food. Pioneering downtowners have a yoga studio, a lingerie boutique, and a multiscreen cinema, but they're still waiting for a major grocery store to arrive. Until then, they have to get in their dreaded cars to stock up elsewhere, or cobble together a meal from the once-weekly farmers market and one tiny gourmet cheese shop.

Meanwhile, downtown is facing competition from a new megadevelopment that could be described as "New Suburbanist": The 13,000-acre Mesa del Sol community, on the south side of the city near the airport, is laid out so that no home is more than 800 yards from groceries. Mesa del Sol's houses are much more familiar to Westerners than downtown's apartments, so this might prove the more popular car-free option. But more simply, Burqueños cannot live on brie alone.

THE UNIVERSITY AND NOB HILL

The state's largest university, another by-product of the railroad boom, was established in 1889 as a tiny outpost on the far side of the tracks. By 1909, under the guidance of its president William George Tight, it had acquired the outline of its distinctive pueblo-inspired architecture (though Tight was then fired in part for his non–Ivy League aesthetics). Pueblo revival pioneer John Gaw Meem carried on the vision through the 1940s, and even with contemporary structures now interspersed among the original halls, it's still a remarkably harmonious vision, uniting the pastoral sanctuary feel of the great Eastern campuses with a soothing, minimalist interpretation of native New Mexican forms. Surrounding the campus is the typical scrum of cheap pizza places, bohemian coffeehouses, and dilapidated bungalow rentals. The next neighborhood east along Central

is the city's best shopping district, Nob Hill, developed around a shopping plaza in the late 1940s and still showing that decade's distinctive style in marquees and shop facades.

The University of New Mexico

Nearly 25,000 students use this campus, which sprawls for blocks beyond the old core bounded by Central Avenue and University Boulevard. Visitors can park in a complex just inside the UNM campus across from Cornell Street; the info center, where you can pick up a detailed map, is in the southwest corner of the structure. Just across the way, the **University Art Museum** (Center for the Arts, 9 A.M.–4 P.M. Tues.–Fri., 1–4 P.M. Sun.) displays treasures from the permanent fine-art collection of more than 30,000 pieces from all over the globe.

Wandering around the grounds, you'll see such classic Meem buildings as **Mesa Vista Hall** (now the Student Services Building) and

Zimmerman Library. Rest up at the bucolic duck pond and then head for the **Maxwell Museum of Anthropology** (off University Blvd., north of M. L. K. Jr. Blvd., 505/277-4405, 9 A.M.–4 P.M. Tues.–Fri., 10 A.M.–4 P.M. Sat., free), a Meem building originally used as the student union. The museum has a particularly good overview of Southwestern Indian culture and a collection of Native American artifacts from university-sponsored digs all over the state.

🄲 Nob Hill

Square frames trimmed in neon mark the Nob Hill district on Central Avenue at Girard Street and at Washington Boulevard. The area began to grow after 1937, when Route 66 was rejiggered to run along Central; the Nob Hill Shopping Plaza, at Central and Carlisle,

signaled the neighborhood's success when it opened as the glitziest shopping area in town a decade later. The area went through a slump from the 1960s through the mid-1980s, but it's again lined with brightly painted facades and neon signs, a lively district where the quirk factor is high—whether you want to buy designer underwear or an antique Mexican mask, you'll find it here. The eastern half of the strip hasn't enjoyed quite the same renaissance, but wander down this way to see the **Aztec Motel** (3821 Central Ave. NE), a bizarre art project/flophouse decorated with an array of tiles, mannequin parts, plastic Christmas decorations, and rain-worn plush animals. Then head off of Central on Monte Vista and keep an eye out for the **Bart Prince house** (3501 Monte Vista Blvd. NE), the home and studio of one of the city's most celebrated contemporary architects,

ROUTE 66 GETS A MAKEOVER

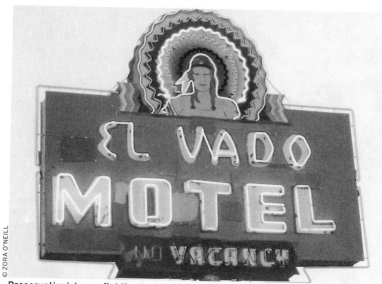

© ZORA O'NEILL

Preservationists are fighting to save Albuquerque's vintage El Vado motel.

Route 66 is one of the biggest repositories of American nostalgia – it symbolizes the country's economic growth in the 20th century, from Depression desperation to postwar optimism to free-wheeling hipness, a little neon-lined ribbon of cool. But the "mother road," on which so many Dust Bowl refugees made their way west and so many beatniks got into their grooves, officially no longer exists. The highway was decommissioned in 1985. Sure, you can still drive Route 66 – look for the brown historic-marker signs – from Chicago to Los Angeles, but it has lost its zip since it was replaced by larger interstate highways. In Albuquerque, I-40 is the conduit for traffic, bypassing Central Avenue, the old Route 66, and the transient-friendly businesses that once thrived there.

Now those businesses – especially the numerous 1950s motel courts – are derelict and have become hot spots for drug deals and other unsavory business. As part of Albuquerque's aggressive urban-renewal program, city planners have been steadily demolishing motels. The east edge of Nob Hill in particular looks like a bit of a graveyard, with dead neon signs standing like tombstones amid the rubble. At the same time, others are putting a great deal of effort and money into restoring the route's icons. The vintage El Vado motel, near Old Town, has been saved from the wrecking ball (though its future as of 2008 was uncertain). More visibly, neon artists have taken the signs on the El Rey theater and the Aztec Motel from dull to dazzling. So even if Route 66 no longer exists, some of its more colorful icons will.

ALBUQUERQUE

COURTESY OF ALBUQUERQUE CONVENTION & VISITORS BUREAU/© NEWMEXICOSTOCK.COM

Shop facades in Nob Hill are as quirky as the goods for sale.

whose favorite forms seem to be spaceships and antennas—it's the residential counterpart to the eccentric businesses that flourish in this area.

ALBUQUERQUE METRO AREA

Beyond the neighborhoods described in the previous pages, Albuquerque is a haze of modern tract houses and shopping centers built during the 1960s and later—decades dubbed Albuquerque's "Asphalt Period" by an unkind local journalist. A few sights, particularly along the edges of the city, are well worth seeking out, however.

National Hispanic Cultural Center

Just south of downtown (but not within walking distance) on 4th Street in the historic, and historically neglected, neighborhood of Barelas, the National Hispanic Cultural Center (1701 4th St. SW, 505/246-2261, www.nhccnm.org, 10 A.M.–5 P.M. Tues.–Sun., $3) is an impressive modern complex that lauds the cultural contributions of Spanish speakers the world over. It has had a huge influence in this down-at-the-heels district (even the McDonald's across the street

mimics its architecture), but numerous houses—occupied by Hispanics, no less—were demolished for its construction. One woman refused the buyout. She has since died, but her two small houses still sit in the parking lot—almost like an exhibit of their own, representing the larger determination of New Mexican Hispanics to hang onto their land through the centuries.

The central attraction is the museum, which shows work varying from traditional santos and *retablos* by New Mexican craftspeople (including Luis Barela, grandson of legendary Taos *santero* Patrocinio Barela) to contemporary painting, photography, and even furniture by artists from Chile, Cuba, Argentina, and more. Three additional rooms house temporary shows—recent exhibits have compared the inspirations of three very different New Mexico artists, for instance. Adjacent to the museum are the largest Hispanic genealogy library in existence and the giant Roy E. Disney Center for Performing Arts.

◖ Sandia Peak Tramway

The longest tramway of its type in the world,

Zip up to Sandia Peak on the world's longest tramway.

the tram (505/856-7325, www.sandiapeak.com, $1 parking, $17.50 round-trip, $9 one-way) whisks passengers 2.7 miles along a continuous line of Swiss-made cables from Albuquerque's northeast foothills 4,000 feet up to the crest in about 15 minutes. If the wind is blowing, the ride can be a bit alarming—or thrilling, depending on your outlook. The service runs frequently all year-round (9 A.M.–9 P.M. daily June–Aug., 9 A.M.–8 P.M. Wed.–Mon. Sept.– May), making it a convenient way to get to the ski area; in the summer, you can ride up to the peak and then hike along the crest or even all the way back down the mountain. Even from the base of the tram, the view across the city is very good—you may want to come to the casual Mexican restaurant here, **Sandiago's** (38 Tramway Rd. NE, 505/856-6692, 4:30 P.M.– midnight, $10), for a sunset margarita (one of which, the Doogie, honors Albuquerque actor Neil Patrick Harris, who attended a nearby high school).

Petroglyph National Monument
Albuquerque's west side is bordered by this national reserve area, 7,500 acres of black boulders that crawl with about 20,000 carved lizards, birds, and assorted odd beasts. Most of the images, which were created by chipping away the blackish surface "varnish" of the volcanic rock to reach the paler stone beneath, are between 400 and 700 years old, while others may date back three millennia. A few more recent examples of rock art include Maltese crosses made by Spanish settlers and initials left by explorers (not to mention a few by idle 21st-century teenagers).

Stop in first at the **visitors center** on Unser Boulevard at Western Trail (505/899-0205, www.nps.gov/petr, 8 A.M.–5 P.M. daily) for park maps, flyers on flora and fauna, general orientation, and free activities on the weekend. You can see some of the largest groupings on two major trails: **Boca Negra Canyon,** a short paved loop, and in **Rinconada Canyon,** a 1.25-mile one-way hike. Boca Negra Canyon is the only fee area ($1/car on weekdays, $2 on weekends), and there are restrooms and water in the parking area. The Rinconada trailhead is less developed; the walk can be tedious going in some spots because the ground is sandy, but it's relatively flat. The clearest, most impressive images are in the canyon at the end of the trail. Keep an eye out for millipedes, which thrive in this stark environment; dead, their curled-up empty shells resemble the spirals carved on the rocks—coincidence? You can also explore in the northernmost section of the reserve, **Piedras Marcadas Canyon,** on a few trails that start in the backyards of the homes bordering the area; maps are available at the visitors center.

The back (west) side of the parkland, the **Volcanoes Day Use Area** (9 A.M.–5 P.M. daily) is also a great place to survey the city. Access is via Paseo Volcan (Exit 149) off I-40; turn right (east) 4.3 miles north of the highway at an unmarked dirt road to the parking area. From the base of three cinder cones, you can look down on the city and see "fingers" stretching east, their crumbled edges forming the escarpment where the petroglyphs are found. They formed when hot lava flowed between sandstone bluffs that later crumbled away. If you go in the winter, you'll see that the volcanoes, which were last reported emitting steam in 1881, are still not entirely dead: Patches of green plants flourish around the steam vents that stud the hillocks, particularly visible on the middle of the three volcanoes.

◖ Anderson-Abruzzo Albuquerque International Balloon Museum

Boosters of Albuquerque's hot-air balloon scene—which has been flourishing since the first rally in 1972—include locals Ben Abruzzo, Larry Newman, and Maxie Anderson, who in 1978 made the first Atlantic crossing by balloon in the *Double Eagle II* helium craft. Abruzzo and Anderson then also crossed the Pacific and set a long-distance record (5,678 miles) in the *Double Eagle V.* These pioneers, and many others, are honored at the Anderson-Abruzzo Albuquerque International Balloon Museum (505/768-6020, www.balloon museum.com, 9 A.M.–5 P.M. Tues.–Sun., $4, $3 for New Mexico residents, free Sun. morning),

Critters adorn the rocks at Petroglyph National Monument.

in Balloon Fiesta Park just off East Alameda Avenue. The displays are a great mix of historical background, interactive physics lessons and games, and inspiring footage of record-setting balloon ventures. As long as you don't dwell too long on the zeppelin exhibit, complete with salt-and-pepper cellars from the *Hindenburg,* you'll definitely come away inspired by the grace of balloons and wanting to take a ride in one yourself.

Los Ranchos and Corrales Scenic Byway

For a pretty drive (or bike ride) through these villages that have been all but consumed by greater Albuquerque, head north from Old Town on Rio Grande Boulevard; you first reach Los Ranchos, then cross the river at Alameda to Corrales Road, and continue up the west bank. These districts remain pockets of pastoral calm where horses graze and 18th-century acequias water organic herb gardens—a practical melding of old agricultural heritage with modern suburban bliss. The only real sights are in central Corrales, two blocks west of the main road. The folk Gothic **Old San Ysidro Church** (505/897-1513, 1–4 P.M. Sat. and Sun. June–Oct.) stands where the center of the village was in 1868, when its bulging adobe piers were first constructed. Across the road is the village cemetery, a typically New Mexican *camposanto,* where graves are trimmed with plastic flowers and votive candles. Next door, **Casa San Ysidro** (973 Old Church Rd., 505/898-3915, www.cabq.gov/museum, tours 9:30 A.M. and 1:30 P.M. Wed.–Sat. and 2 P.M. Sun. Feb.–Nov., plus 10:30 A.M. Sat. July–Aug., $4) was owned by obsessive collectors Alan and Shirley Minge, who lived in the place for nearly 40 years, heating with firewood and squirreling away New Mexican antiques and craftwork. The Albuquerque Museum gives tours several times per week—very much worth reserving if you know you'll be coming up this way.

Coronado State Monument

Though named for Spanish explorer Francisco Vásquez de Coronado, who camped on this

inside the kiva at Coronado State Monument in Bernalillo

lush spot by the river during his 1540 search for gold, the monument (485 Kuaua Rd., Bernalillo, 505/867-5351, 8:30 A.M.–4:30 P.M. daily, $3) is actually a Native American relic, the partially restored pueblo of Kuaua (Tiwa for "evergreen"), which was inhabited between 1300 and the early 1600s. The centerpiece is the partially sunken square kiva, its interior covered with murals of life-size human figures and animals in ritual poses. What you see are only reproductions—the originals have been removed for preservation, and a few are on display in the visitors center. While not exactly worth its own special trip, the site is a good place to stop on your way up to Jemez, and the setting is good for a picnic. Seated on a bench facing the river and the mountains, with the city hidden from view behind a dense screen of cottonwoods, you get a sense of the lush, calm life along the Rio Grande in the centuries before the Spanish arrived. To reach the monument, exit I-25 in Bernalillo and head west on Highway 550; Kuaua Road is on your right, before the Santa Ana Star casino. The monument is closed Tuesdays during the winter.

Gruet Winery

The Spanish planted the first vineyards in North America in New Mexico in the 17th century, and the industry persisted until a series of floods finally wiped out the vines by the 1920s. So New Mexico's current wine scene, while strong, is still somewhat young.

One of the best wineries, Gruet (8400 Pan American Fwy. NE, 505/821-0055, www.gruet winery.com), began producing its excellent sparkling wines (the Gruet family hails from Champagne) only in 1987; look out especially for its nonvintage sparkling rosé, which is delicious and affordable. Tours run at 2 P.M. every day but Sunday; the tasting room (five pours for $6) is open 10 A.M.–5 P.M. weekdays and noon–5 P.M. on Saturday.

Entertainment

BARS AND CLUBS

Albuquerque's downtown is the city's main bar and club scene, all packed in a few square blocks, which makes for handy hopping (or staggering) from place to place. Here and nearer to UNM, a lot of the bars cater to students, with plentiful beer and other happy-hour specials but with a somewhat generic atmosphere. But the more distinctive places are pure Albuquerque: unpretentious, with a remarkably varied clientele. Because there aren't enough members of any one particular subculture to pack a whole bar, even the most chic-appearing places will see an absent-minded professor and a veteran Earth First–er propping up the bar next to well-groomed professionals.

Old Town and the Rio Grande

This neighborhood doesn't offer much in the way of nightlife. The few exceptions are the rooftop patio at **Seasons** (2031 Mountain Rd. NW, 505/766-5100, 4 P.M.–midnight daily), where there's live jazz on weekends and happy hour 4–6:30 P.M. Monday through Friday, and **Q Bar** (800 Rio Grande Blvd. NW, 505/843-6300, 4 P.M.–1 A.M. daily) in the Hotel Albuquerque at Old Town, a swank little lounge filled with low couches and little nooks for sipping sweet and deadly cocktails. As Albuquerque's most dimly lit nondive bar, it seems to inspire decadent behavior among those who don't normally indulge; there's also a VIP room—possibly the only one in the city.

Just over the west side of the river at Alameda, **Elliott's** (10200 Corrales Rd. NW, 505/898-5555, 11 A.M.–2 A.M. Mon.–Sat., noon–midnight Sun.) is the only bar of any note near Los Ranchos and Corrales. It's tucked in a strip mall, but that's easy to forget on the huge back patio overlooking river-fed greenery; a good chunk of the regulars are staff and patrons of the highly lauded Star Tattoo in the same complex, which means an eclectic jukebox, generous beer specials, and plenty to feast your eyes on, and if that doesn't satisfy, there's decent bar food too. Weekends see occasional costume dance parties, such as a hip-hop luau.

Downtown

The best all-purpose bar in the neighborhood is the second-floor **Anodyne** (409 Central Ave. NW, 505/244-1820), a long, wood-floor room filled with pool tables and a younger crowd sprawled on the thrift-store sofas. Choose from more than 100 beers, and get some quarters to plug into the good collection of pinball machines.

To catch the latest touring indie-rock sensation or the local crew about to hit it big, head to the very professional **Launchpad** (618 Central Ave. SW, 505/764-8887, www.launch padrocks.com). For absolutely free live music and a pool table, **Burt's Tiki Lounge** (313 Gold Ave. SW, 505/247-2878, www.burts tikilounge.com, 8 P.M.–2 A.M. Mon.–Sat.) has a funky feel and a very eclectic bill, with everything from British psychedelia to reggae on the roster. Its next-door neighbor, **Atomic Cantina** (315 Gold Ave. SW, 505/242-2200, www.atomiccantina.com), is a good bet too.

The University and Nob Hill

Upstairs, **Zinc** (3009 Central Ave. NE, 505/254-9462, 5 P.M.–1 A.M. Mon.–Sat.) is a sit-down restaurant and a long bar. Those in the know, however, head to the cellar bar, where they might find anything from special flights of wines and a jazz band to martini specials and classic films. In the Nob Hill shopping plaza, **Gecko's** (3500 Central Ave. SE, 505/262-1848, 11:30 A.M.–late Mon.–Fri., noon–late Sat. and Sun.) is a good place for a snack (anything from Thai curry shrimp to chipotle hot wings) and a drink on the patio. Sporting its own breezy patio, **O'Niell's** (4310 Central Ave. SE, 505/255-6782, 11:30 A.M.–2 A.M. Mon.–Sat., 11:30 A.M.–midnight Sun.) is a great Irish pub that draws a varied crowd, whether for quiz night or weekend folk bands; the kitchen is open until midnight.

PERFORMING ARTS AND LIVE MUSIC

Albuquerque's arts scene graces a number of excellent stages. The most beautiful of them all, the city-owned **KiMo Theater** (423 Central Ave. NW, 505/768-3544, www.cabq.gov/kimo) often hosts locally written plays and dance, as well as the occasional musical performance. Bigger acts visit the **Roy E. Disney Center for Performing Arts** at the National Hispanic Cultural Center (1701 4th St. SW, 505/724-4771, www.nhccnm.org), a modernized Mesoamerican pyramid that contains three separate venues, the largest of which is a 691-seat proscenium theater; this is the place to catch a performance by visiting or local flamenco artists—with the National Institute of Flamenco headquarters in Albuquerque, there's often someone performing. UNM's **Popejoy Hall** (UNM campus, 505/277-4569, www.popejoyhall.com) hosts the New Mexico Symphony Orchestra (which also plays at the Rio Grande Zoo in the summer).

Albuquerque is usually a stop for many bands' national tours. Check the schedules at the casinos, which offer not only the enticing jingle of slot machines but also excellent stages. These relatively intimate auditoriums, with low ticket prices, are where you might catch a legend such as Merle Haggard or Etta James. The ritzier **Sandia Casino** (I-25 at Tramway, 800/526-9366, www.sandiacasino.com, 8 A.M.–4 A.M. Mon.–Thurs., open 24 hours Fri.–Sun.) has a great outdoor space, while Laguna Pueblo's **Route 66 Casino** (14500 Central Ave. SW, 866/352-7866, www.rt66casino.com, 8 A.M.–4 A.M. Mon.–Thurs., open 24 hours Fri.–Sun.) is smaller and funkier. Also see what's on at **El Rey Theater** (620 Central Ave. SW, 505/242-2353, www.elreytheater.com) and **Sunshine Theater** (120 Central Ave. SW, 505/764-0249, www.sunshinetheaterlive.com)—both converted movie houses, they have excellent sightlines. **Outpost Performance Space** (210 Yale Blvd. SE, 505/268-0044, www.outpostspace.org) books very good world music and dance acts.

You can catch local thespians at **Albuquerque Little Theater** (224 San Pasquale St. SW, 505/242-4750, www.swcp.com/~alt), founded in 1930, and the **Vortex** (2004 1/2 Central Ave. SE, 505/247-8600, www.thevortextheater.org), near the university. The latter is Albuquerque's longest-running avant-garde space, putting up everything from Beckett to local playwrights' work in its black box since 1976. The **Filling Station** (1024 4th St. SW, www.fillingstation-abq.com) hosts another local theater company, as well as the Sunday Church of Beethoven (10:30 A.M.) and occasional hijinks by improv geniuses The Pajama Men.

CINEMAS

Century 14 Downtown (100 Central Ave. SW, 505/243-7469) devotes most of its screens to blockbusters, while the latest indie and art films are shown at **The Guild** (3405 Central Ave. NE, 505/255-1848, www.guildcinema.com).

ALBUQUERQUE

CEREMONIAL DANCES

This is only an approximate schedule for ceremonial dances at Albuquerque-area pueblos – dates can vary from year to year. Annual feast days typically involve carnivals and markets in addition to dances. Confirm details with the Indian Pueblo Cultural Center (505/843-7270, www.indianpueblo.org) before setting out.

JANUARY 1
- Santo Domingo: corn dance

JANUARY 6
- Sandia and Santo Domingo: various dances

FEBRUARY 2
- San Felipe: various dances for Candlemas (Día de la Candelaria)

MARCH 19
- Laguna (Old Laguna): Feast of Saint Joseph

EASTER (MARCH/APRIL)
- Most pueblos: various dances

MAY 1
- San Felipe: Feast of San Felipe

JUNE 13
- Sandia: Feast of San Antonio
- Santa Clara: Los Comanches

JUNE 29
- Santa Ana: Feast of San Pedro

JULY 14
- Cochiti: Feast of San Bonaventura

JULY 26
- Laguna: harvest dances
- Santa Ana: Feast of Santa Ana

AUGUST 4
- Santo Domingo: Feast of Santo Domingo

AUGUST 10
- Acoma (Acomita): Feast of San Lorenzo

AUGUST 15
- Laguna (Mesita): various dances
- Zia: Feast of the Assumption of Our Blessed Mother

AUGUST 28
- Isleta: Feast of Saint Augustine

LABOR DAY
- Santo Domingo: arts and crafts market

SEPTEMBER 2
- Acoma (Sky City): Feast of San Estevan

SEPTEMBER 4
- Isleta: Feast of Saint Augustine

SEPTEMBER 8
- Isleta (Encinal): Feast of the Nativity of the Blessed Virgin

SEPTEMBER 19
- Laguna (Old Laguna): Feast of Saint Joseph

SEPTEMBER 25
- Laguna (Paguate): Feast of Saint Elizabeth

OCTOBER 17
- Laguna (Paraje): Feast of Saint Margaret Mary

OCTOBER 24-27
- Laguna (Old Laguna): harvest dance

DECEMBER 24
- San Juan: Los Matachines and torchlight processions
- Acoma (Sky City): luminaria display
- Laguna and Santa Ana: dances after evening Mass

DECEMBER 25
- Santo Domingo, San Juan, and Zia: various daytime dances

FESTIVALS AND EVENTS

The city's biggest annual event is the **Albuquerque International Balloon Fiesta** (888/422-7277, www.balloonfiesta.com), nine days in October dedicated to New Mexico's official state aircraft, with more than 700 hot-air balloons of all colors, shapes, and sizes gathering at a dedicated park on the north edge of town, west of I-25. During the fiesta, the city is packed with fanatical "airheads," who claim this is the best gathering of its kind in the world. If you go, don't miss an early-morning mass ascension, when the balloons glow against the dark sky, then lift silently into the air in a great wave.

You'll catch an equally colorful show at the **Gathering of Nations Powwow** (www.gathering ofnations.com), the largest tribal get-together in the United States, with more than 3,000 dancers and singers in full regalia from more than 500 tribes crowding the floor of the University Arena. Miss Indian World earns her crown by showing off traditional talents such as spearfishing or storytelling. The event takes place the last weekend in April.

The state's agricultural roots get their due at the **New Mexico State Fair** (www.exponm .com), a 17-day festival of fried foods and prizewinning livestock that begins immediately after Labor Day. It's your usual mix of midway craziness and exhibition barns, along with really excellent rodeos, which often end with shows by country music legends such as Willie Nelson.

Around November 2, don't miss the **Day of the Dead** parade in the South Valley, also known as the Marigold Parade, for the bright-orange flower that's associated with this Mexican festival for honoring the departed. A procession of skeletons and cars bedecked in marigolds begins by the sheriff's station on Isleta Boulevard, south of Arenal Boulevard, winds through the neighborhood, and ends with a big party at the Westside Community Center (1250 Isleta Blvd. SW, 505/768-5500); call for the exact date and time.

The rest of the year is crowded with specialist get-togethers, such as the **New Mexico Wine Festival** (505/867-3311, www.newmexicowine festival.com), which takes place in Bernalillo over Labor Day weekend—it's well attended by a wide swath of Burqueños; the Rail Runner runs on a special schedule, sparing stress on designated drivers. Also look out for the **National Fiery Foods Show** in March, where capsaicin fanatics try out hot new products; the **Bernalillo Art Car Parade** in early October; the **Mariachi Spectacular** in early July; and the weeklong **International Flamenco Festival** (www.nationalinstituteofflamenco .org) in June, the largest event of its kind in the United States, with performances and workshops sponsored by the National Institute of Flamenco, which has its conservatory here.

Shopping

Albuquerque doesn't have Santa Fe's exotic treasure troves and tony galleries, but it doesn't have the high prices either. Old Town and the environs are where you can pick up traditional American Indian jewelry and pottery for very reasonable prices, while Nob Hill is the commercial center of Albuquerque's counterculture, with body-piercing studios adjacent to comic book shops next to herbal apothecaries. There are a number of **farmers markets** throughout the city; one of the largest is downtown at Robinson Park on Central Avenue at 8th Street (7–11 A.M. Sat. June–Oct.), and there's another good one in Los Ranchos (6718 Rio Grande Blvd. NW, 7–11 A.M. Sat. May–Oct., 10 A.M.–noon every second Sat. Nov.–Apr.). For more info, see www.farmersmarketsnm.org.

OLD TOWN AND THE RIO GRANDE

The galleries and gift shops packed around the plaza can blur together after just a little bit of browsing, but a few places stand out: **Saints & Martyrs** (404 San Felipe St. NW, 505/224-9323, 10 A.M.–5 P.M. Mon. and Wed.–Sat., noon–5 P.M. Sun.) specializes in traditional religious art from Spain and elsewhere; some one-of-a-kind santos are quite pricey, but other trinkets are more affordable. **Hispaniae** (410 Romero St. NW, 505/244-1533, 10 A.M.–5:30 P.M. Mon.–Sat., noon–5 P.M. Sun.) is three rooms crammed with Mexican craftwork—you can get far finer stuff at ¡Que Chula! (see *The University and Nob Hill*), but the prices here are surprisingly reasonable. For American Indian jewelry and other crafts, visit the vendors set up under the *portal* on the east side of the plaza.

Just outside of Old Town's historic zone, the **Gertrude Zachary** showroom (1501 Lomas Blvd. NW, 505/247-4442, 10 A.M.–6 P.M. Mon.–Sat., 10 A.M.–5 P.M. Sun.) is the place to go for turquoise-and-silver jewelry, whether you want a traditional squash-blossom necklace or a contemporary reimagining of that design studded with other semiprecious stones. Among other things, the shop specializes in rare, antique turquoise—the variety of colors is astounding—but everything's sold at wholesale prices, so you can get some great treasures for cheap. A branch in Nob Hill (3300 Central Ave. SE) stocks antique furniture along with jewelry. For strictly traditional work, head to the gift shop at the **Indian Pueblo Cultural Center** (2401 12th St. NW, 505/843-7270, www.indianpueblo.org, 9 A.M.–4:30 P.M. daily); not only are its prices reasonable, but the staff are happy to explain the work that goes into various pieces.

DOWNTOWN

Sears Roebuck and JCPenney have moved on, but a few interesting shops still occupy the curved show windows along Central. An emporium of American Indian goods, **Skip Maisel** (510 Central Ave. SW, 505/242-6526, 9 A.M.–5:30 P.M. Mon.–Fri., 9 A.M.–5 P.M. Sat.) feels like a relic from downtown's heyday—whether you want a war bonnet, a turquoise-studded watch, or deerskin moccasins, it's all here in a vast, overstocked shop with kindly salespeople. Don't miss the beautiful murals above the display windows in the foyer; they were painted in the 1930s by local Indian artists such as Awa Tsireh, whose work hangs in the New Mexico Museum of Art in Santa Fe. Another throwback: **The Man's Hat Shop** (511 Central Ave. NW, 505/239-9871, 9:30 A.M.–5:30 P.M. Tues.–Fri., 9:30 A.M.–5 P.M. Sat.), which stocks just what it promises, from homburgs to ten-gallons. Zip back to the present day at **Visiones Gallery** (212 Gold Ave. SW, 505/242-9267, 9 A.M.–5 P.M. Mon.–Fri.), run by a local nonprofit and showing fresh artwork by Latino, African American, and American Indian artists, usually priced quite reasonably.

THE UNIVERSITY AND NOB HILL

Start your stroll on the west end of the Nob Hill district, near Girard. **Stone Mountain Bead Gallery** (3100 Central Ave. SE, 505/260-1121, 11 A.M.–6 P.M. Mon.–Sat., noon–4 P.M. Sun.) and **Larry's Hats** (3102 Central Ave. SE, 505/266-2095, 10 A.M.–6 P.M. Mon.–Sat., noon–4 P.M. Sun.) both provide intriguing browsing even if you're not in the market for baubles or haberdashery (the latter also has some beautiful vintage jewelry).

Farther along, the best Mexican import store in Albuquerque is **¡Que Chula!** (3410 Central Ave. SE, 505/255-0515, 10:30 A.M.–5:30 P.M. Tues.–Sat.), where vibrantly colored furniture, tableware, and trinkets are arrayed for maximum visual impact. In particular, don't miss the ceramics by Ken Edwards, who learned his craft in Asia but practices in Tonalá, producing delicate paintings of birds on sturdy Mexican-style pottery.

Down the block, tasteful (and expensive) **Hey Jhonny** (3418-B Central Ave. SE, 505/256-9244, 10 A.M.–6:30 P.M. Mon.–Sat., 11 A.M.–6 P.M. Sun.) stocks gorgeous sushi sets, hip handbags, and travel guides to only the coolest destinations.

On the next corner, **Mariposa Gallery** (3500 Central Ave. SE, 505/268-6828, 11 A.M.–6 P.M. Mon.–Sat., noon–5 P.M. Sun.) is one of the city's longest-established art vendors, dealing since 1974 in jewelry, fiber art, and other crafts. If you're looking for unusual postcards, head south one block to **Papers!** (114 Amherst Dr. SE, 505/254-1434, 10:30 A.M.–6:30 P.M. Mon.–Sat., 11 A.M.–5 P.M. Sun.), where the greeting cards are great, but the array of blank sheets may inspire you to make your own missives home. **A, the Albuquerque Store** (3500 Central Ave. SE, 505/266-2222, 10 A.M.–6 P.M. Mon.–Sat., noon–5 P.M. Sun.) specializes in home furnishings for the Southwestern hipster—you'll find some pricey items but also some more affordable bits with excellent design sensibility, such as colorful flower-print Mexican tablecloth fabric and handmade candles; the jewelry here, much of it by local designers, is very good, too.

Nob Hill's hip businesses expand a little farther east every year—now "upper Nob Hill" extends east of Carlisle, and you can keep strolling this way for highlights such as the **Absolutely Neon** gallery of new and vintage signs (3903 Central Ave. NE, 505/265-6366, 11 A.M.–6 P.M. Mon.–Sat.), the **Seventh Goddess** lingerie shop (3901 Central Ave. NE, 505/268-1981, 11 A.M.–6 P.M. Mon.–Sat.), and, farther on, a whole slew of antiques marts.

ALBUQUERQUE METRO AREA

Every Saturday and Sunday, Albuquerque's **flea market** (505/265-3976, 9 A.M.–4 P.M., $2 parking) takes place at the fairgrounds (enter at Gate 9, on Louisiana just north of Central). There are more established vendors

loose turquoise for sale at the Albuquerque flea market

© ZORA O'NEILL

ALBUQUERQUE

than individuals selling off the contents of their garages, but it's still an interesting outlet where you can pick up anything from new cowboy boots to loose nuggets of turquoise; socks and beef jerky are also well represented. Head to the northwest corner for the better collections of secondhand junk, and stop off at one of the myriad food stands for a snack—refreshing *aguas frescas* (fresh fruit juices, in flavors such as watermelon and tamarind) and Indian frybread are the most popular.

Sports and Recreation

Albuquerque is a perfect city for outdoor enthusiasts, with several distinct ecosystems and plenty of trails running through them. Late spring and summer are the best times to head to the higher elevations on the Sandia Mountains; once the cool fall weather sets in, the scrub-covered foothills and the bare, rocky West Mesa are more hospitable. The Rio Grande Valley, running through the center of the city, is remarkably pleasant year-round: mild in winter and cool and shady in summer. As everywhere in the desert, always pack extra layers of clothing and plenty of water before you set out, and don't go charging up to Sandia Peak (10,678 feet above sea level) your first day off the plane.

BALLOONING

You don't have to be in town for the Balloon Fiesta to go up, up, and away: Take a morning hot-air balloon ride with **Rainbow Ryders** (505/823-1111, www.rainbowryders.com, $160 per person) to get a true bird's-eye view of the city. Typically, you're up in the balloon for an hour or so, depending on wind conditions, and you get a champagne toast when you're back on earth.

SKIING

Sandia Peak Ski Area (505/242-9052, www.sandiapeak.com, $43 full-day lift ticket) is open from mid-December through mid-March, though it takes until about February for a good base to build up; the 30 trails, serviced by four lifts, are not dramatic, but they are long. The area is open daily in the holiday season, then Wednesday through Sunday for the remainder of the winter.

Sandia Peak also has plenty of opportunities for cross-country skiing. The most popular place is the **Capulin Snow Play Area** ($3 parking), nine miles up Highway 536 to the crest, where there are also big hills for tubing and sledding. About six miles of trails are groomed here, or you can bushwhack—just be wary of sudden drop-offs. Farther up on the mountain, **10K Trail** is usually groomed for skiers, as is a service road heading south to the upper tramway terminal; the latter is wide and relatively level—good for beginners. You can check the status of the trails at the Sandia ranger station (505/281-3304) on Highway 337 in Tijeras.

HIKING

Between the West Mesa and the East Mountains, Albuquerque offers a huge range of day hikes. The easiest option is the *bosque* (the wooded area along the Rio Grande), where level paths lead through groves of cottonwoods, willows, and olive trees; the **Rio Grande Nature Center,** at the end of Candelaria, is the best starting point for any walk around the area. Anyone looking for some elevation gain will want to head to the Sandias; note that camping is forbidden in the borders of the wilderness area,

though, so there's really no place for backpacking. On the city side, the foothills are ideal in the winter but a little hot in the summertime—the best access is at **Elena Gallegos Open Space** (7 A.M.–9 P.M. Apr.–Oct., 7 A.M.–7 P.M. Nov.–Mar., $1 weekdays, $2 weekends), east of Tramway Boulevard and north of Academy, at the end of Simms Park Road.

The foothills are also the starting point for a much more challenging hike: **La Luz Trail,** a 7.5-mile ascent to the Sandia Crest Visitor Center. The trail has a 12 percent grade at certain points, but the views are worth the effort, as is the experience of hiking through four climate zones (pack lots of layers) as you climb 3,200 vertical feet. The trail is perhaps the best known in the Sandias, so it's well worn; the only potentially confusing part is after about two miles, where the trail crosses a streambed and makes a sharp turn south. Near the top, you can take a spur that leads north to the Sandia Crest observation point or continue on the main trail south to the ski area and the Sandia Peak Tramway, which you can take back down the mountain. Ideally you'd have someone pick you up at the bottom end of the tram, because the 2.5-mile trail along the foothills from the tram back to the trailhead is dusty and lacking in shade. (You might be tempted to take the tram up and hike down, but the steep descent can be deadly to toes and knees.) La Luz trailhead is at **Juan Tabo Picnic Ground** ($3 parking), at the far north end of Tramway Boulevard just before the road turns west.

If you want to enjoy the views without quite so much effort, you can drive up the east face of the mountain (I-40 to Highway 14) via scenic byway Highway 536, a.k.a. the Crest Road, and park at the Sandia Crest Visitor Center at the top ($3 day-use fee). From there, an easy loop of a little more than two miles runs south along the **Crest Spur Trail,** which dips below the ridgeline to connect to **La Luz,** which in turn goes on to the tram terminal. Then you can hike back to your car via the **Crest Trail.** This is the single-most-traveled stretch on Sandia Peak; if you want to avoid the crowds, start on some of the trails lower down the mountain—**Tree Spring Trail,** in particular, five miles up the mountain, heads up to the crest and is also a convenient link to other trails. See www.sandiahiking.com for more details on this and other trails, plus printable maps of the more than 180 miles of hiking available in the mountains.

BIKING

Albuquerque maintains a great network of paved trails for cycling in the city, and the mountains and foothills are lined with challenging dirt tracks. The city publishes a map of designated on-street bike routes, off-road recreational trails, and other bike-friendly spots around town; download it at the city's bike info page (www.cabq.gov/bike), or pick up a copy at any bike shop. But recreational cyclists need head no farther than the river, where the **Paseo del Bosque,** a 16-mile-long, completely flat biking and jogging path, runs through the Rio Grande Valley State Park. The natural starting point is at **Alameda/Rio Grande Open Space** (7 A.M.–7 P.M. daily) on Alameda Boulevard; you can also reach the trail through the **Rio Grande Nature Center** (8 A.M.–8 P.M. daily, $3 parking), at the end of Candelaria and at several other major intersections along the way.

Corrales is also good for an afternoon bike ride: The speed limit on the main street is low, and you can dip into smaller side streets. The excellent **Stevie's Happy Bikes** (4583 Corrales Rd., 505/897-7900, 10 A.M.–7 P.M. Tues.–Sat. May–Sept., 10 A.M.–6 P.M. Tues.–Sat. Oct.–Apr.) can rent comfy cruisers ($25/day), and even tandems ($35/day), and advise on the best routes on and around the river. You could bike along the road one direction, perhaps stopping at the church and Casa San Ysidro, and then loop back on the riverfront path, an extension of the Paseo del Bosque.

Mountain bikers can take the Sandia Peak Tramway to the ski area and then rent a bike to explore the 30 miles of wooded trails. Bikes aren't allowed on the tram, though, so if you have your own wheels, you can drive around

ALBUQUERQUE

The Sandia foothills are criss-crossed with mountain-bike paths.

the east side of the mountain. Advanced riders will appreciate the challenge of rocky **Faulty Trail,** which runs about 11 miles north–south along the lower elevations of Sandia Peak, connecting with other trails that lead down to main roads as well as higher up the mountain. One access point, midway along the route, is from Highway 14: Coming from I-40, turn left after 3.4 miles onto Cañoncito Road (*not* Corte de Cañoncito); stay on this main road for half a mile, bearing right at a fork partway along; just as the paving ends, bear left onto Cole Springs Road, and then park at the pull-out here. Continue up to the road, past some fencing, to a locked gate; the next mile of road is private property (which you may cross on foot), and then you reach the Cañoncito trailhead. This trail leads up 0.75 mile to the intersection with Faulty, just after Cañoncito Spring—the more challenging sections are to the north, or right (heading left brings you into the Sandia Mountain Wilderness, where mountain biking is prohibited). You can also get access to the trail near its north end, via the Sulphur Canyon Trail that leads out of Doc Long Picnic Ground, off the Crest Road.

Or you can stay in the city and explore the foothills. Locals built the small but fun **Embudo Mountain Bike Terrain Park** at the end of Indian School Road; it is packed with jumps and berms. For a longer cruise, head for the **foothills trails,** a web of dirt tracks all along the edge of the Northeast Heights. **Trail 365,** which runs for about 15 miles north–south from near the tramway down to near I-40, is the best run. You can start at either end (near the tramway is the easiest—park in the lot here and ask for directions), or go to Elena Gallegos Open Space, off the north end of Tramway Boulevard at the end of Simms Park Road, where there's access to the midpoint of the trail. Elena Gallegos in particular is very popular, so go on a weekday if you can, and always look out for hikers and other bikers. Aside from the occasional sandy or rocky patch, none of the route is technical, nor is it steep. More complex trails run off to the east; pick up a map at the entrance booth at Elena Gallegos.

For hard-core road bikers, a popular tour is up to **Sandia Peak** via the Crest Road on the east side—you can park and ride from any point, but cyclists typically start somewhere along Highway 14 (the Turquoise Trail) north of I-40 and then ride up Highway 536, which winds 13.5 miles along increasingly steep switchbacks to the crest. The New Mexico Touring Society (www.nmts.org) lists descriptions of myriad other ride options and organizes group rides.

SPECTATOR SPORTS

Minor-league baseball thrives in Albuquerque, apparently all because of some clever name: The so-so Dukes petered out a while back, but a fresh franchise, under the name of the **Albuquerque Isotopes,** has been drawing crowds since 2003. It's hard to judge whether the appeal is the cool Isotopes Park (1601 Avenida Cesar Chavez NE, 505/883-7800, www.albuquerquebaseball.com), the whoopee-cushion theme nights, or just the name, drawn from an episode of *The Simpsons.* Regardless, a

Root for the home team at Isotopes Park.

© ZORA O'NEILL

ALBUQUERQUE

summer night under the ballpark lights, cheering for the 'Topes, is undeniably pleasant; it helps that you can get in the door for $6, and the best seats are just $24.

For an even smaller-scale ball game, you can head up to the ball field at Santa Ana pueblo (near Bernalillo), home of the Tamaya Tigers, where semipro pueblo teams, as well as Navajo teams from Shiprock and Gallup, face off all summer long. (Isotopes Park then hosts the All-Indian All-Star Playoffs when the pueblo tournament season wraps up in mid-September.)

Albuquerqueans also go crazy for UNM Lobos **basketball,** packing the raucous University Arena, a.k.a. "The Pit" (Avenida Cesar Chavez at University Blvd., 505/925-5626, www.golobos.com). In the winter, you can catch a **hockey game,** represented by the New Mexico Scorpions (www.scorpionshockey.com) at Santa Ana Star Center in Bernalillo.

SPAS AND SPORTS FACILITIES

Betty's Bath & Day Spa (1835 Candelaria Rd. NW, 505/341-3456) is the place to get pampered, whether with a massage and a facial or with an extended dip in one of two outdoor communal hot tubs, one co-ed and one for women only and both with access to dry saunas and cold plunges—a bargain at just $11. Private reservations are available most evenings. Also look out for **The Albuquerque Baths** (1218 Broadway NE), set to open as this book was going to press—in a handy location near downtown, the place was planned as a casual, not-at-all-ritzy escape, complete with hot tubs, saunas, and massage space.

Beat the heat at the **Rio Grande Pool** (1410 Iron Ave. SW, 505/848-1397, noon–5 P.M. daily, $2.25), one of Albuquerque's nicest places to take a dip; the outdoor 25-meter pool is shaded by giant cottonwoods.

Accommodations

Because Albuquerque isn't quite a tourist mecca, its hotel offerings have languished a bit. Generic, chain-operated towers are the norm, and some of the bed-and-breakfasts have a haphazard air. But a few places, particularly the inns in the bucolic areas of Los Ranchos and Corrales, on the north edge of the city, are quite nice, and you'll pay substantially less here than you would in Santa Fe for similar amenities.

UNDER $50

Funky and affordable, the **Route 66 Hostel** (1012 Central Ave. SW, 505/247-1813, www.rt66hostel.com) is the kind of place you might get settled into and never leave. This century-old house midway between downtown and Old Town has been offering bargain accommodations since 1978, and it's very clean despite years of budget travelers traipsing through. Upstairs, along creaky wood hallways, are private rooms ($25–35) with various configurations, including the tiny "monk cell," perfect for the broke solo traveler; others have bathtubs and room for three to sleep comfortably. Downstairs and in the cool basement area are single-sex dorms ($20 pp). Guests have run of the kitchen (an optional free dinner is served every night), and there are a laundry and plenty of room to lounge. Some visitors have reported frustratingly flaky communications with the staff, who aren't on hand throughout the night—this can be a liability if you're arriving late or leaving early. The most useful city bus lines run right out front.

The only criticism to muster against the **Sandia Peak Inn** (4614 Central Ave. SW, 505/831-5036, $49 d) is that it's nowhere near the mountain; in fact, it's on the west side of the city, just over the river from Old Town. In all other respects, it's more than you could want in a bargain hotel: Two wings have large, spotless rooms decorated in a homey fashion, all with bathtubs, fridges, microwaves, and huge TVs. (One suite has a whirlpool tub;

another has an extra daybed, handy for families.) An indoor pool and hot tub provide year-round relaxation, and breakfast is included in the rate. The near-obsessive owner lives on the premises with his family and is very proud of his creation.

Conveniently situated in Nob Hill, **Hiway House** (3200 Central Ave. SE, 505/268-3971) retains a bit of the Route 66 motel-court flair, at least on the outside. Rooms are fairly generic, but most all of them have been overhauled since 2005. The place is kept quite clean, however, and you're within easy walking distance of the university as well as all of the Nob Hill attractions. The owners are cagey about their prices, which they tend to change according to demand—feel free to haggle.

If you're on a budget but have your own car, you can also stay in the community of Cedar Crest, on the east side of the Sandias, about a half-hour drive from the city. The **Sandia Mountain Hostel** (12234 Hwy. 14, 505/281-4117) is peaceful and well kept, even if its yard is filled with rusting trucks and live burros; two single-sex dorms ($14 pp) open onto a big shared kitchen with a woodstove, and a separate house has three private rooms ($32) with porches overlooking the back canyon. Just up the road on the west side, the **Turquoise Trail Campground** (22 Calvary Rd., 505/281-2005, May–Oct.) has tree-shaded spots for tents ($15) as well as small cabins ($28), along with showers and laundry facilities.

$50-100

Central Avenue is strewn with motels, many built in Route 66's heyday. Almost all of them are unsavory, except for **Monterey Non-Smokers Motel** (2402 Central Ave. SW, 505/243-3554, $75 d), which is as practical as its name implies. The place doesn't really capitalize on 1950s kitsch—it just offers clean, good-value rooms with no extra frills or flair. The location near Old Town is very convenient.

The Hotel Blue (717 Central Ave. NW, 877/878-4868, www.thehotelblue.com, $82 d) offers decent value downtown, billing itself as a "boutique hotel" but really just a spruced-up chain motel. The low rates include parking, and rooms, decorated in a vaguely art deco style using black-and-white and vintage travel posters, have good-quality beds, refrigerators, and plasma TVs—though they are not always as sparkling as one would hope. There's also a small pool. Request a room on the northeast side for a mountain view.

Hidden on a narrow road in Los Ranchos, **Casita Chamisa** (850 Chamisal Rd. NW, 505/897-4644, www.casitachamisa.com, $95 d) is very small—only one bedroom, and one guesthouse for four people—but it's wonderfully private and the sort of place that could exist only in New Mexico: The 150-year-old adobe house sits by an old acequia, as well as the remnants of a Pueblo community established seven centuries ago and partially excavated by the owner's late wife, an archaeologist. There are also a heated pool and a glass-covered patio—both lovely in the wintertime.

$100-150

The heart of **Cinnamon Morning** (2700 Rio Grande Blvd. NW, 800/214-9481, www.cinnamonmorning.com, $110 d), about a mile north of Old Town, is its lavish outdoor kitchen, with a huge round dining table and a fireplace to encourage lounging on nippier nights. Rooms are simply furnished, with minimalist Southwestern detail—choose from three smaller rooms in the main house, each with a private bath, or the guesthouse across the garden, which has a two-bedroom suite and another separate bedroom with a corner kiva fireplace.

Yes, it's a highly standardized and fairly typical chain hotel, but the **Best Western Rio Grande** (1015 Rio Grande Blvd. NW, 505/843-9500, www.riograndeinn.com, $120 d) is a better deal than the Hotel Albuquerque across the street, and it's one of the cleanest properties in town. A free airport shuttle, a small pool, and laundry facilities are bonuses; request an upper-floor room for a bit of a view.

On the west edge of downtown you'll find the Queen Anne–style **⊂ Mauger Estate** (701 Roma Ave. NW, 505/242-8755,

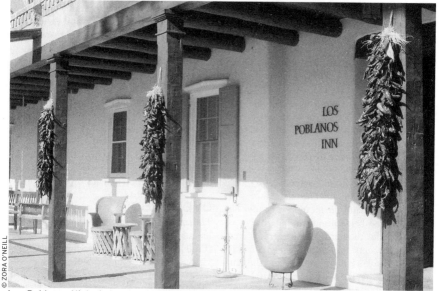

Los Poblanos Historic Inn was built by noted architect John Gaw Meem.

© ZORA O'NEILL

www.maugerbb.com, $129 d), a historic inn that fortunately has a light hand when it comes to lace—it gleams with polished dark wood paneling and floors. Luxe touches such as triple-sheeted beds and fresh flowers contribute to an overall feeling of elegance.

There are two excellent properties in the rural-feeling Los Ranchos district. **Sarabande B&B** (5637 Rio Grande Blvd. NW, 505/345-4923, www.sarabandebb.com, $100 d) offers six rooms in three configurations. Choose from a skylight, brick floors, and a potbellied woodstove; a private garden and a gas fireplace; or a wood-burning kiva fireplace and a soaking tub. They're all done in subdued Southwestern style. A small lap pool takes up the backyard, and a flower-filled patio with a fountain is the breakfast venue.

At Albuquerque's nicest place to stay, you really feel you're nowhere near the city. **Los Poblanos Historic Inn** (4803 Rio Grande Blvd. NW, 505/344-9297, www.lospoblanos.com, $145 d) sits on 25 acres, the largest remaining plot of land in the city, and a nearby public plot of 50 acres preserves wetlands and bird-migration routes. The rooms are tucked in various corners of a sprawling *rancho* built in the 1930s by John Gaw Meem for city bigwig Albert Simms and his wife, Ruth McCormick, former U.S. legislators who contributed enormously to the city's social and economic life. The subsequent owners have been dedicated to maintaining the historic status of the home—even the huge old kitchen ranges are still in place, as are murals by Taos artist Gustave Baumann and frescoes by Peter Hurd. Main-house guest rooms, accented with Spanish colonial antiques and arrayed around a central patio, retain their old wood floors and heavy viga ceilings; a big sunny guesthouse is filled with colorful folk art. Guests are welcome in the extensive gardens and the organic lavender farm (the produce of which goes into the soap, shampoo, and lotion in guest rooms) and the community-supported agriculture (CSA) plots that take up much of the acreage. At the time of research, there were only eight rooms, but plans were in the works to add more. (Note that the majority of the rooms are in the $150–250 range.)

$150-250

Just two short blocks from the plaza in Old Town, **Böttger Mansion** (110 San Felipe St. NW, 505/243-3639, www.bottger.com, $159 d) is the epitome of Victorian, inside (flower prints and lace) and out (pink with white trim). The lavish Stephanie Lynn room features a giant bath lit by a chandelier, while the snug Molly Jane, with two twin beds, has a great view of the mountain and a clawfoot bathtub; it's ideal for friends traveling together.

Hotel Albuquerque at Old Town (800 Rio Grande Blvd. NW, 505/843-6300, www.hotel abq.com, $209 d) got a facelift in 2005; it's a little pricey, though rates are much lower when booked online, and the location is handy. The brick-red-and-beige rooms are relatively spacious. Opt for the north side (generally, even-numbered rooms) for a view of the mountains.

You can save a bit by heading out of the main tourist areas. On the north side of town, **Nativo Lodge** (6000 Pan American Fwy. NE, 505/798-4300, www.nativolodge.com, $179 d) is conveniently situated only for the Balloon Fiesta or an early start to Santa Fe, but once you're inside, it's very nice (it's under the same management as Hotel Albuquerque). The place was completely overhauled in 2005, with new pillow-top beds, sepia-tone decor, and a dramatic lobby and atrium. Definitely get a room in the back, so you're not overlooking I-25, and try to book online, where the rates can drop by nearly half.

The historic former La Posada de Albuquerque (125 2nd St. NW) is Conrad Hilton's first hotel and the city's only remaining relic of early 20th-century travel. Its lobby alone, filled with murals and big wood bar, is worth a visit. It was undergoing a much-needed renovation (and name change, to **Andaluz**) as of press time—do check if it has reopened by the time you're reading this, as it's potentially the best place to stay in the city, with its combination of location and atmosphere.

OVER $250

The smell of piñon smoke and the sound of flute music set the tone at the **Hyatt Regency Tamaya** (1300 Tuyuna Tr., Santa Ana Pueblo, 505/867-1234, www.hyatt.com, $295 d), an impeccably designed resort that's a cooperative project between Santa Ana Pueblo and the Hyatt chain; Hyatt supplies training and experience, and the pueblo dictates aesthetic choices. Even the standard rooms are quite large, with either terraces or balconies. Three swimming pools and a full spa offer relaxation; the more active can play golf or tennis, take an archery class, or attend an evening storytelling program with a pueblo member.

Food

Although Albuquerque has a few dress-up establishments that merit a little bit of credit-card debt, the real spirit of the city's cuisine is in its low-rent spots where dedicated owners follow their individual visions. If you're in search of authentic New Mexican, definitely plan on lunch in one of the many neighborhood, family-run favorites—with a very few exceptions, any New Mexican joint open for dinner is just not good.

OLD TOWN AND THE RIO GRANDE

Aside from those recommended here, the restaurants in the blocks immediately adjacent to the Old Town plaza are expensive and only so-so; better to walk another block or two for real New Mexican flavor, which can be found in a number of local hangouts around Old Town and up Rio Grande Boulevard in the North Valley.

Cafés

In the Old Town area, **Chef du Jour** (119 San Pasquale Ave. SW, 505/247-8998) is a cozy operation, with a big chunk of the floor space occupied by the open kitchen. The weekly lunch menu (served 11 A.M.–2 P.M. Tues.–Fri., $10) is hearty and unpretentious, and always features a couple of great veggie options. Bottomless herbal ice tea and service direct from the owner, who calls everyone "dear," are just icing on the cake. Dinner (5–9 P.M. Thurs.–Sat., $20) is a bit more showy, but the vibe is still very down to earth.

Good for a lunch break, or just a break from chile, **La Crêpe Michel,** tucked in a courtyard on the back side of the art museum (400 San Felipe St. NW, 505/242-1251, 11:30 A.M.–2 P.M. and 6–9 P.M. Tues.–Sat., 11:30 A.M.–2 P.M. Sun., $9), serves French standards—not just crepes, but also quiches and *croque monsieurs*—in a snug front room and a covered back patio.

With sandwiches made from house-smoked meats and mellow hip-hop on the stereo, the **Sunshine Café** (1134 Mountain Rd. NW, 505/242-1499, 6:30 A.M.–8 P.M. Mon.–Thurs., 6:30 A.M.–9 P.M. Fri., 8 A.M.–9 P.M. Sat., 8 A.M.–2 P.M. Sun.) is a cool spot in an up-and-coming area midway between Old Town and downtown. Every night there's a different special hot dish—a creative pasta, say—plus those sandwiches with house-smoked meats. Occasionally a band sets up in one corner.

New Mexican

Not far from the plaza, 🄲 **Duran Central Pharmacy** (1815 Central Ave. NW, 505/247-4141, 9 A.M.–6:30 P.M. Mon.–Fri., 9 A.M.–2 P.M. Sat., $6) is an old-fashioned lunch counter hidden behind the magazine rack in this big fluorescent-lit drugstore. Regulars pack this place at lunch for all the New Mexican staples: huevos rancheros, green-chile stew, and big enchilada plates. Cash only.

Hybrid New Mexican cuisine, the blend of indigenous ingredients such as pinto beans into Mexican dishes such as enchiladas, is everywhere; **Pueblo Harvest Café** (2401 12th St. NW, 505/843-7270, 8 A.M.–3 P.M. Mon.–Fri., 8 A.M.–5 P.M. Sat. and Sun., $8), at the Indian Pueblo Cultural Center, is one of the few places you can get "pure" American Indian food. Along with the usual enchiladas, expect earthy flavors, such as strong lamb and rich hominy, as well as frybread, the deep-fried delight that transcends all cultures. Breakfast is also good, with blue-corn pancakes and apple-raisin "Indian toast."

Steaks and Burgers

A big brown cinder-block building containing a package-liquor store, **Monte Carlo Steakhouse** (3916 Central Ave. SW, 505/831-2444, 11 A.M.–10 P.M. Mon.–Thurs, 11 A.M.–11 P.M. Fri. and Sat., $18) is not a gourmet experience—it's more of a time machine. Inside, it's a dim room full of vintage Naugahyde booths. Go for the prime rib if you're there for dinner Thursday through Saturday; otherwise, it's another cut of steak or a softball-size green-chile cheeseburger, served with hand-cut fries. Greek ownership means you get a tangy feta dressing on your salad and baklava for dessert. And even though the place adjoins a bar, you're still welcome to buy wine from the package store up front and have it with your dinner, for a nominal markup.

Despite the retro name and the menu of burgers and fountain treats, the **Route 66 Malt Shop** (1720 Central Ave. SW, 505/242-7866, 11 A.M.–8 P.M. Mon.–Sat., $5) is no hokey 1950s-theme diner. It's simply the real deal: an unpretentious short-order grill run by friendly people who work hard to make good food. For lunch, get a big BLT ("lots of bacon!" promises the menu) or a cheeseburger topped with extra-savory green chile. Then wash it down with a "black cow" (a Coke float with chocolate syrup and chocolate ice cream) or any other combo of syrup and ice cream you can dream up. An absolute must: the house-made root beer, an invigorating, not-too-sweet brew that's great on a hot day.

Dog House (1216 Central Ave. SW, 505/243-1019, $4) specializes not just in hot dogs, but in chile dogs, and has been doing so since the 1960s. (Don't like wieners? Get a green-chile cheeseburger instead. Or some tater tots.) The place is worth a visit for its neon sign alone: A dachshund wags its tail as it swallows up a link of sausages.

Fine Dining

The dressiest spot in Old Town, **Seasons**

(2031 Mountain Rd. NW, 505/766-5100, 5–9:30 P.M. daily, $23) focuses on grilled meats, and a slightly old-school menu (mmm—hot artichoke dip!), and loads of wine. Although the formal dining area is very nice (helped along with excellent service), the real treat is the rooftop cantina area, where you can enjoy tasty finger food and a view of Albuquerque's skyline. With lunch entrées around $10, this is also a good place for a midday treat (11:30 A.M.–2:30 P.M. Mon.–Fri.).

DOWNTOWN
With so many bars in this area, there's not much room left for food, beyond a couple of solid cafés.

Cafés
For either coffee and pastry or a full dinner with a glass of wine, head to **Gold Street Caffè** (218 Gold Ave. SW, 505/765-1633, 7 A.M.–2 P.M. Mon., 7 A.M.–10 P.M. Tues.–Fri., 8 A.M.–10 P.M. Sat., 8 A.M.–2 P.M. Sun., $10), where you can monopolize a sidewalk table while you sample food that tends toward light and fresh, from tuna niçoise salad to mussels in a red chile broth. It also serves full breakfasts—the de rigueur huevos rancheros alongside innovations such as poached eggs on green-chile brioche, as well as the dangerously addictive honey-chile glazed bacon.

A branch of **Flying Star** (723 Silver Ave. SE, 505/244-8099, 6 A.M.–10 P.M. Sun.–Thurs., 6 A.M.–11 P.M. Fri. and Sat., $9) occupies a hiply restored 1950 John Gaw Meem bank building—stop here for sustenance any time of day. See *The University and Nob Hill* listings for more on this minichain.

If you're on the go—or just prefer to soak up the sun on the 4th Street pedestrian walk—you can grab a delectable sandwich, hot or cold, from **❰ Relish** (411 Central Ave. NW, 505/248-0002, 11 A.M.–5 P.M. Mon.–Fri., $8)—its *cubano* is succulent, and even the coleslaw, studded with slices of green apple, has a special savor. Or you can pick up a cheap slice at **JC's New York Pizza Department** (215 Central Ave. NW, 505/766-6973,

11 A.M.–11 P.M. Sun.–Thurs., 11 A.M.–3 A.M. Fri. and Sat., $6), which specializes in thin-crust pies named after the five boroughs (Da Bronx: cured pepperoni and mozzarella).

Past the railroad tracks in EDo (East Downtown), **The Grove** (600 Central Ave. SE, 505/248-9800, 7 A.M.–4 P.M. Tues.–Sat., 8 A.M.–3 P.M. Sun., $9) complements its local-organic menu with an indoor-outdoor feel, with big front windows facing Central and a screened-in patio. The chalkboard menu features big, creative salads (spinach, orange slices, and dates is one combo) as well as sandwiches and cupcakes; breakfast, with farm-fresh local eggs and homemade English muffins, is served all day. It's a notch above Flying Star in price, but you're paying for the very high-quality ingredients.

A couple of blocks west, **Standard Diner** (320 Central Ave. SE, 505/243-1440, 11 A.M.–9:30 P.M. Mon.–Thurs., 11 A.M.–10 P.M. Fri. and Sat., 9 A.M.–9:30 P.M. Sun., $15) satisfies dinner cravings too. The place is in fact far from standard, with cucumber slices in the water and cotton dish towels for napkins. Each plate, from chicken-fried steak to a pork chop with baked beans, has special touches; there's also a big Sunday brunch menu. With deep booths, exposed brick walls, and flattering lighting, it feels more special than the menu prices would suggest, but it's still family friendly.

New Mexican
Even though it's in the middle of Albuquerque's main business district, **Cecilia's Café** (230 6th St. SW, 505/243-7070, 7 A.M.–2:30 P.M. Mon.–Fri., 8 A.M.–2 P.M. Sun., $7) feels more like a living room than an office. Maybe it's the woodstove in the corner—but more likely it's the personal attention from Cecilia and her daughters and the food that's clearly made with care. The rich, dark red chile really shines here.

Mexican
From the outside, **Juanita's** (910 4th St. SW, 505/843-9669, 7:30 A.M.–4:30 P.M. Mon.–Fri., 8 A.M.–4 P.M. Sat., $5.50) looks like an abandoned Dairy Queen. Inside, though, it's all color and activity—flower-print tablecloths

and lots of sizzle from the half-open kitchen, where hairnetted ladies build giant burritos, crispy tacos, and (most recommended) savory Mexican-style *tortas* (sandwiches) on pillowy white rolls. Jarritos sodas and imported, all-cane-sugar Coca-Cola wash it down. If you're getting your order to go, make sure you get some of the sharp red salsa.

Fine Dining

Since it opened in 1989, the **Artichoke Café** (424 Central Ave. SE, 505/243-0200, 11 A.M.–2:30 P.M. and 5:30–10 P.M. Mon.–Fri., 5:30–10 P.M. Sat., 5:30–9 P.M. Sun., $25) has been top on locals' lists for a dinner treat, largely because the husband-and-wife owners have varied the menu with the times without seeming desperately trendy—influences come from all over the globe (five-spice rubbed duck, pumpkin ravioli with ricotta), but dishes remain simple and unfussy. The blue-tinged dining room is simple without being austere, and the crowd is varied. Reservations are recommended—the 60 seats fill fast even on weeknights.

Dessert

For a sweet treat, stop in at **Cake Fetish** (3rd St. at Copper Ave., 505/243-3612, 7:30 A.M.–4 P.M. Mon.–Fri.) for a "Sleepless in Albuquerque" coffee cupcake, or **Theobroma** (319 Central Ave. NW, 505/247-0848, 10 A.M.–6 P.M. Mon.–Fri., noon–5 P.M. Sat.) for hand-dipped bonbons and other chocolaty delights, such as the UFO bar, a chocolate disk covered with pecans and covered in white chocolate. The shop also serves scoops of rich and creamy Taos Cow ice cream.

THE UNIVERSITY AND NOB HILL

Because of the large student population, this area has some great and varied spots to grab a cheap bite, but Nob Hill has some upscale options too.

Cafés

When you walk into **❰ Flying Star** (3416 Central Ave. SE, 505/255-6633, 6 A.M.–11:30 P.M. Mon.–Thurs., 6 A.M.–midnight Fri. and Sat., $9), you'll be mesmerized by the pastry case, packed with triple-ginger cookies, lemon-blueberry cheesecake, and fat éclairs. But try to look up to appreciate the range on the menu boards: Asian noodles, hot and cold sandwiches, mac-and-cheese, and enchiladas. With speedy service and a huge magazine selection, it's a great place to zip in or to lounge around (wireless Internet access is free). This is the original location of a long-running (20-plus years) minichain that's now all over the city—you'll find one in nearly every neighborhood, including the North Valley (4026 Rio Grande Blvd. NW, 505/344-6714) and downtown.

Just a few blocks from the university, **Annapurna Chai House** (2201 Silver Ave. SE, 505/262-2424, 7 A.M.–8 P.M. Mon.–Wed., 7 A.M.–9 P.M. Thurs.–Sat., 10 A.M.–2 P.M. Sun., $6) is a vegetarian's delight, serving a menu that's compatible with Ayurvedic dietary recommendations, with giant *masala dosas* (rice-flour crepes) as well as less strictly Indian dishes such as cardamom pancakes with maple syrup. Or just stop in for a refreshing spicy mango *lassi* or chai (distinctly different from the sort peddled in Starbucks). There's also free wireless access.

Pick up goods for a picnic at **La Montañita Co-op** (3500 Central Ave. SE, 505/265-4631, 7 A.M.–10 P.M. Mon.–Sat., 8 A.M.–10 P.M. Sun.), where quinoa salads and stuffed grape leaves are all the rage; look in the dairy section for "sampler" pieces of locally made cheese. There's a bigger branch just north of Old Town (2400 Rio Grande Blvd. NW, 505/242-8800, 8 A.M.–10 P.M. daily).

New Mexican

You haven't been to Albuquerque unless you've been to **❰ The Frontier Restaurant** (2400 Central Ave. SE, 505/266-0550, 5 A.M.–1 A.M. daily, $6), a mammoth diner across from UNM. Everyone in the city passes through its doors at some point in their lives, so all you have to do is pick a seat in one of the five Western-theme rooms (hmm, under the big portrait of John Wayne? Or maybe one of the

ALBUQUERQUE

© ZORA O'NEILL

The Frontier is the city's best spot for green-chile stew and people-watching.

smaller ones?) and watch the characters file in. You'll want some food, of course: a green-chile–smothered breakfast burrito filled with crispy hash browns, or a grilled hamburger, or one of the signature cinnamon rolls, a deadly amalgam of flour, sugar, and some addictive drug that compels you to eat them despite the hydrogenated goo they're swimming in. If you feel a little unhealthy, you can always get some fresh orange juice and restore your balance by vegging out in front of the mesmerizing tortilla machine.

Near the university, **El Patio** (142 Harvard Dr. SE, 505/268-4245, 11 A.M.–9 P.M. Mon.–Thurs., 11 A.M.–9:30 P.M. Fri. and Sat., noon–9 P.M. Sun., $9) is the kind of old-reliable place that ex-locals get misty-eyed about after they've moved away; the green-chile-and-chicken enchiladas are high on many citywide favorite lists. It doesn't hurt that the setting, in an old bungalow with a shady outdoor space, feels like an extension of someone's home kitchen.

Mexican
A branch of the popular Santa Fe purveyor of fresh and fast Mexican, **Bumble Bee's Baja Grill** (3423 Central Ave. NE, 505/262-2862, 11 A.M.–8 P.M. daily, $5) specializes in grilled fish tacos, but the meatier ones, including a stewed lamb filling, are delicious too. It also does roast chicken, grilled trout, and a couple of other full entrées ($11); there's also a great fresh salsa selection.

Brewpubs, and Just a Pub
Two places in Nob Hill make their own beer but have more of a restaurant feel. **Kelly's** (3222 Central Ave. SE, 505/262-2739, 8 A.M.–midnight daily, $9), formerly a gas station, is the city's most popular spot for patio dining and schmoozing. The rich Kelly Porter washes down beer-friendly food such as bison burgers and curly fries—not entirely inspired and often served by distracted waitstaff—but you're really here for the scene, the sun, and the suds.

Il Vicino (3403 Central Ave. NE, 505/266-7855, 11 A.M.–11 P.M. Sun.–Thurs., 11 A.M.–midnight Fri. and Sat., $7) has better food but lacks the expansive feel of Kelly's. Order at the front counter from the list of high-grade pizza toppings, and the dough promptly gets slid into the wood-fired oven at the back—or opt for a grilled *panino* sandwich or a big fresh salad. Then squeeze into your seat and enjoy your pint of Wet Mountain IPA while you wait; in keeping with the upscale pizza-joint feel, there are also wine and Italian sodas.

And one place doesn't make its own beer but has legions of fans for its fish-and-chips and other bar snacks: **O'Niell's** (4310 Central Ave. SE, 505/255-6782, 11:30 A.M.–2 A.M. Mon.–Sat., 11:30 A.M.–midnight Sun., $8), an Irish pub that also happens to have a very nice patio. It's packed for lunch, and the kitchen is open late.

Fine Dining
Even if you're not hankering for a big slab of meat, check out the classy **Gruet Steak House** (3201 Central Ave. NE, 505/256-9463, 5–10 P.M. daily, $29), housed in the pueblo-look Monte Vista fire station, built by the WPA in 1937. Though you can pick from six cuts of beef and a very tasty iceberg-and-blue-cheese

salad, you might want to stick just to appetizers, such as the grilled oysters, and a glass of wine as an excuse to enjoy the great patio that now occupies the spot where the fire trucks used to roll in and out. Local Gruet vintages are the centerpiece of the wine list, but you've got plenty of other options too.

All sleek black and silver inside, stylish **Nob Hill Bar & Grill** (3128 Central Ave. SE, 505/266-4455, 11 A.M.–10 P.M. Mon.–Sat., 11 A.M.–9 P.M. Sun.) is the domain of Sam Etheridge, renowned for his previous restaurant, Ambrozia. His newer effort is more casual, with hardly anything over $20 (or "20 bucks," in the folksy menu's parlance), and familiar dishes get a little twist of fancy: a crab BLT, for instance, or steak *frites* with a trio of homemade ketchups; salads are only "6 bucks." All-you-can-eat Sunday brunch ($20) is a gourmand's undoing: chocolate croissants alongside mole enchiladas and crab-cake Benedict.

ALBUQUERQUE METRO AREA

Great places to eat—particularly the best New Mexican places—are scattered all over the city, just as often in unlikely-looking strip malls as in intimate and luxurious historic properties. These places are worth making a trip for or will provide a pick-me-up when you're in a strange part of town.

Cafés

Stuck on a barren stretch of North 4th Street in Los Ranchos, where neighboring businesses are feed stores and car-repair shops, **Sophia's Place** (6313 4th St. NW, 505/345-3935, 7 A.M.–3 P.M. Mon., 7 A.M.–3 P.M. and 5–9 P.M. Tues.–Fri., 9 A.M.–2 P.M. and 5–9 P.M. Sat., 9 A.M.–2 P.M. Sun., $8) is a colorful gem that's well worth the drive, the sort of bohemian café that serves fresh farm eggs but doesn't brag about it. Get those eggs on a breakfast sandwich, which you're really ordering for the side of highly addictive red-chile-dusted home fries. If it's lunchtime, you can opt for a big bowl of noodles or a fat sandwich stuffed with your choice of grilled meats, and at dinner, there are duck tacos and other delicious things. In

any case, this is the sort of place where you'll want to laze around, reading the newspapers strewn about and musing over the oddball art and vintage calendars on the walls.

If, for some crazy reason, you're in Corrales and don't want to eat enchiladas at Perea's (page 172) for lunch, you can get a somewhat lighter meal at **Hannah & Nate's Market Café** (4512 Corrales Rd., 505/898-2370, 7 A.M.–2 P.M. daily, $7), which specializes in elaborate sandwiches, such as a New Mexico BLT (green chile, naturally, goes along with the holy trinity of sandwich components) and one made of *porchetta* (boneless pork roasted with herbs). There's also a full breakfast menu, with all manner of egg dishes as well as a dazzling variety of burritos.

New Mexican

Don't confuse the old location of **Los Cuates** (5016 Lomas Blvd. NE, 505/268-0974, 11 A.M.–9 P.M. daily, $8) with the newer place across the street. You want the 1979 original, which is an archetypal New Mexican restaurant. Its red vinyl booths have saggy springs; pebbled plastic water cups scrape on the glass tabletops; and you can hear the clink of ceramic and silverware from the dishwasher. The vinyl-encased menus offer combination plates and smaller choices *para los niños*. Everything's tasty, and make sure you get a basket of hot, puffy sopaipillas to mop it all up.

Experts agree: **Mary & Tito's Café** (2711 4th St. NW, 505/344-6266, 9 A.M.–6 P.M. Mon.–Thurs., 9 A.M.–8 P.M. Fri. and Sat., $7) is the place to go for *carne adovada,* the dish of tender pork braised in red chile. The only thing better is the "Mexican turnover," an uncooked flour tortilla filled with *carne adovada* and then deep-fried. But in fact, everything with red chile is delicious at this simple, home-style place north of downtown. You'll see locals cashing in their frequent-diner cards—even if you're in town for a short stay, you might want to get one.

Cruise down by the rail yards south of downtown to find **El Modelo** (1715 2nd St. SW, 505/242-1843, 7 A.M.–6:45 P.M. daily, $5), a local go-to for a hangover-curing *chicharrón* burrito, chile-smothered spare ribs, or tamales for the whole family. Because it's really a front for a tortilla factory, the flour tortillas are particularly tender, and you can order either a taco or a whole platter of food. If the weather's nice, grab a seat at a picnic table outside and watch the freight trains go by.

Just two blocks north of the National Hispanic Cultural Center, popular **❰ Barelas Coffee House** (1502 4th St. SW, 505/843-7577, 7:30 A.M.–3 P.M. Mon.–Fri., 7:30 A.M.–2:30 P.M. Sat., $6) can be confusing to the first-timer: The attraction is chile, not coffee—especially the red, which infuses hearty, timeless New Mexican standards such as posole, *chicharrones,* and menudo. The restaurant occupies several storefronts, and even then there's often a line out the door at lunch. But it's worth the wait—this is timeless food.

Out in Corrales, **Perea's Tijuana Bar & Restaurant** (4590 Corrales Rd., 505/898-2442, 11 A.M.–2 P.M. Mon.–Sat., $7) serves food at lunch only, but it's worth scheduling around if you know you'll be out this way. Everything's home cooked, from Frito pie to *carne adovada,* which has an earthy kick. You can eat inside the old adobe, with the regulars at the bar, or outside on a small patio.

Finally, **K & I Diner** (2500 Broadway SE,

505/243-1881, 6 A.M.–3 P.M. Mon.–Sat., 8 A.M.–2 P.M. Sun., $6) serves perhaps the most massive meal you will eat anywhere in New Mexico. It's a single dish, the Travis, an enormous burrito, bigger even than the heads of the high-school football players who come here to bulk up, is slathered in chile and topped with French fries. You can order a half-Travis, or even a quarter-Travis, but you'd better have a damn good excuse, such as a stapled stomach, if you opt for the eighth-Travis.

Asian

Can't decide what kind of food you're craving? Cruise the aisles of **Talin Market World Food Fare** (88 Louisiana Blvd. SE, 505/266-0755, 8:30 A.M.–8 P.M. Mon.–Sat., 9 A.M.–7 P.M. Sun.), a megamarket stocked with items from Bombay to the United Kingdom. Its Asian stock is the largest, though, and you can get a variety of hot Laotian, Korean, and Filipino lunch items from the small cafeteria section in one corner and sweets such as pumpkin custard from the bakery. A bubble-tea joint outside rounds out the meal. This corner across from the fairgrounds may be home to other ethnic eateries as part of the city's plan to develop the zone as a larger internationally flavored district.

Outside Albuquerque

In every direction from the city, you'll find some great natural attractions. To the west lies Acoma, an ancient pueblo that seems to have grown out of the tall, windswept mesa on which it's built, and the dramatic, wide-open scenery out this way is the stuff of movie backdrops. A winding road through the mountains southeast of town brings you past the ruined Salinas pueblo missions—an intriguing bit of early conquest history and little visited. South along I-40, the Rio Grande continues through its fertile valley to the Bosque del Apache, a lush network of marshlands maintained for migrating birdlife; the drive down is a long one, but you can make a day of it with stops

at out-of-the-way eateries and a scenic dirt-road route back. To the east is the start of one of three routes to Santa Fe, the Turquoise Trail, which leads through the vestiges of New Mexico's mining past. An equally scenic route north is the more circuitous Jemez Mountain Trail, past red rocks and hot springs. Or you can zip directly up the main highway, where you'll pass another remarkable bit of scenery, the windswept region known as Tent Rocks.

WEST TOWARD ACOMA

Heading out from Albuquerque, I-40 climbs the West Mesa and heads dead straight across

OUTSIDE ALBUQUERQUE

ALBUQUERQUE

© AVALON TRAVEL

a plateau lined with flat mesas—archetypal Southwest scenery. Although it's somewhat dull freeway driving, the trip out this way is well worth it, as ancient Acoma Pueblo is built on top of one of these mesas, an amazing place to visit and meet the people whose ancestors have lived here for nearly a thousand years.

Laguna Pueblo

About 18 miles west of Albuquerque, I-40 crosses the border onto the 45 square miles of Laguna Pueblo (505/552-6654, www.laguna pueblo.org), on which nearly 8,000 Keresan-speaking Ka-waikah (Lake People) live in six villages. From the highway, the only impression you get of Laguna is its Dancing Eagle Casino, but if you have time, it's worth getting off at Exit 114 to visit the **San José Mission Church** (8 A.M.–4:30 P.M. Mon.–Fri.). Built around 1700, it is immediately distinguished by its stark white stucco coating, but this is a relatively recent addition. Inside is the really distinctive element of the church: Between a packed-earth floor and a finely wrought wood ceiling, the fine late-18th-century altar screen commands the full focus of the room. It's the work of the unknown "Laguna Santero," an innovative painter who placed his icons inside a crowded field of decorative borders and carved and painted columns, creating a work of explosively colorful folk art that was copied elsewhere in the region in subsequent decades.

Each of the six villages of Laguna celebrates its own feast day, and then the whole pueblo turns out at the church September 17–19 for the Feast of San José, one of the bigger pueblo events in the Albuquerque area. Along with traditional dances and an arts-and-crafts market, the pueblo hosts the All-Indian Baseball Tournament, in which the very sports-minded pueblo fields five semipro teams.

◀ ACOMA PUEBLO

At Exit 102 off I-40, visitors to Acoma turn south. The road soon crosses up and over a ridge, and you may feel as though you've crossed through a pass into a Southwestern Shangri-La, for none of this great basin is

adobe houses at Acoma Pueblo

COURTESY OF ALBUQUERQUE CONVENTION & VISITORS BUREAU/© LYNN BAKER

visible from the highway. The route runs directly toward a flat-topped rock that juts out of the plain like a tooth.

Atop this rock is the original Acoma Pueblo, the village known as Sky City. The community covers about 70 acres and is built entirely of pale, sun-bleached adobe, as it has been since at least 1100. Given the hardships of no running water or electricity, only 50 or so people live on the mesa top year-round. But many families maintain homes here, and the place is thronged on September 2, when the pueblo members gather for the Feast of San Esteban. The rest of the 2,800 Acoma (People of the White Rock, in their native Keresan) live on the valley floor, which is used primarily as ranchland.

Visiting Sky City

The fragile nature of the windswept village accounts in part for the particularly stringent tourism policies. All visitors must stop at the **Sky City Cultural Center and Haak'u Museum** (Indian Rte. 23, 800/747-0181, www .skycity.com, 8 A.M.–7 P.M. daily May–Oct.,

8 A.M.–4 P.M. Nov.–Apr.) on the main road, which houses a small café and shop stocked with local crafts, along with beautiful rotating exhibits on Acoma art and tradition. From here, they must join a guided tour ($10), which transports groups by bus to the village. The one concession to modernity has been the carving of this road to the top; previously, all goods had to be hauled up the near-vertical cliff faces. The tour lasts one hour, after which visitors must return by bus, or they may hike down one of the old trails, using hand- and footholds dug into the rock centuries ago.

The centerpiece of the village is the **Church of San Esteban del Rey,** one of the most iconic of the Spanish missions in New Mexico. Built between 1629 and 1640, the graceful, simple structure has been inspiring New Mexican architects ever since. (Visitors are not allowed inside, however, nor into the adjoining cemetery.) As much as it represents the pinnacle of Hispano-Indian architecture in the 17th century, it's also a symbol of the Spanish brutality exercised in the early colonial period, as it rose in the typical way: forced labor. The men of Acoma felled and carried the tree trunks for the ceiling beams from the forest on Mt. Taylor, more than 25 miles across the valley, and up the cliff face to the village.

Acoma is well known for its pottery, easily distinguished by the fine black lines that sweep around the curves of the creamy-white vessel; on the best works, the lines are so fine and densely painted they appear almost like a moiré. Additionally, the clay particular to this area can be made extremely thin to create a pot that will hum or ring when you tap it. Throughout the village, you have opportunities to buy samples. Given the constraints of the tour, this can feel a bit high pressure, but in many cases, you have the privilege of buying a piece directly from the artisan who created it.

Accommodations and Food

The cultural center contains the **Yaak'a Café** ($6), which serves earthy local dishes such as mutton stew, posole, and bread made in traditional *horno* ovens—as well as Starbucks coffee. Acoma Pueblo operates the small-scale **Sky City Casino & Hotel** (888/759-2489, www.skycity.com, $69 s, $79 d), also at Exit 102. Its hotel rooms are a bit cookie-cutter but are reasonably priced.

SALINAS PUEBLO MISSIONS NATIONAL MONUMENT

Set on the plains behind the Manzano Mountains, the scenically decaying mud-brick buildings at Quarai, Gran Quivira, and Abó represent one of the Franciscans' bigger challenges during the early years of the conquest. The national monument designation actually applies to three separate sites. Visiting them all will take a full day, and the route (Highway 337, beginning in Tijeras, just east of the city) also passes by the little town of Mountainair, as well as one of the area's most beautiful fall hiking spots.

Tijeras

To reach Highway 337, take I-40 east to Exit 179. Settled in the 1850s, the village of Tijeras (Scissors, for the way the canyons meet here) is still a stronghold of old Hispano traditions, though it doesn't look too distinctive on the surface. Beginning the ascent along the mountains, you'll leave it behind in a matter of minutes. Very soon you'll pass the **Ponderosa Steakhouse** (10676 Hwy. 337, 505/281-8278, 4–11 P.M. Mon.–Fri., noon–midnight Sat. and Sun., $8), which is really more of a bar, populated by mountain men far more grizzled than you'd expect this close to the big city—this place represents the East Mountains of old, before the area was considered a suburb. But the steak is good—worth driving this route backward, in fact, if you want to end your day with dinner or a drink here.

Fourth of July Canyon

Past the Spanish land grant of Chililí (its terms have been contested ever since the Treaty of Guadalupe Hidalgo), Highway 337 runs into Highway 55—bear right and head to Tajique, and then turn onto Forest Road 55 to reach Fourth of July Canyon. The area in the foothills of the Manzanos, seven miles down the dirt road, is a destination in late September and early October, when the red maples and oak trees turn every shade of pink, crimson, and orange imaginable. (Amazingly, the place got its name not for this fireworks-like show of colors, but for the date an Anglo explorer happened across it in 1906.) It's also pretty in late summer, when the rains bring wildflowers. You can explore on the short **Spring Loop Trail** or **Crimson Maple Trail,** or really get into the woods on **Fourth of July Trail** (no. 173), which wanders into the canyon 1.8 miles and connects with **Albuquerque Trail** (no. 78) to form a loop.

Forest Road 55 loops back to meet Highway 55, but the second half, after the campground, can be very rough going. It's usually maintained in the fall, but at other times of the year, you might want to backtrack rather than carry on, especially if you're in a rental car.

Quarai

The first ruins you reach are those at Quarai (505/847-2290, 8:30 A.M.–5 P.M. daily in summer, 9 A.M.–5 P.M. daily in winter, free), a pueblo inhabited from the 14th to the 17th century. Like the other two Salinas pueblos, Quarai was a hardscrabble place with no natural source of water and very little food, though it did act as a trading outpost for salt, brought from small salt lakes farther east (hence the name). When the Franciscans arrived, then, they put more than the usual strain on this community of 400 or so Tiwa-speakers; they nonetheless managed to build a grand sandstone-and-adobe mission, the most impressive of the ones at these three pueblos. In addition to a struggle with the local population, the priests found themselves at odds with the Spanish governors, who helped protect them but also undermined their conversion work by encouraging ceremonial dances. At the same time, raids by Apaches increased because any crop surplus no longer went to them in trade, but to the Spanish. Oh, and there were terrible famines between 1663 and 1670. No wonder, then, that the place was abandoned even before

the Pueblo Revolt of 1680. Only the mission has been excavated; the surrounding hillocks are all pueblo structures.

Mountainair

Highway 55 meets U.S. 60 in the village of Mountainair, which hosts the **Salinas Pueblo Missions Visitors Center** (505/847-2585, 8 A.M.–5 P.M. daily), on U.S. 60 west of the intersection—though it offers not much more information than what's available at the small but detailed museums at each site. The **Mountainair ranger station** (505/847-2990, 8 A.M.–noon and 12:30–4:30 P.M. Mon.–Fri.) is also here.

Mountainair is home to the weird architectural treasure that is the **Shaffer Hotel** (103 Main St., 888/595-2888, www.shafferhotel .com), a 1923 pueblo deco confection with a folk-art twist, built by one Clem "Pop" Shaffer, who had a way with cast concrete—look for his name in the wall enclosing the little garden. Redone in late 2005, the hotel rooms ($79 s, $89 d) have dull beige carpet but beautiful antiques, old oil paintings, and attractive pedestal sinks in the bathrooms, some of which are shared. At last pass, there was no firm tenant in the hotel's dining room—if there's no café open, ask to look in at Shaffer's masterpiece: an elaborately carved and painted wood ceiling that's crawling with turtles, snakes, lizards, and other critters.

Gran Quivira

South from Mountainair 26 miles lies Gran Quivira—a bit of a drive, and you'll have to backtrack, but on the way you'll pass **Rancho Bonito,** another Pop Shaffer creation—his actual home. As it's private property, you can't go poking around, but from the road you can see a bit of the little log cabin painted in black, red, white, and blue. (If you happen to be in Mountainair in May for its art tour, the house is open to the public then.)

Where Highway 55 makes a sharp turn east, Gran Quivira (505/847-2770, 8:30 A.M.–5 P.M. daily in summer, 9 A.M.–5 P.M. daily in winter, free) looks different from the other two Salinas

© ZORA O'NEILL

a warren of interconnected rooms at Gran Quivira

pueblos because it is built of gray San Andres limestone slabs, not sandstone, and finished with plaster that was painted with symbols. It's the largest of the three, with an estimated population between 1,500 and 2,000, likely devoted to trade, as the large array of feathers and pottery styles found here indicate. Like the people of Abó, the residents spoke Tompiro, and the Spanish dubbed them Los Rayados (The Striped) for the decorations they wore on their faces. It appears they outwardly accepted the Franciscan mission after the first sermon was preached here in 1627. But they took their own religion literally underground, building hidden kivas underneath the residential structures even as they toiled on two successive missions ordered by the Catholics. Nonetheless, the place was deserted by 1671, after more than a third of the people had starved to death.

Abó

From Gran Quivira, drive back the way you came and turn west on U.S. 60 in Mountainair to reach Abó (505/847-2400, free), nine miles on. The visitors center here has the same hours as the other sites (8:30 A.M.–5 P.M. daily in summer, 9 A.M.–5 P.M. daily in winter), but the ruins themselves are open all the time— it's nice to drop by here just as the setting sun is enhancing the red glow of the rocks. Abó was the first pueblo the Franciscans visited, in 1622; the mission here, constructed over more than 60 years, shows details such as old wood stairs leading to the choir loft. (The Franciscans were so dedicated to re-creating the Catholic church experience here in the desert that they brought in portable pipe organs and trained their converts to sing.) Unlike Gran Quivira, though, Abó seems to have had some agreement regarding kivas, as there is one built right in the center of the *convento* (the compound adjoining the mission), dating from the same period—something that no archaeologist or historian has yet explained. The excellent condition of all of these ruins is due in part to a family that owned the land from the mid-19th century on—one member, Federico Sisneros, is buried near the mission, at his request.

From Abó, you can continue west through the mountain pass and then down into the

© ZORA O'NEILL

the ruins at Abó

long, flat Rio Grande Valley on U.S. 60, which runs straight into I-25 at Bernardo; if you're heading back to Albuquerque, you can take Highway 47 northwest to Belén, about 25 miles closer to the city.

SOUTH TO THE BOSQUE DEL APACHE

If you haven't gotten enough of the area's bird-life along the Rio Grande in the city, head to the Bosque del Apache bird sanctuary, which is the site of an awe-inspiring fly-in of giant sandhill cranes during November and hosts hundreds of other migratory species in the fall and winter. On the way there or back, you can strike out into truly remote New Mexico along the Quebradas Scenic Backcountry Byway.

Socorro

Once a pueblo that offered food to conquistador Don Juan de Oñate, Socorro (Succor, or Relief) now shelters the students of the **New Mexico Institute of Mining & Technology** (a.k.a. New Mexico Tech, 575/835-5011, www.nmt.edu),

which has been training engineers since 1889. The town has a small time-warp historic plaza, but the mission-style campus is scenic as well. To reach it, turn west from the main north–south route, California Street, onto Bullock Street and follow it toward the hills.

Wet your whistle at the **Capitol Bar** (575/835-1193, noon–2 A.M. Mon.–Sat., noon–midnight Sun.) on the plaza, which doesn't seem to have changed much in its century of doing business—this is one of those dim, swinging-door saloons that you thought existed only on movie sets. **Manzanares Street Coffeehouse** (110 Manzanares St., 575/838-0809, 6 A.M.–10 P.M. daily), just off the plaza, is a popular non-alcoholic hangout.

For a full meal, try the **Stage Door Grill** (115 Abeyta St., 866/889-7124, 11 A.M.–1 P.M. Mon.–Sat., $10), just off the plaza, or **Socorro Springs** (1012 N. California St., 575/838-0650, 6:30 A.M.–10 P.M. Mon.–Fri., 8 A.M.–10 P.M. Sat. and Sun., $9), a brewpub on the north end of the main drag through town that serves everything from morning coffee and omelets to late-night flame-grilled burgers and creative pizzas. Another local favorite is **Frank & Lupe's El Sombrero Café** (210 Mesquite St. NE, 575/835-3945, 11 A.M.–9 P.M. daily, $7), where the salsa verde is especially tasty; it's just east of I-25 on the north side (Exit 150).

As for accommodations, chain motels are the only real options here; if you want something with a bit more character, head down the road to Magdalena.

San Antonio

Even though it's just a blip on the map, this town supports two great burger joints: the ◖ **Owl Bar & Café** (U.S. 380, 575/835-9946, 8 A.M.–9 P.M. Mon.–Sat., $5), which has always gotten all the press, and the lesser-known **Manny's Buckhorn** (U.S. 380, 575/835-4423, 11 A.M.–8 P.M. Mon.–Sat., $5), just across the street. Both serve beer and green-chile cheeseburgers, both have chummy local staff and plenty of lore—so how to choose? Go to the Owl if you like your burgers thin, to Manny's if you like them a little fatter. Actually, the Owl gets an extra point for historic detail: The bar here is from the world's first Hilton hotel—not part of Conrad Hilton's international chain, but the one opened by his father when he moved here in the 1880s; Conrad was born shortly thereafter, grew up to be his father's business partner, and went on to develop hotel properties around the world. The Owl's owners salvaged the bar after the structure surrounding it burned.

If you want to wake up and get straight to the birds, **Casa Blanca B&B** (13 Montoya St., San Antonio, 575/835-3027, www.casablanca bedandbreakfast.com, $80 d) can put you up for the night in one of three cozy rooms in an 1880 Victorian farmhouse; it's open only October–May. You can camp at the **Bosque Birdwatchers RV Park** (575/835-1366, open year round, $20), just 100 yards north of the reserve border on Highway 1.

Bosque del Apache National Wildlife Refuge

Occupying 57,191 acres on either side of the Rio Grande, this bird sanctuary is in a sense a manufactured habitat: Controlled flooding creates the marshes that draw the birds, which find food on farm plots dedicated to tasty grains. But this is really restoring a process that happened naturally before the Rio Grande was dammed. The birds certainly have no objection. Arctic geese, sandhill cranes, bald eagles, and a whole variety of ducks happily settle in for the winter. In the spring, migratory warblers and pelicans stop off on their way back to points north, while great blue herons make their spring nests here. Summer is relatively quiet, as only the year-round species remain: hummingbirds, swallows, flycatchers, and the like.

Five miles inside the north border of the reserve, you pass the **visitors center** (7:30 A.M.–4 P.M. Mon.–Fri., 8 A.M.–4:30 P.M. Sat. and Sun.), where you can pick up maps and find out which birds have been spotted that day. A bit farther south on Highway 1, a 12-mile paved car loop passes through all the marshlands and the grain fields; at certain points along the drive, you can get out and

hike set trails, such as a quarter-mile boardwalk across a lagoon or a trail to the river. Some areas are open to mountain bikers. The loop drive opens when birdlife is at its best, one hour before sunrise; cars need to be out by an hour after dark. With all its marshland, the *bosque* could just as well be called a mosquito sanctuary—slather on plenty of repellent before you start your drive.

The biggest event of the year is the arrival of the sandhill cranes—they were the inspiration for the refuge, as their population had dwindled to fewer than 20 in 1941, but now more than 15,000 of these graceful birds with six-foot wingspans winter over in the *bosque*. They're celebrated annually at the five-day **Festival of the Cranes** (www.friendsofthe bosque.com) in November, when birders gather to witness the mass morning liftoffs and evening fly-ins.

Quebradas Backcountry Scenic Byway

This 24-mile dirt road cuts across several deep arroyos, or natural drainage channels—these are the *quebradas* ("breaks") in the earth that give the area its name. The rounded hills here are striped with rainbow hues, and the scrub desert teems with hawks, mule deer, and foxes. The route makes a good slow way back to Albuquerque if you've come down early in the morning to see the birds (though you could just as easily drive down this way and hit the *bosque* near sunset). The drive takes between two and three hours, but bear in mind that this is remote wilderness—be sure you have extra food and water, as well as a spare tire. Don't attempt it if it has rained very recently, as the mud can be impossible to pass, and look out for sandy patches at all times.

From the intersection of the *bosque* road (Highway 1) in San Antonio, in front of the Owl Café, head east on U.S. 380 for 11 miles; then turn north on County Road A-129, the beginning of the byway. Coming from Albuquerque is a little trickier: Leave I-25 at Escondida (Exit 152, south of Lemitar) and then go north on the east frontage road; turn east after you pass Escondida Lake, cross the river, and continue for about two miles to Pueblito, where you turn right at a T intersection. After about a mile, you will see a sign for the byway beginning on your left (east).

THE TURQUOISE TRAIL

This scenic back route to Santa Fe, which runs along the east side of the Sandia Mountains and up across high plateaus, revisits New Mexico's mining history as it passes through a series of ghost towns. Take I-40 east from Albuquerque to Exit 175. Bear right to go into the village of Tijeras and the **Sandia ranger station** (505/281-3304) if you want to pick up hiking maps to the area. Otherwise, bear left to continue directly to the junction with Highway 14, the beginning of the Turquoise Trail.

The four-lane road heads north through alternating communities of old Spanish land grants and modern subdivisions collectively referred to as the East Mountains. Practically an Albuquerque suburb, the area still preserves its independence—this might be the only place in the United States that a Blockbuster was forced to close because of a community boycott. Meet the feisty locals at the **Greenside Café** (12165 Hwy. 14, 505/286-2684, 11 a.m.–8 p.m. Mon.–Thurs., 11 a.m.–9 p.m. Fri., 8 a.m.–9 p.m. Sat., 8 a.m.–8 p.m. Sun., $8), a casual place with fresh American standards; it's just south of the Triangle Grocery in Cedar Crest.

◖ Tinkertown Museum

Six miles up Highway 14, you come to a large triangle intersection—to the left is Highway 536, the Crest Road up to Sandia Peak, a beautiful winding drive through steadily thinning forests until you reach the exposed top of the mountain, more than 10,000 feet above sea level and more than 5,500 feet above the center of Albuquerque. Even if you don't drive to the peak, do head 1.5 miles up the Crest Road to Tinkertown Museum (505/281-5233, 9 a.m.–6 p.m. daily Apr.–Oct., $3), a temple to efficient use of downtime. Ross Ward, an artist and sign painter who learned his trade doing banners for carnivals, was also a master

THE TURQUOISE TRAIL

© AVALON TRAVEL

SALINAS PUEBLO MISSIONS NATIONAL MONUMENT

Quarai Ruins

SALINAS PUEBLO MISSIONS National Monument
New Mexico

The majestic Spanish mission church of Nuestra Señora de la Purísima Concepción de Cuarac (ca. 1630-77). Here Franciscan friars labored to convert the Tiwa-speaking Pueblo Indians of Quarai to Christianity. The Tiwa people who lived in the surrounding pueblo (unexcavated) built the church. Photographer – Baker Aerial Photography

19171

www.impactphotographics.com

THIS AREA FOR OFFICIAL POSTAL USE ONLY

0 45622 90012 3

BIRDING ON THE PEAK

Sandia Peak in the dead of winter does not seem hospitable to life in any form, much less flocks of delicate-looking birds the size of your fist, hopping around cheerfully in the frigid air. But that's precisely what you'll see if you visit in the iciest months, particularly right after a big snowfall. The feathered critters in question are rosy finches, a contrary, cold-loving variety (sometimes called "refrigerator birds") that migrate from as far north as the Arctic tundra to the higher elevations of New Mexico, which must seem relatively tropical by comparison.

What's special about Sandia is that it draws all three species of rosy finch, which in turn draws dedicated birders looking to add the finches to their "life lists." *Birder's World* magazine praises Sandia Peak as "the world's most accessible location to see all three species of rosy finches." This is a boon for people who are more accustomed to kayaking through swamps and slogging through tropical forests to spot rare species. So if you see the finches – they're midsize brown or black birds with pink bellies, rumps, and wings – you'll probably also spy some human finch fans. But they might not have time to talk, as it's not unheard-of for the most obsessive birders – those on their "big year," out to spot as many species as possible in precisely 365 days – to fly into Albuquerque, drive to the crest, eyeball the finches, and drive right back down and fly out in search of even more obscure varieties.

odd collectibles, for instance; the museum, like an amoeba, even seems to have taken over a friend and neighbor's 35-foot wooden boat. Ward died in 2002; his family keeps up the museum, and even though it's no longer growing as it used to, it remains a remarkable piece of pure folk art.

Golden

Back on Highway 14, continue north through rolling hills and ever-broader sky. After 15 miles, you reach the all-but-gone town of Golden—so named because it was the site of the first gold strike west of the Mississippi, in 1825. But all that's left now is a handful of homes, an attractive adobe church, and one store, **Golden General Merchandise** (10 A.M.–3:30 P.M. Tues.–Sat.), open since 1918. Pop in if you happen to be there during its limited opening hours; it's largely given over to Indian jewelry and pottery, but prices are reasonable and quality is generally quite high. Antique trinkets line the upper shelves, remnants of Golden's moment of glory.

Madrid

Thirteen miles beyond Golden, and about midway along the drive, Madrid (pronounced MAD-rid by locals) is a ghost town back from the dead. Built by the Albuquerque & Cerrillos Coal Co. in 1906, it once housed 4,000 people, but it was deserted by the end of World War II, when natural gas came into use. By the late 1970s, though, a few of the swaybacked wood houses had been reoccupied by hippies who were willing to live where indoor plumbing was barely available. Through the decades, Madrid slowly revived; portable toilets are still more common than flush models, but the arts scene has flourished, and a real sense of community pervades the main street, which is dressed in gaudy lights at Christmas and lined with pretty painted bungalows. Galleries line the main street—the typical itinerary is just a stroll down and back, perhaps with a stop on the porch of the Old Boarding House Mercantile to chat with various bearded "Madroids," the old-timers who may or may not be models for

ALBUQUERQUE

whittler and creative engineer who built, over 40 years, thousands of elaborate miniature figures and dioramas out of wood, some of which he animated with tiny pulleys and levers: a man with a cleaver chases chickens in a circle, circus performers soar, the blacksmith's bellows huff and puff. Many of the buildings themselves are also Ward's creations—undulating walls made of bottles and studded with the locally produced *Nude Geezers* pinup calendar. Particularly outside the summer months, try to come through on a weekend, as opening hours can be erratic otherwise.

You can learn more about Madrid's history at the **Old Coal Mine Museum** (Hwy. 14, 505/438-3780, 9:30 A.M.–5:30 P.M. daily June–Aug., 10 A.M.–5 P.M. Sat. and Sun. Sept.–May, $5), where you can wander among sinister-looking machine parts and even walk partway down an abandoned mine shaft—a great disciplinary tool for kids who've been acting up in the car. You'll feel the "ghost" in "ghost town" here. If the Old West costume photo studio in the lobby doesn't sate your desire for old-timey fun, you can stay for a show at the **Engine House Theatre** (505/438-3780, 3 P.M. and 7 P.M. Sat., 3 P.M. Sun., $10), where local hams play out a classic melodrama inside an atmospherically drafty repair shed (call ahead to reserve).

A more vibrant remnant of Madrid's company-town days is the **Mine Shaft Tavern**

© ZORA O'NEILL

Belly up to the 40-foot-long pine-pole bar at the Mine Shaft Tavern.

(2846 Hwy. 14, 505/473-0743, 11 A.M.–10 P.M. Mon.–Sat.), where you can belly up to a 40-foot-long pine-pole bar, over which hang murals by local artist Ross Ward, who built the Tinkertown Museum in Sandia Park. "It is better to drink than work," reads the Latin inscription interwoven among the mural panels, and certainly everyone in the bar, from long-distance bikers to gallery hoppers, is living by those encouraging words.

As for food, head straight to **Mama Lisa's Ghost Town Kitchen.** When it's open (seemingly not on a regular basis, but chances are better in the summer), it's a true treat, a cozy place with an all-over-the-map menu: buffalo chalupas, Austrian-style pork chops, rhubarb pie, and hibiscus mint tea, which you can enjoy out on the tree-shaded front patio (entrées are about $10). When it's closed, all you can do is press your face against the window and dream—or go down the street to **Java Junction** (2855 Hwy. 14, 505/438-2772, from 7:30 A.M. daily) for coffee.

During summers only, the **Miner's Chuckwagon,** midway through town, sells cheap and tasty sausage biscuits and coffee in the mornings and doles out pit barbecue for lunch, for less than $10.

Cerrillos

By contrast with Madrid, Cerrillos, once the source of turquoise that has been traced to Chaco Canyon, Spain, and Chichén Itzá in Mexico's Yucatán Peninsula, hasn't been gallerified like its neighbor down the road. A trading post sells cow skulls, antique bottles, taxidermied jackalopes, and turquoise nuggets; an adjacent petting zoo has a llama and a sheep. And there's one bar, **Mary's,** whose proprietress is into her 10th decade of life and has been running the place since 1977. The bar doesn't look particularly open from the outside, but do stop in and have a beer and a chat with Mary Mora, who can tell some fine tales of putting unruly drunks in their place (including the cast of *Young Guns,* which was filmed here). You can go **horseback riding** through the canyon (Broken Saddle Riding Co., 505/424-7774, the oldest watering hole on the Turquoise Trail

© ZORA O'NEILL

www.brokensaddle.com, $75 for two hours) and in **Cerrillos Hills Historic Park** (head north across the railroad tracks; www.cerrillos hills.org), more than 1,000 acres of rolling hills and narrow canyons that are also good for mountain biking.

After ascending from the canyons around Cerrillos onto a high plateau (look out for antelope), you're on the home stretch to Santa Fe—but you'll pass one more dining option, the (**San Marcos Café** (3877 Hwy. 14, 505/471-9298, 8 a.m.–2 p.m. Tues.–Sun., $10), which shares space with a working feed store where vain peacocks have replaced the usual farm chickens. Breakfast in the country-style dining room (a potbellied stove lurks in one corner) is especially delicious, with deliciously flaky cinnamon rolls, homemade chicken sausage, and a variety of fresh-tasting egg dishes.

From here, Highway 14 continues to become Cerrillos Road, the very slow and unscenic way into Santa Fe; the more direct route is via I-25 to Old Santa Fe Trail. Keep an eye out for the highway on-ramp—signs point to Las Vegas.

THE JEMEZ MOUNTAIN TRAIL

Beginning just northwest of Albuquerque, the Jemez (HAY-mez) Mountain Trail is an exceptionally beautiful drive through Jemez Indian Reservation, the Santa Fe National Forest, and the Valles Caldera National Preserve. It's the most roundabout way of getting to Santa Fe—you actually wind up near Los Alamos and must backtrack a bit south to reach town—but nature lovers will want to set aside a full day for the trip, which is especially beautiful in the fall, when the aspen leaves turn vivid yellow against the rich red stones. The drive begins on U.S. 550, which goes northwest out of the satellite town of Bernalillo, just west of I-25. At the village of San Ysidro, bear right onto Highway 4, which forms the major part of the route north.

Jemez Pueblo

This community of about 3,000 tribal members settled in the area in the late 13th century, and Highway 4 runs through the middle of

Battleship Rock is a landmark north of Jemez Springs.

the 89,000 acres it still maintains; before the Spanish arrived, the Hemish people (which the Spanish spelled Jemez) had established more than 10 large villages in the area. One of the few pueblos in the area that has not opened a casino, it's quite conservative and closed to outsiders except for ceremonial dances; because Jemez absorbed members of Pecos Pueblo in 1838, it celebrates two feast days, San Diego's (November 12) and San Persingula's (August 2). It's also the only remaining pueblo where residents speak the Towa language, the rarest of the related New Mexico languages (Tewa and Tiwa are the other two). The pueblo operates the **Walatowa Visitors Center** (505/834-7235, www.jemezpueblo.org, 8 A.M.–5 P.M. daily Apr.–Dec., 10 A.M.–4 P.M. daily Jan.–Mar.), about five miles north of San Ysidro. The center is easy to miss because you'll be gawking off the east side of the road at the lurid red sandstone cliffs at the mouth of the **San Diego Canyon;** vendors selling traditional Indian frybread are another tasty distraction. The visitors center has exhibits about the local

geology and the people of Jemez and doubles as a ranger station, dispensing maps and advice on outdoor recreation farther up the road, such as hiking trails, campgrounds, fishing access points, and the various hot springs that well up out of crevices all through the Jemez Mountains.

Jemez Springs

This charming small resort town—really just a handful of little clapboard buildings tucked in the narrow valley along the road—is the most convenient place to indulge in some of the area's springs, which are a stew of minerals and trace elements such as lithium that have inspired tales of miraculous healing since tourists began visiting in the 1870s. **Giggling Springs** (Hwy. 4, 575/829-9175, www.giggling springs.com, 11 A.M.–sunset Tues.–Sun. June–Aug., Wed.–Sun Sept.–May, $15/hour or $35/day), built in the 1880s, has a luxe-meets-rough feel, with a relatively small spring-fed pool enclosed in an attractively landscaped flagstone area right near the Jemez River. The **Jemez Springs Bath House** (Hwy. 4, 505/829-3303, www.jemezspringsbath house.com, 10 A.M.–8 P.M. daily May–Sept., 10 A.M.–6 P.M. Mon.–Thurs., 10 A.M.–8 P.M. Fri. and Sat. Oct.–Apr., $15/hour) is operated by the village; here, the springs have been diverted into eight individual private soaking tubs; call ahead to reserve. Massages and other spa treatments are available.

For a bite to eat, **Consetta's, the Green Restaurant** (Hwy. 4, 505/829-4455, 11 A.M.–8 P.M. Wed.–Mon. May–Oct., $12), on the south edge of town, serves veggie-friendly fare such as miso pesto, as well as eggplant parmesan and crisp-crust pizzas from its solar-powered kitchen; in the spring and fall, call first to check hours. Just south of the two bathhouses, the **Laughing Lizard** (Hwy. 4, 505/829-3108, $10) is also tasty, and open a bit more of the year than Consetta's. If you're just craving a burger after your bath, head to **Los Ojos Restaurant & Saloon** (Hwy. 4, 505/829-3547, 11 A.M.–8:30 P.M. Sun.–Thurs., 11 A.M.–9 P.M. Fri. and Sat., $8), where horseshoes double as window grills and the atmosphere hasn't changed in decades.

If you're planning to explore the wilderness and missed the Walatowa Visitors Center at Jemez Pueblo, you can stop at the **Jemez Ranger District Office** (Hwy. 4, 505/829-3535, 8 A.M.–5 P.M. Mon.–Fri.) for info. There's also a **visitors center for Valles Caldera National Preserve** (Hwy. 4, 505/661-3333, 8 A.M.–4:30 P.M. Mon.–Fri.) here too—stop in to arrange reservations for the park, or to see if there are last-minute openings. Both are on the north edge of town.

Jemez State Monument

Just north of Jemez Springs, you pass this set of ruins (Hwy. 4, 505/829-3530, 8:30 A.M.–5 P.M. daily, $3), where the ancestors of the present Jemez people settled more than 700 years ago and lived until the Pueblo Revolt of 1680. More striking than the old pueblo, which was named Giusewa, is the crumbling Franciscan mission that rises in the middle of it. The convent and church of San José de los Jémez were built around 1620, using forced labor from the pueblo; the result was remarkably lavish, but the friars had abandoned their work by 1640, probably because they'd thoroughly antagonized their would-be parishioners. Today the remnants of the two different cultures have nearly dissolved back into the earth from which they were both built, but the church's unique octagonal bell tower has been reconstructed to good effect. The place is closed Tuesdays in the winter; pay $5 admission, and you can also visit Coronado State Monument, on the north edge of Albuquerque, on the same day.

A couple of curves in the highway past the monument, you pass the rocks of **Soda Dam** off the right side of the road. The pale, bulbous mineral accretions that have developed around this spring resemble nothing so much as the top of a root-beer float, with a waterfall crashing through the middle. You can't really get in the water here, but it's a good photo op.

Hot Springs

Outside of the town of Jemez Springs, there

are several other places you can take a dip. Five miles north, where the red rocks of the canyon have given way to steely-gray stone and Battleship Rock looms above the road, is the trail to **McCauley Springs.** These require a two-mile hike along East Fork Trail but are an excellent motivator for a not-too-strenuous climb. The day-use parking area (no fee) is just north of the turn for Battleship Rock Picnic Area; follow signs from here for trail no. 137. Follow the trail until it meets a small stream flowing down from your left (north) and then walk up the creek about a quarter mile to the spring, which has been diverted so it flows into a series of pools of ever-cooler temperatures (only 85°F at most points). Because the trail runs along the streambed, though, it's usually impassable in the high-flow winter and spring.

The most accessible pools are **Spence Springs,** about 1.6 miles north of the parking area for the McCauley Springs Trail. A sign marks a parking area on the east side of the road, and the trail to the springs starts immediately south of the dirt pullout. A short hike (0.4 mile) leads down to the river and then up the steep hillside to two sets of 100°F pools. The place is well known, and although there are signs insisting on clothing, don't be surprised if you encounter some people bathing nude.

San Antonio Springs require the most effort to reach, but they're a good reward for the trek, five miles up Forest Road 376 (closed to motor vehicles). To reach the road, first turn off Highway 4 at La Cueva Lodge, continuing on Highway 126 for about 3.5 miles and parking at the gate blocking the forest road. From there, it's a straight shot until a smaller road near a cabin leads downhill to the right; cross the creek and head straight uphill, about a quarter mile, to the pools, which enjoy great views of the valley.

Hiking

Several trails run through Jemez, but the best one for a day hike is the **East Fork Trail** (no. 137), which runs from Battleship Rock Picnic Area to Las Conchas. At 10 miles one-way, the full route is a bit ambitious for a full day, so it's preferable to start the trail where it crosses Highway 4, about three miles after the highway makes its hairpin turn southeast, when you descend a bit and enter a small valley. From this point, the eastern half of the trail, about 4.5 miles one-way, is the most scenic, following a stream up through a pine forest, where wild berries grow in the summer; or you can head west one mile to Jemez Falls, where water cascades through a narrow canyon.

◖ Valles Caldera National Preserve

Spreading out for 89,000 acres to the north of Highway 4, this protected parkland (866/382-5537, www.vallescaldera.gov) is a series of vast green valleys, rimmed by the edges of a volcano that collapsed into a huge bowl millennia ago. At the center is rounded Redondo Peak (11,254 feet). It was originally a private ranch—the U.S. government bought the land in 2000 and then created an experimental structure to manage the new preserve, with

the goal of making the area self-sustaining, independent of government funds. To this end, use fees are high (starting at $10 per person), and you must make reservations at least 24 hours ahead of time online, as there are restrictions on how many people may enter the park each day. The reward is a hike through land that feels utterly untouched, where you might see herds of elk grazing and eagles winging across the huge dome of the sky. Hiking is best June–September, but the park is open in winter for cross-country skiing, and there are limited elk-hunting and fishing seasons. In addition to exploring on your own, a full roster of guided activities is available: group day hikes, full-moon snowshoeing and sleigh rides, overnight winter yurt camping, tracking classes, horseback riding, and more.

If you haven't planned for a stop here, you can still use the **Coyote Call Trail,** a 3.5-mile loop off the south side of Highway 4, and the **Valle Grande Trail** (two miles round-trip), off the north, without reservations.

Past Valles Caldera, Highway 4 goes into

the basin of Valles Caldera

© ZORA O'NEILL

© ZORA O'NEILL

Kasha-Katuwe Tent Rocks National Monument

Bandelier National Monument (covered in detail under *Outside Santa Fe* in the *Santa Fe* chapter). If you're carrying on to Santa Fe, go through White Rock and join Highway 502, which leads through Pojoaque to U.S. 285, which then goes south to the capital.

THE INTERSTATE TO SANTA FE

The most direct route north to Santa Fe is along I-25, a drive of about 60 miles. The road, which passes through the broad valley between the Sandia and Jemez mountain ranges, is not as scenic as other routes, but it does cross wide swaths of undeveloped pueblo lands (Sandia, San Felipe, and Santo Domingo) with impressive vistas. You also have the opportunity to detour to one of the region's most striking natural phenomena, **Kasha-Katuwe Tent Rocks National Monument** (Forest Rd. 266, 7 A.M.–7 P.M. daily Apr.–Oct., 8 A.M.–5 P.M. daily Nov.–Mar., $5/car), where the wind-whittled clusters of volcanic pumice and tuff do indeed resemble enormous tepees, some up to 90

feet tall. To reach the parklands, leave I-25 at Exit 259 and head west toward Cochiti Pueblo on Highway 22, and then turn south in front of Cochiti Dam, which blots out the horizon around mile 15. From the parking area, you have the choice of two short trails: an easy, relatively flat loop runs up to the base of the rocks, passing a small cave, while a longer option runs 1.3 miles into a narrow canyon where the rock towers loom dramatically on either side. The latter trail is level at first, but the last stretch is steep and requires a little clambering.

On your way out from the hike, you can drive through **Cochiti Pueblo,** the northernmost Keresan-speaking pueblo, which claims its ancestors inhabited some of the ruins found at Bandelier National Monument. The traditional core of the community is still two ancient adobe kivas; the people who live in the surrounding houses sell craftwork. Nearby **Cochiti Lake** (reached by continuing along Highway 22 past the dam) is a popular summer destination for boaters, though it's not particularly scenic.

Information and Services

TOURIST INFORMATION

The Albuquerque Convention and Visitors Bureau (800/284-2282, www.itsatrip.org) offers the most detailed information on the city, maintaining a kiosk on the Old Town plaza in the summer and a desk at the airport near the baggage claim (9:30 A.M.–8 P.M. daily). The New Mexico Tourism Department has an office at the Indian Pueblo Cultural Center (2401 12th St. NW). The City of Albuquerque website (www.cabq.gov) is very well organized, with all the essential details about city-run attractions and services.

Books and Maps

Albuquerque's largest independent bookstore is **Page One** (11018 Montgomery Blvd. NE, 505/294-2026, 9 A.M.–10 P.M. Mon.–Sat., 9 A.M.–8 P.M. Sun.), which has given the megachains a run for their money since 1981. More centrally located, the **University of New Mexico bookstore** (2301 Central Ave. NE, 505/277-5451, 8 A.M.–6 P.M. Mon.–Fri., 10 A.M.–5 P.M. Sat.) maintains a good stock of travel titles and maps, along with state history tomes and the like. On the west side, **Bookworks** (4022 Rio Grande Blvd. NW, 505/344-8139, 9 A.M.–9 P.M. Mon.–Sat., 9 A.M.–7:30 P.M. Sun.) is a great resource, with a large stock of New Mexico–related work as well as plenty of other titles, all recommended with the personal care of the staff.

Local Media

Albuquerque supports the daily *Journal,* which publishes cultural-events listings in its Friday entertainment supplements. On Wednesdays, pick up the new issue of the free weekly *Alibi* (www.alibi.com), which will give you a hipper, more critical outlook on city goings-on, from art openings to city council debates.

Radio

KUNM (89.9 FM) is the university's radio station, delivering eclectic music, news from NPR and PRI, and local-interest call-in shows such as *Native America Calling.* KANW (89.1 FM) is a project of Albuquerque Public Schools, with an emphasis on New Mexican music of all stripes, but particularly mariachi and other traditional forms; it also carries a lot of the most popular NPR programs.

SERVICES
Banks

Banks are plentiful, and grocery stores and pharmacies increasingly have ATMs inside. Downtown, look for **New Mexico Bank & Trust** (320 Gold Ave. SW, 505/830-8100, 9 A.M.–4 P.M. Mon.–Thurs., 9 A.M.–5 P.M. Fri.). In Nob Hill, look for **Wells Fargo** on Central at Dartmouth (3022 Central Ave. SE, 505/265-0365, 9 A.M.–5 P.M. Mon.–Thurs., 9 A.M.–6 P.M. Fri., 9 A.M.–1 P.M. Sat.). Both have 24-hour ATMs.

Post Offices

Most visitors will find the **Old Town Plaza Station** the most convenient (303 Romero St. NW, 505/242-5927, 10 A.M.–6 P.M. Mon.–Fri., noon–5 P.M. Sat.). The **Downtown Station** (201 5th St. SW, 505/346-1256, 9 A.M.–5 P.M. Mon.–Fri.) and **University Station** (115 Cornell Dr. SE, 505/346-0923, 8 A.M.–5 P.M. Mon.–Fri.) are also handy.

Internet

The main branch of the **Albuquerque Public Library** (501 Copper Ave. NW, 505/768-5141, 10 A.M.–6 P.M. Mon. and Thurs.–Sat., 10 A.M.–7 P.M. Tues. and Wed.) offers Internet access with the one-time purchase of a $3 card that's good for three months for out of towners; wireless access is completely free. City-maintained Wi-Fi hot spots are listed at www.cabq.gov/wifi; quite a few businesses around town also provide the service.

Laundry

Mountain Road Laundromat (1134 Mountain

Rd. NW, 505/247-0164, 8 A.M.–8:30 P.M. daily) is midway between Old Town and downtown. **Allstar Cleaners** (800 Central Ave. SE, Ste. D, 505/242-8888, 7 A.M.–6 P.M. Mon.–Fri., 10 A.M.–1 P.M. Sat.) offers same-day laundry and dry cleaning.

Getting There and Around

BY AIR

Albuquerque International Sunport (ABQ; 505/244-7700) is a pleasant single-terminal airport with four runways. It's on the south side of the city, just east of I-25, about four miles from downtown. The Sunport is served by all of the major U.S. airlines. There's free wireless Internet access throughout the complex and a nice collection of art on the walls; look up while descending to the bag claim to see the original carved wood vigas from the 1965 structure. Also near baggage claim, you'll find a desk maintained by the convention and visitors bureau.

A city bus ($1), Route 50, runs from the airport to the main bus hub downtown, the Alvarado Transportation Center at Central and 1st Street. Buses depart the airport weekdays every half hour 7 A.M.–8:30 P.M., but service is much more limited on the weekends: There's none on Sunday, and service is only every hour and 10 minutes on Saturday, 9:45 A.M.–7:05 P.M.

A shuttle bus also runs from the airport to the **Rail Runner** (505/245-7245, www.nmrailrunner.com, $2), Albuquerque's commuter-rail service that runs north–south through the city. Downtown is only a 10-minute ride north, but service does not run very frequently, so it is not a vast improvement over the bus.

BY CAR

All of the major car-rental companies have offices in a single convenient complex adjacent to the airport, connected by shuttle buses. **Hertz** and **Enterprise** offer service at the Amtrak depot, and Hertz also has several other locations around town—less expensive, because you bypass the airport service fee, but less convenient too.

BY BUS

With **ABQ Ride** (505/243-7433, www.cabq.gov/transit) public buses, it's possible to reach all of the major sights along Central Avenue, but you can't get to the Sandia Peak Tramway or anywhere in the East Mountains.

Visitors benefit most from the bus that runs up and down Central Avenue—fittingly, it's Route 66—that links Old Town, downtown, and Nob Hill. For faster service along Central, hop on one of the double-length **Rapid Ride** buses (Route 766), which speed between the most popular stops from Unser Boulevard on the west side up to Wyoming in the heights; service runs until 3 A.M. on summer weekends. The fare for all buses, regardless of trip length, is $1; a **three-day pass** is a bargain at $4 from the ABQ Ride office downtown (100 1st St. SW) and the UNM bookstore. The free **Downtown Get Around** bus makes a loop between Lomas and Silver via 3rd and 5th Streets.

TNM&O/Greyhound (800/231-2222, www.tnmo.com) runs buses from all major points east, west, north, and south, though departures are not frequent. The bus station (505/243-4435) is at 320 1st Street NW, just south of the Alvarado Transportation Center. Cheaper *and* nicer are the bus services that cater to Mexicans traveling across the Southwest and into Mexico, though they offer service only to Santa Fe, not Taos; **El Paso-Los Angeles Limousine Express** (1611 Central Ave. SW; 505/247-8036) is the biggest operator.

BY TRAIN

The city's commuter rail, **Rail Runner** (505/245-7245, www.nmrailrunner.com, $2), runs north–south from Bernalillo down to

Belén, stopping at the Alvarado Transportation Center downtown. It runs infrequently, however, and stations outside of downtown are geared for car commuters rather than for walking around sightseeing.

Amtrak (800/872-7245, www.amtrak.com) runs the Southwest Chief through Albuquerque, arriving daily in the afternoon from Chicago and Los Angeles. The depot is just south of the Alvarado Transportation Center, on 1st Street, in the same complex with TNM&O/ Greyhound.

BACKGROUND

The Land

Sharp peaks, windswept cliffs, deep gorges—everything about northern New Mexico's landscape is dramatic and severe. The light glints off surfaces at surprising angles, and the scenery can change at any bend in the road. The altitude ranges from around 6,500 feet in Albuquerque to more than 13,000 (at Wheeler Peak, the state's highest, north of Taos)—so if you're not gasping for breath from the scenery alone, you almost certainly will be from the thin air.

GEOGRAPHY AND GEOLOGY

Much of northern New Mexico's landscape is the product of volcanic activity, beginning hundreds of millions of years back and ceasing (at least for now) only about 3,000 years ago. The region's main mountain ranges are relatively young, pushed up in the Eocene era between 55 million and 34 million years ago, when shock waves from the collision of the North American plate and the Farallon plate caused the continent to heave. Just a few million years later, the Rio Grande Rift—one of the biggest rift valleys in the world—formed, as eras' and eras' worth of accumulated rock was pulled apart by shifting faults, leaving the perfect path for the river when it began to flow about three million years ago. The water carved deep canyons, perfect slices of geologic time,

© ZORA O'NEILL

where you can see layers of limestone, sandstone, clay, and lava stacked up. The best example is the 800-foot-deep Rio Grande Gorge, cut through the lava plateau that stretches west from Taos. Just 1.2 million years back, a volcano's violent eruption and subsequent collapse created the huge Valles Caldera, and the jagged edges of the crater have barely softened in the intervening time. A very tangible benefit of the state's volcanic activity is the numerous hot springs, especially in the very young Jemez Mountains (15 million years old).

Below all this, though, is evidence of a more stable time. For about four billion years, the land was completely underwater, and then it spent hundreds of millions of years supporting a range of prehistoric sea life—hence the marine fossils found at the top of the Sandia Mountains, 10,000 feet above the current sea level. Dinosaurs, too, flourished for a time—in particular, one of the first, *Coelophysis,* a nimble meat eater, lived during the Triassic area around Abiquiu. In 1947, paleontologists found the largest collection of *Coelophysis*

skeletons in the world, about 100, all of them seemingly killed at once, perhaps by a flash flood. Another product of the dinosaur age (specifically, the Jurassic) was the lurid red, pink, and orange sandstone. It began as a vast desert, then petrified into the very symbol of the American Southwest, and is visible around Abiquiu and Jemez Pueblo.

CLIMATE

Much more than simple latitude, the relative altitude determines the climate in northern New Mexico, where river-bottom central Albuquerque can be crisp and cloudless while Sandia Peak, 20 miles away and almost 5,000 feet up, is socked in by a blinding snowstorm. Nowhere, though, is it a particularly gentle or mild climate—expect sudden changes in weather and extremes of heat and cold.

At the lower elevations, winter is cold—days usually between 40°F and 55°F—but rarely cloudy, with a few snowstorms that never add up to quite as much moisture as people hope for. Come spring, which starts in late April or

winter on Sandia Peak outside Albuquerque

May, the number of wildflowers that dot the hills is a direct reflection of the previous winter's precipitation. Little rain falls in May and June, typically the hottest months of the year, with temperatures climbing into the 90s.

But by early July, the "monsoon" season (as locals call it) brings heavy, refreshing downpours and thunderstorms every afternoon for a couple of months. It's remarkable—if a bit dismaying—to see how quickly all the water vanishes after each torrential rain. (If you're out hiking in this season, steer clear of narrow canyons and arroyos during and after rains, as they can fill with powerful, deadly flash floods in a matter of minutes.) September, October, and November are again dry, with the temperature dipping lower each month.

The higher the elevation, the later the spring: At 8,500 feet, snow could still be on the ground in May. Summer nights are rarely warm, and winter chill sets in sooner too, with fresh snow often falling in late October or November, although it usually takes well into December for a good base layer to build up at the ski areas.

ENVIRONMENTAL ISSUES

New Mexico's unforgiving climate and geography have made it a perpetual challenge for human inhabitants. For thousands of years, New Mexicans have been facing the same problem: never enough water. In prehistoric times, farming in the river valley was relatively easy, if subject to erratic flooding, but at higher elevations, mountain streams had to be channeled into irrigation ditches. This system was perfected by the Spanish settlers, who called their ditches acequias, a word they'd learned from the Arabs (al-saqiya), who used the system to cultivate the Iberian Peninsula.

But now, as an ever-growing population demands more amenities, the traditional ways of managing water have given way to more complex legal wranglings and general hostility ("No chingen con nuestra agua"—don't f—k with our water—reads a license plate on some farmers' trucks in northern New Mexico). Some 49 billion gallons of water are pumped out of the middle Rio Grande aquifer every year, and only

The risk of wildfires is almost always high in New Mexico.

a part of that is replenished through mountain runoff. Albuquerque was set to start using filtered river water by early 2009, but some areas are already on chronic alert. Santa Fe, for instance, already has the lowest per-capita water use in the country, and it doesn't have any more resources to tap. "Smart growth" gets lip service in city council meetings, and neo-homesteaders on the fringes are installing cisterns to catch rain and systems to reuse gray water, but construction continues apace on Albuquerque's arid West Mesa.

Another result of northern New Mexico's dry climate is that years of relative drought have made tinderboxes of the forests. In 2000, the National Forest Service started a "controlled burn" (a hotly debated strategy for thinning invasive undergrowth in choked woodlands) that got very out of control and nearly destroyed the town of Los Alamos, along with 45,000 acres of trees. It was the largest wildfire ever in New Mexico, and the smoke and flames could be seen in Albuquerque. The mountain behind Los Alamos is still bald and brown, spiked with burnt tree trunks. Pecos

LEAVE NO TRACE

So as not to upset the rather precarious environmental balance in much of New Mexico, you should internalize the ethic of "leave no trace," whether you're out for a day hike or a weeklong backpacking trek. The idea should first guide your trip in the planning stages, when you should equip yourself with good maps and GPS tools or a compass, to avoid relying on rock cairns or blazes, and repackage food and other items to minimize the waste you'll have to pack out. Also try to keep your group size under six people, and don't take pets with you.

On the trail, resist the urge to cut across switchbacks. Stick to the center of the trail to minimize further erosion. Be quiet and courteous to avoid disturbing wildlife and other hikers. Leave what you find, whether plants, rocks, or potsherds or other relics of the past.

Camp only where others have, in durable areas, at least 200 feet from water sources; dig cat holes 200 feet away, too. Pack out your toilet paper and other personal waste, and scatter dishwater and toothpaste. Safeguard food in "bear bags" hung at least 15 feet off the ground. Campfires are typically banned in New Mexico – please honor this policy, and keep a close eye on camp stoves. Pack out all cigarette butts.

While most leave-no-trace ethics apply to backpackers, day hikers should follow the same policy. Even though tossing an orange peel, apple core, or other biodegradable item along the trail won't cause an environmental disaster, it does remind other hikers that humans have been there and intrudes on the natural solitude of New Mexico's wilderness.

Wilderness Area, too, suffered from fire in 2000 and is still recovering.

Visitors to New Mexico can help the picture by following local environmental policies—complying with campfire bans in the wilderness, for instance, and keeping showers short. Golfers may want to consider curtailing their play here. New courses are springing up everywhere, especially as part of casino resort complexes on American Indian reservations, and most are intense draws on the water table, with little thought to sustainability (one exception is Santa Fe's municipal course, which was planned with water restrictions in mind).

Flora and Fauna

Just as humans have managed to eke a life out of northern New Mexico, so have plants and animals—and a rather large variety of them, considering the circumstances. In fact, New Mexico has one of the most diverse arrays of wildlife in the United States.

FLORA

Although much of the plant growth in New Mexico is nominally evergreen, the overall aspect of the landscape can skew toward brown, until you get up into the relatively lush alpine elevations.

Vegetation Zones

New Mexico's **Upper Sonoran** zone, covering the areas between 4,500 and 7,000 feet, is the largest vegetation zone in the state and includes most of Albuquerque and Santa Fe, where the Sandia and Sangre de Cristo foothills are covered with juniper and piñon trees. The **Transition** zone, from 7,000 feet to 8,500 feet, sees a few more stately trees, such as ponderosa pine, and a lot of the state's colorful wildflowers: orange Indian paintbrush, bright red penstemon, purple lupine. Above 8,500 feet, the **Mixed Conifer** zone harbors just that sort of tree—along with clusters of aspens. The **Subalpine** zone, starting at 9,500 feet, is home to Engelmann spruce and bristlecone pine, while 11,500 feet marks the tree line in most places and the beginning of the **Alpine** zone, where almost no greenery survives.

Trees and Grasses

Trees are the clearest marker of elevation. In very low areas—such as on Albuquerque's West Mesa—you'll see very few trees, only some of the more desertlike plants that are more prevalent in the southern part of the state, but not in the northern: assorted cactuses, such as the common **cane cholla;** the spiky **yucca** plant, which produces towering stalks of blooms in May; and the humble **tumbleweed.** Along the river, thirsty **cottonwoods** provide dense shade; many of the biggest trees, with their gnarled, branching trunks, have been growing for centuries. In the spring, their cotton fills the air—hell for the allergic, but source of a beautiful fragrance—and in the fall, their leaves turn pure yellow. Willow and olive are also common.

In the foothills, **piñon** (also spelled pinyon), the official state tree, is everywhere, as a slow-growing, drought-resistant scrub tree tailor-evolved for the New Mexican landscape. Its wood produces the distinctive scent of a New Mexico winter night, and its pinecones yield tasty nuts. Alongside piñon is **shaggy-bark juniper,** identifiable by its loose strips of bark, its soft, fanlike needle clusters, and branches that look twisted by the wind; in season, it's studded with purple-gray berries—another treat for foraging humans and animals alike. On the ground in the foothills, also look for clumps of sagebrush and bear grass, which blooms in huge creamy tufts at the ends of stalks up to six feet tall.

Up in the mountains, the trees are a bit taller—here you'll find the distinctive, towering **ponderosa** pine, the bark of which smells distinctly of vanilla. Look for tall trees with thick, almost crusty chunks of reddish-black bark. At slightly higher elevations, dense stands of **aspen** trees provide a rare spot of fall color

in the evergreen forests—the combination of their golden leaves and white bark creates a particularly magical glow, especially in the mountains near Santa Fe. The highest mountain areas are home to a number of dense-needled hardy pines, such as blue-green **Engelmann spruce, corkbark fir, bristlecone pines,** and **subalpine fir,** with its sleek, rounded pinecones. Hike your way up to stands of these, which are all tall but with sparse branches, and you'll know you're close to the peak.

ATTACK OF THE BARK BEETLES

Piñon is the most prevalent tree in New Mexico's foothills – or it *was*, until the bark-beetle blight first struck in 2002. Since then, the invasive bugs have killed an estimated 43 million trees, leaving whole swaths of hillsides an eerie shade of gray. The hardy trees were felled not so much by the beetles, which are always present, as by drought. Ordinarily, the piñon's sticky sap protects it by smothering the insects, but years of abnormally dry weather meant it could no longer produce as much sap. No larger than grains of rice, the beetles bored under the bark and laid eggs; the larvae feasted on the soft inner bark, while the adults spread a blue fungus that helped kill off the tree.

New Mexicans fight the invaders using tactics straight out of a zombie movie: Living trees have to be felled at the first sign of infestation and then chopped into tiny pieces and buried. The other option is to seal the bug-filled wood in heavy plastic and leave it in the sun to effectively smother and cook the beetles. Wet weather in 2004 briefly slowed the plague, but subsequent drought years – and ever-warmer winters – have given them the edge again. Santa Fe composer David Dunn has recorded the chattering of the beetles in the trees and mixed it into an arrangement called *The Sound of Light in Trees* – the soundtrack of global warming.

just one of the scores of varieties of yucca, the state flower

FAUNA

As with plants, what you see depends on where you are on the mountain slopes. And you'll have to look very carefully, because a lot of the animals that have survived this long in dry, harsh New Mexico are the sort that have blended in with their surroundings—in short, there are a lot of brown critters.

Mammals

In the open, low-elevation areas on Albuquerque's fringes (and sometimes in the occasional vacant urban lot), look for **prairie dogs,** which live in huge communities of underground warrens. If you're camping, the first little creatures you'll meet are **squirrels** and **chipmunks**—at higher elevations, look out for Aber's squirrel, with its tufted ears and particularly fluffy tail. Long-haunched, clever, and highly adaptable, **coyotes** roam the lower elevations and are not shy about nosing around backyards; they make a barking yelp at night. On the plains just south of Santa Fe,

you may see **pronghorns** (often called pronghorn antelopes, though they are not true antelopes) springing through the grasses, while hefty **mule deer** flourish in mountain forests, such as the Pecos Wilderness area. Herds of even larger **elk** live in the high valleys; Rocky Mountain elk are common, thanks to an aggressive reintroduction effort in the early 20th century to make up for overhunting. A group of the largest variety, Roosevelt elk, whose fan-like antlers are the stuff of dreams for trophy hunters, roams in Valles Caldera. **Bighorn sheep** live in the mountains around Taos.

Black bears crash around the forests, though their name is misleading—at any given time, they can also be brown, cinnamon-red, or even nearly blond. Smokey Bear, the mascot of the National Forest Service, was from New Mexico, a cub rescued from a forest fire in Capitan. Drought has on many occasions driven the omnivorous beasts into suburban trash cans to forage, with tragic results; if you're camping, take thorough measures to keep your food away from your camp and out of reach of animals.

And then there's the elusive **jackalope,** a jackrabbit hare sporting elaborate antlers. Alas, it seems now to appear only on postcards, although you may occasionally see a taxidermied head in a curio shop.

Birds

New Mexico's state bird is the **roadrunner,** which can grow to be up to two feet long; it lives in the lower desertlike elevations (Coronado State Monument, north of Albuquerque, is home to a few), nesting in the ground and feeding on insects and even rattlesnakes. Blue-and-black **Steller's jays** and raucous all-blue **piñon jays** are some of the most common birds in the foothills and farther up in the mountains, where you can also see **bluebirds, black-masked mountain chickadees,** and **Clark's nutcrackers,** which hoard great stashes of piñon nuts for winter. Also look around for varieties of **woodpeckers,** including the three-toed variety, which lives at higher elevations. On the very highest peaks

a roadrunner in a rare moment of repose

© ZORA O'NEILL

are **white-tailed ptarmigans,** which blend in with their snowy environment. But you can't miss the bright-yellow-and-red **Western tanager,** a shot of tropical-looking delight in the Transition zone forests.

In the late summer, keep an eye out for tiny, red-throated **Rufous hummingbirds** on their way to Mexico for the winter. The Sandia Mountains are part of the migratory corridor for **red-tailed hawks, eagles,** and other raptors—they're especially numerous in the springtime.

With more than 450 species spotted in New Mexico, this list is only scraping the surface. If you're a dedicated birder, first contact the **Randall Davey Audubon Center** (505/983-4609, nm.audubon.org) in Santa Fe, which leads bird walks, or the **Rio Grande Nature Center** in Albuquerque. **Bosque del Apache National Wildlife Refuge,** south of Albuquerque, is a must-visit, especially in the winter when thousands of **sandhill cranes**— and even the occasional rare **whooping crane**—rest in the wetlands. You may want to take a trip with Jim West of **WingsWest Birding** (800/583-6928, http://home.earthlink.net/~wingswestnm), who has been leading groups around New Mexico, from the Pecos to Las Vegas, since 1996. He offers four-hour, eight-hour, and full dusk-till-dawn outings to some of the best spots all over the state, and he's also willing to take people out for several days at a stretch.

Fish

Trout are the major endemic fish, found in the cold waters of the Rio Grande as well as the Chama River, the Pecos River, and the Rio Chiquito and Rio Pueblo around Taos. The cutthroat is particularly beloved in New Mexico—the only variety of trout that was originally found on the eastern side of the Continental Divide, whereas the more aggressive rainbow and brown trout are interlopers. The Rio Grande cutthroat, the official state fish, is now quite uncommon. Another local fish in jeopardy is the **Rio Grande silvery minnow,** listed as endangered since 2004. The

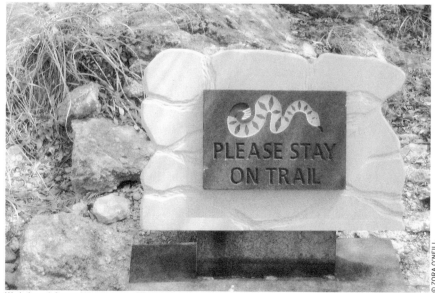

© ZORA O'NEILL

Watch out for rattlesnakes whenever you hike.

last of the Rio Grande's five native fish, it's in such a dire state that biologists are scooping them out of the water individually during bad dry spells and taking them to the Albuquerque Aquarium for safekeeping. The hope is that they will breed and be able to be returned to their original habitat during wetter conditions.

Reptiles

One can't step foot in the desert without thinking of **rattlesnakes,** and New Mexico has plenty of them, usually hidden away under rocks and brush, but very occasionally sunning themselves in full view, much to hikers' alarm. The New Mexico ridgenose variety is an endangered species, while the predominant species in the Rio Grande Valley, the Western diamondback, can grow to be seven feet long. Although its venom is relatively weak, it has an impressive striking distance of almost three

feet. Around Taos and Santa Fe, the main species is the prairie rattlesnake, which is only about four feet long at most.

More benign cold-blooded critters include all manner of **lizards,** including the short-horned lizard (a.k.a. horny toad), a miniature dinosaur, in effect, about as big as your palm—you'll see them primarily in the scrubby foothills.

Insects and Arachnids

Because it's so dry, New Mexico isn't too infested with bugs. The ones that are there, however, can be a bit off-putting to a visitor, particularly if you chance upon the springtime **tarantula** migration, usually in May around Albuquerque—it's not a true seasonal relocation, just all of the male tarantulas coming out of their dens to go on the prowl for mates. The fist-size spiders move in huge waves, hundreds at a time, and occasionally roads are closed to let them pass. Though they're big and hairy, they're not poisonous.

History

The historical and cultural continuity in New Mexico is remarkable. Although the state has been transformed from ice-age hunting ground to home of the atom bomb, many people claim roots that stretch back hundreds, even thousands, of years.

ANCIENT AND ARCHAIC CIVILIZATION

New Mexico was one of the first places to harbor humans after the end of the last ice age. Archaeological findings indicate that about 12,000 years ago, people were hunting mastodons and other big game across the state. Mammoth bones, arrowheads, and the remains of campfires have been found in Folsom, in northeastern New Mexico; Clovis in the south;

and the Sandia Mountains east of Albuquerque. Sometime between 8000 and 5000 B.C., these bands of hunters formed a small temporary settlement just north of Albuquerque, but it was not enough to stave off the decline of that ancient culture, as climatic shifts caused the big game to die off. Nomadic hunter-gatherers, seeking out smaller animals as well as seeds and nuts, did better in the new land, and by 1000 B.C., they had established communities built around clusters of pit houses—sunken, log-covered rooms dug into the earth.

Along with this new form of shelter came an equally important advance in food. Mexican people gave corn kernels (maize) and lessons in agriculture to their neighbors, the Mogollon, who occupied southern New Mexico and

---

THE ANASAZI AND THE CANNIBALISM DEBATE

The Anasazi – the culture that established the elaborate condolike community of Tyuonyi and the cliff dwellings at Bandelier National Monument – have long been a mystery and a topic of debate among archaeologists because their society appears to have collapsed abruptly in the 13th century.

The popular conception of the Anasazi has long been of a peaceful, egalitarian society based on agriculture, an image further enhanced by the Pueblo Indians' push to rename the Anasazi (an old Navajo word meaning "ancient enemies") "ancestral Puebloans." The Puebloans point out that the Anasazi are not some foreign, archaic people who mysteriously vanished but the forebears of today's American Indians in the Southwest.

But a theory advanced by physical anthropologist Christy Turner suggests the Pueblo Indians might be better off disavowing their ancestors. In his 1999 book *Man Corn: Cannibalism and Violence in the Prehistoric American Southwest,* Turner proposed that the Anasazi culture was a violent one obsessed with ritual consumption of human flesh. His

theory neatly suggests yet another stress that could have contributed to the Anasazi collapse and answers another nagging question: What about all those piles of mangled human bones and fire-blackened skulls found at Chaco Canyon, Mesa Verde, and other Anasazi sites?

Many of Turner's colleagues were highly skeptical, and Pueblo Indians were, and still are, outraged at the accusations about their ancestors – Turner and other archaeologists were banned from their excavations in Mesa Verde. In the years since Turner published *Man Corn,* however, the evidence to support his theory seems to have grown – for instance, he discovered a coprolite (preserved human feces) that tests positive for human proteins. Turner now posits that the cannibalism was introduced by a Mexican culture, perhaps the Toltecs, and used against the Anasazi as a means of terrorizing them into submission. This puts the ancestral Puebloans in a somewhat better light but still paints a bleak and violent picture of life in what today are lush, peaceful valleys and canyons.

Arizona; by A.D. 400, the Mogollon had begun growing squash and beans as well and had established concentrated communities all around the southern Rio Grande basin. This culture, dubbed the Basketmakers by archaeologists, also developed its own pottery, another skill learned from the indigenous people of Mexico. So when the Mogollon made contact with the Anasazi (the ancestors of today's Puebloans) in the northern part of the state, they had plenty to share.

THE PUEBLOS FORM

The year 700 marks the beginning of the **Pueblo I** phase—the time when disparate groups began to form larger communities in the upland areas on either side of the northern Rio Grande. Pit houses were still in use, but aboveground buildings of clay and sticks were erected alongside them. Increasingly, the pit houses were sacred spaces, chambers in which religious ceremonies were carried out; these are now known as kivas and are still an integral part of pueblo life. The **Pueblo II** era dates from 850 and is distinguished by the rise of Pueblo Bonito in Chaco Canyon, northwest of Santa Fe, into a full-scale city and perhaps capital of a small state. It was home to an estimated 1,500 people ruled by a religious elite. But Chaco began to crumble abruptly around 1150 (perhaps because of drought, famine, or warfare), marking the beginning of the **Pueblo III** period, when the people who were to become today's Puebloans began building their easily defended cliff dwellings— most famously in the Four Corners area, at Mesa Verde, but also farther south, on the Pajarito Plateau in what's now called Bandelier National Monument, and in Puyé, on Santa Clara Pueblo land. A drought at the end of the 13th century cleared out the Four Corners, marking the start of the **Pueblo IV** era and provoking the population to consolidate along the Rio Grande in clusters of sometimes more than 1,000 interconnected rooms. These communities dotted the riverbank, drawing their sustenance both from the river water and from the mountains behind them.

THE SPANISH ARRIVE

These settlements were what the Spanish explorer Francisco Vásquez de Coronado and his crew saw when they first ventured into the area in 1540. Their Spanish word for the villages, *pueblos,* stuck and is still the name for both the places and the people who live in them. Coronado wasn't all that impressed, however, because the pueblos were made out of mud, not gold as the Spanish had been hoping—so after two years and a couple of skirmishes with the natives, the team turned around and headed back to Mexico City. It took another half a century for the Spanish to muster more interest in the area—this time, in 1598, Juan de Oñate led a small group of Spanish families to settle on the banks of the Rio Grande, at a place they called San Gabriel, near Ohkay Owingeh (which they called San Juan Pueblo). About a decade later, the settlers moved away from their Indian neighbors, to the new villa of Santa Fe. The territory's third governor, Don Pedro de Peralta, made

Santa Fe's Old Cross of the Martyrs commemorates Spaniards killed in the Pueblo Revolt.

© ZORA O'NEILL

it the official capital of the territory of Nuevo México, which in those days stretched far into what is now Colorado and Arizona.

This time the colonists, mostly farmers, were motivated not so much by hopes of striking it rich but simply of making a living. Moreover, they were inspired by Catholic zeal, and Franciscan missionaries accompanied them to promote the faith among the Puebloans.

It was partly these missionaries and their ruthless oppression of the native religion that drove the Indians to organize the Pueblo Revolt of 1680. The Franciscans' "conversion" strategy involved public executions of the pueblos' medicine men, among other violent assaults on local traditions. But the Spanish colonists were no help either. In their desperation to squeeze some wealth out of the hard land, they exploited the only resource they had, the slave labor of the Indians, who were either conscripted for projects or stolen from their families (though the Indians did their share of poaching from Spanish families, creating a sort of cultural exchange program).

The leader of the Pueblo Revolt was a man named Popé (also spelled Po'pay), from San Juan Pueblo. Using Taos Pueblo as his base, he traveled among the other communities, secretly meeting with leaders to plan a united insurrection. Historians theorize he may have used Spanish to communicate with other Puebloans who did not speak his native Tewa, and then he distributed among the conspirators lengths of knotted rope with which to count down the days to the insurrection. Although the Spanish captured a few of the rope-bearing messengers (Isleta Pueblo may never have gotten the message, which could explain its being the only pueblo not to participate), they could not avert the bloodshed. The Puebloan warriors killed families and missionaries, burned crops, and toppled churches. Santa Fe was besieged, and its population of more than 1,000 finally evacuated in a pitiful retreat.

The Spanish stayed away for 12 years, but finally a new governor, Diego de Vargas, took it upon himself to reclaim the land the Spanish had settled. He managed to talk many pueblos into peaceful surrender, meeting resistance only in Taos and Santa Fe, where a two-day fight was required to oust the Indians from the Palace of the Governors. The Spanish strategy in the post-revolt era was softer, with more compromise between the Franciscans and their intended flock, and a fair amount of cultural and economic exchange. The threat of raiding Comanche, Apache, and Navajo also forced the Spanish and Indians to cooperate. Banding together for defense, they were finally able to drive the Comanche away, culminating in a 1778 battle with Chief Cuerno Verde (Green Horn). The decisive victory is celebrated in the ritual dance called Los Comanches that's still performed in small villages by Spanish and Indians alike.

The other bonding force was trade. The Spanish maintained the Camino Real de Tierra Adentro (Royal Road of the Interior), which linked Santa Fe with central Mexico—the route follows roughly the line carved by I-25 today. Caravans came through only every year or two, but the profit from furs, pottery, textiles, and other local goods was enough to keep both cultures afloat, if utterly dependent on the Spanish government.

MEXICAN INDEPENDENCE AND THE FIRST ANGLOS

Spain carefully guarded all of its trade routes in the New World, even in a relatively unprofitable territory such as New Mexico. Interlopers were certainly not welcome—only a few enterprising fur trappers, lone mountain men in search of beaver pelts, slipped in. Spy-explorer Zebulon Pike and his crew were captured (perhaps intentionally, so Pike could get more inside information) and detained in Santa Fe for a spell in 1807. But in 1821, Mexico declared its independence from Spain, liberating the territory of Nuevo México along with it—and one of the first acts of the new government was to open the borders to trade. Initially just a trickle of curious traders came down the rough track between St. Louis and Santa Fe, but soon a flood of commerce flowed along the increasingly rutted and broad Santa Fe Trail, making the territory's capital city a meeting place between Mexicans and Americans swapping furs, gold, cloth, and more.

THE MEXICAN-AMERICAN WAR AND AFTER

Pike's expedition, conducted just as Lewis and Clark were returning from their march across the Louisiana Purchase, not only gave the U.S. government new information on the locations of Spanish forts and other details, but it also helped fuel the country's general expansionist fervor. By the 1840s, "manifest destiny" was the phrase on every American's lips, and the United States was eyeing the Southwest. It annexed Texas in 1845, but New Mexico, with its small population and few resources, didn't figure heavily in the short-lived war that resulted—the Mexican governor surrendered peacefully to General Stephen Kearny when he arrived in Santa Fe in 1846. In Taos, though, the transition was not accepted so readily, as a brief but violent uprising instigated by Hispano business leaders with help from Taos Pueblo Indians resulted in the beheading of the first American governor, Charles Bent.

During the Civil War, New Mexico was in the way of a Texan Confederate strategy to secure the Southwest, but the rebels were thwarted in 1862 at the Battle of Glorieta Pass. The territory stayed in the hands of the Union until the end of the war, and people were more concerned with the local, increasingly brutal skirmishes caused by the arrival in Santa Fe of Bishop Jean Baptiste Lamy, a tyrannical—or at least very out-of-touch—Frenchman who tried to impose a European vision of the Catholic church on a populace that had been far beyond centralized control for centuries.

More significant to New Mexico's development was the arrival of the railroad in 1880, as it was laid through Raton Pass, near Santa Fe, and very close to Albuquerque. Virtually overnight strange goods and even stranger people came pouring into one of the more remote frontier outposts of the United States. Anglo influence was suddenly everywhere, in the form of new architecture (redbrick was

an Eastern affectation) and new business. Albuquerque, almost directly on the new railway tracks, boomed, while Santa Fe's fortunes slumped and Taos all but withered away (its peak had been back in the late days of the Camino Real).

But while wheeler-dealers were setting up shop in central New Mexico, some more intrepid souls were poking around in the less-connected areas farther north. These tourists were artists who valued New Mexico not for its commercial potential but for its dramatic landscapes and exotic populace who seemed untouched by American ways. From the early 20th century on, Santa Fe and Taos were cultivated as art colonies, a function they still fulfill today.

FROM STATEHOOD TO WORLD WAR II

Based on its burgeoning economy, New Mexico became the 47th state in the union in 1912, effectively marking the end of the frontier period, a phase of violence, uncertainty, and isolation that lasted about 300 years, longer here than in any other state. In addition to the painters and writers flocking to the new state, another group of migrants arrived: tuberculosis patients. Soon the state was known as a health retreat, and countless people did stints in its dry air to treat their ailing lungs. One of these people was J. Robert Oppenheimer, whose mild case of TB got him packed off to a camp near Pecos for a year after high school. He loved northern New Mexico and became familiar with some of its more hidden pockets, so when the U.S. Army asked him if he had any idea where it should establish a secret base for the Manhattan Project, he knew just the place: a little camp high on a plateau above Santa Fe—its name was Los Alamos. This was the birthplace of the atomic bomb, a weird, close-knit community of the country's greatest scientific minds (and biggest egos), all working in utter secrecy. Only after Fat Man and Little Boy were dropped over Japan was the mysterious camp's mission revealed.

RECENT HISTORY

With the invention of the A-bomb, New Mexico was truly ushered into the modern era—not just because it produced world-changing technology, but also because the high-paying jobs at Los Alamos and Kirtland Air Force Base in Albuquerque helped pull some of the population out of subsistence farming and into a life of car driving and electricity using. Even with these modern trappings, though, the character of the state remained very conservative and closed, so when the 1960s rolled around and New Mexico looked like the promised land to hippies, the culture clash was fierce. Staunch Catholic farmers even took potshots at their naked, hallucinogen-ingesting neighbors who fantasized about getting back to the land but had no clue how to do it. After a decade or so, though, only the hardiest of the commune dwellers were left, and they'd mellowed a bit, while the locals had come to appreciate at least their enthusiasm. Even if the communes didn't last, hippie culture has proven remarkably persistent—even today, distinctly straight Hispanos can be heard saying things such as, "I was tripping out on that band, man," and the state still welcomes Rainbow Gatherings, would-be Buddhists, and alternative healers.

The end of the 20th century saw a sudden burst of growth in both Albuquerque and Santa Fe. As usual, Albuquerque got the practical-minded development, such as the Intel plant and the financial headquarters for Gap Inc., while Santa Fe was almost felled by its own artsiness, turned inside-out during a few frenzied years when movie stars and other moneyed types bought up prime real estate. In just a matter of months in the early 1990s, rents

"What Is Past Is Prologue" reflects New Mexican history at Santa Fe's old archives.

went up tenfold and houses were selling for more than $1 million. The city has yet to work out the imbalance between its creative forces, which did save the city from utter decline, and the weird economic ones through which the richest people live in faux-adobe homes on real dirt roads, and the poorest put a fresh coat of mud on their houses every year, but at least the paving runs up to their doors.

Meanwhile, Taos has grown slowly but steadily, as have the pueblos, thanks to the legalization of gambling on their lands, but all of these communities have a touch of old New Mexico about them, where the frontier flavor and solitude can still be felt.

Government and Economy

Up until very recently, New Mexico hasn't looked so good on paper, what with high statistics for corruption, nepotism, and poverty. But that has also inspired a good deal of activist sentiment, and politics are lively as the economy has begun to slip out of some of its old restrictive patterns.

GOVERNMENT

New Mexico's political scene is as diverse as its population, a fractious mix of Democrats, Republicans, Greens, Libertarians, anarchists, independents, and irredeemable cranks. The presidential contests of 2000 and 2004 were too close to call on Election Day, requiring recounts to determine the winners by a hair (Gore in 2000, Bush in 2004). Governor Bill Richardson, a Democrat who previously served as the U.S ambassador to the United Nations and secretary of the Department of Energy, was elected in 2002 by 17 percentage points (56 percent vs. 39 percent), the widest margin in any race since 1964. Don't be fooled by his Anglo last name: Richardson is Mexican American, born in Pasadena and raised in Mexico City. A fluent Spanish speaker who has lived in New Mexico since 1978, he's the only Hispanic governor in the United States, and was the first Hispanic to run for the Democratic nomination for president, as he entered the 2008 primary.

The state political scene is a mix of entrenched cronyism and activism. On the one hand, Senator Pete Domenici (Republican), a former pitcher for the Albuquerque Dukes, held his seat from 1972 to 2008; on the other, former governor Gary Johnson is an advocate for marijuana legalization, and the Santa Fe city council passed a living-wage law in 2008. But nepotistic assignments of highway repair contracts are common enough—as are politicians repeatedly arrested for DUIs and then cleared—that pundits often quip, "New Mexico is a third-world country."

The system is even more muddled by the Indian reservations, each of which acts as a sovereign nation, with its own laws, tax regulations, police forces, and government. Indians vote in U.S. and state elections, but in the pueblos, most domestic issues are decided by each pueblo's tribal governor, war chief, and a few other officials elected by a consensus of men in the kiva.

ECONOMY

New Mexico has always lagged at the bottom of the country's economic ratings: In 2006, 18.5 percent of the population was living below the poverty level, giving the state a bigger proportion of working poor than any other. It's also 46th out of 50 in the number of high school graduates and the number of college graduates per capita.

But at least as of 2007, the state was in an upswing, with overall unemployment down to 3.8 percent, and the average income among the 10th fastest-growing in the country. As the

state government buildings in Santa Fe

© ZORA O'NEILL

a faux café built for a movie shoot in Madrid

and an aerospace manufacturing park growing on the west side. On the horizon: a solar farm that would produce electricity for 300,000 homes and, under the direction of the New Mexico Space Commission, the development of spacecraft by private companies at the New Mexico Spaceport south of Albuquerque.

Significant profits from coal, copper, oil, and natural-gas extraction—most in the southern part of the state, as well as in the northwest—actually put the state economy well in the black in 2006. That's the big money, but the agricultural sector, from apple orchards along the Rio Grande to beef jerky from the numerous cattle ranches, contributes a decent amount to the pot. And Santa Fe's arts sector shouldn't be overlooked—galleries post sales of $200 million every year, though they're criticized for sending much of that money right back out of the state to artists who live and work elsewhere. Finally, Governor Richardson has been actively courting the **film industry,** leading to a boom in movies shot against the dramatic backdrops around Albuquerque and Santa Fe — now referred to locally as "Tamalewood."

Even if the economic situation isn't ideal, it's nothing New Mexicans aren't used to—low income has been the norm for so long that a large segment of the population is, if not content with, at least adapted to eking out a living from almost nothing (the median family income is only around $37,000). In this respect, the state hasn't lost its frontier spirit at all.

manufacturing center for all manner of things, from computer chips to mattresses to specialty running shoes, Albuquerque leads the state's economy. And the city where Microsoft was founded (then Bill Gates and Paul Allen moved back to Seattle to be close to their families) is doing better at fostering technology development these days, as home to a range of tech specialists catering to Sandia National Labs

The People

New Mexico's 1.9 million people have typically been described as a tricultural mix of Indians, Spanish, and whites, though that self-image has slowly begun to expand as residents have delved deeper into history and seen that the story is a bit more complex.

DEMOGRAPHY
The typical labels of Indians, Spanish, and Anglo are used uniquely in New Mexico.

First, **Indians:** New Mexicans generally don't use the term "Native American." So you'll see "American Indian" in formal situations, but even the "American" part is a bit laughable, considering "America" wasn't so named until Christopher Columbus made his voyage west. In any case, "Indian" refers to a number of different peoples who do not share a common culture or language: Navajo on the west side of the state, Jicarilla and Mescalero Apache, and the Puebloans of the Rio Grande and west as far as Acoma and Zuni. (The latter term, Pueblo, is another problematic one, as it refers not to a particular tribe but to a larger group of people who speak four distinct languages but are banded together by a common way of living.) With about 10 percent of the population claiming American Indian ancestry, traditions are still strong—though of course they've changed, as neon-dyed feathers trim kids' ceremonial headdresses, and wealth from casinos funds elaborate museums as well as new housing projects.

Spanish really means that: the people, primarily in northern New Mexico, whose ancestors were pure-blood Spaniards rather than the mestizos of Mexico. For many families, it's a point of pride similar to that of Mayflower descendants. Through the years, particularly during the 20th century, a steady influx of Mexican immigrants has blurred racial distinctions a bit, but it has also helped preserve the local Spanish culture, in that it has reinforced the use of Spanish as a daily language and spurred pride in the culture's music and other folkways. Increasingly, the word "Hispano" is being used to label New Mexico's distinct culture with centuries-old Spanish roots, though this still doesn't accurately cover the Basques, who came here both during the conquest (Juan de Oñate, the first Spanish governor, was Basque) and in the early 20th century as sheepherders. And the recent discovery of families of crypto-Jews (Spanish Jews who nominally converted to Catholicism but fled here to avoid the Inquisition) has added another fascinating layer to the Spanish story.

Anglo is the most imprecise term of all, as it means anyone who's not Spanish or Indian. Originally used to talk about the white traders who came to hunt and sell furs and trade on the Santa Fe Trail, it still refers to people who can't trace their roots back to the conquistadors or farther. If you're a Vietnamese immigrant in Albuquerque, you're an Anglo. If you're a Tibetan refugee in Santa Fe, you're an Anglo. And if you're an African American farmer who settled here after the Civil War, you're an Anglo. (According to the 2000 census, about 45 percent of the population is white; Asians are only 1 percent, and African Americans make up 2 percent.) But all Anglo culture is shot through with Spanish and Indian influence, whether among the organic garlic farmers from California who rely on their acequias for water or the New Age seekers who do sweatlodge rituals.

Even with this liberal application of "Anglo," the tricultural arrangement is a bit limiting, as it doesn't assign a place to contemporary immigrants from Mexico and other Latin American countries, and their numbers are growing steadily. It also doesn't acknowledge the strong Mexican-American Chicano culture that's shared across the Southwest, from Los Angeles through Texas. The U.S. census form lumps both newer arrivals and old Spanish under "Hispanic"—a category (distinct from race) that made up about 42 percent of the population in 2000.

LANGUAGE
English is the predominant language, but once you get off the beaten track, you'll hear **Spanish** used more and more—about 29 percent of the population speaks it. Spanish speakers in northern New Mexico were for centuries only the old Hispano families, speaking a variant of Castilian with a distinct vocabulary that developed in isolation. This "Quixotic" dialect changed little until the 20th century, when immigrants began to arrive from Mexico and elsewhere in Latin America—a development that changed the old-fashioned New Mexican dialect but also helped encourage the use of Spanish all over the state. For much of the 20th century, though, English was the only permissible classroom language, although many school districts required Spanish as a foreign language. Since the 1990s, education policy has shifted to include bilingual classrooms.

Additionally, you'll occasionally hear the Pueblo Indians speaking their respective languages, of which there are four main ones. **Tewa, Tiwa,** and **Towa** are part of the Tanoan family of languages (Kiowa, spoken by Plains

LUMINARIAS OR *FAROLITOS*?

The cultural differences between Santa Fe and Albuquerque don't apply just to the number of art galleries per square block and whether you eat posole or rice with your enchiladas. Every Christmas, the eternal debate rears its head: What do you call a paper bag with a bit of sand in the bottom and a votive candle inside? These traditional holiday decorations, which line the driveways and flat adobe rooftops in both cities in December, are known as luminarias in Albuquerque and most towns to the south, and as *farolitos* in Santa Fe and all the villages to the north.

To complicate matters, another common holiday tradition in Santa Fe and other northern towns is to light small bonfires of piñon logs in front of houses. And Santa Feans call these little stacks of wood...luminarias. *Faroli-*

tos, they argue, are literally "little lanterns," an accurate description of the glowing paper bags – and under this logic, the use of *farolito* has spread a bit in Albuquerque, at least among people who weren't raised saying luminaria from birth.

But Albuquerqueans have Webster's on their side; the dictionary concurs that luminarias are paper-bag lanterns and notes the tradition comes from Mexico, where the bags are often colored and pricked with holes. (Perhaps Albuquerque's relative proximity to the border – and its larger proportion of Mexican immigrants – has shaped the language through the years?) In any case, because this author's loyalties are to Albuquerque, the argument is settled, at least in these pages: Luminaria it is.

Indians, is the fourth member). They are all somewhat related but mutually unintelligible, roughly equivalent to, say, French, Spanish, and Italian. Tewa is the most widely spoken, used in all of the pueblos just north of Santa Fe: Ohkay Owingeh, San Ildefonso, Santa Clara, Pojoaque, Tesuque, and Nambé. Four pueblos speak Tiwa—Taos and Picurís share one dialect, while Isleta and Sandia, in an odd pocket near Albuquerque, speak a different dialect. Towa is now spoken only at Jemez Pueblo.

Keresan (spoken in Laguna, Acoma, Cochiti, Santo Domingo, San Felipe, Santa Ana, and Zia) is what linguists call an "isolate." Like Basque, it is unconnected not only to neighboring languages but also to any other language. Additionally, each pueblo has developed its own dialect, such that immediately adjacent communities can understand each other, but those farthest apart cannot.

One interesting phenomenon of the Pueblo languages is that their speakers have managed to keep them relatively pure. Despite centuries of Spanish and English influence, Tewa vocabulary is still less than 5 percent loan words—probably because of the way speakers

have long been forced to compartmentalize it, using it for conversation at home and switching to English or Spanish for business and trade. For centuries, the Franciscan priests and then the U.S. government attempted to stamp out Native American languages. After the Civil War, Puebloan children were moved forcibly to boarding schools, where they were given Anglo names and permitted to speak only English, a policy that continued for decades.

Only in 1990, with the passage of the Native American Languages Act, were American Indian languages officially permitted in government-funded schools—indeed, they are now recognized as a unique element of this country's culture and encouraged. This has created an interesting practice in Taos, where the Tiwa language is a ritual secret that outsiders are not permitted to learn. But one Taos public school has Tiwa classes for younger students, open only to tribe members and taught only by approved teachers; as an added measure against the language being recorded, the classroom has no chalkboard. Less formal instruction within the pueblos has also helped the Pueblo languages enjoy a renaissance lately.

THE SECRET BROTHERHOOD: NEW MEXICO'S PENITENTES

In almost every small Hispano village in northern New Mexico is a modest one-story building called a *morada* – the meeting place of Los Hermanos Penitentes (The Penitent Brothers), a lay Catholic fraternity with deep roots in medieval Spain and a long and varied history that has often put it at odds with the church itself.

The Penitentes developed in New Mexico in the early colonial era and were at the height of their influence during the so-called Secular Period (1790-1850), when the Franciscans had been pushed out by church leaders in Mexico but no new priests were sent to the territory. The brotherhood, likely modeled after penitential fraternities in the Old World, cared for the ill, conducted funerals, and settled petty disputes and even elections. They generally maintained the spiritual and political welfare of their villages when there were no priests or central government to do so.

What the Penitentes are best known for, however, is their intense religious ritual, which includes self-flagellation, bloodletting, and mock crucifixion – activities that apparently took place in public processions for centuries but were driven underground after official church condemnation in the late 19th century. The secrecy, along with sensational journalism by visitors from the East Coast, fueled gruesome rumors about the brotherhood. Penitentes used real nails in their crucifixion reenactments, people said, and the man drawn by lot to be the *Cristo* had a good chance of dying (no eyewitness recorded the practice on paper, though). One particularly morbid – and well-documented – ritual involves pulling *la carretera del muerte*, an oxcart filled with rocks and a wooden figure of Doña Sebastiana, the Angel of Death. Morbid imagery bred morbid curiosity: Photos in a *Harper's* magazine story from the early 20th century show Anglos looking on agog as Penitentes clad in white pants and black hoods whip themselves.

In 1947, after years of concerted lobbying (but not an official renunciation of its bloody rituals), the Penitentes were again accepted into the fold of the Catholic church; the *hermanos mayores* (head brothers) from all of the *moradas* (meetinghouses) convene annually in Santa Fe, and the group, which has an estimated 3,000 members, has the outward appearance of a political and public-service club.

The rituals, though, do continue, most visibly during Holy Week. This is when the group's devotion to the physical suffering of the human Jesus is at its keenest. The Penitentes reenact the stations of the cross and the crucifixion, and although ketchup is more prevalent than real blood now and statues often stand in for the major players, the scenes are solemn and affectingly tragic. On some days during Holy Week, the *morada* is open to non-Penitentes for various rituals – a rare chance for outsiders to see the meeting place of this secretive group.

RELIGION

Four hundred years after the arrival of the Franciscan missionaries, New Mexico is still a heavily **Catholic** state—even KFC offers a Friday-night fish fry during Lent. But the relative isolation of the territory produced some variances that would no doubt disturb the Vatican. In both Indian and Spanish churches, the pageantry of medieval Christianity is preserved. Las Posadas, the reenactment of Mary and Joseph's search for lodging in Bethlehem, is a festive torch-lit tradition every December, and during the annual Holy Week pilgrimage to Chimayó, devoted groups stage the stations of the cross, complete with 100-pound wood beams and lots of fake blood.

The Pueblo Indians play on church-as-theater too: During Christmas Eve Mass, for instance, it's not uncommon for the service to come to an abrupt end as the priest is hustled off the pulpit by face-painted clown figures who make way for the parade of ceremonial dancers down the aisle. In both cultures, the Mexican Virgin of Guadalupe is highly revered, and a number of saints are honored as intercessors for all manner of troubles, from failing crops to false imprisonment.

Eastern religions have a noticeable presence as well, and even a bit of political clout—a community of American-born converts to **Sikhism** in Española, for example, is a major donor to both big political parties.

Santa Fe is home to a substantial number of **Buddhists,** both American converts and native Tibetan refugees who have relocated to this different mountainous land. Stupas can be found up and down the Rio Grande, the largest at Santa Fe's KSK Buddhist Center, which hosts many of the most influential Tibetan teachers.

Food

New Mexicans love their food so much, they put it on lottery tickets, with scratch cards named Chile Cash, Chips and Salsa, and Sopaipilla Dough (promising "lots of honey and plenty of money"). The state cuisine is a distinctive culinary tradition that shouldn't be confused with Tex-Mex or south-of-the-border Mexican—even though most locals will say they're going out for "Mexican" when they mean they want a bowl of purely *New* Mexican green-chile stew. (But if you're eating *mole* or *ceviche,* that's called "Mexican-Mexican.")

ALL CHILE, ALL THE TIME

The cuisine's distinguishing element is the **New Mexico chile pepper,** also called the Hatch chile, for the name of the southern New Mexican town that's the center of the industry. In the north, Chimayó is another big chile-producing town. When the chile is picked green, it is roasted and frozen, to be used whole to make chiles rellenos (stuffed with cheese and fried in batter) or cut into chunks and blended into sauces or used as the base of a meaty green-chile stew. Other chiles are left to ripen and

preparing a *horno* (adobe dome oven) for baking

RED CHILE SAUCE

Use only freshly ground New Mexico red chile for this sauce – not the "chile powder" sold in most grocery stores. The sauce will keep in the refrigerator for a month, and you can use it to top eggs or steaks, or devote the whole batch to a tray of enchiladas. (If you're doing the latter, you'll want to keep the sauce relatively runny, so you can easily coat the tortillas with sauce before filling them.) The flavor is best if it is prepared ahead and left to sit overnight.

½ c. New Mexico red chile powder

1 tsp. ground cumin

1 tsp. ground coriander

2 Tbsp. all-purpose flour

2 Tbsp. vegetable oil (or lard)

2 or 3 cloves garlic, crushed or minced

1 tsp. dried oregano

2 c. water or chicken stock

Measure the chile, cumin, coriander, and flour into a heavy-bottomed saucepan and place over medium-high heat. Stirring frequently, toast the spices until they are just fragrant and the flour has darkened slightly. Turn the heat down to medium-low and make a well in the center of the spices, pushing the powder to the sides of the pan so it is not directly over the flame. Pour in the oil then add the garlic. When the garlic is fragrant, stir the spices into the oil-garlic mixture – you will have a very coarse paste. Stirring constantly, slowly add half of the water or stock. The mixture should thicken and become velvety. Add the remaining water or stock, mix well, turn heat to low, and let sauce simmer for about 20 minutes, until it is somewhat reduced and thickened to your liking. If the mixture becomes too thick, simply add more water.

then dried in the sun, where they turn dark red and leathery. The dry red chiles are then ground into powder or strung up whole in long chains called *ristras* to be used later in sauces or marinades. While some dishes, such as *carne adovada* (pork shoulder marinated with red chile), are only ever made with one type, most other items—enchiladas, burritos, and eggs (huevos rancheros), to name a few—can be ordered with either variety, so a standard question in restaurants is "Red or green?"

The chile is coupled with the traditional Native American triad of **corn, squash,** and **beans.** The beans are typically brown, meaty pintos, served whole in a stew or mashed up and "refried" (not actually fried twice—the term is a mistranslation of Spanish *refrito*, which means "really fried"). Corn makes its way into tortillas as well as into hulled kernels of hominy, called posole here and often cooked into a hearty stew with lamb or beef, chile, and oregano. Ground corn paste (masa) is whipped with lard (or Crisco, if you're "healthy") and wrapped around a meaty filling, then tied in a corn husk and steamed to make a tamale (a local corruption of the Spanish *tamal*). Squash comes in a common side dish called *calabacitas*, sautéed with onions and a touch of green chile. Spanish settlers brought lamb, which crops up in tacos and stews.

Traditional Puebloan cuisine isn't so distinct from what everyone else eats—its one major element is **frybread,** a round of deep-fried dough served with honey or filled with ground meat, cheese, and lettuce to make an "Indian taco"; bread baked in a traditional domed adobe *horno* oven is also popular. Game meat, such as deer, is also a major component of Indian cooking, though you'll rarely see it in restaurants.

Green chile makes its way into standard American fare as well. It's a popular **pizza** topping (great with pepperoni or ham), and the **green-chile cheeseburger** is a top choice at fast-food restaurants. Try the statewide Blake's Lotaburger minichain for excellent fresh burgers, as well as hand-cut fries and cherry Coke with extra syrup. Also look out for **breakfast**

burritos, big flour tortillas filled with scrambled eggs, hash browns, and some kind of meat—bacon, crumbled sausage, or sometimes Mexican chorizo, a spicy pork sausage. Some places sell them as on-the-run food, in which case, green chile is added to the mix, and the whole thing is wrapped in foil. At sit-down places, you can opt to get the thing smothered in either red or green chile sauce and topped with cheese.

Sopaipillas are another New Mexican invention—they're little square bits of dough that puff up like pillows when deep-fried. They're used to mop up chile and beans during the main meal and then slathered with honey for dessert. (In a disturbing trend, some restaurants are switching to a honey-flavored corn syrup, because it's cheaper and doesn't crystallize—if you encounter this, complain at top volume.) **Bizcochitos,** little anise-laced butter cookies, are the state's official sweet treat. Wash it all down with a **margarita,** which purists insist should involve only lime, tequila, and triple sec and be served on the rocks in a salt-rimmed glass. You can get a slushy frozen margarita, but it's usually the mark of a restaurant that's pandering to tourists.

HOW TO TAKE THE HEAT
When your server plunks down a heavy white ceramic plate covered in melted cheese and oozing chile sauce, the words "this plate is very hot" cover only half of the story. Every year the harvest varies a bit, and the chile can be mild or so spicy as to blister lips and produce a dizzying (and addictive) endorphin rush. Locals look back on particularly incendiary seasons with that mixture of awe, fear, and longing that junkies reserve for their best scores. In general, green chile tends to be hotter than red, but it's a good idea to ask your server what to expect.

You can protect yourself against chile-induced burns by ordering a side of sour cream with your enchiladas or burrito—although be warned that this is seen as a "Texan" affectation and may be derided by your fellow diners. Locals usually just reach for a sopaipilla, the starch from which can absorb some of the chile oils. But don't gulp down water, which only spreads the searing oils around your mouth. Beer is a marginal improvement. If all else fails, there's the distracting power of margaritas.

FINE DINING
While there are plenty of time-warp diners and mom-and-pop hole-in-the-wall joints, the dining scene can also be very sophisticated, keeping pace with the national trend toward local and organic produce—a movement that hasn't been such a huge leap in New Mexico, as many small family farms didn't have to "go organic" because they were never industrialized in the first place. At white-tablecloth places, Southwestern fusion is the byword, with chile working its way into foie gras appetizers and even high-concept desserts. The fine-dining scene is enhanced by a burgeoning wine industry, the product of Spanish settlers in the 17th century but enjoying a resurgence since the 1980s. Gruet Winery in Albuquerque is the best-known New Mexico producer, known for its excellent sparkling wine. This is a boon to dining out, because you can get inexpensive fizzy wine by the glass almost everywhere. *Local Flavor,* a monthly tabloid magazine, and the glossy quarterly *Edible Santa Fe* cover artisanal food and high-end dining, which is centered in Santa Fe but has its proponents in Taos and Albuquerque.

VEGETARIAN FOOD
New Mexican food isn't a meat-centric cuisine, but vegetarians will have to be vigilant, as many chile dishes are traditionally made with beef or chicken stock as well as lard for flavoring. Decades of hippie influence, though, have resulted in many menus that state clearly whether the chile is meatless. And quite a lot of restaurants have an unreconstructed 1970s worldview, with alfalfa sprouts and squash casseroles galore.

Arts and Crafts

Northern New Mexico is a hotbed of creativity, from Santa Fe's edgy contemporary art scene to traditional Spanish folk artists working in remote villages, using the same tools their great-grandfathers did. Here's what to look out for in the more traditional arenas of pottery, weaving, jewelry, and wood carving.

POTTERY

New Mexico's pottery tradition is perhaps the state's most thriving one, drawing on millennia of craftsmanship. About 2,000 years ago, the **Mogollon** people in the southern part of the state began making simple pots of brown coiled clay. A thousand years later, the craft had developed into the beautiful black-on-white symmetry of the **Mimbres** people. Later, each of the pueblos developed its own style; by the 20th century, some traditions had died out, but almost all felt some kind of renaissance after the work of **María Martínez** in the first half of the 20th century. A San Ildefonso potter, Martínez developed, along with her husband, Julian, a lustrous black pottery painted with geometric designs to make a subtle matte-on-shiny finish. The elegant pieces, at once innovative and traditional, inspired Anglo collectors (who saw the couple's work at the 1934 Chicago World's Fair, among other places) as well as local potters. Today, many artists make their livings from pottery, sold both in galleries and out of people's homes in the pueblos.

The various pueblo styles are distinguished by their base clay, the "slip" (the clay-and-water finish), and particular shapes. Taos and Picurís pueblos, for instance, are surrounded by beds of micaceous clay; the mica helps the pots withstand heat well (they're renowned for cooking beans) and lends the pottery a subtle glitter. Acoma Pueblo specializes in intricate black-and-white painted designs; pottery from Ohkay Owingeh (formerly called San Juan) is typically reddish-brown with incised symbols; and Santa Clara Pueblo developed the "wedding jar," a double-neck design with a handle.

COURTESY OF ALBUQUERQUE CONVENTION & VISITORS BUREAU/© NEWMEXICOSTOCK.COM

traditional clay pot shapes with striking modern geometric designs

If there's a particular style that catches your eye in city galleries, then you can visit the specific pueblo, where you may be able to buy directly from the artisan and perhaps see where the piece was made.

A whole other field of contemporary design is thriving too, with artists working in glass, for instance, or applying traditional decorative motifs to large-scale sculpture. Non-Indian artists are producing beautiful work, sometimes incorporating local forms, sometimes using Asian techniques. Many of them have open studios—you can even tour the New Mexico Potters Trail (www.newmexicopotterstrail.org) around Santa Fe.

TEXTILES

After pottery, weaving is probably the state's largest craft industry. Historically, Indian and Spanish weaving styles were separate, but they have merged through the centuries to create some patterns and styles unique to the Rio Grande Valley. Before the arrival of the Spanish, American Indians had already developed a weaving tradition—the Spanish explorers marveled especially at the Navajo cotton blankets, woven in whole panels on wide looms (Spaniards had been working with narrow looms and stitching two panels together) and featuring patterns of stepped diamonds. Spanish weavers introduced the hardy Churro sheep, with its rough wool that was good for hand-spinning, as well as new dyes, such as indigo (although the blue-tinted rugs are often called **Moki** rugs, using a Navajo word).

In the early 1800s, in an attempt to make a better product for trade, the Spanish government sent Mexican artists north to work with local weavers. Out of this meeting came the distinctive **Saltillo** styles (named for the region the Mexican teachers came from), such as the running-leaf pattern, which Rio Grande weavers alternated with solid-color stripes. In the 1880s, New Mexican artisans first saw quilts from the Eastern United States, and they adapted the eight-pointed star to their wool rugs; another popular motif from the 19th century is a zigzag pattern that resembles lightning. One item that crops up in antique shops is the **Chimayó blanket,** an invention of the tourist age in the early 20th century, when Anglo traders encouraged local Hispano weavers to make an affordable souvenir to sell to visitors looking for "Indian" blankets. They're handsome, single-width rugs with a strong central motif, perhaps the iconic Southwestern-look rug. Also look for **colcha** work, a Spanish style in which a loose-weave rug is decorated with wool embroidery. It was revived in the 1930s by Mormons, and you will occasionally see beautiful examples from this period in collectors' shops. Contemporary weaving can draw on any and all of these innovations and can be practiced just as often by a young Anglo as a Hispano grandmother. A strong small-batch wool industry in New Mexico helps the scene tremendously—expect to see vivid color-block contemporary pieces alongside the most traditional patterns.

JEWELRY

The Indians of New Mexico have been making jewelry for thousands of years, though the familiar forms seen today date only from the mid-19th century, when the Navajo of western New Mexico pioneered silversmithing and taught it to the Pueblo Indians. The most iconic piece of Southwestern jewelry is the turquoise-and-silver **squash-blossom necklace,** a large crescent pendant decorated with flowerlike silver beads. Actually derived from Spanish pomegranate decorations, rather than native plant imagery, it's readily seen in every Santa Fe jewelry store. Look also for shell-shape **concho belts** (also spelled concha), silver "shells" linked together or strung on a leather belt, and **heishi,** tiny disks made of shell and threaded to make a ropelike strand. The Zuni carve small animal **fetishes**—bears, birds, and more—often strung on necklaces with *heishi.* In addition to turquoise, opals are a popular decorative stone, along with brick-red coral, lapis lazuli, and black jet and marble. Whatever you buy, the gallery or artisan should supply you with a written receipt of its components—which stones, the grade of silver (sterling, ideally), and so forth.

Shopping for Turquoise

Although New Mexico's turquoise is all mined out, the stone is still an essential part of local jewelry making; most of it is imported from mines in China. It is available in shades from lime-green to pure sky-blue, and much of it has been subjected to various processes to make it more stable and versatile, which affects the price.

Rare gem-grade turquoise is the top of the line—a piece from now-empty mines such as Lander or Lone Mountain can cost $40 per carat. "Gem-grade" applies only to **natural stones**—those that have not been chemically treated in any way—and is based on the piece's matrix (the spiderweb of dark veins running through it, which you should be able to feel in any natural turquoise, regardless of grade), luster, and hardness. Gem-grade turquoise pieces from still-functioning mines in China or Tibet will cost significantly less ($10–20 per carat) but will be of the same quality as some premium American stones. Slightly less splendid natural stones are graded jewelry-quality, high-quality, or investment-quality—but they are not quite hard enough to guarantee they will not change color through the decades. They cost $2–5 per carat. For any natural stone, the seller must provide you with a written certificate of its status.

Turquoise that has been **stabilized,** or submerged in epoxy resin to prevent color change, makes up the bulk of the market. Because good natural turquoise is increasingly difficult to come by and turquoise is such an unstable stone, stabilization is a perfectly acceptable way of making a great deal of the stuff usable. Because it's less expensive, it allows for a little waste in the carving process, and good-quality stabilized turquoise is often found in expensive jewelry with elaborate inlay. Average-quality stabilized stone, the next grade down, is used by perhaps 70 percent of American Indian artisans—it can stand up to being carved and is very well priced. Though it ranks relatively low in the range of turquoise available, it produces an attractive piece of jewelry—perhaps not with the elaborate spiderwebbing of a rare piece, but with an overall good color and luster.

Below this are low-quality stabilized stones that have been artificially colored (often called "color shot," or, more confusing, "color stabilized"). **"Synthetic"** stones are actually real turquoise—small chunks mixed with a binding powder of ground turquoise or pyrite and then pressed into shapes and cut. The result is surprisingly attractive, with natural spiderwebbing, but it should be clearly labeled as synthetic. **Treated** turquoise has been submerged in water or oil to make it heavier and shinier, a scam with only temporary results—best avoided, but by its nature, it's seldom honestly labeled.

Aside from the treated stuff, don't worry too much about getting "bad" or "cheap" turquoise—because each stone is different, the more important thing is to find a piece that's attractive to you and is priced to reflect its quality. Just remember that the words "genuine," "authentic," or "pure" have no real meaning—only "natural" commands a premium. Shopping in New Mexico provides many opportunities to buy direct from the artisan—under the *portal* at the Palace of the Governors in Santa Fe, for instance. Otherwise, just avoid shopping in too-good-to-be-true stores that are perpetually "going out of business" or "in liquidation."

WOOD AND TINWORK

When Spanish colonists arrived in New Mexico, they had few resources, little money, and only the most basic tools. The first group of settlers included one carpenter, whose skills helped the group both fill their houses with heavy wood **furniture** (still made today) and worship—for chief among the wood-carvers was (and is) the *santero* or *santera,* who carves images of saints out of wood. These images, called **santos,** can be either flat *(retablos)* or three-dimensional *(bultos)* and are typically painted in lively colors, though some outstanding work has been produced in plain, unpainted wood. Santo styles have shown remarkable continuity through the centuries—the most notable break from tradition was *santero* Patrocinio Barela, whose work, sponsored by the WPA in the 1930s, employed fluid, modernist shapes that use the natural curves and grains of the wood. His sons and grandsons practice the art today. For centuries, the piousness of the *santero* was valued at least much as his skill in carving, though many contemporary carvers do their work for a large market of avid collectors. One popular figure is San Isidro, patron saint of farmers, from 12th-century Spain.

Look also for **straw marquetry,** another product of hard times in the colonial period, in which tiny fibers of "poor man's gold" replaced precious metals as inlay to make elaborate geometric designs on dark wood. Tinwork is another ubiquitous craft, found in inexpensive votive-candle holders as well as elaborately punched and engraved mirror frames and chandeliers.

ESSENTIALS

Getting There

BY AIRPLANE

Albuquerque International Sunport (ABQ) is served by all major U.S. air carriers. Southwest Airlines runs occasional direct flights from the East and West Coasts; otherwise, you'll have to fly through a hub. Fares fluctuate on the same schedule as the rest of the country, with higher rates in summer and over holidays. **Santa Fe** (SAF) has a small municipal airstrip that at press time was set to start receiving flights from Dallas, Los Angeles, and Salt Lake City on Delta and American. In general, though, you're better off taking one of the frequent and not terribly expensive shuttle vans from Albuquerque.

BY BUS

TNM&O (800/231-2222, www.tnmo.com), the local Greyhound affiliate, connects New Mexico with adjacent states and Mexico—along either I-40 or I-25. Coming from elsewhere in the Southwest, you may want to investigate **El Paso-Los Angeles Limousine Express** (915/532-4061 in El Paso, 626/442-1945 in Los Angeles), the biggest operator of bargain bus service for the Mexican immigrant population—its route runs east–west from El Paso to Los Angeles but also connects Denver and Albuquerque. It's both less expensive and more comfortable than TNM&O, but it helps to have some basic Spanish when calling.

Albuquerque's Sunport is the gateway to the state.

Arriving by car is very straightforward: I-40 and I-25 cross in the center of Albuquerque; I-25 runs straight north to Santa Fe. Two scenic but well-traveled roads run between Santa Fe and Taos (take the low road, Highway 68, in winter to avoid snow closures).

BY TRAIN

Amtrak (800/872-7245, www.amtrak.com) runs the Southwest Chief daily between Chicago and Los Angeles, stopping in Lamy (18 miles from Santa Fe) and Albuquerque. Traveling by train, if you have the time to do it, is a rewarding experience, as you'll get a great sense of New Mexico's isolation—and of what a dramatic change the railroad made when it arrived in 1880.

Arriving in Albuquerque, you're in the middle of downtown, but Lamy is little more than a depot and a café. Amtrak provides shuttle service to Santa Fe hotels, or you can connect with a tour run by **Santa Fe Southern Railway** (505/989-8600, www.sfsr.com), though the schedule varies significantly according to the day and the season. If you're coming from Chicago, know that Amtrak pads its schedule heavily between Lamy and Albuquerque—so if the train is running behind, you'll be late arriving in Lamy, but generally will still get to Albuquerque on schedule.

At press time, Albuquerque's **Rail Runner** commuter-rail service was being extended to Santa Fe, with direct service between the cities' downtowns set to start in late 2008. It should be a solid transit option by the time you read this. Check www.nmrailrunner.com for details.

Getting Around

This book covers a relatively small area—about 200 miles from north to south, easily covered by car or bus. Within each city, you can often get around by walking, biking, or public transport.

BY CAR

If you want to explore at all beyond the town centers, you will have to do it by car—but driving New Mexico's scenic byways is definitely one of the pleasures of traveling here. Parking can be somewhat limited in Santa Fe, and you can get around the center of town very easily on foot, so you may want to rent a car only for the days you plan to go out of the city. In Taos, though, only the very dedicated can get around by bus, and in Albuquerque, a car can give you a great deal more flexibility in your day. All of the major car-rental chains are at Albuquerque's airport, in a single building;

see the respective city chapters for other rental companies and offices.

All but a few roads described in this book are passable year-round and don't require four-wheel-drive, but be prepared in winter for ice and snow anywhere other than central Albuquerque. Plan on an hour's drive from Albuquerque to Santa Fe via I-25, and an hour and a half from Santa Fe to Taos via the low road.

BY BUS

TNM&O/Greyhound (800/231-2222, www .tnmo.com) connects Albuquerque, Santa Fe, and Taos, with either two (Taos) or three (Santa Fe) buses daily. The buses run along I-25 between Albuquerque and Santa Fe and up Highway 68 (the low road) to Taos, with stops in Española and Pilar. If you're just going north to Santa Fe, an airport shuttle is preferable. If

A handy hub in downtown Albuquerque, the Alvarado Transportation Center is where to hop on a bus or train.

you're already in downtown Albuquerque, away from the airport, try **El Paso-Los Angeles Limousine Express** (1611 Central Ave. SW, 505/247-8036), which also runs to Santa Fe; unfortunately, it doesn't stop in Taos.

BY BIKE

With beautiful vistas, often-deserted roads, and a strong community of cyclists, northern New Mexico can be a great place to get around on two wheels, as long as it's not your main form of transport. Whether you'll be riding your own bike or renting one in New Mexico, always pack a patch kit—goat-head thorns and broken glass are particular scourges of the highway shoulder. You may want to install tire liners.

Central Albuquerque and Santa Fe are both very manageable by bicycle, with separate lanes in many cases; Taos is less accommodating, and traffic on the main street through town can be unpleasantly heavy and fast.

TOURS

If you have a particular interest, such as art or archaeology, or just a limited amount of time to see the area, you may want to arrange a custom tour. **Destination 505** (505/424-9500, www.destination505.com), a Santa Fe–based company, has a roster of area-savvy experts in archaeology, Pueblo Indian culture, and history to act as guides. Daylong tours or walking tours are recommended in earlier chapters.

Accommodations

Throughout the book, distinctive, privately run accommodations are emphasized over chain options. This author prefers the historic and even odd over a cookie-cutter chain hotel—but you might prefer the latter, especially if you like to have a lot of room to spread out. Almost any hotel or bed-and-breakfast that touts its location in a historic adobe will have very snug rooms (usually with small windows as well).

The prices listed are the official high-season rack rates—that is, what you'd pay if you just walked in off the street, with no discounts; tax is not included. Most often, the numbers are the least expensive room for one person in one bed (a single, abbreviated *s*) and two people in

two beds (a double, abbreviated *d*). High season is typically June–August and, in the mountains, the ski season January–March. Expect even higher rates during special events, such as Indian Market in Santa Fe.

Note that while many hotels tout their swimming pools, they are often forced to leave them empty because of water restrictions during severe droughts (which, these days, is nearly all the time). If you've booked at a hotel specifically for the pool, you might want to check the status before your trip, so you don't wind up paying a premium for a service you can't use. Santa Fe is usually the strictest area in the state, and it also limits hotels to changing bed linens only every third day.

Conduct and Customs

New Mexico is a part of the United States, but it can sometimes feel quite foreign, particularly in the high mountain Spanish villages and in the Indian pueblos. Basic courtesy still rules—starting with limiting your cell-phone use in public, which is looked on with a bit of derision in both the cities and the small towns. Also, women should dress somewhat modestly for visiting the older Catholic churches—at least put a layer over a tank top.

New Mexico is not a wealthy state, and the gap between rich and poor can be very wide. People don't generally appreciate conspicuous displays of wealth, and it's doubly rude to flash cash, fancy gadgets, and jewelry in tiny villages and pueblos. (On the flip side, well-off tourists who dress in tattered jeans and beat-up shoes are also a bit confounding; locals tend to dress as well as they can.) Be thoughtful when taking photos, particularly of people's homes—always ask permission, and consider that some of the more "scenic" elements of New Mexico are also the products of poverty, which some people may not be proud of your capturing on film.

You can help the local economy by favoring New Mexican–owned businesses, rather than chain operations. Also try to buy directly from artisans wherever possible. In these situations, don't get too bent on bargaining—the item you're buying represents not just raw materials and hours of work, but a person's particular talent, skill, and heritage; insisting on an extra-low price belittles not just the item but the artisan as well.

PUEBLO AND RESERVATION ETIQUETTE

Visiting pueblos calls for particular behavior. Remember that you are not at a tourist attraction—you are walking around someone's neighborhood, so peeking in windows and wandering off the suggested route isn't polite. If you want to take photos, you'll need a camera permit, for an additional fee; always ask permission before taking photos of people, and ask parents, rather than children, for their consent. Most pueblos ban alcohol as well—if not all the time, then certainly on feast days.

Some pueblos are more welcoming than others—San Ildefonso, for instance, is open year-round, whereas Jemez is completely closed, except for some feast days. It doesn't pay, then, to go in the off times in order to have a less "touristy" experience, because the more private pueblos will not be at all welcoming to strangers poking around among their homes. The most rewarding time to visit *is* on a big feast day. You won't be the only tourist there, but you have a better chance of being invited into a local's home. Some Pueblo Indians find loud voices, direct eye contact, and firm handshakes off-putting and, by the same token, may not express themselves in the forthright way a lot of other Americans are used to. Similarly, a subdued reaction doesn't necessarily mean a lack of enthusiasm.

Tips for Travelers

STUDY AND VOLUNTEEERING
From afternoon cooking classes to a semester-long intensive on adobe building techniques, the opportunities to learn in northern New Mexico are broad. Santa Fe and Albuquerque are both home to renowned alternative healing and massage schools, more than can be listed here; if you're interested, visit www.natural healers.com for a list.

General Education
Look first into the art, music, and outdoors programs at **Ghost Ranch** (877/804-4678, www.ghostranch.org), both at the beautiful

property in Abiquiu and at the Santa Fe campus; of particular interest is **Zoukfest** (www .zoukfest.com), a world folk-music workshop, in November. The El Rito campus of **Northern New Mexico College** (575/581-4115, www.nnmc.edu), north of Abiquiu, runs the **Heritage Retreat Center,** offering Spanish immersion classes and short-term workshops in traditional crafts.

Cooking Classes

Santa Fe School of Cooking (116 W. San Francisco St., 505/983-4511, www.santafe schoolofcooking.com) offers day classes not only in contemporary Southwestern cuisine, but also in traditional Native American cooking (author Lois Ellen Frank instructs) and New Mexican standards; nice farmers market trips are offered too.

In Albuquerque, learn to fry the perfect sopaipillas at **Jane Butel Cooking School** (2655 Pan American Hwy. NE, 800/473-8226, www.janebutel.com), presided over by a Tex-Mex maven who has written numerous cookbooks; day, weekend, and weeklong classes are available.

For a more rural experience, **Comida de Campos** (877/552-4452, www.comidade campos.com) is based in Dixon, north of Santa Fe—a stay at this school involves learning about the working farm it's set on. Day classes cover basic dishes such as tamales and lessons in how to bake in a traditional *horno.*

Permaculture and Alternative Construction

At Santa Fe's **Ecoversity** (2639 Agua Fria St., 505/424-9797, www.ecoversity.org), you can dip in with daylong sessions topics such as making your own biodiesel or buying a goat, or stay for a semester and get a certificate in permaculture or beekeeping. **Lama Foundation** (575/586-1269, www.lamafoundation.org) in San Cristobal, north of Taos, hosts a weeklong permaculture get-together, with hundreds of people swapping tips on solar design, organic gardening, and water catchment. You can also be a summer steward at the foundation, for two weeks or the full season, and learn organic gardening and land-preservation techniques this way, along with plenty of yoga and quiet time.

In the same vein, you can take a three-day **Earthship Seminar** (575/751-0462, www .earthship.org), a crash course in building the off-the-grid rammed-earth houses that are springing up around Taos. The Earthship Biotecture organization also accepts volunteers. If you're very interested in local building styles, look into the intensive semester-long classes in adobe construction at **Northern New Mexico College** (575/581-4115, www.nnmc.edu).

Seeds of Change (888/762-7333, www .seedsofchange.com) is an organization dedicated to preserving biodiversity in agricultural products and promoting organic farming practices; the group occasionally calls for volunteers on its six-acre research farm in El Guique, just outside of Santa Fe near Ohkay Owingeh (San Juan Pueblo).

FOREIGN TRAVELERS

As for any destination in the United States, check before departure whether you'll need a **visa** to enter; most European and Latin American nationals do not need one, however.

New Mexico uses the United States dollar, and currency exchange is available at most banks as well as in better hotels, though the rates in the latter case will not be as good. For the best rates and convenience, withdraw cash from your home account through **automatic teller machines** (ATMs), in bank lobbies and, increasingly, in shops and restaurants; check first, though, what fee your home bank will charge you for the transaction. Otherwise, **travelers' checks** are widely accepted— American Express and Visa are well known, Thomas Cook less so. It's best if you can buy them in U.S. dollar amounts, rather than British pounds, to avoid an additional transaction while traveling.

Tipping etiquette is similar to elsewhere in the country: 15–20 percent on restaurant bills (though often restaurants will add 15 percent or so to the bill for groups of six or more); $1

Don't worry – you can get cash from an ATM almost anywhere.

© ZORA O'NEILL

or so per drink when ordered at the bar; 15 percent to cab drivers; $1 or $2 to staff who handle your luggage in hotels; and $1 or $2 per day to housekeeping in hotels—envelopes are often left in rooms for this purpose, though if you don't see one, don't assume a tip won't be appreciated. **Bargaining** is usually accepted only if you're dealing directly with an artisan, and sometimes not even then—it doesn't hurt to ask, but don't press the issue if the seller won't budge. **Electricity** is 120 volts, with a two-prong, flat-head plug, the same as Canada and Mexico.

TRAVELERS WITH DISABILITIES

Wheelchair access can be a little frustrating in some historic properties and on the narrower sidewalks of Santa Fe and Taos, but in most other respects, travelers with disabilities should find no more problems in northern New Mexico than elsewhere in the United States. Public buses are wheelchair-accessible, for instance, and you can even get out

in nature on paved trails such as the Santa Fe Canyon Preserve loop or the Paseo del Bosque in Albuquerque. If you'll be visiting a lot of wilderness areas, get the National Park Service's **Golden Access Pass** (888/467-2757, www.nps.gov), a free lifetime pass that grants admission for the pass holder and family to all national parks and forests, as well as discounts on interpretive services, camping fees, fishing licenses, and more. Apply in person at any federally managed park; you must show medical documentation of blindness or permanent disability.

The **Governor's Committee on Concerns for the Handicapped** (491 Old Santa Fe Tr., 505/827-6465 voice, 505/827-6329 TDD) occasionally publishes a print guide outlining accessibility features of major sights, restaurants, and more, but you may still want to call places ahead to make sure they can accommodate you.

SENIORS

Senior discounts are available at most museums and other attractions. If you'll be visiting a number of wilderness areas, get a **Golden Age Passport,** a lifetime pass for people 62 and older that grants free admission for the pass holder and any additional passengers in the vehicle to national parks, National Forest Service lands, and many other areas, as well as a 50 percent discount on activities such as camping and boat launching. You can buy the pass, in person only, at a federally managed wilderness area for just $10; for more information, contact the **National Parks Service** (888/467-2757, www.nps.gov).

The **Elderhostel** (877/426-8056, www .elderhostel.org) program runs more than 40 group trips in northern New Mexico, from a five-day general introduction to Santa Fe history to slightly longer tours focusing on the legacy of Georgia O'Keeffe, for instance, or issues in Native American museum curation and conservation. Prices are very reasonable, and, as the emphasis of Elderhostel trips is on education, tour guides are generally excellent.

TRAVELING WITH CHILDREN

Hispanic and American Indian cultures are typically very child friendly, so your little ones will be welcome in most environments, including restaurants and hotels. The only exception would be some of the more formal restaurants in Santa Fe and Taos. Kids are sure to be fascinated by ceremonial dances at the pueblos, but be prepared with distracting games and the like, as long waits are the norm. Prep children with information about American Indian culture beforehand, and brief them on the basic etiquette at dances, which applies to them as well. Kids will also enjoy river rafting (relaxing, less risky "floats" along placid sections of the Rio Grande and Rio Chama are best) and skiing; Taos Ski Valley in particular has a strong program of classes for youngsters. Though the specific prices are not listed in this guide, admission at major attractions is almost always lower for children than for adults.

GAY AND LESBIAN TRAVELERS

Santa Fe is one of the major gay capitals in the United States, second only to San Francisco in the per-capita rates of same-sex coupledom, and particularly popular with lesbians. There are no designated "gay-borhoods" (unless you count RainbowVision Santa Fe, a retirement community) or even particular bar scenes—instead, gay men and lesbian women are well integrated throughout town, running businesses and serving on the city council. Two weeks in June are dedicated to Pride on the Plaza, a whole array of gay-pride arts events and parades.

Albuquerque also has a decent gay scene, especially if you want to go out clubbing, which is not really an option in quieter Santa Fe. Taos isn't antigay in any way—it just doesn't have a big organized community. As for smaller towns and pueblos, they're still significantly more conservative.

Gay culture in the state isn't all about cute shops and cool bars. One big event is the annual **Zia Regional Rodeo,** sponsored by the **New Mexico Gay Rodeo Association** (505/720-3749, www.nmgra.com). It takes place every June in Albuquerque, with all the standard rodeo events, plus goat dressing and a wild drag race.

Health and Safety

Visitors to New Mexico face several unique health concerns. First and foremost are the simple environmental hazards of **dehydration, sunburn,** and **altitude sickness.** The desert climate, glaring sun, and thin ozone layer conspire to fry your skin to a crisp and drain you of all moisture. (On the plus side, sweat evaporates immediately.) Apply SPF 30 sunscreen daily, even in winter, and try to drink at least a couple of liters of water a day, whether you feel thirsty or not; remember to ask for water in restaurants—it's frequently brought only on demand to cut down on waste. After you start feeling thirsty, you're already seriously dehydrated and at risk of further bad effects: headaches, nausea, and dizziness, all of which can become full-blown, life-threatening

heatstroke if left untreated. It doesn't even take serious exertion—just lack of water and very hot sun—to develop heatstroke, so if you're feeling at all woozy or cranky (another common symptom of a lack of water), head for shade and sip a cold drink. Gatorade or a similar electrolyte-replacement drink is a good option, but avoid caffeine- and sugar-laden soft drinks or iced coffee.

Staying hydrated will also help stave off the effects of the high elevation, which most visitors will not be used to. The mildest reaction to being 7,000 feet or more above sea level is simple lethargy or lightheadedness—you will probably sleep long and soundly on your first night in New Mexico. Some people do have more severe reactions, such as a piercing headache or intense nausea, especially if they engage in strenuous physical activity. Unfortunately, there's no good way to judge how your body will react, so give yourself a few days to acclimate, with a light schedule and plenty of time to sleep.

More obscure hazards include **West Nile virus** (wear a DEET-based repellent if you're along the river in the summer); **hantavirus,** an extremely rare pulmonary ailment transmitted by rodents; and the even rarer **bubonic plague** (a.k.a. The Black Death), the very same disease that killed millions of Europeans in the Middle Ages. Only a case or two of the plague crops up every year, and it's easily treated if diagnosed early. **Lyme disease** is so far nonexistent, as deer ticks do not flourish in the mountains.

If you'll be spending a lot of time hiking, take precautions against **giardiasis** and other waterborne ailments by boiling your water or treating it with iodine—even the clearest mountain waterways may have been tainted by cows upstream. **Snake bites** are also a small hazard in the wild, so wear boots that cover your ankles, stay on trails, and keep your hands and feet out of odd holes and cracks between rocks. Only the Western diamondback is aggressive when disturbed; other snakes will bolt, and will certainly not bite if you simply back away quietly.

And the general **outdoor safety rules** apply: Don't hike by yourself, always register with the ranger station when heading out overnight, and let friends know where you're going and when you'll be back. Pack a good topographical map and a compass or GPS device; people manage to get lost even when hiking in the foothills, and if you're at all dehydrated or dizzy from the altitude, any disorientation can be magnified to a disastrous degree. Also pack layers of clothing, and be prepared for cold snaps and snow at higher elevations even in the summer.

CRIME AND DRUGS
Recreational drug use is not uncommon in New Mexico—generally in a relatively benign form, with marijuana fairly widespread. But as in much of the United States, crystal methamphetamine is an epidemic, and some villages in northern New Mexico have also been devastated by heroin use, with overdose deaths at a rate several hundred times higher than the national average. A side effect has been a lot of petty theft, especially in isolated areas such as trailheads; always lock your car doors, and secure any valuables in the trunk. Don't leave anything enticing in view.

Drinking and driving is unfortunately still very common, especially in rural areas; be particularly alert when driving at night. A distressing number of crosses along the roadside *(descansos)* mark the sites of fatal car accidents, many of which involved alcohol.

Information and Services

MAPS AND TOURIST INFORMATION
The website of the **New Mexico Tourism Board** (800/733-6396, ext. 0643, www.newmexico.org) is packed with background information and listings of special events. The organization also publishes the monthly *New Mexico* magazine (www.nmmagazine.com), which covers both mainstream attractions and more obscure corners of the state. If you plan to do a lot of hiking, order detailed topographical maps from the **National Forest Service** office in New Mexico (505/842-3292) or from the Bureau of Land Management's **Public Lands Information Center** (www.publiclands.org). Santa Fe's Travel Bug bookstore also stocks an excellent selection of maps; see the *Santa Fe* chapter for details.

TELEPHONE AND INTERNET
Albuquerque and Santa Fe use the area code 505, while Taos numbers (and most of the

rest of the state) start with 575—this is a relatively recent split, effective as of January 2009, so businesses may not have updated their information.

Mobile phones on the GSM network (Cingular, T-Mobile) get very poor or no reception in rural areas, though this is steadily improving. The corridor between Albuquerque and Santa Fe is fine, but if you'll be spending a lot of time outside of these two cities, you might consider a CDMA phone (Verizon is reliable).

Internet access is widespread, and many cafés have wireless networks. But thick adobe walls and chicken wire inside faux-adobe walls conspire against the wireless waves, so hotels can have erratic service, if they have it at all. There are not many Internet cafés with computers for public use; when in doubt, head to the public library.

TIME ZONE

New Mexico is in the mountain time zone, one hour ahead of the West Coast of the United States and two hours behind the East Coast. It's -7 GMT during the winter and -6 GMT in summer, when daylight saving time is followed statewide.

RESOURCES

Glossary

abierto Spanish for "open"

acequia an irrigation ditch, specifically one regulated by the traditional Spanish method, maintained by a *mayordomo*, or "ditch boss," who oversees how much water each shareholder receives

adobe a building material of sun-dried bricks made of a mix of mud, sand, clay, and straw

arroyo a stream or dry gully where mountain runoff occasionally flows

asado pork stew with plenty of red chile

atrio the churchyard between the boundary wall and the church entrance, usually used as a cemetery

bizcochito anise-laced hard cookie, traditionally made with lard but now more commonly baked with butter

bosque Spanish for "forest," referring specifically to the cottonwoods and other wetlands growth along a river

bulto a three-dimensional wood carving, typically of a saint

caldera a basin or crater formed by a collapsed volcano

canal a water drain from a flat roof; pl. *canales*

carne adovada pork chunks marinated in red chile and then braised; the result is meatier and dryer than *asado*

cerrado Spanish for "closed"

chicharrón fried pork skin, usually with a layer of meat still attached, incorporated into burritos and bowls of chile

chile not to be confused with Texas-style meat-and-beans chili; refers to the fruit of the chile plant itself, eaten green (picked unripe and then roasted) or red (ripened and dried)

chimichanga a deep-fried burrito; allegedly invented in Arizona

colcha a style of blanket, in which loom-woven wool is embellished with long strands of wool embroidery

convento residential compound adjoining a mission church

enchilada a corn tortilla dipped in chile sauce, then filled with cheese or meat, and then topped with more chile; can be served either rolled or flat (stacked in layers)

farolito in Santa Fe and Taos, a luminaria

genízaro during Spanish colonial times, a detribalized Indian who lived with Spaniards and followed Catholic tradition, usually because of having been taken as a slave

heishi fine disk-shaped beads carved from shells

horno a traditional dome-shaped adobe oven

jerga a Spanish-style wool blanket or rug, usually loosely woven and barely decorated, meant for daily use

kachina an ancestral spirit of the Pueblo people as well as the carved figurine representing the spirit; also spelled katsina

kiva the sacred ceremonial space in a pueblo, at least partially underground and entered by a hole in the ceiling; only men are allowed in the kiva, and outsiders are never permitted to enter

latillas thin saplings cut and laid across vigas to make a solid ceiling

lowrider an elaborately painted and customized car with hydraulic lifts

luminaria in Albuquerque, a lantern made of a sand-filled paper bag with a votive candle set inside; in Santa Fe and Taos, refers to small bonfires lit during the Christmas season

menudo tripe soup, said to be good for curing a hangover

morada the meeting space of the Penitente brotherhood

nicho a small niche in an adobe wall, usually meant to hold a santo

Penitente a member of a strict Catholic brotherhood

petroglyph a rock carving

pictograph a painting on a rock surface

portal the covered sidewalk area in front of a traditional adobe structure; pl. *portales*

posole stew of hominy (soaked, hulled corn), pork, and a little chile, either green or red

pueblo literally Spanish for "village," the word for the various communities of American Indians settled along the Rio Grande Valley; also identifies the people themselves, though they are not of the same tribe and speak several different languages

rajas rough-hewn slats laid over vigas to form a ceiling; also, strips of roasted chile

ramada a simple structure built of four sapling posts and topped with additional saplings laid flat to form a shade structure and a place to hang things to dry

reredos an altar screen, usually elaborately painted or carved with various portraits of Christ and the saints

retablo a flat portrait of a saint, painted or carved in low relief, usually on wood

ristra a string of dried red chiles

santo a portrait of a saint, either flat (a *retablo*) or three-dimensional (a *bulto*)

sipapu the hole in the floor of a kiva, signifying the passage to the spirit world

sopaipilla square of puffed fried dough, served with honey for dessert and with the main meal for wiping up sauces

tamale a corn husk filled with masa (hominy paste) and a dab of meat, vegetables, or cheese, and then steamed; usually made in large quantities for holidays

terrón a building material of bricks cut out of sod and dried in the sun – similar to adobe, but much more rare in New Mexico

Tewa the language spoken by the majority of Pueblo Indians; others in the Rio Grande Valley speak Tiwa, Towa, and Keresan

torreón a round defensive tower built in Spanish colonial times

vato a cool Chicano, usually driving a lowrider

viga a ceiling beam, usually made of a single tree trunk and cut to extend outside the building walls on either side

zaguán a long central hallway

Suggested Reading

In addition to the books listed here, check out *La Herencia,* a quarterly journal that covers New Mexico's unique Hispanic heritage, through history articles, personal memoirs, and more — any given issue covers some fascinating topics. Pick one up at better bookstores and newsstands in New Mexico, or order the latest from www.herencia.com.

HISTORY

Deutsch, Sarah. *No Separate Refuge.* New York: Oxford University Press USA, 1989. Not a light read because of its scholarly tone, but the definitive history on the transition from Hispano to Anglo dominance in New Mexico and the power struggles involved, beginning with the railroad's arrival in 1880.

Hordes, Stanley. *To the Ends of the Earth: The History of New Mexico's Crypto-Jews.* New York: Columbia University Press, 2005. A rather exhaustive but nonetheless intriguing account of the Jewish families who fled the Inquisition and lived in the Southwest as Catholic converts. The communities, some still practicing distinctly Jewish rituals, came to light only a few decades ago.

Horgan, Paul. *Great River*. Middletown, CT: Wesleyan University Press, 1991. Two enormous tomes (*Vol. 1: The Indians and Spain* and *Vol. 2: Mexico and the United States*) that won the Pulitzer Prize for history, and deservedly so: They're packed with drama and intrigue, all on a base of meticulous analysis of primary sources. Horgan's *Lamy of Santa Fe* (Wesleyan, 2003) is also highly recommended as a balanced examination of the contentious archbishop's life in New Mexico.

Martinez, Esther. *My Life in San Juan Pueblo*. Champaign: University of Illinois Press, 2004. Born in 1912, Martinez has a lot of stories to tell. This free-flowing book incorporates her memories with larger pueblo folklore, and a CD with recordings of some of her stories is included.

Poling-Kempes, Leslie. *Valley of Shining Stone: The Story of Abiquiu*. Tucson: University of Arizona Press, 1997. Georgia O'Keeffe fans will like the personal stories of those in her circle in the 1930s, while historians will appreciate the detailed, linear second half of the book, which gives a more objective overview of the transformation of this remote valley into an artists' haven.

Salaz-Marquez, Ruben. *New Mexico: A Brief Multi-History*. Albuquerque: Cosmic House, 1999. A good introduction with an easy-to-follow timeline format; very thorough, though not much analysis.

Sides, Hampton. *Blood and Thunder: An Epic of the American West*. New York: Doubleday, 2006. Working from the story of Kit Carson and the campaign against the Navajo, including the Long Walk, Sides tells the gripping story of the entire American West. He's an excellent storyteller, and the 480 pages flow by in a rush of land grabs, battles on horseback, and brutality on both sides.

Simmons, Marc. *New Mexico: An Interpretive History*. Albuquerque: University of New Mexico Press, 1988. The state's historian laureate presents an easy, concise overview of the major historical events. Also look into his more specialized titles, such as *The Last Conquistador: Juan de Oñate and the Settling of the Far Southwest* (Norman: University of Oklahoma Press, 1993).

Smith, Mike. *Towns of the Sandia Mountains*. Charleston, SC: Arcadia, 2006. This slim volume of vintage photographs and juicy stories in extended captions is about a very specific region, but it could tell the story of much of New Mexico in its shift to modernity.

Usner, Donald J. *Sabino's Map: Life in Chimayó's Old Plaza*. Santa Fe: Museum of New Mexico Press, 1995. A balanced and gracefully written history of the author's hometown, illustrated with fond photos of all the craggy-faced characters involved. Usner's follow-up, *Benigna's Chimayo: Cuentos from the Old Plaza* (Santa Fe: Museum of New Mexico Press, 2001), is equally good, relating his grandmother's story of the village and her trove of folktales.

LITERATURE AND MEMOIRS

Anaya, Rudolfo. *Bless Me, Ultima*. New York: Warner, 1994. Anaya's story of a young boy coming of age in New Mexico in the 1940s is beautifully told and an interesting depiction of life in that era. The book, first published in 1973, launched Anaya into his role as Chicano literary hero; his later books, such as *Alburquerque* (1992) are not quite so touching, but they always have a lot of historical and ethnic detail.

Hillerman, Tony. *Skinwalkers*. New York: HarperTorch, 1990. Hillerman's breakout detective novel, set on the Navajo Nation, weaves a fascinating amount of lore into the plot—which all comes in handy when Tribal Affairs police Joe Leaphorn and Jim Chee investigate three homicides. Hillerman spun Leaphorn and Chee into a successful franchise, and all of the books show the same cultural depth.

Nichols, John. *The Milagro Beanfield War.* New York: Henry Holt, 2000. The first title in Nichols's "New Mexico Trilogy" is also the best, a ripping tale of comic intrigue in a small Hispano village, all started by a little dispute over acequia access. First published in 1974, it was made into a film by Robert Redford in 1988.

Pillsbury, Dorothy. *Roots in Adobe.* Santa Fe: Lightning Tree Press, 1983. Pillsbury's charming stories (which occupy three other *Adobe*-based titles) capture the strangeness and warmth of Santa Fe culture in the 1940s. The author tells hilarious stories of settling into her little adobe home and all the characters she meets. The books can be hard to find but are worth seeking out for their excellent vignettes.

Silko, Leslie Marmon. *Ceremony.* New York: Penguin, 1988. Silko's classic novel about the impact of the atomic bomb on Native Americans' worldview (and that of all Americans) is brutal, beautiful, and bleak.

Waters, Frank. *The Woman at Otowi Crossing.* Athens, OH: Swallow Press, 1987. Longtime Taos resident Waters fictionalizes the story of a woman whose isolated café catered to Los Alamos scientists during the bomb-building years. Waters is particularly fascinated with the often mystical relationship between the land of the Southwest and the people who live on it—his *The Man Who Killed the Deer* (Athens: Ohio University Press, 1970), about a crime in the Taos Pueblo community, does the same.

ART AND CULTURE

Clark, Willard. *Remembering Santa Fe.* Layton, UT: Gibbs Smith, 2004. A small hardback edition of selections from the Boston artist who stopped off in Santa Fe in 1928 and stayed to learn printmaking and produce a series of charming etchings depicting Santa Fe life.

Gandert, Miguel. *Nuevo México Profundo: Rituals of an Indo-Hispanic Homeland.* Santa Fe: Museum of New Mexico Press, 2000. Like Enrique Lamadrid's work, but with a slightly broader scope. There's an attempt at scholarly analysis in the text, but it's really about the 130 beautiful photographs.

Hammett, Kingsley. *Santa Fe: A Walk Through Time.* Layton, UT: Gibbs Smith, 2004. A light, largely visual tour of the capital's history and rich trove of weird legends, as told through its buildings.

Lamadrid, Enrique. *Hermanitos Comanchitos: Indo-Hispano Rituals of Captivity and Redemption.* Albuquerque: University of New Mexico Press, 2003. Fascinating documentation, in descriptive prose and rich black-and-white photos, of the traditional Spanish dances of northern New Mexico, such as Los Comanches and Los Matachines.

Lummis, Charles F. *A Tramp Across the Continent.* Lincoln: University of Nebraska, 1982. In 1884, fledgling journalist Lummis decided to walk from Cincinnati to his new job in Los Angeles; this book chronicles his trip. The sections on New Mexico really shine, and Lummis was so entranced that he later moved to the territory. He wrote a number of other books about American Indian culture, and he was the first to write stories about the Penitente brotherhood in the national press.

Padilla, Carmella, and Juan Estevan Arellano. *Low 'n Slow: Lowriding in New Mexico.* Santa Fe: Museum of New Mexico Press, 1999. Lovingly lurid color photographs by Jack Parsons are the centerpiece of this book, which pays tribute to New Mexico's Latino car culture—an art form that has even landed a lowrider from Chimayó in the Smithsonian.

Price, V. B. *The City at the End of the World.* Albuquerque: University of New Mexico Press,

1992. Journalist and poet Price writes a travel guide to New Mexico's biggest metropolis but disguises it as a discourse on urban theory, recommending his favorite spots in the context of the city's unique position and growth processes—sometimes a little dense and overblown, but interesting nonetheless. Black-and-white photographs by Kirk Gittings highlight the stark landscape.

Robinson, Roxana. *Georgia O'Keeffe: A Life.* Lebanon, NH: University Press of New England, 1998. A strong and intimate biography, focusing on the celebrated painter's role as a protofeminist and her difficult relationships.

NATURE AND THE ENVIRONMENT

Coltrin, Mike. *Sandia Mountain Hiking Guide.* Albuquerque: University of New Mexico Press, 2005. Basically a print version of Coltrin's meticulously maintained website (www.sandiahiking.com), with thorough trail descriptions, GPS coordinates, and a foldout map of the east and west slopes of the mountain.

Julyan, Robert, and Mary Stuever, eds. *Field Guide to the Sandia Mountains.* Albuquerque: University of New Mexico Press, 2005. A thorough guide illustrated with color photographs, detailing birds, animals, plants, even insects of the Sandias—worth picking up even if you'll be in the Santa Fe area, as much of the wildlife is the same.

Kricher, John. *A Field Guide to Rocky Mountain and Southwest Forests.* New York: Houghton Mifflin, 2003. Part of the Peterson Field Guide series, this comprehensive book covers both flora and fauna: trees, birds, mammals, you name it. It's illustrated with both color photos and drawings. It's not encyclopedic, but it's a great basic reference. Peterson guides are also available for narrower categories—reptiles and amphibians, for instance, and butterflies.

Reisner, Marc. *Cadillac Desert: The American West and Its Disappearing Water.* New York:

Penguin, 1993. Not specifically about New Mexico, but an excellent analysis of the Southwest's water shortage and how the U.S. government's dam-building projects exacerbated it. Apocalyptic, sarcastic, and totally compelling.

Sibley, David Allen. *The Sibley Field Guide to Birds of Western North America.* New York: Knopf, 2003. The New Mexican birder's book of choice, with 810 species listed, about 4,600 color illustrations, and a handy compact format. Generally beats out Peterson's otherwise respectable series.

Tekiela, Stan. *Birds of New Mexico: Field Guide.* Cambridge, MN: Adventure Publications, 2003. A great book for beginning birders or curious visitors, with 140 of the state's most common species listed, many illustrated with photographs.

FOOD

Frank, Lois Ellen. *Foods of the Southwest Indian Nations.* Berkeley, CA: Ten Speed Press, 2002. Beautiful photographs are a highlight of this thorough documentation of a little-covered cuisine—they help make an ancient culinary tradition accessible and modern without subjecting it to a heavy-handed fusion treatment. For good reason it earned a James Beard Award.

Kagel, Katharine. *Café Pasqual's Cookbook: Spirited Recipes from Santa Fe.* San Francisco: Chronicle, 1993. Re-create your best meals from the legendary restaurant that set the standard for Santa Fe fusion cooking. Chef Kagel is a charming contrarian, too, which makes for great reading.

Sharot, Scott. *New Mexico Chow: Restaurants for the Rest of Us.* Branford, CT: Intrepid Traveler, 2004. Sharot, a former reviewer for Albuquerque's weekly *Alibi,* strikes out all over the state in search of obscure restaurants with proud chefs, whether they're Vietnamese or Mexican.

Internet Resources

TRAVEL INFORMATION

Use official sites produced by chambers of commerce and convention bureaus to look up specific businesses or to find out what special events will be going on during your trip. If you want more opinionated information, look to privately run sites.

Official Tourism Sites

Albuquerque Convention and Visitors Bureau
www.itsatrip.org

The basic official intro to the city and surrounding areas, with events listings and hotel-booking services. A good starting point for research.

New Mexico Board of Tourism
www.newmexico.org

The best of the official sites, this one has very thorough maps, suggested itineraries, and background info such as weather. You can even do a live online chat with the New Mexico Visitors Center in Santa Fe.

Santa Fe Convention and Visitors Bureau
www.santafe.org

Near-exhaustive listings of tourist attractions and services on this slickly produced site. Primarily, though, you'll just want to order the CVB's visitors guide.

Taos Chamber of Commerce
www.taoschamber.com

Nice background information, a thorough business directory, and events listings, but the chamber's office, in Taos itself, is handier.

Visit Los Alamos
http://visit.losalamos.com

The online version of the chamber of commerce's nice handbook, with business listings and an events calendar.

Other Sites

Digital Abiquiu
www.digitalabiquiu.com

A community-maintained website with lots of information about local galleries, as well as good detailed maps and directions around the Chama Valley area.

Hiking in the Sandia Mountains
www.sandiahiking.com

Mike Coltrin hiked every trail in the Sandias during the course of a year, covering about 250 miles. He detailed each hike, complete with GPS references, here.

Public Lands Information Center
www.publiclands.org

Buy USGS, Forest Service, and other topographical maps online from the Bureau of Land Management's well-organized website. Good stock of nature guides and other travel books too.

Sangres.com
www.sangres.com

Scores of articles and travel details about the mountain communities, culture, and history of northern New Mexico, and of southern Colorado.

NEWS AND CULTURE

Albuquerque Journal
www.abqjournal.com

The state's largest newspaper is available free online only for the day of publication—reading the archives requires an annual subscription or an ad-supported day pass.

Alibi
www.alibi.com

Albuquerque's free weekly has been cracking wise since 1992, taking a critical look at politics as well as restaurants. Sometimes the staff are too hung over to list all the movie times, but otherwise they're right on target. Its annual "Best of Burque" guide is a good listing of local recommendations.

Duke City Fix
www.dukecityfix.com

This Albuquerque-centric blog covers everything from politics to gossip about the restaurant scene.

Free New Mexican
www.freenewmexican.com

The free online version of the *Santa Fe New Mexican* requires registration, but its archives contain good restaurant reviews, trail descriptions, and weekend outings, as well as all the news about the city.

My Strange New Mexico
www.mystrangenewmexico.com

Book author and newspaper columnist Mike Smith unearths the state's weirdest lore, from folk legends to UFO sightings.

New Mexico Passport
www.newmexicopassport.com

Feeling as if you could be a New Mexico native? Apply for your official papers here, to be presented to any baffled American who's not sure what country you've just been to.

New Mexico Politics with Joe Monahan
www.joemonahan.com

Analyst Monohan's obsessive, snarky blog charts the circus that is state politics, with plenty of examples of why New Mexico still can't shake its "third-world country" rep.

Santa Fe Reporter
www.sfreporter.com

Santa Fe's weekly, like Albuquerque's, is politically sharp and often funny. Get opinionated reviews and news analysis here.

Smithsonian Folkways
www.folkways.si.edu

At this enormous online music archive, download two excellent albums: *Music of New Mexico: Hispanic Traditions,* and *New Mexico: Native American Traditions.*

Stephen T. Terrell's Web Log
www.steveterrell.blogspot.com

A music critic for the *Santa Fe New Mexican,* Terrell also watches politics like a hawk, so his blog mixes reviews of new albums with reports on Senate intrigue.

Taos Horse Fly
www.taosdaily.com

Rumor mongering, way-left-of-center political commentary, and listings of activist meetings—check the pulse of Taos here.

Index

Map Index

Acknowledgments

Thanks first to the staff at Avalon, who do such great work with words, graphics, and maps to really pull the whole book together. I'm grateful to my mother, Beverly McFarland, whose car once again got a workout—too bad you weren't there for what was a relatively leisurely trip, for once! Thanks too to the usual round-the-dinner-table crew: Sandra Stengel, Tony Geller, Barbara Sundberg, Melu Uriate, and Kent Caldes. Other old NM hands, such as Jesse Wood, Jenna Hansche, and Susan Loubet shared great information, as did Gwyneth Doland, Heidi Ernst Jones, JoAnn Lysne, Judy Herzl, Matthew Rembe, and Robert(o) Gurule. Casey McFarland provided crucial services in positive critter identification.

I've also had quite a few readers write in, and I am glad to have their feedback more than anything—it's always great to hear the book has wound up in good hands!

www.moon.com

DESTINATIONS | ACTIVITIES | BLOGS | MAPS | BOOKS

MOON.COM is all new, and ready to help plan your next trip! Filled with fresh trip ideas and strategies, author interviews, informative blogs, a detailed map library, and descriptions of all the Moon guidebooks, Moon.com is all you need to get out and explore the world—or even places in your own backyard. As always, when you travel with Moon, expect an experience that is uncommon and truly unique.

MAP SYMBOLS

Expressway	Highlight	Airfield	Golf Course
Primary Road	City/Town	Airport	Parking Area
Secondary Road	State Capital	Mountain	Archaeological Site
Unpaved Road	National Capital	Unique Natural Feature	Church
Trail	Point of Interest		Gas Station
Ferry	Accommodation	Waterfall	Glacier
Railroad	Restaurant/Bar	Park	Mangrove
Pedestrian Walkway	Other Location	Trailhead	Reef
Stairs	Campground	Skiing Area	Swamp

CONVERSION TABLES

°C = (°F – 32) / 1.8
°F = (°C x 1.8) + 32
1 inch = 2.54 centimeters (cm)
1 foot = 0.304 meters (m)
1 yard = 0.914 meters
1 mile = 1.6093 kilometers (km)
1 km = 0.6214 miles
1 fathom = 1.8288 m
1 chain = 20.1168 m
1 furlong = 201.168 m
1 acre = 0.4047 hectares
1 sq km = 100 hectares
1 sq mile = 2.59 square km
1 ounce = 28.35 grams
1 pound = 0.4536 kilograms
1 short ton = 0.90718 metric ton
1 short ton = 2,000 pounds
1 long ton = 1.016 metric tons
1 long ton = 2,240 pounds
1 metric ton = 1,000 kilograms
1 quart = 0.94635 liters
1 US gallon = 3.7854 liters
1 Imperial gallon = 4.5459 liters
1 nautical mile = 1.852 km

MOON SANTA FE, TAOS & ALBUQUERQUE
Avalon Travel
a member of the Perseus Books Group
1700 Fourth Street
Berkeley, CA 94710, USA
www.moon.com

Editors: Kevin McLain, Annie M. Blakley
Series Manager: Kathryn Ettinger
Copy Editor: Karen Bleske
Graphics Coordinators: Stefano Boni,
    Kathryn Osgood
Production Coordinator: Darren Alessi
Cover Designer: Stefano Boni
Map Editor: Albert Angulo
Cartographer: Chris Markiewicz
Proofreaders: Jamie Andrade, Kia Wang
Indexer: Greg Jewett

ISBN-10: 1-59880-158-9
ISBN-13: 978-1-59880-158-3
ISSN: 1557-7163

Printing History
1st Edition – 2006
2nd Edition – March 2009
5 4 3 2 1

Front cover photo: old town Albuquerque Mexican
crafts for sale, © Walter Bibikow/Danita delimont
Agency

Title page photo: the ruins of a Franciscan mission,
© Zora O'Neill

Additional color photos: Page 4 © JoAnn Lysne;
pages 5-7 © Zora O'Neill; page 7 © Patrick
McCormick; pages 8 and 9 © Zora O'Neill; page 10
© Jay Blackwood & Jeff Greenberg/courtesy of
Albuquerque Convention & Visitors Bureau; page 12
© Zora O'Neill; page 13 (top) © Zora O'Neill; page 13
(bottom) © Jay Blackwood/courtesy of Albuquerque
Convention & Visitors Bureau; page 14 © Chris
Corrie/courtesy of Santa Fe Convention & Visitors
Bureau; page 16 © Zora O'Neill; page 17 (top) © Easy
Traveler; page 17 (bottom) © Lynn Baker/courtesy
of Albuquerque Convention & Visitors Bureau; page
18 © Petroglyph National Monument/courtesy of
Albuquerque Convention & Visitors Bureau; page 19
© Chris Corrie/courtesy of Santa Fe Convention &
Visitors Bureau; page 20 © Zora O'Neill

Printed in the United States by RR Donnelley

KEEPING CURRENT

If you have a favorite gem you'd like to see included in the next edition, or see anything
that needs updating, clarification, or correction, please drop us a line. Send your
comments via email to feedback@moon.com, or use the address above.